THE STORY OF
THE GREEN HOWARDS

H.M. KING HAAKON, VII, OF NORWAY
COLONEL IN CHIEF
THE GREEN HOWARDS.

THE STORY OF
THE GREEN HOWARDS

1939 - 1945

by

CAPT. W. A. T. SYNGE

1952

THE GREEN HOWARDS

RICHMOND - YORKSHIRE

This book gives the story of
The Green Howards during the
World War II.

It depicts the gallantry with
which the men of this Regiment
fought in order to save their
country and to restore freedom
to those conquered and enslaved.

I am proud to be the Colonel-
in-Chief of The Green Howards.

FOREWORD

by

GENERAL SIR HAROLD E. FRANKLYN, K.C.B., D.S.O., M.C.
Colonel, The Green Howards.
1939 - 1949

The record of the regiment in the 1939-45 war was one of which all Green Howards can justly feel very proud.

It was my good fortune to have some units of the regiment serving under my command almost throughout the war. Naturally I looked for the very highest standard of efficiency from them and I can honestly say that I was never disappointed.

Looking back on the war years I can so well remember seeing the 1st Battalion off to Norway and welcoming it back again in Scotland. Later I had it under my command in Ireland when it had become so very good that I could afford to tell the officers and men that they were not nearly good enough. I had the 4th and 5th Battalions with me at the counter-attack at Arras in May, 1940, and in 1942 said farewell to them, and to the 6th and 7th Battalions in Somerset just before they left for the Middle East. All four of those units were composed of first class fighting material. Again I saw the 6th and 7th Battalions at Southampton in 1944 just before " D " Day and I was not alone in being much impressed by their magnificent bearing and self confidence. Throughout the war I constantly visited Richmond, where the foundations were well and truly laid for many of the successes achieved in battle.

The other Battalions of the Green Howards all played their part worthily. Although the prowess of a battalion means much, and rightly so, to the members of that unit, the main significance lies in the lasting glory which each battalion contributes to the regiment as a whole.

In reading the story of the Green Howards we can never forget those who did not come back, and, although they are worthily commemorated in the regimental chapel in Richmond Parish Church, this book is also a memorial to their valiant spirit.

I must pay a tribute to the author, Captain W. A. T. Synge, who has taken endless trouble to collect accurate accounts of events, and who has succeeded so well in giving us our story in the form and style which we want.

I hope that this story will be an inspiration to future members of the regiment and a source of satisfaction to present Green Howards. I purposely do not refer to past members for there are none such. It has been truly said and I make no apology for repeating it :

" Once a Green Howard, always a Green Howard."

EDEN FISHER & COMPY., LTD., LONDON, E.C.4.

AUTHOR'S PREFACE

" It is the true office of history to represent the events themselves, and to leave the observations and conclusions thereupon to the liberty and faculty of every man's judgement."—FRANCIS BACON.

In the following pages I have endeavoured to carry out this precept, with the assurance that the Green Howards can safely commit themselves to every man's judgement, upon the events themselves, as chronicled in this book.

No one can read these stories of heroism and devotion to duty without a feeling of pride in his fellow countrymen and, if a Green Howard, in his comrades and his Regiment.

This story has been built up around the deeds of the individuals who made it. In order to give as much space as possible to these, I have made the accounts of the strategy of campaigns and the tactics of battles as succinct as possible. For the same reason, only the briefest references have been made to those other regiments and arms of the service, who fought so gallantly side by side with the Green Howards.

My one regret is that so much remains untold, but a historian can only write upon facts, of which there is evidence.

In writing this story I have had to rely mainly on the War Diaries, and on accounts given to me by individuals. The information contained in the former is, on the whole, very brief and impersonal, while the memories of those who fought have, not unnaturally, faded over the years. In some cases I have found very conflicting evidence upon facts between the statements contained in the War Diaries and those made by individuals, and have had to use my own judgment as to the probability of which is most likely to be correct.

There will, therefore, be found in this book some omissions and mistakes, particularly in the names, ranks, and initials of individuals. Every endeavour has been made to reduce these to a minimum, and I hope that any one, who can do so, will send to the authorities at the Regimental Depot any facts which will help towards the greater accuracy of a more complete history of the Regiment, which may be written one day, when the official War History of these days is published.

The Regiment owes a great debt to those Green Howards, and members of other regiments who served with them, who have helped me by supplying information. On its behalf I would like to thank them for all the time and care which they have expended on this work.

I must also acknowledge my thanks to the Imperial War Museum for the gift of the photographs included in this book, and to Mr. C. V. Owen, and his staff in the Historical section of the Cabinet Office.

Finally I would like to say how much I appreciate the honour of having been entrusted with the task of writing the Green Howards' story, and to express the hope that this trust has not been misplaced.

W. A. T. SYNGE

The Old Hall,
   Barford,
      Norfolk.

CONTENTS

xi

CHAPTER FOURTEEN
FEBRUARY–MAY 1945

CHAPTER FIFTEEN
1939–1945

CHAPTER SIXTEEN

APPENDICES

INDEX

LIST OF ILLUSTRATIONS

LIST OF MAPS
(*Designed by the Author*)

CHARTS

showing the location of

THE GREEN HOWARDS BATTALIONS

during each month from

AUGUST 1939 to JUNE 1945

b

CHARTS *showing the location of The Green Howard Battalions during each month from August 1939 to June 1945*

1939

Month	1st Bn.	2nd Bn.	4th Bn.	5th Bn.	6th Bn.	7th Bn.	8th} 13th} 30th Bn.	9th Bn.	2nd E. Riding Yeomanry (10th Bn.)	11th Bn.	12th Bn.
Aug.	Catterick Lt.-Col. Robinson	Ferozepore Lt.-Col. Peddie	Guisborough Lt.-Col. Ridley	Scarborough Lt.-Col. Russel	Middlesbrough Lt.-Col. Steel	Bridlington Lt.-Col. Richmond Brown	Middlesbrough Lt.-Col. Pennyman		Hull Lt.-Col. Birch		
Sept.	Mobilisation Waitwith Camp	Ferozepore	Mobilisation Middlesbrough	Mobilisation Cottingham	Mobilisation Middlesbrough	Mobilisation Middlesbrough	Mobilisation Middlesbrough		Mobilisation Hull		
Oct.	4. To France L'Arquenay Le Boujon	Ferozepore	Lt.-Col. Littleboy Moreton in the Marsh	Moreton in the Marsh	Middlesbrough	Bridlington	Middlesbrough		Hull		
Nov.	Le Boujon	Ferozepore	Moreton in the Marsh	Chipping Campden	Middlesbrough	Bridlington	Middlesbrough		Hull		
Dec.	Armentieres	Ferozepore	Moreton in the Marsh	Lt.-Col. Bush Chipping Campden	Middlesbrough	Bridlington	Middlesbrough		Hull		

1940

Month	1st Bn.	2nd Bn.	4th Bn.	5th Bn.	6th Bn.	7th Bn.	8th} 13th} 30th Bn.	9th Bn.	2nd E. Riding Yeomanry (10th Bn.)	11th Bn.	12th Bn.
Jan.	Armentieres 25. Metz	Major Hawkins Ferozepore	Moreton in the Marsh 26. To France Conlie	Chipping Campden 26. To France Rouez	Middlesbrough	Bridlington	Middlesbrough		Hull		Lt.-Col. Bright Wetherby as 5 Holding Bn.

xviii

Feb.	"Ligne de Contacte" Armentieres	Ferozepore	Longny Vaux	Tourouvre La Vacquerie	Hull	Hull	Middlesbrough	Dover	Hull		Wetherby
Mar.	Armentieres	Ferozepore	Vaux Wavrin	Belleuse Sainghin	Hull	Hull	Middlesbrough	Dover Lt.-Col. Belcher	Tidworth		Wetherby
Apr.	17. To England 25. to May 3. Norway	Lt.-Col. Hawkins Ferezepore	Wavrin	Sainghin	24. To France Irles	24. To France Farbus	Middlesbrough	Dover	Tidworth		Wetherby
May	Galashiels	Ferozepore	Wavrin 16. Retreat to Dunkirk	Sainghin 16. Retreat to Dunkirk	Irles 16. Retreat to Dunkirk	Farbus 16. Retreat to Dunkirk	Middlesbrough	Dover	Tidworth		Wetherby
June	Galashiels	Ferozepore	Knutsford Sherborne	Knutsford Sherborne	Launceston Hinton Admiral	Launceston Parkstone	Neasham	Dover	Tidworth became 10th Bn. Green Howards		Ripon became 50 Green Howards
July	Ringwood	Ferozepore	Sherborne	Sherborne	Hinton Admiral	Parkstone	Neasham	Dover	Tidworth Lt.-Col. Moorhead	Gandale Camp Lt.-Col. Parry	Ripon
Aug.	Ringwood	Ferozepore	Sherborne Weymouth	Winfrith Newburgh	East Moors Farm Camp	Parkstone Wimborne	Neasham	Dover	Tidworth	Gandale Camp	Ripon
Sept.	Hatton Castle	Ferozepore	Weymouth	Winfrith Newburgh	Studland	Canford Cliffs	Neasham split 1/8 Lt.-Col. Pennyman 2/8 Lt.-Col. Barber	Dover	Tidworth	Gandale Camp	Ripon became 12 Green Howards

Month	1st Bn.	2nd Bn.	4th Bn.	5th Bn.	6th Bn.	7th Bn.	8th⎰13th⎱30th Bn.	9th Bn.	10th Bn.	11th Bn.	12th Bn.
Oct.	Pilsworth Lt.-Col. Shaw	Ferozepore	Weymouth	Steepleton	Studland Swanage	Canford Cliffs	1/8 Middlesbrough 2/8 becomes 13th Bn. Spalding	Dover	Tidworth	Warkworth	Redcar
Nov.	Pilsworth	Ferozepore	Weymouth Weston Super Mare	Steepleton Cheddar	Swanage Frome	Canford Cliffs Castle Cary	8th Middlesbrough 13th Spalding	Dover Deal	Warminster	Warkworth	Redcar
Dec.	Pilsworth	Ferozepore	Weston Super Mare	Cheddar	Frome	Castle Cary	8th Middlesbrough 13th Spalding	Deal	Warminster	Warkworth	Redcar

Month	1st Bn.	2nd Bn.	4th Bn.	5th Bn.	6th Bn.	7th Bn.	8th⎰13th⎱30th Bn.	9th Bn.	10th Bn.	11th Bn.	12th Bn.
Jan.	Pilsworth	Ferozepore	Weston Super Mare	Cheddar	Frome	Castle Cary	8th Middlesbrough 13th Spalding	Deal Sheppey	Warminster	Warkworth	Redcar
Feb.	Pilsworth	Ferozepore	Weston Super Mare	Cheddar	Frome	Castle Cary	8th Middlesbrough 13. Mablethorpe Doncaster	Sheppey Aberdeen	Shorncliffe	Warkworth	Redcar
Mar.	Pilsworth	Ferozepore	Weston Super Mare	Cheddar	Frome Lt.-Col. Chads	Castle Cary	8th Middlesbrough 13th Doncaster	Lerwick	Shorncliffe Folkestone	Seaton Delaval	Redcar

Apr.	Redcar	Seaton Delaval	Folkestone	Lerwick	8th Middlesbrough 13th Doncaster	Castle Cary Lt.-Col. MacDonnell	Frome Lt.-Col. Cooke-Collis	Cheddar 23. Embarked at Liverpool	Weston Super Mare 23. Embarked at Liverpool	Ferozepore	Pilsworth Omagh
May	Redcar Thirsk	Woodhouse Homes	Folkestone	Lerwick	8th Middlesbrough 13th Doncaster	Castle Cary 31. Embarked at Gourock	Frome 31. Embarked at Gourock	At Sea Freetown Capetown Durban	At Sea Freetown Capetown Durban	Bakarial Camp	Omagh
June	Thirsk	Chester le Street S. Shields	Folkestone	Lerwick	8th and 13th amalgamated into 30th under Lt.-Col. Barber Doncaster	At Sea Freetown	At Sea Freetown	Port Tewfik Qassasin	Port Tewfik Qassasin	Bakarial Camp	Omagh
July	Thirsk	S. Shields	Folkestone	Lerwick	Doncaster	Durban Port Tewfik Qassasin	Durban Port Tewfik Qassasin	El Daba	Fuka	Bakarial Camp	Omagh
Aug.	Thirsk	Gosforth Park	Folkestone Hawkinge	Lerwick	Doncaster	7. Embarked at Port Said Cyprus Limassol	5. Embarked at Port Said Cyprus Limassol	15. Embarked at Port Said Cyprus Larnaca	13. Embarked at Port Said Cyprus Ailasyka	Bakarial Camp	Omagh
Sept.	Thirsk	Gosforth Park	Hawkinge	Lerwick	Doncaster	Cyprus Limassol	Cyprus Limassol	Cyprus Larnaca	Cyprus Ailasyka	Bakarial Camp	Omagh
Oct.	Thirsk	Gosforth Park	Hawkinge Shorncliffe	Lerwick	Doncaster	Cyprus Limassol	Cyprus Limassol	Cyprus Larnaca Ailasyka	Cyprus Larnaca	Ferozepore	Omagh
Nov.	Thirsk	Gosforth Grimsby	Shorncliffe	Lerwick Felton Ashington	Doncaster	7. Sailed for Palestine Acre 28. Moved to Irak	7. Sailed for Palestine Acre 28. Moved to Irak	7. Sailed for Palestine Mt. Carmel 28. Moved to Egypt	7. Sailed for Palestine Mt. Carmel 28. Moved to Egypt	Jubblepore	Omagh
Dec.	Thirsk Malton	Marsh Chapel	Folkestone	Ashington Became 108 L.A.A. Regt. R.A.	Doncaster	Kirkuk	Kirkuk	Sidi Haneish Bir Thalata	Sidi Haneish Bir Thalata	Jubblepore	Omagh

Month	1st Bn.	2nd Bn.	4th Bn.	5th Bn.	6th Bn.	7th Bn.	30th Bn.	108 L.A.A. Regt. R.A.	10th Bn.	11th Bn.	12th Bn.
Jan.	Omagh	Vadaubhui Camp	27. Crossed the Libyan Frontier Bir Tengedir	27. Crossed the Libyan Frontier Garat El Auda	Kirkuk 24. Syria El Aïne	Kirkuk 30. Syria Djeideide	Doncaster	Ashington Carlisle	Folkestone	Marshchapel Lt.-Col. Evans	Malton
Feb.	Omagh	Jubblepore	Bir Hacheim Alem Hamza	Bir Hacheim Bir El Naghia	12. Moved to Egypt 16. El Daba 22. Gazala Line	12. Moved to Egypt 16. El Daba 22. Gazala Line	Doncaster	Carlisle	Folkestone Lt.-Col. Herbert	Marshchapel	Malton
Mar.	Omagh 16. Embarked at Liverpool	Jubblepore	Alem Hamza	Bir El Naghia	Alem Hamza	Alem Hamza	Doncaster	Tillicoultry	Folkestone	Skegness	Malton
Apr.	At Sea Freetown Capetown	Jubblepore	20. Got El Ualeb Lt.-Col. Cooper	20. Got El Ualeb	Alem Hamza	Alem Hamza	Doncaster	Meldrum Fortrose	Folkestone	Spilsby	Malton
May	Mombasa 19. India Bombay Poona	Jubblepore	Got El Ualeb	Got El Ualeb	Alem Hamza Bir Aslagh Knightsbridge Alem Hamza	Alem Hamza	Doncaster	Fortrose Finedon	Folkestone Hawkinge	Spilsby	Malton
June	Ranchi	Jubblepore	1. Bn Captured Cadres Major Lacy Sidi Bengallad	1. Bn Captured	14. Break Out 16.BirThalata 21. Buq Buq 26. Mersah Matruh Major Brunton	6. Sidra 14. Break Out 16.BirThalata 22. Mersah Matruh	Doncaster	Finedon Flookborough	Hawkinge	Marshchapel	Malton Whitby

Month	Whitby	Marshchapel	Sutton at Hone	Orton	Doncaster	Mareopolis Lt.-Col. Gibbon	Mareopolis Lt.-Col. Eden	Sidi Bishr	Jubblepore	Ranchi
July					Doncaster	Egypt	21. El Taqa 25. Alem Dakar	Amirya	Jubblepore	Ranchi
Aug.	28. Converted into 161 Recce Regt. (Green Howards) Scarborough	Marshchapel	Dartford	Orton Lt.-Col. Bowie	Doncaster	Egypt	Egypt	In Nile defence lines	Jubblepore	Ranchi 24. Embarked Bombay
Sept.	Scarborough	Spilsby	Hythe Ottley	Orton	Doncaster	Egypt	Egypt	23. Embarked for England	Jubblepore	Persia Kermanshah
Oct.	Scarborough	Spilsby	Ottley Withernsea	Orton Buckie	Doncaster	Lt.-Col. Seagrim 14. Munassib Depression	Lt.-Col. Lance 14. Munassib Depression	At Sea	Razmak	Kermanshah
Nov.	Scarborough	Spilsby Skegness	Cottingham	Buckie	Doncaster	Deir El Mireir	Deir El Mireir	19. Arrived at Richmond Disbanded	Razmak	Kermanshah
Dec.	Scarborough	Skegness	Cottingham Truro	Buckie	Doncaster	El Adem Benghazi	El Adem Benghazi		Razmak	Qum

xxiii

1943

Month	Scarborough	Burgh	Truro	Buckie/Brighton	Doncaster	Benghazi Regima	Benghazi Regima	Razmak	Qum
Jan.	Scarborough	Burgh	Truro Lt.-Col. Parker	Buckie Brighton	Doncaster	Benghazi Regima	Benghazi Regima	Razmak	Qum
Feb.	Scarborough Lt.-Col. Savill	Burgh	Truro	Brighton Clacton	Doncaster	Regima	Regima	Razmak	Qum

1943

Month	1st Bn.	2nd Bn.	4th Bn.	5th Bn.	6th Bn.	7th Bn.	30th Bn.	108 L.A.A. Regt. R.A.	10th Bn.	11th Bn.	161 Recce Regt.
Mar.	Qum 16. Kabrit	Razmak			Tripoli Mareth	Tripoli Mareth	Doncaster	Clacton Doncaster Carlisle Buckie	Truro	Burgh	Scarborough Trowbridge
Apr.	Damascus	Razmak Lt.-Col. Walton			Akarit Enfidaville	Akarit Lt.-Col. Jebb Enfidaville	Doncaster	Hamble	Truro Gear Sands	Burgh	Trowbridge
May	Damascus	Razmak			Benghazi Tobruk Sidi Bishr	Benghazi Tobruk Sidi Bishr	Doncaster	Peterhead Lt.-Col. Elliot	Gear Sands Larkhill Became 12th Bn. (Yorkshire) Parachute Regt.	Burgh	Trowbridge
June	Damascus El Shatt	Razmak 6/7 Action at Dosali			Kabrit Lt.-Col. Smith 30. Embarked at Suez	Kabrit 30. Embarked at Suez	Doncaster	Peterhead Otterburn		Burgh	Trowbridge
July	5. Sailed from Port Said 10. Landed in Sicily	Razmak			5. Sailed from Port Said 10. Landed in Sicily Major Brunton Primosole Lt.-Col. Hastings	5. Sailed from Port Said 10. Landed in Sicily Primosole	Doncaster	Peterhead Clacton	Larkhill	Burgh	Trowbridge
Aug.	Sicily Lt.-Col. Bulfin	Razmak			Sicily	Sicily Lt.-Col. Richardson	Doncaster Queensbury	Lyndhurst Canterbury New Radnor	Larkhill	Burgh	Trowbridge

xxiv

1943–1944

Sept.	3. Landed in Italy / Picerno	Razmak		Sicily	Sicily	Queensbury / 14. Embark Glasgow / 22. Algiers	Canterbury / New Radnor	Larkhill	Burgh / Lt.-Col. Keating	Trowbridge / 23. Became 161 Recce Regt.
Oct.	Italy / R. Biferno	Razmak		Sicily / 23. Embarked at Augusta	Sicily / 23. Embarked at Augusta	Manouba	New Radnor / Seaford	Larkhill	Burgh	Trowbridge
Nov.	Italy / R. Sangro	Razmak		5. Arrived at Liverpool / Thetford	5. Arrived at Liverpool / Thetford	Manouba	Carnoustie	Larkhill	Burgh	Trowbridge / Ballymena
Dec.	Italy / Lanciano	Razmak / Peshawar		Thetford	Thetford	Manouba	Carnoustie	Larkhill	Burgh	Ballymena

1944

Jan.	Italy / Minturno / Trimonsuoli	Peshawar		Thetford	Thetford	3. Embark at Bizerta / Taranto	Carnoustie	Larkhill	Burgh	Ballymena / Lt.-Col. Kidston
Feb.	Italy / Trimonsuoli / Lt.-Col. Perreau	Peshawar		Southwold	Southwold	Taranto	Carnoustie	Larkhill / Lt.-Col. Johnson	Burgh	Ballymena
Mar.	Italy / 3. Sailed for Anzio	Peshawar		Inverary	Boscombe	Taranto	Carnoustie	Larkhill / Bulford	Burgh	Ballymena / Lt.-Col. Turner
Apr.	Italy / Anzio	Peshawar		Winchester	Winchester	Taranto	Carnoustie	Larkhill / Bulford	Burgh	Ballymena
May	Italy / R. Moletta	Ranchi		Romsey	Romsey	Taranto / Bari	Carnoustie	Bulford	Burgh	Ballymena

Month	1st Bn.	2nd Bn.	4th Bn.	5th Bn.	6th Bn.	7th Bn.	30th Bn.	108 L.A.A. Regt. R.A.	12th (Yorkshire) Parachute Regt.	11th Bn.	161 Recce Regt.
June	19. Embarked Naples 27. Cairo	Ranchi			1. Embarked at Southampton 5. Sailed for Normandy 6. Landing at La Riviere Oristot La Taille	1. Embarked at Southampton 5. Sailed for Normandy 6. Landing at La Riviere Bronay Les Orailles	Bari	Carnoustie	Landed by air in Normandy Maj. Stockwell Maj. Harris	Burgh	Ballymena
July	Cairo Palestine Kafar Yona	Ranchi Lohardaga			Lt.-Col. Exham Les Landes	Lt.-Col. Cox Les Landes	Bari	Carnoustie	France		Ballymena 'B' Sqdn. mobilised goes to Normandy under Maj. Graham
Aug.	Jebel Mazar Ar Rama	Lohardaga			Tracey Bocage Pierre La Vieille Advanced to Villers Bretonneux	Tracey Bocage Pierre La Vieille Advanced to Villers Bretonneux	Bari	Carnoustie Wooton Underwoods	France		
Sept.	Ar Rama	17. Moved to Arakan Goppe Bazaar			Crossing of the Albert Canal Lt.-Col. Hutchinson Nijmegen Baal	Crossing of the Albert Canal Nijmegen Heuval	Bari	Newark	3. Return to U.K. Larkhill		

1945

Oct.	Ar Rama Julis	Goppe Bazaar		Nijmegen and "The Island"	Nijmegen and "The Island" Lt.-Col. Wilson	Bari	Newark Ostend Axel	Larkhill Pickering Scarborough
Nov.	Julis	Colaba			Nijmegen and "The Island" 28. Moved to Roulers	Bari	Axel Jagerbosch	
Dec.	Julis Lt.-Col. Waldron	Nidania		13. Embarked Ostend 15. Arrived at Malton	13. Embarked Ostend 15. Arrived at Malton Lt.-Col. Barlow	Bari	Jagerbosch Brunssum	Larkhill Lt.-Col. Darling 25. France

1945

Jan.	Julis	16. Chitta- gong 21. Kyaukpyu Minbyin				Bari	Brunssum Wehr	Givet Holland Baarlo
Feb.	Julis 24. Embarked at Haifa	Minbyin Kalabon Kyaukpyu Gonchwein				Bari	Venray Gennep	Baarlo 22. Return to Larkhill
Mar.	3. Disem- barked at Marseilles Schellbelle	Pyin Wan				Bari	Gennep Burlo	Larkhill 14. Landed by air Hammin- kelin

Month	1st Bn.	2nd Bn.	4th Bn.	5th Bn.	6th Bn.	7th Bn.	30th Bn.	108 L.A.A. Regt. R.A.	12th (Yorkshire) Parachute Regt.	11th Bn.	161 Recce Regt.
Apr.	Grossethorndorf Mucklingen 30. Crossed the R. Elbe	Taungup Kyetkiang					Bari	Burlo Bremen Lt.-Col. Lawson	Osnabruck Celle Radenbeck		
May	Buchen Lt.-Col. Scrope	Lt.-Col. Philpots Green Sandoway					Bari Maj. Farmer	Bremen Halberstadt	1/2 Crossing of R. Elbe Luneberg 21. Larkhill		
June		Sandoway July 12. Sailed for Madras					Bari Lt.-Col. Tucker	Halberstadt Middlekirke	Larkhill	Rothbury Lt.-Col. Morogh-Bernard	
							10. Naples 14. Algiers	Middlekirke Langenberg	Larkhill 19. Sailed for India		

CHAPTER ONE

" The Green Howards Prepare for War "

September, 1939

THIS story of an English County Regiment, the 19th Foot, The Green Howards, Alexandra, Princess of Wales' Own Yorkshire Regiment begins, as chance fell out, in the fine old town of Richmond in the North Riding of Yorkshire, with which the Regiment has been so intimately and uniquely associated for nearly a hundred years. In the summer of 1939, just before the war clouds broke, the 1st (Regular) Battalion, having recently returned from Palestine, was stationed at Catterick Camp, which lies across the river at the foot of Richmond hill. It was, therefore, in close proximity to its spiritual home, the Regimental Depot on the top of the hill, where in their early days of soldiering both officers and men had so quickly found themselves to be members of a family, those roots were firmly established in the past, and of whose glorious traditions they were soon made aware.

The story will show how a blend of county pride, regimental heritage, good comradeship, and discipline can unite thousands of men of different callings, creeds, and orders of society into an individual fighting unit ; and how, as has happened so often before in the annals of the British Army, this blend provided that little extra strength and staying power, which turned defeat into victory.

There is in Richmond Church a beautiful Chapel, dedicated to the Green Howards, and on the wall beside the altar hangs a poem, written by a Green Howard Officer, the words of which must have been read by many before they went out to battle, and which surely helped to inspire the gallant deeds which they accomplished.

> " Here is a noble heritage
> Who kneel in Richmond at this hour "
>
> .   .   .   .   .
>
> " Yours is the privilege and the power
> To make that record brighter yet
> Do not forget, lest later men forget ! "

When this story has been read, it will be seen that those who wore the badge of the Green Howards from 1939 to 1945 did

B

1

not forget ; indeed they added further glory to that record.
Again, how many young soldiers must have been roused by
these lines :—

> " You shall be more than what you are—
> Young men, caught up, and bound, and blind—
> Obedient as the northern star :
> Adventurous as the wind, resigned
> And passionless as mountains are.
> These, and more things you shall find
> Before you die : and should that be
> You pass in more than lordly company."

> .   .   .   .   .

> " You stand for more than your own name
> Than your own life ; for many lives . . ."

> .   .   .   .   .

> " You were a boy. Become a man,
> Immune to failure or success.
> Do what you can as best you can.
> Give of your best, and give no less."

3 *Sept* 39   On that fine Sunday morning of September 3, 1939, when
at 11 a.m. the Prime Minister announced over the wireless that
a state of war existed between Great Britain and Germany,
there were thousands of men living peaceably in the North
Riding of Yorkshire, who never dreamed that, in the course
of the next six years, fate would lead them to widely scattered
regions of the earth. Men from the dales, and from the rich
central plain of York ; men from the mines of Cleveland, and
from the industrial town of Middlesbrough, from the market
towns of Thirsk and Northallerton, and from the seaside
towns of Scarborough, Redcar, Whitby and Bridlington, all
joined or rejoined the Green Howard family. Those who were
too old proudly took up arms in 1940 as members of the
Home Guard, ready to face any invader who should dare to
attempt to put a foot on Yorkshire soil.

The young men in the course of their adventures were to
experience the snows of Norway, the burning heat and bitter
cold of the North African desert, the scorching plains of
India, and the barren heights of Persia. They were to sail
round the Cape of Good Hope, traverse Cyprus, Palestine,
Sicily and Italy, and finally be launched from the sea onto the
coast of a German-held France, and pursue their enemy across
the Elbe, almost to the gates of his capital. Others endured for
a short time the steamy heat of the Burmese jungle, while many

were to experience the worst fate of all—long years in prison camps in Italy or Germany.

Before, however, starting to tell the story of their adventures, it will be as well to describe in outline the manner in which the Regiment was organised in those pre-war days, and the location of all the battalions at the beginning of the war, since, alas—it is to be hoped only temporarily—the individuality of county regiments possesses today but a feeble flicker of life, and those who only know the army of today may not understand the links—strong as steel—which in those days joined one battalion of a regiment to another.

The 1st (Regular) Battalion, commanded by Lt.-Col. A. E. Robinson, was, as has been stated, stationed at Catterick Camp, forming part of the 15th Brigade of the 5th Division. This Division happened to be commanded by Major-General H. E. Franklyn, D.S.O., M.C., the Colonel of the Green Howards, as his father had been before him.

The 2nd (Regular) Battalion, commanded by Lt.-Col. A. W. Hawkins, was stationed at Ferozepore in the Punjab, having recently taken part in a brief but arduous campaign on the North West frontier of India.

The 3rd Battalion, originally Militia, had been placed in suspended animation after the 1914/1918 war and had never been resuscitated.

The 4th (Territorial) Battalion, commanded by Lt.-Col. T. K. G. Ridley, M.C., T.D., which recruited largely from Middlesbrough and Cleveland, was embodied on September 1, 1939, at Middlesbrough.

The 5th (Territorial) Battalion, commanded by Lt.-Col. J. R. Russell, was embodied at Scarborough on the same date.

These two battalions formed, together with the 4th Battalion, East Yorkshire Regiment, the 150th Brigade, commanded by Brigadier H. S. Kreyer, O.B.E., D.S.O., who had previously commanded the 1st Battalion, Green Howards. This Brigade formed part of the 50th (Northumbrian) Division, commanded by Major-General G. Le Q. Martel, D.S.O., M.C.

Under the then existing scheme of army expansion, the 4th and 5th Battalions duly gave birth to the 6th and 7th Battalions respectively, which were raised in the same areas as their parent battalions. The 6th Battalion, commanded by Lt.-Col. M. R. Steel, D.S.O., M.C., was embodied at the beginning of September at Middlesbrough, and the 7th Battalion, commanded by Lt.-Col. C. F. Richmond-Brown, at Bridlington at

the same time. These two Battalions, together with the 5th
Battalion, East Yorkshire Regiment, formed the 69th Brigade
of the 23rd Division, commanded by Major-General W. N.
Herbert, C.B., C.M.G., D.S.O.

The 8th Battalion was formed in November, 1939, under
Lt.-Col. J. B. W. Pennyman, late K.O.S.B., from the National
Defence Companies, an offshoot of the Territorial Army.

In September, 1940, this Battalion was split into two
battalions, the 1/8th, under Lt.-Col. Pennyman, and the 2/8th,
under Lt.-Col. V. J. Barber.

In June, 1941, these two battalions were amalgamated at
Doncaster, and became the 13th Battalion, under Lt.-Col.
Barber.

About twelve months later all Home Defence Battalions
were re-designated the 30th Battalion, and under this title it
served until it was disbanded in 1945.

The 9th Battalion was not formed until March, 1940, when
it was stationed at Dover, and commanded by Lt.-Col. A. E.
I. Belcher, M.C.

The 10th Battalion came officially into being in June, 1940,
when it was formed at Tidworth from the 2nd Line East
Riding Yeomanry, which had moved there from Hull in
March, 1940. The first commanding officer of this Battalion
was Lt.-Col. W. B. Moorhead of the King's Regiment.

The 11th Battalion was formed under the command of
Lt.-Col. A. C. L. Parry, M.B.E., M.C., at Gandale in July,
1940.

The 12th Battalion, formed at about the same time, was
first stationed at Redcar under the command of Lt.-Col. H. N.
Bright, M.B.E.

All these Battalions depended in various degrees upon the
Regimental Depot at Richmond, which was commanded in
August, 1939, by Major A. E. I. Belcher, M.C. This officer,
however, handed over his command on the outbreak of war
to Lt.-Col. B. V. Ramsden, a retired officer, who carried it
on until July, 1944. The Depot, shedding its familiar title,
became known as The Infantry Training Centre (The Green
Howards), with the role of receiving and training recruits for
all battalions, and of generally administering the affairs of the
whole regiment.

Although the story of the regiment between the years 1939
and 1945 cannot be complete without fuller accounts of those
units which for various reasons were not destined for the
battlefield, it is proposed to give them in a later chapter,

and to take the reader as rapidly as possible to the point where the Green Howards first met the enemy in battle, in the Second World War.

The first Green Howards to go overseas were the 1st Battalion, which crossed over to France in October, 1939, to be followed by the 4th and 5th Battalions in January, 1940, and the 6th and 7th Battalions in April, 1940. All were fated to be back in England again by June 3, 1940, having, in their respective theatres of war, carried out a gallant retreat in the face of overwhelming opposition.

Many of the epic achievements in the annals of the British Army have consisted of similar retreats, and it will be seen that these battalions of the Green Howards in no way fell short of the dogged determination, fortitude, and bravery which their forerunners had displayed in the past. Since the 1st Battalion was the first to go, and, incidentally, the first to return, as it did from Norway on May 3, 1940, its story shall be told first.

CHAPTER TWO

" THE 1st BATTALION IN FRANCE AND NORWAY "

" The Battle of Otta "

October 1939—*May* 1940

4 Oct 39 IN the evening of October 4, 1939, the terminus station at Richmond was once again the scene of those conflicting emotions which are engendered by the departure of soldiers going to war. As the 1st Battalion, headed by Lt.-Col. A. E. Robinson, marched into the station yard, there must have been some who gave a thought to all those Green Howards who had gone the same way before them to South Africa, or to the battlefields of the 1914-1918 war ; and who felt resolved thereby to uphold the traditions of the Regiment. Others, the younger of them, doubtless only looked to the future, excited by the novelty of the situation, and looking forward eagerly to putting their training into practice. The onlookers, those who had come to say goodbye, theirs was the most poignant emotion, since their lot was to wait bravely and patiently for the return of those they loved. But it is not the custom of the British people to allow their feelings to show overmuch, and it was to the accompaniment of cheering from both sides that the train eventually moved out on its journey to Southampton.

On the 5th the Battalion, 21 officers and 655 other ranks in strength, embarked at Southampton on the S.S. *Manxman,* and sailed across the channel to Cherbourg. There it entrained for Meslay, where it arrived on the 7th. Battalion headquarters was established at L'Arquenay, with the companies billeted in the neighbourhood, and they stayed there until October 11.

The first reinforcements were now left behind, and the remainder of the Battalion entrained for its concentration area. Alighting the next day at Raches, some six miles north of Douai, it marched to its billeting area at Le Boujon, where it remained until after Christmas. There is little to be said of this period, which was spent in training, reconnaissance, and in digging a Corps reserve defence line.

In November Captain C. S. Scrope took over the duties of Adjutant from Captain P. G. J. M. D. Bulfin, and on Christmas Eve the Battalion was inspected by Major-General

6

Franklyn, its Colonel and Divisional Commander. Immediately after Christmas it moved to Armentieres, where it remained for three weeks before proceeding by train to the Metz area.

It was snowing heavily when, on February 2, 1940, the Battalion relieved the 1st Battalion, York and Lancaster Regiment in the " Ligne de Contacte " at Waldweistroff. Here it stayed for about a fortnight, and the only entry of interest in the war diary reads : " Enemy activity nil—enemy movement, two men and one black dog seen entering Lomuhl ". So it can be recorded that the first sight of the enemy by the Green Howards took place on February 3. On February 15 they returned to Armentieres, and spent the next seven weeks in training and preparing various defence positions.

On April 7 they were inspected by the Corps Commander and, when this visit was followed by ten days of intensive training, there must have been some feeling of surprise when on the 17th they entrained for Boulogne, and crossed the 17 *Apr* 40 Channel back again to England. The next day they continued their journey from Dover to Dunfermline, and, after five days there, embarked at Rosyth on April 24 for Norway.

Seldom in the annals of the British Army has a more ill-prepared expedition left our shores, as the account of the following week will show. Whatever the reasons may have been, and to discuss them is outside the scope of this book, the result was to give British Infantry yet another opportunity of showing its outstanding qualities of courage and endurance in fighting a losing battle against outstanding odds. In its initial clash with the enemy, the 1st Battalion Green Howards set an example of discipline and determination, which was to be maintained by the Regiment in many other theatres of war.

Of the original force allotted on paper to Major-General B. C. T. Paget, D.S.O., M.C. for these operations, only a small proportion ever reached the forward areas in Norway at all, namely the 148th Brigade (less one battalion), the 15th Brigade, made up of the 1st Green Howards, the 1st York and Lancasters, and the 1st King's Own Yorkshire Light Infantry, the 168th Light A.A. Battery (less 2 troops), the 55th Field Company R.E. (less one section), and the Brigade Signal Section.

There was also a Brigade Anti-Tank Company, formed of men from each of the three battalions in the Brigade, which was commanded by Captain P. H. D. Dessain of the Green Howards. To this officer fell the distinction of being the first Green Howard to be decorated for bravery in the war. He was awarded the Military Cross for the part which he played in the fighting on April 26. To quote his citation : " Three of his gun detachments were situated in the front line ; the approach to these was along the main road, on which the enemy had established heavy machine-gun fire. Throughout the day Captain Dessain visited his detachments, and by his example and personal disregard for danger he encouraged his gun teams to hold on, and bar the way to any advance by hostile armoured fighting vehicles. In particular, in the afternoon, when the situation was becoming critical, the sight of this officer riding a lady's cycle up the road under heavy machine-gun fire and some shelling encouraged all who saw him ".

There were no artillery, no tanks, practically no signals behind Brigade H.Q., no medical services beyond the base, and no air defence or air support.

The expedition was despatched with such urgency that the two battalions of the 148th Brigade, under Brigadier H. de R. Morgan, had landed on the night of April 19-20 and secured Dombaas on the 20th. By the time Major-General Paget, the commander of the expedition, arrived in Norway (on the evening of the 25th), this Brigade had already moved up into line with the Norwegian Army beyond Lillehammer, suffered severely in retreat, and by the 26th, when it arrived back at Dombaas, was reduced to five officers and four hundred other ranks. They were exhausted and had had very little food for three days, consequently all the ensuing fighting fell on the 15th Brigade.

This Brigade, commanded by Brigadier H. E. F. Smyth, M.C., landed at Aandalsnes on the 23rd, having left the Green Howards at Rosyth to follow. This Battalion, commanded by Lt.-Col. A. E. Robinson, had, on receipt of sailing orders, been hurriedly reorganised at Dunfermline.

It had been allotted one cruiser, H.M.S. *Birmingham*, and three destroyers, H.M.Ss. *Acheron*, *Arrow* and *Griffin*, each of the latter being only capable of taking 66 men. Lt.-Col. Robinson had received orders to be prepared for an opposed landing, or to fight immediately on landing. In order to fulfil these conditions, the complement allotted to each ship had to be made up of a tactical unit, and this necessitated the formation of an additional company, " Y " Company, composed of transport drivers, despatch riders, and odd drafts which arrived at the last moment. No transport whatever was to be taken, and so all stores had to be made up into one-man loads, in case it proved impossible to get alongside a quay on arrival in Norway.

24 *Apr* 40   When they sailed on the 24th, Battalion Headquarters, the Headquarters Company, " D " Company, " Y " Company,

and one platoon each from " A ", " B " and " C " Companies were on board H.M.S. *Birmingham*, 3 officers and 63 other ranks of " A " Company on H.M.S. *Acheron*, 3 officers and 61 other ranks of " B " Company on H.M.S. *Arrow*, and 3 officers and 60 other ranks of " C " Company on H.M.S. *Griffin*.

The thirty-six hour journey across the North Sea was by no means calm, particularly in the destroyers, and the troops were very ill. However, when the calmer waters of the fiords were reached, the Navy produced a good meal and a generous tot of rum, which soon put everyone on their feet, and ready for landing. The only enemy action against them consisted of four bombs from an aeroplane, which dropped harmlessly into the sea near H.M.S. *Birmingham*.

As the ships steamed up the fiord, the snow-capped mountains could be seen in the half light, and a deep silence took the edge off the excitement and anticipation of the future. The first sight of Aandalsnes was of a tiny quay backed by a patchwork of houses rising up the hill behind. Some of the houses were still burning, the result of a bombing attack on the previous day.

The Battalion disembarked in the early hours of April 26, 26 *Apr* 40 and found a red cross train waiting in the station. Everything, including mortars and ammunition, had to be manhandled from ship to train, and considerable time and effort were expended in tying tarpaulins over the roof of the train to cover the red cross markings. A few Norwegian lorries were also impressed but, so important was it to get away—and if possible, reach their destination before daylight—some of the stores were inevitably left behind. A start was eventually made at about 3 a.m. on April 26.

In order to follow the sequence of events during the next few days, a brief description of the theatre of war, and of the objects of the campaign are necessary. The operations of Major-General Paget's force were confined to the Ramsdal and Gudbrandsdal valleys between Aandalsnes and Kvam, a distance of just over a hundred miles. Except in the neighbourhood of Lesjaskogen, the valley is nowhere more than a mile wide—in places only a few hundred yards—and the railway, road and river intertwine throughout its length. The valley is flanked by snowclad mountains, thickly wooded in many places up to a considerable height. Although the snow had melted on the floor of the valley—except in the shade—it was still lying to a depth of from two to three feet at no great distance up the hill-sides, and the side roads leading out of it were impassable except for ski-troops. During the day the sun melted the top layer of snow, which froze into a hard crust at night. This crust was just not firm enough to support the body and, at each step, the foot had to be lifted clear of the crust, and then sank some two or three feet. This form of progress added greatly to the exhaustion of the troops.

During the time the British were fighting in the valley their flanks were guarded by Norwegian ski-troops. It will readily be seen that these lines of communication were particularly vulnerable to air attack, and they were continually exposed to heavy bombing and machine-gun attacks throughout the hours of daylight. There was no anti-aircraft defence, and the key town of Dombaas was soon completely destroyed.

With complete command of the air the Germans made full use of adventitious methods of harassing the British troops. These were provided by the natural features of the country. They frequently bombed the tops of the mountains along the sides of the valley in order to bring down avalanches upon the troops below. This was particularly nerve wracking at Otta, when the infantry were under effective shell and small arms fire at the same time.

The enemy also made good use of incendiary bombs, setting the forest alight on more than one occasion. Since all the houses were made of wood, the enemy airmen made a dead set at them and, when the Battalion arrived back at Aandalsnes, it found the town a smouldering mass, and the village across the harbour a flaming furnace which lit up the whole country-side.

One other natural circumstance must be mentioned as affecting the trials to which the Green Howards were exposed. Sunrise, at that time of the year, was at about 4 a.m. and sunset at 9.30 p.m. This meant, in fact, eighteen hours of daylight, during which the troops were almost continuously bombed or machine-gunned from the air. Only troops with first-rate discipline and morale could have stood up to this assault by nature, of fire, avalanche, and lack of sleep, in addition to continuous attack from the air, and occasional fighting on the ground.

The main object of the expedition was to co-operate with the Norwegian Army in preventing the northward advance of the Germans based in Southern Norway. A secondary objective, namely to encircle Trondheim, in co-operation with General Carton de Wiart's force from Namsos, could not be put into operation.

Immediately on landing on the 24th the Advanced Head-quarters of the 15th Brigade, with the 1st Battalion K.O.Y.L.I.

and the Anti-Tank Company, were rushed up by train and lorries to Otta, and later in the day to Kvam, at which place the whole battalion of the K.O.Y.L.I. was in position by about 2.30 a.m. on the 25th. The Brigadier was wounded by shrapnel early in the day, and the command devolved on Lt.-Col. A. L. Kent Lemon, Officer Commanding the 1st Battalion, York and Lancasters. The York and Lancasters were by this time in a support position some two miles in the rear.

Such was the situation when the Green Howards arrived by train at Dombaas at 7.30 on the morning of the 26th. The Battalion immediately took cover from aircraft in the neighbouring woods, with the exception of " B " Company which was left to unload the train. 26 *Apr* 40

Dombaas station was in a state of chaos, as a Battalion of the 148th Brigade had recently been caught by enemy aircraft whilst detraining. The scene was one of burning wagons, shattered buildings and scattered equipment.

" A " Company, under the command of Major C. W. D. Chads, was sent off about a mile up the road leading to Hjerkinn to guard the left flank of the Dombaas defences, which were in the hands of Brigadier Morgan, with the remnants of his Brigade. Reports had come in of enemy movements in the adjoining Osterdalen valley.

It was subsequently learnt that a German Force, Group Fischer, consisting of three infantry battalions accompanied by tanks, was within twenty miles of Hjerkinn on April 27.

At 3 o'clock in the afternoon " B " Company, under Capt. Bulfin, together with Nos. 2 and 3 sections of the Composite Platoon (Carriers) under Capt. G. R. Lidwill, moved off in lorries to Kvam to support the York and Lancasters. The composite platoon was, of course, without its Bren carriers. In the course of this journey of some fifty miles, the column, which was widely dispersed, was subjected to several bombing and machine-gun attacks from the air. The smouldering wrecks of many Norwegian trucks and clearly marked ambulances were passed on the road side. The company arrived just west of Kvam at about 7 p.m., without sustaining any casualties, but with the loss of two vehicles.

Lt.-Col. D. C. Tennent was commanding the York and Lancasters, and Capt. Bulfin was met by him at his Battalion Headquarters on arrival. These Headquarters were situated near the road which, at this point, ran along the north side of the valley. To get to its positions " B " Company had to go forward about threequarters of a mile to a point where there was a suitable crossing over the ice-bound river. It then climbed up, and came back to a position in support of the two right-hand Companies of the York and Lancasters, and about level with their Battalion Headquarters.

The country was heavily wooded with fir trees, but there were a certain number of rides and clearings. The Company position was just inside a wood with a clear field of fire of about two hundred yards straight to the front. The right flank rose steeply up to the mountain top, from which it was difficult to get any observation or field of fire. The left flank dropped away to the river at the bottom of the valley, whence there was excellent long-range observation.

The whole of that night was spent in digging in. This was not easy since only in a few places was there any soil, and most of the work consisted in picking away at rocks and stones; but by daybreak everyone was behind cover of some sort. This work was to repay them on the morrow, although, as no one had any rest, it was an unpopular order at the time.

Throughout the night the enemy's fire could be seen like some huge pyrotechnical display reflected against the mountain side, as they began to follow up the withdrawal of the K.O.Y.L.I. Spirits rose with the dawn when the ever-cheerful Captain Fanshawe appeared, touring the platoon localities with a large jar of rum tucked underneath his arm.

27 Apr 40   At about 7 a.m. on the 27th the enemy started deploying against the left flank of the York and Lancasters, and during the rest of the day could be seen steadily pushing forward until they appeared to be right up to Battalion Headquarters and level with " B " Company, Green Howards. There was no road on the south of the valley, and activity developed later on the right flank of " B " Company. During the morning British prisoners could be seen being marched back along the road, whilst enemy armoured cars and troops were coming up.

Captain Bulfin had always been worried about his right flank, and had sent a standing patrol from the carrier platoon fairly wide up the mountain to watch it. As pressure increased against the York and Lancasters, the Green Howards could not tell, from their position, what was happening in front, and so No. 10 Platoon, less one section, under Lt. J. S. Bade, was sent forward to reconnoitre.

This party left at about 3 p.m. and, after floundering through deep snow and pinewoods, eventually gained contact with the York and Lancasters at about 5 p.m. Spasmodic firing was going on, and the forward companies had received considerable casualties.

Shortly after the arrival of Lt. Bade's party the officer commanding the York and Lancaster group decided to withdraw, and asked the Green Howard patrol to give covering fire.

The first York and Lancaster platoon extricated itself without casualties, but, as it came up a steep ravine against a snow background, the enemy was presented with a good target and took a heavy toll. Of the last two sections which came away from the forward position, only one man escaped.

The actual orders for withdrawal, which had been given out the previous evening, were for the two leading Companies of the York and Lancasters to withdraw through " B " Company at 10 p.m., and for " B " Company to pull out at 11 p.m. In fact, both these forward Companies passed back through " B " Company's position at approximately 6 p.m., but the Green Howards held on, and did not withdraw until 11 p.m. as originally ordered.

Capt. Bulfin had received a very garbled signal, from which he gathered that the suspension bridge over the river at Sjoa was to be blown up at 1 a.m. on the 28th, and that, if his men did not reach this in time, they would have to continue on the south side of the valley as best they could.

They started back in single file with Company Headquarters leading, followed by the three platoons. The men were told that, if there was any doubt of the way, all they had to do was to keep their right shoulder to the river, and keep going until they came up to the bridge. They hoped to make the best time by keeping down by the river, and making as much use of the level surface of the ice as possible but, to begin with, they took a route slightly above and amongst the trees, since they knew that the Germans were somewhat behind them on the other side of the river. The first time they dropped down into the open they drew fire from an enemy patrol, attracted by the noise of the troops scrambling over the ice-covered rocks. The company deployed and, after a while, moved on in small groups. By this time the platoons were inextricably mixed owing to the darkness of the night and the very rough going. Apart from this one occasion, there was no further trouble on this account. The thaw had set in and the frozen river was only usable in parts, so that they were forced to cover a considerable distance on the broken ground, which made the going very heavy and slow. Ultimately they caught sight of the bridge and cut up on to the higher ground, to try to pick up the road which was shown on the map as leading from it.

At this stage Capt. Bulfin got separated from his Company, which failed to find the road. However, he himself finally got on to the bridge where he found a sapper, who cheerily told him that the bridge was not to be blown up after all. There was, as yet, no sign of the Company, so he trudged on up to the crossroads in Sjoa, where he met the Brigade Major, who informed him that " B " Company was required to move forward, and take up a rear-guard position on the north side of the river, covering the withdrawal of the remainder of the York and Lancasters, and the entrance to Sjoa.

28 *Apr* 40   The first part of the missing Company came in at about 2 a.m. and by 5 a.m. the last remnants of the exhausted troops had arrived, and were collected under cover near the bridge as dawn broke. Capt. Bulfin, having arranged for their reorganisation, had meanwhile gone forward to make a reconnaissance. He had been told that the rear-guard must have anti-tank rifles, and this led him to select the carrier platoon for the task, since it was strong in weapons and filled this requirement. This platoon got into position at 6 a.m.

In the meantime some transport had been organised to ferry the Company back to Otta to rejoin the Battalion, but, on this occasion, Company Headquarters went last. No. 10 Platoon, under Lt. Bade, was ordered to take up a position in support of the carrier platoon, and from then onwards the two platoons were to leap-frog back through each other, until the remainder of the Company in transport were well clear of possible interference from enemy armoured cars. No. 10 Platoon proceeded to improvise a road block with a farm cart, and waited for Capt. Lidwill and the carrier platoon to pass through. After about half an hour Capt. Bulfin returned in a truck to find that Capt. Lidwill was now long overdue. He and Lt. Bade walked to a spot from which a long stretch of road could be observed but nothing was seen or heard. Capt. Bulfin could then only assume that they had in fact withdrawn unnoticed, and had gone back in the transport. Accordingly, Capt. Bulfin, with Lt. Bade and his party, started to drive back, with an anti-tank rifle pointed out of the back of the truck. They arrived at Otta just in time to jump out of their transport and into another Company's slit trenches, as a squadron of enemy aircraft bombed the battalion positions.

What exactly happened to the Carrier Platoon is unknown, but it appears that it must have been completely surprised by one or more German armoured cars. Capt. Lidwill, who was killed, was one of the first to be hit, and the cars moved up and down the road machine-gunning the men lying on the ground either dead or wounded. Of this party, only Corporal C. L. Horner managed to escape alive and rejoin the Battalion at Otta.

For his leadership and courage in this action Capt. Bulfin was awarded the Norwegian Military Cross.

While " B " Company had been fighting this spirited rearguard action, and helping to extricate the York and Lancasters, orders had been issued during the night of April 26/27 for the K.O.Y.L.I. to be withdrawn to Dombaas some five miles behind the position held at that time by the York and Lancasters. " B " Company, less the carrier platoon, arrived at Otta at about 7 a.m., and moved straight into positions which had been prepared for them.

The Otta position required two battalions to hold it, and the York and Lancasters had been ordered to withdraw during the night to reinforce the Green Howards. Unfortunately the former Battalion suffered heavy losses in extricating itself from its position near Sjoa, and, in the words of the Force Commander, " The Otta position would thus have to be held solely by the Green Howards. The Green Howards are in good heart, but all too few to cover this extensive position."

The German force which was advancing up the Gubransdal valley, after the defeat of Brigadier Morgan's force and the Norwegian troops near Lillehammer, was the Group Pellenghar.

This force consisted of seven infantry battalions, including one of mountain troops, a motorised machine-gun battalion, a troop of tanks, some artillery and smaller units—in all about nine thousand men. It was the spearhead of this force which bumped up against the Green Howards on April 28, and which the latter held at bay without any support either from artillery or from the air.

Actually a Brigade Headquarters platoon was formed, which took up a position behind No. 19 platoon of " Y " Company, but it can be said that throughout April 28 the Green Howards stood alone, with the Brigade Anti-Tank Company, and held the Gudbrandsdal valley without artillery or air support against a well-equipped German force opposed to them. Again, to use the words of the Force Commander, " During the afternoon and evening the Green Howards fought splendidly. There is no doubt that the enemy suffered many casualties in this battle, and in his subsequent actions showed little desire or ability to press home an attack."

It must be remembered that the Battalion was still without
" A " Company, left behind at Dombaas, and the Carrier
Platoon which had been destroyed.

See MAP
No 1
The Otta position was naturally strong. It lay across a
deep gorge in which the main river was joined by a tributary
from the west, thus forming a natural obstacle. The village
of Otta was situated north of the river junction. The battalion
was disposed with " D " Company—Major C. E. W. Holds-
worth, and " C " Company—Capt. E. R. P. Armitage, the
Royal Scots, in front, both south of and flanking the village.
" D " Company was on the right and " C " Company on the
left. " B " and " Y " Companies were in the village ; " Y "
Company—Capt. G. F. P. Worthington, M.C.—having a
detached platoon on the high ground, east of the village,
behind " C " Company. Battalion Headquarters, with the
mortars and fighting patrol troops, were situated in the
northern outskirts of the village.

At 7 o'clock in the morning the first reconnaissance plane
came over, followed by bombers, which dropped their bombs,
and then flew low machine-gunning the positions. This
went on throughout the day at intervals, and very soon the
enemy artillery came into action. Against these forms of
attack there could be no retaliatory action, except by small
arms fire against low-flying aircraft. The men were, however,
fairly well protected in trenches and sangars which had been
constructed the day before, and eagerly awaited the arrival
of ground troops with whom they were in a position to deal.

They did not have long to wait, as, at about 10.30, some
hundred and fifty enemy infantry, accompanied by tanks and
armoured cars, advanced up the track in front of " D "
Company. " D " Company, as well disciplined troops will,
withheld its fire until the enemy were within four hundred
yards. They then opened fire with every available weapon and
this body of troops was easily driven off with heavy casualties.

" D " Company was in action throughout the day. No. 16
Platoon on the right flank was heavily bombarded early on,
and withdrew further up the hill. Although runners were
sent on three occasions to try to locate this Platoon, it was lost
for the remainder of the day as far as the Company Commander
was concerned.

No. 17 Platoon was the centre Platoon. At about 11.30
a.m. enemy infantry, accompanied by tanks, armoured cars
and artillery, advanced up the road to the west of the Company
position. No. 17 Platoon withheld its fire until the enemy were
a hundred yards away, and the Germans withdrew leaving
many casualties. This was repeated again at about 3 p.m.

A PATROL MOVING OFF FROM THE MAGINOT LINE.

A SECTION POST IN THE MAGINOT LINE.

Face page 16

At about 6 p.m. the enemy started to advance up the hill towards 17 and 18 Platoons under cover of artillery and machine-gun fire. L./Sgt. J. Barnes was wounded during this attack. At about 6.30 p.m. orders were given to withdraw, and while passing on the order to his sections the Platoon Commander, P.S.M. A. H. Malcolm, was wounded. Pte. G. Potts was killed at the same time. Pte. R. Elwin took command of Ll/Sgt. Barnes' section, and displayed great presence of mind and leadership in extricating the section. The enemy had advanced to within hand-grenade range, and Pte. Elwin, by his resource and courage, not only got the section safely back, but left many dead and wounded Germans on the field of battle.

No. 18 Platoon, commanded by 2/Lt. M. R. Newman, was on the left, and, although the enemy could be seen, they did not come within range until about 5 p.m. Throughout the day this platoon was exposed to constant bombardment from the air, and from artillery and machine-gun fire.

At about 4.30 p.m. large numbers of the enemy, accompanied by two tanks, were seen advancing along the road on the west bank of the river. These were fired upon and dispersed, leaving many casualties.

At 6 p.m. a determined attack was made by the enemy up the hill, and at 6.30 the platoon was withdrawn. 2/Lt. Newman and Sgt. C. Peacock, M.M. visited their section posts throughout the day under heavy fire and set a fine example of coolness and courage. Later the whole company withdrew across the river on ice, which was thin in many places and made the crossing difficult, and took up a position with " B " Company to cover the withdrawal of the remainder of the Battalion. All day long, C.S.M. H. Dinsdale visited the platoons under heavy fire and encouraged their power of resistance. Sgt. Peacock was awarded the Norwegian Military Cross for bravery in this action.

On the east bank of the river light tanks were seen advancing along the road from Kringen in front of " Y " Company at about 1.30 p.m. As they appeared, the leading tank was knocked out by Lt. E. G. Harrison with an Anti-Tank Rifle, and this successfully blocked the road. Lt. Harrison was wounded in the early hours of the next morning. The enemy then attempted to cross the river in collapsible boats, but well-directed fire from " Y " Company soon put a stop to this move. Four men were shot, and seen to fall before they could embark, while the boat, from which two men landed, drifted away down stream.

c

During the fighting at Otta P.S.M. W. H. B. Askew of
" Y " Company, who was in charge of the right half company,
controlled his command with conspicuous skill and a total
disregard of personal danger. He effected the withdrawal of
his men in perfect order, and throughout the action, set a
splendid example to all ranks. He was awarded the Distinguished Conduct Medal. Others of this Company who were
specifically mentioned for the part which they played were :
Sgt. D. Turner, Corporals W. N. Brown and R. C. Angel,
L/Cpls. J. J. Smith and W. A. Dale, and Pte. D. Simmonds.

Meanwhile another body of Germans, pursuing their
usual tactics, was observed trying to filter through the woods
above " C " Company's left flank. Capt. Armitage accordingly
sent No. 15 Platoon up the hill to protect his flank. Contact
with this platoon was never made again.

While the frontal attacks on all companies were being so
successfully repulsed, Capt. Armitage was becoming very
worried about his Company's left flank, when at 5 o'clock
there were no less than four enemy groups on the fringe of
his position. He accordingly sent Lt. J. H. Rawson with two
sections to get in touch with Battalion Headquarters to find
out the position of affairs, and to ask for two platoons as
reinforcements, if he was expected to hold out during the
night. This patrol was not heard of again, and Capt.
Armitage soon afterwards shortened his line. Although enemy
posts of double his strength were entrenched on the verge of
his position, they were entirely dominated by " C " Company's
sangars, and great execution was done amongst them,
including the shooting of an officer in black uniform at point
blank range.

Meanwhile Lt.-Col. Robinson had, at 5 p.m., issued
orders for a withdrawal from the position ; the forward
companies were to start at 9 p.m., and the remainder at 11 p.m.
The rendezvous was Rudi station, from which the Battalion
was to move back to Dombaas, partly by rail and partly by
road transport. These orders reached everyone except " C "
Company, whose adventures will be told later, and No. 19
Platoon of " Y " Company.

There was a lull in the activity of the enemy ground
troops until about a quarter past nine, when a patrol
approached the bridge in front of " B " Company. It was
fired on by No. 10 Platoon and dispersed. It was at this
juncture that Sgt. T. W. Dickinson, of No. 10 Platoon, decided
to uncork a bottle of whiskey marked " Johnny Walker ",
which he had found that morning in a deserted building.

His first swig produced such a look of horror on his face that the platoon runner thought he had been poisoned. The contents turned out to be some immature elderberry wine, which failed to give the expected " fortification ". Half an hour later, this road and rail bridge was blown up, and " D " Company had to ford the river at a point about half a mile above it, which had been previously reconnoitred, to effect its withdrawal.

As soon as " D " Company had vacated the spur on which it had fought all day, the Mortars laid down a barrage, while " B " and " Y " Companies opened rapid fire. The enemy probably took this to be the prelude to a counter attack, and the battalion was able, with the exception of " C " Company and No. 19 Platoon, to get clear away.

At the last moment it had been decided that " B " Company should withdraw by road in Norwegian trucks. Shortly after they had started marching back Captain Scrope, the adjutant, arrived with changed orders, and proceeded to guide the company along the west bank of the river to find a crossing in order to reach the rendezvous, which was across the river. The ice was thin, and several vain attempts were made to get across. The final attempt resulted in Capt. Scrope and Lt. Bade, who were leading, falling through the ice into deep water. They were hauled out by Capt. Bulfin and Pte. White, who extended rifles to them across the ice.

After this unpleasant experience " B " Company moved back over frozen bogland to the railway, where, fortunately, the Norwegians produced another train. At one rendezvous a train was waiting complete with sleeping cars, which, the Norwegian guard announced, were reserved for officers. The beds were made up with clean sheets, but this luxury accommodation was rather wasted ! They reached Dombaas without further incident at 7 o'clock the next morning, April 29.

There is no account of what happened to No. 19 Platoon, except that it managed to disengage, and arrived safely at Dombaas later in the day.

" C " Company, however, did not escape so easily. At about 9.30 p.m. Capt. Armitage went out with a section escort to try to locate No. 15 Platoon, which, under Lt. A. D. Mackenzie, Royal Scots, had last been seen moving up the hillside to protect the left flank. Unsuccessful, Capt. Armitage returned to find an action drawing to an end in which his company had beaten off an attack by an enemy formation of double its own numbers.

He then decided to break off the action and withdraw. He divided his company into four groups and took a course back to Otta some thirty to a hundred yards below the crest of the hill. This proved to be very strenuous ; the route was chosen as being so steep that the enemy were unlikely to be in position across it, but it took seven hours to traverse—half the time the men were travelling on hands and knees on ice or bare rock. It says a great deal for their determination and grit that they arrived complete in numbers, and with all their arms and heavy equipment intact.

When they reached Otta, of course, the enemy were in possession, and, finding his line of retreat cut off, Capt. Armitage divided his company into small parties, and instructed them to get through as best they could to Dombaas, where they arrived successfully in their small parties later in the day.

The following members of " C " Company were especially recommended for the part they played in the defence of Otta. L/Cpl. C. E. Headley of No. 13 Platoon, when it was attacked by a superior force of Germans during the evening, seized the Bren gun from his No. 1, and, on his own initiative, ran out some twenty yards to the flank, under heavy enemy fire, and brought a deadly enfilade fire to bear on the attackers. This action was largely instrumental in making the enemy withdraw, and in enabling " C " Company to break off the action without loss.

Sgt. F. M. Roche, of the same platoon, on more than one occasion during the day, advanced out from his post and drove the enemy back with grenades. For his bravery and initiative Sgt. Roche was awarded the Military Medal, to which he was to add a Bar nearly four years later in Italy.

2/Lt. P. R. Meldon was left in charge of the Company, which by then was reduced to twenty-three all ranks, when Capt. Armitage went out to look for the missing No. 15 Platoon. While Capt. Armitage was away about fifty of the enemy attacked and reached the edge of the position. 2/Lt. Meldon not only held on, but eventually drove off the enemy.

Throughout the day Lt. Rawson, commanding No. 14 Platoon, displayed great coolness and courage. During the afternoon a conference of about thirty German officers was observed some distance in front of " C " Company's line. Lt. Rawson, with a small party and a Bren gun, managed to creep up to within effective range, and inflicted heavy casualties upon them. Shortly after this he directed the fire of his platoon on a body of twenty Germans who were erecting a pontoon on the river bank. Several of the enemy were seen to fall, and the remainder fled, giving up their attempt to cross the river. When the enemy guns registered on his positions, he had got his men into alternative positions, and so did not lose a single man under heavy shelling. When Capt. Armitage decided to send back a fighting patrol to try to contact the Battalion Commander in Otta, Lt. Rawson immediately volunteered, well knowing the risks of such a venture in broad daylight. He and his party were never seen again. Capt. Armitage, who, throughout the day and night, had commanded his Company with great determination and bravery, was awarded the Military Cross.

While the rest of the Battalion was fighting the battle of Otta, a force composed of " A " Company and all available men, collected from the details in Dombaas, commanded by Major A. C. L. Parry, had been sent out to cover a demolition party of the 55th Field Company R.E. near Rosti Gorge. The bridge across the gorge was successfully blown up at 5.45 on the morning of the 29th, after the road and train 29 *Apr* 40 parties from Otta had passed over, and this party rejoined the remainder of the Battalion in Dombaas at about 8 o'clock.

Until 8 o'clock in the evening of the 29th the Green Howards enjoyed a well-earned rest in the woods, but were then ordered to take up a position astride the Hjerkinn road about one mile east of Dombaas.

The British Commander had undertaken not to withdraw from Dombaas before the night of April 30/May 1, in order to give the Norwegian troops the opportunity of retiring. Actually the latter passed through the Green Howards' position during the night of April 29/30, and their withdrawal was completed by mid-day on the 30th. All was now clear, therefore, for the withdrawal of the British troops, and this was ordered to take place at 11.30 that night by train to Aandalsnes.

However, at about half-past three, the enemy gained 30 *Apr* 40 contact with the K.O.Y.L.I., who were in position on the Dombaas-Otta road, about one and a half miles south of Dombaas. " Y " Company of the Green Howards was therefore sent up under command of the K.O.Y.L.I. to prolong their right flank, while " A " and " D " Companies, under Major Chads, took up a rearguard position just south of Dombaas station.

The enemy were, however, beaten off, and the withdrawal successfully accomplished. The train left at about 11 o'clock, and " A " and " D " Companies followed shortly afterwards

in lorries. The latter parties went straight through to Aandalsnes, but the train party were to have one more Norwegian
adventure.

1 May 40   At one o'clock in the morning the train crashed near
Lesjaskogen. Both engines overturned, and there were many
casualties in the leading coaches. The first truck of the train,
in which the train guard was travelling, also contained all the
reserve Mortar bombs, grenades and S.A.A. This immediately
caught fire and the ammunition started to explode, and
most, if not all, of the train guard were killed. It was pitch
dark except for the blazing trucks and flashes from the
exploding ammunition, and, to make it worse, the snow at the
sides of the line was waist deep. It was therefore a considerable feat to have been able to clear the train of all troops,
arms, and equipment, and get them on the march within
forty-five minutes of the accident, especially as, at the time of
the accident, they were all dog tired and fast asleep in the
train. The nearest cover from the air attacks, which were
bound to start at daylight, was the railway tunnel at Verma,
some seventeen miles further down the line towards Aandalsnes. The troops accomplished this march along a snow and
ice covered road, starting at 1.45 a.m. and carrying all arms,
Bren guns, Anti-Tank guns and equipment, and were safely
in the tunnel by 8 a.m. A platoon of " D " Company was left
behind, with a detachment of Royal Marines, to cover the
scene of the train wreck.

Quarters inside the tunnel were very cramped, as, in
addition to fifteen hundred troops, there was also a loaded
ammunition train. It was very fortunate that there was this
train available, as the troops were very exhausted, not only
from their seventeen mile march in the snow and ice but,
owing to the intense cold, they had had very little sleep for
days, and a very large proportion of them had frost-bitten
feet. Despite a few bombs dropped near the mouth of the
tunnel during the day, the men managed to snatch a well-
deserved rest, and quickly recovered their spirits.

At about 5.30 in the afternoon the train began to get
up steam, and the resultant fumes made the position in the
tunnel untenable. The troops, therefore, were moved out
to previously reconnoitred positions in the open, risking
detection from the air in preference to suffocation. Reports
came in shortly after this that the enemy had broken through
the Marines some three to four miles down the road, and
" B " Company was sent out to reinforce the platoon of " D "
Company which was doing outpost duty. This company,
together with a small but very gallant party of one officer and

four men of the Royal Marines, successfully held off the enemy until the train left at 8.30 p.m. This rear party then embussed in mechanical transport, which was waiting for them near the church at Verma, and arrived later at Aandalsnes without further incident.

All embarked safely on board H.M.Ss. *Birmingham, Manchester* and *Calcutta*, with the rear parties in H.M.S. *Auckland.* The last ship sailed at 2 o'clock on the morning of 2 *May* 40
May 2. The embarkation was carried out in the light from burning villages. As the troops wound down the hill to the waterside, they were a very weary body of men. Their spirits were, however, still undaunted, as is reflected in the fact that there was great argument between the members of the rear party as to who should have the privilege of being the last man out !

The return voyage was uneventful, and the Battalion arrived in Scapa Flow at 11 o'clock in the morning of May 3. It at once transferred to H.M.T. *Lancastria*, which sailed for Glasgow, and tied up in King George V dock at noon on May 6. The next day the Green Howards disembarked and entrained 7 *May* 40
for Galashiels, where they arrived at about 5 p.m.

Later in the year Lt.-Col. A. E. Robinson was awarded the Distinguished Service Order. In the words of his citation : " This officer showed exceptional ability in occupying a defensive position at Otta on April 27, 1940, and holding it throughout the 28th. He extricated his battalion on the night of April 28/29 from very close contact, and succeeded in withdrawing it intact. He set a fine example of courage and devotion to duty which inspired his Battalion."

The following extract from an official account of the operation is a fitting conclusion to this chapter.

Referring to the battle of Otta, the account says :— " Artillery was then employed on a most extensive scale, but none of these expedients could dislodge the Green Howards from their positions. Incendiary bombs set fire to houses behind the leading Companies, aeroplanes dropped their bombs as near the defences as they could, artillery pounded them, but when the hostile infantry came on, they were met by controlled and accurate fire. Special emphasis is laid on this tenacious defence . Anything less good would have cracked."

CHAPTER THREE

"THE TERRITORIAL BATTALIONS IN FRANCE"

"The Retreat to Dunkirk"

January—June, 1940

See MAP
No. 2

WE must now take up the story of the Territorial Battalions.

The 50th (Northumbrian) Division, known as "50 Div." to all who served in it, drew its men from Yorkshire, Durham and Northumberland. The units had kept very well up to strength throughout the inter-war years, and so were in an advanced state of preparedness when the word came to mobilise. In the previous autumn it had been decided to motorise the Division with its own transport for personnel, and, for convenience of handling, the establishment had been cut to two brigades of infantry, two regiments of artillery, two field companies and two field ambulances. The Division had also two mechanised transport companies, and a motorcycle battalion for reconnaissance work. The two Infantry Brigades were the 150th, composed of the 4th Battalion, East Yorkshire Regiment, and the 4th and 5th Battalions, Green Howards, commanded by Brigadier H. S. Kreyer, O.B.E., D.S.O., a Green Howards Officer, and the 151st, composed of the 6th, 8th, and 9th Battalions, Durham Light Infantry, commanded by Brigadier J. A. Churchill, M.C., A.D.C. When the German attack was launched in May, 1940, the 25th Infantry Brigade also formed part of the Division, but, as this Brigade was parted from the Division during most of the fighting and was evacuated independently, its composition does not affect this story. It should be mentioned, however, that it was commanded by Brigadier W. H. C. Ramsden, M.C., who was later to command the 50th Division during an arduous period of the latter's glorious fighting career.

4 *and* 5 *Bns*
22 *Oct* 39

The 4th and 5th Battalions, which we left in Chapter One in the process of mobilising at Middlesbrough and Scarborough respectively, moved to the Cotswold country on October 22, 1939. Two days before leaving Middlesbrough, Lt.-Col. C. N. Littleboy, M.C., T.D., took over command of the 4th Battalion from Lt.-Col. T. K. G. Ridley, M.C., T.D., who was found unfit for service overseas, much to the regret

24

of all ranks. It must be recorded that at the outbreak of war Lt.-Col. Littleboy was a Brevet Colonel on the Territorial Reserve. He had joined the 4th Battalion from the Sherwood Foresters, with whom he had served in the 1914/18 war, as a captain in 1919, and had commanded the Battalion for six years prior to 1937, when he retired. He had always displayed the greatest interest in the Battalion, and, in order to have the opportunity of leading it in the field, he voluntarily resigned his Brevet Colonelcy. Such were his courage and power of leadership, he won the Distinguished Service Order in France, and it was a great disappointment to him, and to his officers and men, when he had to leave his Battalion in the Western Desert in April, 1942, under a compulsory age limit. In December Lt.-Col. W. E. Bush, M.C., who had been Brigade Major, 150th Brigade, took command of the 5th Battalion.

The men of Yorkshire, Durham, and Northumberland settled down to their training, and made many friends amid the Cotswold villages. The links of friendship thus formed are still firm, and the officers of the 5th Battalion, Green Howards, for instance, hold periodic reunions to this day alternately in Chipping Campden and in Scarborough.

On January 17, 1940, both battalions were inspected by *4 and 5 Bns* H.M. The King, and on the 25th embarked at Southampton *17 Jan 40* en route for France. Landing the next day at Cherbourg the 50th Division made its way by slow degrees to its assembly area north of Le Mans. The cold was intense ; truck radiators froze while they were running, and, when the Division started to move up towards the frontier on February 5, the roads became almost impassable, so much so that the 5th Battalion, for instance, was ordered to stay at Tourouvre, until road conditions improved, which was not until a fortnight later.

After spending some weeks in the neighbourhood of Amiens the Division moved up again to the vicinity of Lille. There the 4th Battalion was billetted in Wavrin, and the 5th in Sainghin, where they remained until May 16. Soon after arriving in the Lille area Brigadier Kreyer had to go into hospital, and returned to England. He was succeeded by Brigadier C. W. Haydon, M.C., who commanded the 150th Brigade until he was killed in its midst, when it was finally overrun on June 1, 1942, in the Western Desert. The role of the Division, which was now in G.H.Q. Reserve, during April and the beginning of May, was the construction of the 2nd Corps reserve line, which was a north-western continuation of the Maginot Line. The 50th Division's sector ran from Loos (two miles west of Lille) south-east, for eight miles through Seclin to Wavrin. With this work in progress, intensive weapon training was also carried out, and detachments were sent down for periods of training to ranges at Le Touquet and other places on the coast.

Plans in the event of the German Army invading France by way of Holland and Belgium had been worked out in great detail, and the British Expeditionary Force was to advance sixty miles into Belgium to a strong position on the R. Dyle in front of Brussels, where it was reported that the Belgians had prepared defences. At the outset the 50th Division was to remain in G.H.Q. reserve. On receipt of the code word " Birch " the Division was to be ready for action at six hours' notice.

At 6.30 a.m. on May 10 the code word " Birch " was received. The 1st and 2nd Corps advanced according to plan to the R. Dyle, and, although the Germans crossed the Albert Canal in strength, the B.E.F. held their progress everywhere with confidence. The situation on the right flank, however, soon became serious, and the enemy began to break through further south between the 1st French Army and the French troops on the Maginot Line. On May 16 the G.O.C. in C. of the B.E.F., General Lord Gort, V.C., K.C.B., C.B.E., D.S.O., M.V.O., M.C., received orders to withdraw, and the 50th Division was ordered to take up a defensive rear-guard position on the R. Dendre to the west of Brussels.

Paradoxically, the retreat to Dunkirk really began with the Division's advance into Belgium, and we will therefore start the story of the somewhat confused wanderings and actions of the Green Howards from May 16. On that day they began to move forward ; and, after facing at various times north, south, east and west, they finally got away from Dunkirk on varying dates between May 31 and June 2.

It is a strange story of order and counter order, of marches and counter marches, and of commanding officers at one time separated by seventy miles from their battalions. It is also interesting to see how the four battalions of the Green Howards, the 4th, 5th, 6th and 7th, although originally paired in different divisions, came together at one moment, then split apart, and finally all assembled, those who were left of them, on the beaches at Dunkirk.

In the following pages will be found the names of many places well known in the annals of the Regiment, and doubtless many sons fought over the same soil on which their fathers fell in the years 1914–1918. This double sacrifice, with so few years between, is a melancholy reflection on the statesmen who are ultimately responsible for putting armies into the field.

It is a strange coincidence to read in the Regimental History of 1914–1918 that the 4th and 5th Green Howards took part in the second battle of the Scarpe in April, 1917, within a few miles of where they fought in May, 1940. Ypres and Arras knew the Green Howards well, but there were no woods just north of Poperinghe when last they passed that way in 1918.

How different were the conditions in those days. For four years battalions of the Regiment moved up and down from the R. Yser to the R. Aisne, and, except in the closing stages of 1918, if they advanced half a mile, it was a major action, and a very costly one. This time, in the short space of fifteen days, the four battalions covered hundreds of miles, fighting fiercely whenever they had the opportunity, only to find themselves at the end standing patiently up to their waists in the sea—their transport, guns and equipment destroyed—but proudly holding their rifles above the water.

On May 16 the 50th Division was in billets a few miles west of Lille. The 4th Green Howards were at Wavrin and the 5th at Sainghin as part of the 150th Brigade. Some sixteen miles away to the south, the 7th were at Farbus, and, south again, at Irles were the 6th ; these two battalions forming part of the 69th Brigade of the 23rd Division.

From this day these battalions were almost continually on the move ; often without rations, at times separated from their brigades, and, indeed, with companies and platoons fighting for long periods on their own. It is impossible to tell a coherent story of those chaotic days, but, since it was the first to move, and since, as will be seen, it eventually absorbed the remnants of the 23rd Division, we will begin with the 50th Division.

This Division, under the command of Major-General G. le Q. Martel, D.S.O., M.C., was ordered to advance to the line of the R. Dendre in relief of the 5th Division, and, late on May 16, left its billets in motor transport. The three brigades of the Division were to take up positions guarding the river crossings, with the 25th Brigade on the left at Ninove, the 151st Brigade in the centre at Grammont, and the 150th Brigade on the right at Lessines. Divisional Headquarters was to be established at Everbecq.

The 150th Brigade, under the command of Brigadier C. W. Haydon, M.C., included the 4th and 5th Battalions of the Green Howards, and moved to its new positions via Seclin, Tournai and Renaix. The 4th Battalion, under the command **4 Bn** of Lt.-Col. C. N. Littleboy, M.C., T.D., made a comparatively 16/17 *May* 40 uneventful journey to Lessines, where it arrived just before dawn. It manned the bridges immediately, and took up positions covering the river crossings.

The 5th Battalion, commanded by Lt.-Col. W. E. Bush, M.C., had a more adventurous journey. As it arrived at Tournai, the town was being severely bombed, and was partly in flames, while, to add further to the difficulties of the drivers, still new to driving without lights, a gas alarm was passed down the column. This, however, turned out to be false, and the Battalion reached Renaix at about 10 o'clock on the night of May 16. Here there was some delay, as the advance billeting staff had received three successive orders during the night giving different places each time, and the final destination, Ath, was not reached until the early hours of the 17th.

The billets in which they were finally housed are described as being " of sorts ", which is not surprising, perhaps, since the town was full of refugees " surging about in all directions ". The Battalion, however, proceeded to tackle affairs, and Captain H. I'A. Dennis, who commanded Headquarter Company, was appointed Town Major. Amongst the many troubles of this harassed officer was the investigation into the bona-fides of still more harassed priests. These had been rounded up indiscriminately by enthusiastic soldiers, who had been warned of German Agents in disguise.

2/Lt. Lord Normanby, the Intelligence Officer, exercised his linguistic talents in questioning two German airmen in the local hospital. It is to be hoped that he met with more success than when, on an earlier occasion, in seeking to supply the Commanding Officer with an imposing billet, he became slightly confused between a " Maison de temperance " and a
" Maison de tolerance ". All the preparations to defend the line of the R. Dendre were, however, in vain, as, early on the 18th, the 50th Division, less the 25th Brigade, received orders to withdraw behind the R. Escaut, and to proceed to the Arras area, where a serious threat to the southern flank had developed. And so began the long retreat to Dunkirk.

Rear parties of the 4th Battalion, under Captain I. Donking, and of the 5th Battalion, under Captain F. W. Chadwick, were left behind to guard the bridges across the R. Dendre, and to hand over to incoming troops. Captain Chadwick, who had with him 2/Lt. H. D. G. Greene and eighty men of " D " Company, waited at Ath until a Battalion of the Gloucestershire Regiment, belonging to the 48th Division, arrived shortly after 1 p.m. The latter were in an exhausted condition, and closely pressed by the enemy. One section of Captain Chadwick's command was overrun, all being killed except Cpl. J. Stanfield and L/Cpl. T. W. Holliday, who were captured. The remainder of the party finally got away safely, and reached Pecq some considerable time after the remainder of the Battalion.

Between 6 and 7 a.m. the 5th Battalion marched out of Ath, and at the same time the 4th Battalion started back from its positions on the R. Dendre further north. As far as the 150th Brigade was concerned, this entailed a march of thirty miles, since No. 11 Troop-carrying Company, which had safely delivered them on the R. Dendre, had been rushed away to Brussels on an urgent mission. It was very hot, the road was pavé, a slight breeze disturbed the dust, and the way was crowded with refugees, and parties of Belgian and other troops. Despite these conditions, and the fact that they were supposed to be motorised infantry, the 4th and 5th Green Howards accomplished this march, with a further fourteen miles the next day, without a single man falling out, albeit the 5th confessed to being a trifle footsore. They were, of course, very fit, largely due to the fact that during the earlier months of the year they had been accustomed to march some ten miles every day, to dig a huge anti-tank ditch as a continuation of the Maginot Line.

Comparisons are, of course, odious, but it is an interesting sidelight on modern warfare that this feat should have been worthy of mention in a War Diary, and one can imagine the sarcastic comments of the Peninsular Veterans or the Old Contemptibles could they read it. However, these comments would only be sour grapes, as a Mechanical Troop-carrying Company would, in their day, doubtless have been greeted with enthusiasm.

The night of May 18/19 was spent by the two battalions in the neighbourhood of Pecq, just south of Dottignies, on the R. Escaut. Hurried reconnaissances were made in the midst of scenes of indescribable confusion—civilians abandoning their homes, their shops and their farms, bridges being blown up, and barges sunk in the canal.

They were told that the position was to be held at all costs, but, soon after 9 a.m. on the 19th, warning orders for a move further back were received. *4 and 5 Bns 19 May 40*

The 50th Division was to be relieved by the 1st Division, and, later in the day, together with the 5th Division and other troops, it became part of Frankforce, under the command of Major-General H. E. Franklyn, D.S.O., M.C., for action in the neighbourhood of Vimy.

Soon after mid-day the 150th Brigade moved off on the first stage of its journey south-west to Vimy. The 4th Battalion

marched via Hem to Ascq, and the 5th to Flers, an industrial
village near Lille, and not far from Sainghin, whence it had
set out three days before.

The congestion on the roads was much worse than on the
previous day. The heat was still intense and the pavé no less
4 *and* 5 *Bns* hard. After a good night's rest in billets, however, the
20 *May* 40 battalions were cheered to hear that troop-carrying transport
was available once more, and during the afternoon they
embussed for Vimy, proceeding by way of Seclin, Carvin and
Lens.

The news spread that the situation to the south had
improved, and that it was probable that the Brigade would be
taking offensive action that night. It is typical of the Yorkshireman that, when told he might be fighting at Vimy that
night, one Green Howard said to 2/Lt. E. L. Kirby, the
Intelligence Officer of the 4th Battalion : " Vimy Ridge, Sir !
It's just like being asked to play for England at Lords."

The road to Vimy presented a scene of confusion. In
places vehicles of all descriptions were not only head to tail,
but also abreast to the full width of the road—in broad daylight, and with the enemy in command of the sky. There was
a certain amount of machine-gunning, and 2/Lt. A. J. Clarke
of the 5th Battalion was wounded.

Just before reaching Vimy the 4th Battalion turned off the
main road to Farbus, where it received orders to prepare
defence positions on the south-eastern end of Vimy Ridge,
and to get into touch with the 6th and 7th Green Howards,
who were reported to be holding part of the ridge. The time
was now about 6 p.m., and an hour later the Commanding
Officer was summoned to Brigade Headquarters at Vimy.
Here he was told that the 5th Green Howards had been sent
on into Arras, that the 4th East Yorkshires were moving to
St. Laurent, and that he was to take his battalion at once
on to Athies, and hold the bridges over the R. Scarpe.
Returning to Farbus, Lt.-Col. Littleboy gave orders for the
battalion to move to a crossroads about a mile north of
Athies, and set off himself in his truck, with his Intelligence
Officer (2/Lt. Kirby) and Anti-Tank Platoon Commander
(2/Lt. Roche), for Athies just as it was getting dusk. Their
route lay across by-roads and cart-tracks, and they did not
arrive until nearly midnight—to find Athies deserted. Moving
forward about three-quarters of a mile, they found a French
patrol, who informed them that the main enemy force appeared
to be on a hillside further south. They then drove back through
Athies, but found no signs of life there, nor in Fampoux about

a mile to the east. When they went on to Roueux, however, they were amazed to find that the 6th Battalion had received orders to withdraw.

There was no time for consultation as it was by this time 1 a.m. on the 21st, so Lt.-Col. Littleboy hurried back to Athies, where the sole inhabitants appeared to be two dead cows, and sent off 2/Lt. Kirby to bring up the Battalion.

4 *Bn*
21 *May* 40

His plan of defence was to hold the railway bridge area with " B " Company (Capt. I. Donking) ; Athies and the road bridge over the Scarpe with " D " Company (Major H. Keyworth) ; while he placed " C " Company (Capt. B. J. S. Proud) on the left flank in the outskirts of Fampoux, as the 13th Brigade had not yet arrived. His own headquarters were established in an estaminet by the cross roads in Athies, while, in reserve just behind Athies, he kept " A " Company (Capt. R. W. Metcalfe), the mortar platoon, and the remainder of the Headquarter Company under Major G. I. Mackinlay. The carrier platoon under 2/Lt. U. Alexander was hidden in a sunken road to the north-west of Fampoux as a protection to the left flank.

The Battalion arrived at about 2 a.m. on May 21, and the companies were hurried to their positions. The transport only just got back over the ridge before daylight on its return to Bailleul. (This village of Bailleul must not be confused with the town of the same name, well-known in the 1914–1918 war, through which the 7th Battalion was to pass on May 26.)

The 4th Battalion was now extended over a two-mile front with the R. Scarpe in front of it, and by 10.30 a.m. the Commanding Officer was sufficiently satisfied with his dispositions to allow the French outposts to withdraw. The 2nd Battalion, Wiltshire Regiment, had also arrived by this time in Fampoux, and taken up its positions. During the day the 151st Brigade, with a Brigade of tanks, was making an encircling attack to the west and south of Arras which met with some success, but was forced back to Vimy in the evening.

Coincident with this attack, three German tanks appeared in front of " D " Company, and one was immediately knocked out by P.S.M. G. H. Upton with a Boyes rifle. The remaining two tanks withdrew, after having been fired upon by our artillery. Late in the evening Capt. Donking took out a patrol across the river to investigate P.S.M. Upton's tank, and returned with two crash helmets, a map, a revolver and some papers.

The morning of May 22 passed quietly, and Lt.-Col. Littleboy was able to shorten his front by withdrawing " C " Company and the Carrier platoon from Fampoux, now that

4 *Bn*
22 *May* 40

the Wiltshires were established there. " C Company" took up position in a wooded area on the left of " D " Company, and the Carrier platoon was moved back into reserve behind Athies. At four o'clock in the afternoon orders were received for withdrawal, rather to the surprise of everybody, and at 5 p.m. the transport came hurtling over the ridge under fairly heavy fire. Pte. F. Chaney, Signals Despatch Rider, was killed—the first battle casualty of the 4th Battalion.

The trucks and lorries were loaded under more or less incessant shell fire and hurried back to Bailleul, but, before any troops moved, the enemy put down a heavy barrage of mortar, shell and machine gun fire on to " B " and " D " Companies, and it was reported that the Germans had crossed the canal in front of " B " Company. 2/Lt. A. J. Capps and two other ranks were killed in this brief action, but the attack did not develop. At 11.30 p.m. the orders to withdraw were cancelled, and the transport brought back once more the baggage which it had evacuated earlier in the evening.

4 Bn
23 May 40
The morning of May 23 was hot and sunny, and the men were very tired. Enemy sniping and mortaring of the forward positions increased, and during the afternoon another withdrawal order arrived. Athies was now being heavily shelled, and the transport under L/Sgt. J. W. Peacock suffered some casualties, both in men and vehicles, before it could be extricated. When the Battalion finally got back to England, L/Sgt. Peacock was awarded the Military Medal for the fine leadership which he displayed throughout the operations and, in particular, at Athies, and later at Dunkirk. His calm behaviour under heavy fire had a steadying influence on his drivers, and his bearing and work under very trying circumstances were beyond all praise.

At 7 p.m. reports came in from " D " Company that the enemy were attacking in force across its front towards " C " Company ; a certain number had got across the canal in boats, and the platoon guarding the bridge had been forced to withdraw owing to heavy shell fire.

Athies was by this time partly in flames, and Lt.-Col. Littleboy withdrew his headquarters to a command post further back on the ridge, leaving 2/Lt. Kirby in the attic of the Estaminet to watch the approaches to Athies. It was an unhealthy observation post, which became unhealthier when the Estaminet caught fire. There on the ridge a secondary defensive position was established with the remains of Headquarters Company, and stragglers who were coming in from the forward companies.

DIGGING DEFENCE POSITIONS IN EGYPT.

CAPTURING A RIDGE IN N. AFRICA.

Face page 32

In order to secure a better command of the exits from Athies, and to give some support to " C " Company, P.S.M. T. Fenwick of the Pioneers was sent off with as many men as he could collect to the Athies-Fampoux road. This advance over open country and under heavy rifle fire was successfully accomplished.

As dusk fell figures were seen some thousand yards to the east of the command post, and bullets began to arrive from the rear. Major E. C. Cooke-Collis went out to the east, and Capt. J. B. Mansell to the rear, to investigate, and it soon became apparent that they were encircled on these two sides. It was now 11 p.m., and, as far as was known, " A " and " B " Companies were still holding out in front. A report to this effect was successfully carried to Brigade Headquarters by Cpl. A. T. Heathcock, who drove straight through the enemy in his carrier.

Two patrols were now sent out, under Capt. Donking and 2/Lt. Kirby respectively, to find out the position round the bridge. These patrols met according to plan and re-occupied the bridge. Meanwhile, the Commanding Officer, with Capt. Mansell, covered by a patrol under 2/Lt. P. B. Watson, walked across country to visit " C " Company. Failing to find anybody, and meeting a German patrol complete with a close support gun approaching Athies from the direction of Fampoux, they discreetly withdrew.

At 3 a.m. on the morning of May 24 verbal orders were   4 *Bn* received from the Brigade Major to withdraw forthwith to 24/25 *May* 40 Carvin. Under cover of a thick mist, which lasted well into the morning, the Battalion, except for " C " Company whose fate was then unknown, marched the eighteen miles to Carvin unmolested. Here it was picked up by troop-carrying vehicles and lifted to L'Abrisseau, a suburb of Lille. The 4th Green Howards arrived here at about 4 p.m., were billeted in a large factory, and slept the sleep of exhaustion.

When they took stock on the 25th it was found that their losses had been heavy. Capt. Proud, 2/Lts. B. Winterschladen, P. Forster and D. C. Preston, together with the whole of " C " Company, with the exception of 2/Lt. J. R. Booth and eight other ranks, were missing, and the other companies had lost heavily. But the Battalion had fought well.

Lt.-Col. C. N. Littleboy was later awarded the D.S.O. The following is the official citation for this award :

" During the operations from May 20 until embarkation, Lt.-Col. Littleboy commanded his Battalion with great vigour and initiative. He was always cool and calm. His complete
D

personal disregard of enemy action, no matter in what form, had an excellent effect on all ranks, especially so at Athies on May 23 when this officer's action and deportment undoubtedly saved a very awkward situation, resulting from the combination of enemy ground action and intensive air bombardment. The results achieved by the 4th Green Howards are very largely due to this officer's fine example and leadership."

2/Lt. Kirby was awarded the Military Cross for his leadership of the patrol on May 23, and also for his calm behaviour in remaining in his observation post in the estaminet at Athies on May 21, until the latter was destroyed by artillery fire.

Capt. D. B. Elliott, the padre, did magnificent work in helping to rescue the wounded under fire, and was also awarded the Military Cross.

The task of the despatch riders was a difficult and dangerous one under the conditions which obtained, and Pte. J. A. Scuffham was continually employed carrying messages along roads which were under shell and small arms fire. He never faltered in his duties, and his spirit and carefree riding were an example to all who saw him. He was awarded the Military Medal.

L/Cpl. W. J. Alexander also received the Military Medal. He was a member of one of the patrols on May 23, and volunteered to go forward alone and draw the enemy's fire so as to enable his comrades to locate the enemy position. He displayed great courage and coolness, and complete disregard for his own safety.

5 *Bn*
20 *May* 40   Leaving the 4th Battalion to spend a day's rest in Lille, we must now return to May 20, and to the 5th Battalion, which, on arriving at Vimy just before dark, was ordered to proceed into Arras as part of Petreforce. This garrison of Arras, under the command of Major-General R. L. Petre, D.S.O., M.C., consisted, in addition to the Green Howards, of a battalion of the Welsh Guards, and a detachment of the South Staffordshire Regiment. The Battalion extricated itself somehow from the traffic chaos on the Vimy Road, and, de-bussing outside the town, eventually trickled into Arras at about

5 *Bn*   midnight, in the middle of an aerial bombardment.

21/22 *May* 40   Inevitably the role of the Battalion in Arras was defensive, and each company was allotted one of the main approaches to the city from the west. " B " Company (Capt. W. G. Dumville) guarded the St. Pol road, and suffered the mortification of having its road block demolished by a French civilian, who drove his bus through it. " D " Company (Capt. Chadwick), on the Doullens road, had a more formidable road block composed of steam rollers, which, however, had the disadvantage of being most conspicuous and attractive to enemy bombers. Pte. J. Richardson, who was in a position some hundred yards in front of this road block, had the satisfaction of shooting stone dead a German officer who was reconnoitring the road. " C " Company (Capt. G. A. F. Steede) defended the approaches through the Citadelle, and " A " Company (Major W. Lacy) looked after the road from Achicourt, and the railway sidings on the southern edge of the city.

Regimental Headquarters was established in the Palace St. Vaast, but, unluckily, before they could be unloaded, the Battalion office truck and Officers' Mess truck received a direct hit from a bomb outside the entrance to the cellars. Eleven men were killed or wounded at the same time, and 2/Lt. J. I. A. Russell was also wounded inside " D " Company's H.Q. the same night.

The three days spent in Arras are described by Captain J. M. Whittaker as three of the weirdest days experienced by the Battalion. " The city was in that eerie ' No-man's land ' between the civilian and military worlds. The shop windows were full of pre-war goods, but the streets were deserted. There was little sign of civilians, but there must have been several hundreds in the city who, too feeble or too listless to escape, dragged out a miserable existence in the cellars. Some were, doubtless, there for loot, and some for no good at all from the British point of view, judging from the sporadic sniping after dark, and the mysterious Verey lights which went up at intervals." Bombers flew continually over the city, but only two main attacks were made—a light one on the afternoon of May 22, and a really heavy one on the morning of May 23. Casualties were, however, few, owing to trench and cellar protection, and the " screaming raids ", when the bombers howled over the housetops every evening at 6 p.m., failed to upset the morale of the Green Howards. One serious result, however, of the bombing was the destruction of the sole surviving source of water supply in the city. The shortage of water was severely felt, and it was left to Lt. F. M. Pearce to make the magnificent gesture of shaving in champagne !

A certain grim humour was provided by a statement heard on the B.B.C.'s six o'clock news on May 21 that the French Prime Minister had announced the fall of Amiens and Arras, and the next day that the latter had been recaptured by the French—of whom there had been none in evidence in that area.

5 *Bn*
23 *May* 40

At 7 p.m. on May 23 rumours of evacuation were dispensed with by the publication of an order that " Arras was to be held at all costs ". As so often happened in those hectic days, this order was very soon countermanded by another, to the effect that all bridges were to be blown up, and the town evacuated, by 2.30 a.m. next morning.

The road leading north out of Arras, although subjected to shelling and bombing, was still open, as was proved by Lt. (Q.M.) A. N. Evans, who went to and from La Bassee along it daily, and brought up rations and supplies without fail. The work of the Quarter-master and his men must not go unrecorded. All the way back to Dunkirk the Battalion was supplied with rations and petrol with a regularity which belied the difficulties of obtaining them in a highly confused situation. For this work Lt. (Q.M.) Evans received a mention in despatches.

5 *Bn*
24 *May* 40

As the order for evacuation only reached the Battalion at 2 a.m. on May 24, instructions were rushed out to companies to retire independently. The only order as to destination was " to go to the canal bank area just north of Douai ". Battalion Headquarters moved first, and marched out over the St. Nicholas bridge, which was due to be blown up. Lt.-Col. Bush left a check post here under his second in command, Major P. V. V. Guy, and set out with the remainder of his party to reconnoitre his next position at the rendezvous north of Douai. Soon after leaving St. Laurent Blangy on the Douai road they came to a road junction. The main Douai road at this point went to the left, and a minor road led to the right following the course of the R. Scarpe. Both roads crossed a railway line—the main road over a bridge, which was blown up, and the subsidiary road under a bridge which was intact. Sending back word for the troops which were following to be diverted to a more westerly road by way of Bailleul, Lt.-Col. Bush led his party on foot across the broken bridge, and proceeded another three miles forward to Gavrelle, where he waited a while, hoping to be joined by the rest of the Battalion and the headquarters transport. The latter he had had to send off by the lower road, and they ran into a dawn crossing of the Scarpe by the Germans. The leading vehicles, including the Commanding Officer's car with the Signals Officer, Lt. Pearce, ran straight into the enemy in the heavy mist and were captured.

When Lt.-Col. Bush and his party arrived at Gavrelle it was already daylight, and the enemy could clearly be seen on the high ground to the south, and also on the ridge to the east of the village. There were some elements of the Inniskilling

Dragoons in Gavrelle, and Lt.-Col. Bush decided to make a stand there with a view to protecting the right flank of the remainder of his Battalion which, he hoped, was moving back along the road to Bailleul. Splitting his party into two groups he took command of one himself, and placed the other under his adjutant, Capt. H. D. Whitehead.

All the troops were put into the front line, with no reserve, and they thus covered a maximum of frontage, which had the desired effect of deceiving the enemy. While shelling Gavrelle, he massed troops and machine-guns on the ridge, but hesitated to advance until well after mid-day.

When the Inniskillings withdrew between 10 and 11 a.m. Lt.-Col. Bush conformed, but was unable to get in touch with Capt. Whitehead who, with his small and gallant party, held on for another two hours, and eventually extricated himself with little loss. For his gallantry and leadership in this action, Capt. Whitehead was awarded the Military Cross, and L/Cpl. T. B. Owen of the Intelligence Section, received the Military Medal. Lt.-Col. Bush was awarded the Distinguished Service Order on the recommendation of Major-General Petre. In the words of the official citation accompanying the award : " Lt.-Col. Bush led his battalion into Arras to reinforce the perimeter. The posts held by the Battalion were subjected to heavy air-bombing attacks, followed later by attacks by armoured vehicles. Yet no posts were lost before the final withdrawal, and many casualties were inflicted on the enemy. It was the cheerful and confident presence of Lt.-Col. Bush at points on the perimeter where the danger was greatest that contributed very largely to the success of the Battalion. He was invariably on the spot to encourage his men, with the result that they became imbued with a fine offensive spirit."

Meanwhile the remainder of the Battalion succeeded in getting away from Arras in various independent groups. " A ", " B ", and Headquarter Companies got clear of the town before dawn, and made their way to Oignies. " D " Company, with the exception of Lt. G. H. Chamber's Platoon, left shortly before 5 a.m. But " C " Company, together with Lt. Chamber's Platoon, did not get away until 5.30 a.m. This latter party, under command of Major Guy, pursuing a course of its own, through Vimy, Givenchy, Loos, Hulluch, Wingles and Seclin, arrived in Lille on the night of the 24th. They were enabled to do this largely owing to a fortunate meeting with a Field Park Company, R.E., near Wingles, which not only threw a bridge over the canal, but also lifted them on their vehicles for the rest of the way into Lille.

" D " Company, however, was not so lucky, since it missed Major Guy's control post and, acting on the original orders, proceeded to try and make its way to Douai. Getting clear of the town at about 5 a.m. under cover of the thick mist, it made its way to Thelus and over the Vimy Ridge towards Bailleul. On approaching the village, however, it came under intense fire and was forced north to make a long detour. When eventually it was within a mile of Douai, which was then in flames, it was intercepted by a despatch rider and, as a result of his information, made its way to Flers, where it linked up with another British battalion. The next day was spent in a defensive position, but on the following day it was given a complete platoon of stragglers to make the Company up to strength, and was put into another defensive position at Gargautelle, a village near Oignies. Had they only been sent there twenty-four hours earlier, they would have found the remainder of the 5th Battalion. The next morning a French detachment arrived to take over the position, and Capt. Chadwick sent back for orders to his (temporary) Battalion headquarters. These could not be found, and he was preparing to withdraw his Company, when the French asked him for four Bren guns to guard their right flank. Knowing that time was short, and that they were almost surrounded, Captain Chadwick did not wish to jeopardise the whole of his command, and so called for volunteers. 2/Lt. Greene and seventeen men answered the call, and he sent off the rest of the Company under 2/Lt. P. G. Rickard towards Lille, with orders to join up with any British troops he could find. This party managed to make its way as far as Ypres, where they were all either killed or captured when fighting a desperate action within a quarter of a mile of the positions occupied by the 5th Battalion, but unfortunately with the enemy in between them.

Meanwhile, towards evening, Capt. Chadwick, after holding on all day with his small party, tried to contact the French Headquarters, only to find that it had gone. He then moved back to Seclin and laid up for the night. When they woke up next morning they found Germans all round them, and so lay doggo for the rest of the day. When night came, Capt. Chadwick again split up his force, and sending one section under 2/Lt. Greene to the north-west, he led his own party north towards Lille. Neither party got very far ; 2/Lt. Greene was captured in Armentieres, and Capt. Chadwick before reaching Lille. The latter officer was interviewed by a German Intelligence Officer in Lille next day, who said that he had been a Professor of History at Oxford. When he found that he could extract no information out of Capt. Chadwick, he said : " You will be taken to Germany, where you will have a very good time and be returned to England in September, when the war will be over." To this Capt. Chadwick replied : " Surely, as a Professor of History, you must know that the English always win the last battle ! " The German laughed and said : " As a matter of fact you are right, but this is the exception that proves the rule." Captain Chadwick then had the last word : " And, what is more, I can tell you that this war will last longer than that of 1914–1918 ". During his long term of imprisonment—he was there till the end—he must sometimes have regretted that he was such a good prophet.

It was not until late on the 24th that the Battalion, less all " C " and " D " Companies, came together again at Oignies, from which place it was lifted a further twelve miles to Faubourg Des Douais, a suburb of Lille, where it found *5 Bn* Major Guy and his party, and spent May 25 enjoying a much *25 May* 40 needed rest.

Leaving the 4th and 5th Battalions in Lille, before following them on their move into Belgium on May 26, we must bring the story of the 6th and 7th Battalions up to date.

The 23rd Division, under the Command of Major-General *6 and 7 Bns* Herbert, went to France in April, 1940, with the object of *Apr* 40 supplying working parties on aerodrome construction. When reading in the following pages the exploits of the 6th and 7th Battalions it must always be remembered that they were not fully equipped to fight. The scale of weapons, other than rifles, was approximately two Bren guns and one anti-tank rifle to each rifle Company. There were no carriers, no mortars, and signal equipment was practically non-existent. There were no supporting arms, such as artillery, with the Division. The officers had no equipment such as revolver, binoculars, or compass, except when they had provided their own. It had been intended that the Division should return to England after three months, to complete its training. Fate, however, decreed otherwise and, within a few weeks, these troops, many of whom had hardly fired a rifle and none of whom had been given any training in the use of anti-tank rifles or Bren guns, found themselves fighting for their lives, and holding up the onrushing Germans like seasoned warriors.

On May 16 the 69th Brigade, commanded by Brigadier *6 and 7 Bns* Lord Downe, of which the 6th and 7th Green Howards formed *16/17 May* 40 a part, was at Becourt, with the 6th Green Howards, commanded by Lt.-Col. M. R. Steel, D.S.O., M.C., at Irles, and the 7th Green Howards, commanded by Lt.-Col. Richmond Brown, at Farbus. At 8.30 a.m. on May 17 the Division was ordered to take up positions on the Canal Du Nord between

Ruyaucourt and Arlieux, a front of seventeen miles. This front was divided into two sectors on each side of the Arras-Cambrai road. The 70th Brigade was given the right sector, and the 69th Brigade the sector north of the road.

Warning was received that rations were to be reduced to half scale, and that the troops were to live on the country ; in point of fact no further normal issue of supplies reached the Division during the next fifteen days.

The 6th Battalion had spent the first half of May at Irles, working on the construction of runways for an aerodrome north of Grevilliers Wood. Digging here was full of interest—and also danger. Ammunition of all sorts, dating from the trench warfare of 1914–1918, was constantly being unearthed, and it was found that some of the detonators and explosives had suffered no deterioration after twenty-five years in the earth. Many other relics were also dug up—the most interesting being a set of German Officers' Mess drinking glasses, complete with the Imperial Insignia of a crown over a " W ". There was also considerable activity in searching for fifth columnists, and patrols went out every night, plotting lights seen on the ground when enemy aircraft were overhead. As a result, two of the local inhabitants were arrested, and later shot by the French Security Police.

By mid-afternoon on the 17th the Battalion arrived at its new positions between Marquion and Sauchy Cauchy, and proceeded to dig in and consolidate.

6 *and* 7 *Bns*   The next day passed quietly except for rumours of enemy
18 *May* 40 tanks in Cambrai, but at 5 p.m. orders were received to blow up the bridges over the canal. This was successfully accomplished, although the destruction of the main Arras-Cambrai road bridge unfortunately entailed the death of many civilians, who, although the bridge was cleared several times, persisted in following up the patrol as soon as it withdrew, after setting the charges.

6 *and* 7 *Bns*   The 7th Battalion had also moved on the afternoon of the
19 *May* 40 17th to Ecourt St. Quentin, and taken up positions along the canal on the left of the 6th. On the 19th the 69th Brigade was withdrawn from the Canal du Nord, and the 7th Battalion, less one company, moved back again to the woods on Vimy
7 *Bn*   Ridge near Thelus. Here it remained under cover, until, on
20/22 *May* 40 the morning of May 22, it embussed and was taken to Gondecourt, where it was billeted in houses and farm buildings.

6 *Bn*   Meanwhile the 6th Battalion had withdrawn early on the
19 *May* 40 19th to the village of Saudemont, some three miles to the north-west, where it took up positions in and around the village.

The tactics necessarily devised by the 6th Battalion to defend the locality of Saudemont serve to accentuate the fact that the Battalion, although full of the will to fight, as it was to show later at Gravelines, was ill equipped and only very partially trained. The country around Saudemont was open and undulating, with no natural obstacles, and ideal for an attack by armoured vehicles.

Realising that in such country, and with so few weapons, a normal system of defence would be useless, Lt.-Col. Steel evolved a plan, whereby the Battalion, if attacked, would inflict as much execution as possible on the enemy, albeit it would be a suicidal battle. One rifle company spread itself out in the open country at some distance from the village, its task being to give the alarm on the approach of the enemy. The remainder of the Battalion was confined in the houses of the village. The plan was that, if the enemy attacked with tanks, the Battalion would lie doggo in the houses, allowing the tanks to pass through. If the enemy attacked with infantry, of if infantry followed the tanks, then the Battalion was to rush out of the houses and fight it out. Greatly to the relief of the few experienced soldiers present, no attack took place, and at about 8.30 p.m. orders were received to march to Thelus.

Just as the last company was marching off, Lt.-Col. Steel, who had left in advance to reconnoitre the Thelus position, arrived back with new orders. The Battalion was to plug a gap on the north bank of the R. Scarpe at Roueux. The companies got into their positions just before dawn on May 20. "B", "C" and "D" Companies were in the front line, with "A" and Headquarter Companies in reserve. Two companies of the 11th Battalion Durham Light Infantry were on the Battalion's left flank, with the 5th Battalion East Yorkshires at Plouvain, while on their right was one company of the 7th Green Howards under Capt. A. C. Scott, the remainder of this Battalion having gone too far on the way to Thelus to be recalled when the orders were changed. French light tanks were covering the bridges in front, but were withdrawn by order of the French Higher Command about mid-day. *6 Bn 20 May 40*

In the early hours of May 20 the bulk of the 70th Brigade was overrun by enemy tanks and lost. The 69th Brigade, therefore, held on almost alone.

As soon as it was daylight it was discovered that the enemy were just across the river, and a certain amount of mortar fire was put down on the forward positions. The main Arras road ran along the top of the ridge to the front about a mile away, and this appeared to be the axis of the German advance. These enemy troops were probably a flank guard, as, beyond exchanging a few shots with the Green Howards, they made no attempt to cross the river that day. During the day Private F. Rowan, by good sniping, accounted for at least three of the enemy. The foreground presented an extraordinary sight, as the Germans had evidently cleared the road of refugees, and huge crowds of the latter were swarming across country on foot, pushing handcarts, prams and bicycles, and riding in farm vehicles piled high with their household belongings.

6 Bn
21 May 40   In the early hours of May 21 the 4th Battalion, Green Howards, arrived, and the 6th Battalion received orders to move back to Farbus. Orders were given to march in sections, and to mix freely with the refugee stream to avoid attention from the air, and the Battalion reassembled safely in the Vimy woods late in the afternoon. On the 22nd it moved back again to Gondecourt, and joined up once more with the 7th Battalion.

6 Bn
22 May 40

During May 22 Lt.-Col. Steel took over command of the 69th Brigade ; the command of the 6th Battalion, Green Howards, devolving on Major G. R. Dixon. The 23rd Division, with its Headquarters at Seclin, was now in a sadly depleted condition, and the remnants of the 70th Brigade were used to fill up gaps in the ranks of the 69th Brigade.

On May 22 the 23rd Division was placed directly under G.H.Q., and orders were received to withdraw some seventy miles, and take up positions along the R. Aa, from the sea at Gravelines towards St. Omer. Advance Divisional Headquarters, accordingly, with reconnaissance parties of Brigade Staff, Commanding Officers and Adjutants, set out at once for Gravelines where they arrived safely. By the time, however, that the troops got on the move, reports came in that the enemy were in Hazebrouck, and lying across their route. They were, accordingly, turned back at Estaires, and arrived back at Gondecourt during the afternoon—with the exception of the 6th Green Howards, who had got through safely to Gravelines, with the reconnaissance parties. From this point the 6th Battalion operated independently, and, before taking up the story of the 50th Division, and the remainder of the 23rd Division, we will follow its adventures until it embarked at Dunkirk on May 31.

6 Bn
23 May 40   The Battalion arrived at Gravelines soon after dawn on May 23, and found the fort garrisoned by French reserve gunners, who were apparently out of touch with the situation, and surprised at the arrival of British troops. The elderly Colonel considered himself Garrison Commander, and was only persuaded with great difficulty that the Green Howards

were correct in taking up their positions facing south-west, while his own troops, except for some mortars covering the estuary, were facing east. The front taken up along the canal was a long one, and all the companies, except Headquarter Company in reserve near the fort, were strung out along the canal bank. Lt.-Col. Steel, as he was separated from the rest of his brigade, now resumed command of the Battalion.

All was quiet during the morning, and life in the cafés and shops was practically normal, but in the afternoon a few enemy light tanks appeared from the direction of Calais, and, on approaching the bridge, which had only been barricaded and not blown up owing to lack of explosives, were fired upon by the bridgehead platoon under Lt. J. M. Hewson, commanding No. 13 Platoon of " C " Company. In view of its vital position round the bridge, No. 13 Platoon had been entrusted with the Company's one anti-tank rifle. As this weapon was practically an unknown quantity, and reported to have a terrible " kick ", 2/Lt. Hewson decided to handle it himself. He sited it well forward of his platoon's position in a spot which, had he had the opportunity of knowing the weapon, he would never have chosen. There was no covered line of withdrawal by which to change its position once it had fired its first few tell-tale rounds, and the soil was sandy and dry. But the position fulfilled the one condition typical of 2/Lt. Hewson's spirit, namely that it was one from which he could get at the enemy. When the enemy tanks approached 2/Lt. Hewson held his fire, and then, with his first few rounds, knocked out one tank and hit others. Under small arms fire from the remainder of No. 13 Platoon the enemy withdrew towards the wood from which they had appeared, firing as they went. 2/Lt. Hewson fired again, but, by this time, his position was fully exposed and he was wounded. While he was trying to get the precious anti-tank rifle back to another position, he was hit again, and killed outright. By this gallant action he undoubtedly saved the bridge. Not only did he stop the tanks by his calm and accurate firing, but he also showed the remainder of the Battalion that the Germans could be stopped. His body was recovered two days later and he was buried at Fort Mardick. " B " Company's anti-tank rifle, and some riflemen, were then sent to " C " Company for the further defence of the bridge.

In the very early hours of the next morning more tanks approached along the road from Oye, and were fired upon by this anti-tank rifle section. They immediately withdrew. As soon as it grew light the tanks appeared again, covered with red, white and blue streamers. They turned out to be one cruiser and three light British tanks, which had been cut off

6 Bn
24 May 40

in the tank battle outside Calais. Unfortunately the gunner of the cruiser tank had been killed by the anti-tank rifle fire, and the Commanding Officer slightly wounded. They agreed, however, to join in the defence of Gravelines, and played an important part in repelling a determined attack by the enemy later in the day.

The commander of the cruiser tank asked for a replacement for his gunner, and Sgt. W. Gibson, the Headquarter Company cook, volunteered for the job. Sgt. Gibson had attended a two-day 2-pounder course at Irles, and put his knowledge to good use later in the afternoon by knocking out at least one enemy tank. At the height of the bombardment which accompanied this attack, C.S.M. J. O'Grady of " B " Company made the famous remark, which not only relieved the tension at the time, but was also frequently repeated in the Battalion for years afterwards. Pointing to a forlorn little bird which was hopping about in front of his trench, " Sure," he said, " those —— Boches are putting so much stuff up there today that even the —— birds have to come down and walk !"

After the Germans had been repulsed in the afternoon and things were quiet again, orders were received at about 6 p.m. for the Battalion to march to Bergues, and to become part of Usherforce in the defence of Dunkirk. This news was imparted to the French Garrison Commander by Major Dixon, who found the old gentleman drinking brandy, highly delighted that the attack had been driven off, and quite confident that he could hold on without British assistance.

Some time between 9 and 10 p.m. the Battalion started to move back, but the enemy had by this time got across the canal on the exposed left flank, and some very confused hand-to-hand fighting took place on the outskirts of the town. Captain E. H. Kidd, Commander of the left flank company, after No. 9 Platoon had withdrawn into the town, went back to look for his remaining platoons accompanied by Captain P. B. Foster, who commanded " D " Company. They had the misfortune to run into an enemy patrol. Captain Kidd was wounded by a grenade, and both officers were taken prisoner. Lt. G. F. Farrand, the signals officer, was also badly wounded and captured about this time when making his way to " A " Company to check the signal lines. After the battalion had withdrawn from its forward positions, the enemy halted their attack for a while, and 2/Lt. J. L. Hughes took out a patrol along the canal bank. For his leadership and bravery throughout the day and night, 2/Lt. Hughes was awarded the Military Cross. 2/Lt. P. J. Carr also received the

Military Cross for his coolness and courage throughout the action.

Pte. R. Laidler was awarded the Military Medal. When his section post had been burnt by incendiary ammunition, and there were many casualties from high explosive and machine-gun fire, Pte. Laidler volunteered to lead a party to rescue the wounded. He carried this out under heavy fire, and was only restrained by his Commander from going back for the dead.

Finally, Lt.-Col. M. R. Steel was awarded a bar to his Distinguished Service Order. In the words of his citation : " By his gallantry and resource, the enemy attack upon Dunkirk from the west was considerably delayed ". There can be no doubt that this action, fought so gallantly by the 6th Green Howards, who, it must always be remembered, had only been part of a " pick and shovel brigade " a week previously, compares favourably with anything that a trained and well equipped Battalion might have been expected to carry out, and was worthy of the highest traditions of the Regiment.

It is a noteworthy fact that when, much later, Lord Gort's despatches were published, the 6th Battalion, Green Howards was specifically mentioned by name for its defence of Gravelines.

Lt.-Col. Steel had left Gravelines earlier on the 24th for Bergues, at which place the remainder of the 69th Brigade was expected to arrive during the night. This move was *6 Bn* cancelled later, and, on the afternoon of the 25th, Lt.-Col. *25 May 40* Steel returned to Fort Mardick, to which place the 6th Battalion had been diverted on leaving Gravelines. He brought with him orders for the Battalion to move to Les Moeres, which it did during the night, and by dawn was settling into barns *6 Bn* and farmhouses, with Battalion Headquarters established in a *26 May 40* small house in the village street. Lt.-Col. Steel went off early to Bray Dunes, and during his absence a low-flying aircraft bombed Les Moeres. A direct hit was scored on Battalion Headquarters, and the house was completely demolished. Fortunately, out of about twenty officers and men, only one man was killed and one wounded.

The next day, the 27th, the Battalion spent controlling *6 Bn* traffic on the Bergues-Wormhoudt road. It was relieved of *27 May 40* these duties at about 9.30 p.m. and marched off to billets in Teteghen. The next evening it moved back into the line at *6 Bn* Hague Moelen, facing south-west, and protecting the right *28 May 40* flank of the main axis of withdrawal to Dunkirk. The front was a long one and all companies were in the line.

It was very noticeable, after their successful resistance at Gravelines, how the morale of the troops had risen. Prior to that action, there had often been, particularly after long marches, a certain amount of argument as to who should carry the extra weight of a bren gun or the anti-tank rifle. Now the men were collecting, whenever possible, discarded brens and anti-tank rifles, and, when the Battalion went into the line at Hague Moelen, it fairly bristled with additional weapons. When, on their final withdrawal to Bray Dunes, they were told to hand them over to the Welsh Guards, they would only do so after an order had been given by the Commanding Officer. The Battalion had now found itself, and was thirsting for blood, but had only one more day on which to show its fighting spirit.

The Irish and Welsh Guards were on the Green Howards' left flank, and the right flank was lightly held by the remnants of the Fife and Forfarshire Yeomanry with a few armoured vehicles. Bergues was being heavily shelled and bombed at this time, and one of the forward companies located a German battery position. On this information being given to a troop of 25 pounders which had appeared in the sector, it was discovered that the latter had destroyed their sights, and could only take on targets at point blank range. The 6th Green Howards held on here all through the 29th, and there was a certain amount of confused fighting.

" A " Company, on the right of the line, received a message at one period of the afternoon to withdraw, but, as it passed Battalion Headquarters, it transpired that the message had been a mistake and it was ordered back. Cautiously making their return journey to their positions, which had been untenanted for half an hour, they found that their absence had not been noticed by the enemy. In the words of one of the officers : " The fog of war was as black as the skies above ".

" D " Company, commanded by Captain J. G. Middleditch, was holding the left flank adjoining the 2nd Battalion Welsh Guards. During the afternoon the enemy launched a heavy attack, under cover of a smoke screen, mainly against the Guards, but partly against " D " Company, which was forced to withdraw about half a mile. Capt. Middleditch was ordered by a Brigadier to split his company, which now consisted of only two platoons, and to break through the gap between the Guards and the Green Howards, and engage the enemy. Captain Middleditch took one platoon and what was left of his Company Headquarters, and placed the other platoon under the command of 2/Lt. W. Warrener.

2/Lt. Warrener's party had not proceeded very far before it was attacked by German tanks, which emerged from a wood in front of it. Corporal W. L. Martin was killed, and there were other casualties. Those who were left alive, having fired a few rounds from their revolvers or rifles, which were their sole equipment, feigned death as the tanks approached, and passed through or over them. They lay like this until it was quite dark, when it was found that only 2/Lt. Warrener, Sgt. G. Trainer, B.E.M., Cpl. L. Greco, and one other N.C.O. were still alive. These four men made their own way back as best they could, and eventually met again in England a fortnight later, with the exception of Sgt. Trainer, who was killed on the beaches.

Captain Middleditch and his party also suffered many casualties. He himself was severely wounded, but was rescued under heavy fire by Pte. A. Walker, who was awarded the Military Medal.

Throughout these days of confusion and hazardous moves, one man, although not decorated on this occasion, will remain in the memory of those who fought with the 6th Battalion at that time. He was Pte. S. E. Hollis, the Commanding Officer's personal despatch rider, who, more than four years later, was to win the Victoria Cross as Company Sergeant-Major in the same Battalion. He travelled along roads and through towns reported to be held by the enemy, and arrived sometimes at his destination only to find that the British troops had gone. Yet he always got through, and brought back valuable information. He was always ready to go out again, and it was not an unknown sight to see Hollis asleep from sheer exhaustion in the saddle of his motor cycle outside Battalion Headquarters. His devotion to duty had an inspiring effect on the men of the Battalion, and that it was appreciated is shown by the fact that he was promoted from Private to full Sergeant on his return to England.

At 9 p.m. on the evening of the 29th the Battalion began to pull out, and march the nine miles back to Bray Dunes. *6 Bn*
29/31 May 40

The whole of the next day was spent on the sand dunes, and, although the beach and bridgeheads were by now well organised, no sign of a 23rd Divisional Area, nor of one for G.H.Q. troops, could be located. The next morning found them still waiting, and at 11 a.m. Major L. Petch set out on a further investigation. He had not gone far before he met Major-General Herbert, the Divisional Commander, who was collecting a column to proceed to Dunkirk. He included the 6th Green Howards in his column, and they marched off at about 2 p.m.

They embarked on the *Lady of Man* at the Mole, and sailed from Dunkirk at 6 p.m. that night, arriving at Folkestone early on June 1, where they were met by Major T. F. J. Collins, who was on the Movement Control Staff. In the words of one diarist : " Meeting a Green Howard at this stage was indeed a happy chance ".

6 *Bn*
1 *June* 40

The total casualties suffered by the 6th Battalion during these operations were 1 officer and 15 other ranks killed, 1 officer and 16 other ranks wounded, and 3 officers and 36 other ranks missing.

4 *and* 5 *Bns*
25/26
May 40

We must now return to the 50th Division, and the 4th and 5th Green Howards, whom we left resting in billets near Lille on May 25, incorporating the story of the 7th Green Howards, who came into the 50th Division on May 27, and fought the final phases of the campaign in company with the 4th and 5th Battalions.

During the 25th discussions took place between G.H.Q. and the Divisional Commander with a view to making an attack in a southerly direction towards Cambrai on the following day : but hopes of offensive action were dashed, when, in the early hours of the 26th, orders were received to retire, and take up positions at Bois Grenier, three miles south of Armentieres, in case of enemy penetration across the Belgian frontier. The 150th Brigade actually received orders to be prepared to face east or west !

Later in the day a force was detailed, under the command of Brigadier Haydon, for the defence of Ypres, and, although the 4th Green Howards actually debussed on the Bois Grenier position, both the 4th and 5th Green Howards (the latter going direct), were in Ypres that night.

4 *Bn*
26 *May* 40

Lt.-Col. Littleboy with his Company Commanders, in advance of the Battalion, arrived in Ypres at about 8 p.m., and was given his orders verbally by the Brigadier. His Battalion was to hold the south-eastern end of the town from the southern end of Zillebeeke Lake to the Menin Gate. The 4th Battalion East Yorkshires would be on the left, with the 5th Green Howards holding the western half of the town. He was also informed that the 17th Brigade would be on his right, and that somewhere about were remnants of the Belgian Army. Hurriedly making his dispositions before darkness fell, the Commanding Officer placed " A " Company on the right by Zillebeeke Lake, " D " Company in the centre between the lake and the ramparts, and " B " Company on the left between the Lille and Menin Gates. In reserve he held the remains of " C " Company under 2/Lt. J. R. Booth, reinforced by the Pioneer, Anti-Tank and Mortar Platoons covering Battalion Headquarters at the Trois Bois cross roads, better known to the 1914–1918 soldiers as " Shrapnel Corner ". In Ypres 2/Lt. Booth found some 2-in. H.E. Mortar ammunition. He had been carrying 2-in Mortars all over France with no ammunition except smoke, and, delighted with his find, made good use of it next day.

2/Lt. Booth showed conspicuous gallantry and devotion to duty during the next two days, for which he received the Military Cross. On May 28, when the enemy penetrated a sector of his defences, he did his best to dislodge them by means of his sole remaining mortar, regardless of his own personal safety. Later in the day, when practically surrounded, he maintained his position until he was definitely ordered to withdraw on May 29. In the words of his commanding officer : " 2/Lt. Booth showed a fine example of leadership and initiative throughout the whole period. In spite of his youth he readily assumed the duties and responsibilities of a much older man."

The carrier platoon, now reduced to six vehicles, was hidden in an orchard close by, and the Anti-Tank platoon, under 2/Lt. Watson, was kept at Headquarters. Shortly before midnight the 4th Green Howards marched into Ypres, as thousands of British soldiers had done before them, and many thought, as they marched past the Cloth Hall, and turned right by the Menin Gate in the ramparts, that here, in the town that withstood all assaults from 1914 to 1918, they would fight it out once more. Little did they know that Captain (Q.M.) J. Corner had already received his orders to destroy all unnecessary stores.

Soon after entering the town an unlucky shell landed amongst Battalion Headquarters, killing two men, and wounding Major Mackinlay and eight signallers. Practically at the same time a French or Belgian lorry severely bruised the leg of Major Cooke-Collis, and for some days after this annoying and painful accident Major Cooke-Collis carried a light chair about with him in order to direct operations with greater ease.

Throughout the 27th " A " Company was sniped and mortared. Capt. Metcalfe and 2/Lt. J. L. Stevenson were wounded early on, and Capt. Donking was sent across from " B " Company to take command. Shortly after this 2/Lt. Wright was killed, and odd casualties were continually coming back to the Regimental Aid Post. *4 Bn 27 May* 40

Fearing that the enemy were working their way round his right flank, Lt.-Col. Littleboy sent 2/Lt. Alexander with three

E

carriers to reconnoitre. 2/Lt. Alexander carried out this unpleasant task well, and, although wounded himself and losing one carrier, he brought back exact information as to the whereabouts of the enemy.

Soon after mid-day the Brigade on the right of the Green Howards made a partial withdrawal, and, in order to conform, " A " and " D " companies were brought back, while Battalion Headquarters moved to the south-west corner of Ypres, under orders from the Brigadier. Here they supped of cold ham, washed down by some kind of white wine. These continual moves had at least one compensation—there was no need to wash up ; clean plates could always be found at the next place.

Meanwhile " B " Company of the 5th Green Howards, the remaining platoon of " D " Company, and six carriers had come into line on the right flank of the 4th Battalion.

5 Bn
27 May 40 The 5th Green Howards, after a journey rendered very slow by the congestion on the roads, had entered Ypres at about midnight on May 26/27. During the 27th there was little activity on their front beyond shelling. This however, caused some casualties, including C.Q.M.S. C. Horsley of Headquarter Company, who was killed while bringing up rations.

" B " Company under Captain Dumville, however, and the platoon of " D " Company under Lt. Chambers, which
5 Bn had been sent to prolong the right flank of the 4th Battalion,
28 May 40 met the full force of an enemy attack launched at about mid-day on the 28th. " D " Company's last platoon was overrun, P.S.M. J. Harding was killed, and Lt. Chambers was so badly wounded that he fell into the enemy's hands. " B " Company was forced to make a partial withdrawal up the canal. For his handling of the situation, and the defence of his position against constant pressure, Capt. Dumville was awarded the Military Cross and his runner, Pte. A. L. Fulcher, received the Military Medal. Throughout this, and subsequent days, stirling work in support of the forward companies was done by the Mortar crews under the command of Major Guy.

4 and 5 Bns At 6 p.m. on the 28th orders were received to withdraw
28/29 May 40 to the woods just north of Poperinghe, after first destroying all surplus kit and stores. These orders were a great surprise, as the news of the Belgian surrender and the impending evacuation of the British Army had not yet been received in Ypres. The transport was waiting just outside the town, and the two Battalions of the Green Howards got safely away in the early morning to their positions north of Poperinghe.

It was a wrench to leave Ypres, a name which will always remain high in the annals of the British Army, with all its old associations with 1914–1918. There were still some soldiers of those days fighting with the Green Howards in May, 1940, and they found themselves using the headstones from their comrades' graves in the War Cemeteries as cover against one more German onslaught.

In the meanwhile, the remnants of the 23rd Division (now under the command of the 50th Division), with the 7th Green Howards, were in close proximity.

On May 25 this Battalion left Gondecourt, to which it will *7 Bn* be remembered it had returned after its unsuccessful attempt *25/28 May 40* to reach Gravelines. Moving north by way of Beaucamps, Le Petit Mortier, and Steenewerck, it had arrived in the woods near Peselmoek, north of Poperinghe, on the night of the 27th. The woods were being heavily bombed, and so the battalion spent the night in a farmhouse some two hundred yards west of the Peselmoek road. To make things worse, the weather had broken temporarily, and it was raining hard.

The next morning it moved back a further three miles to the west, and dispersed in a large wood, where it was fortunately found by the Transport, which provided a very welcome meal. In the afternoon all surplus stores and equipment were destroyed and the battalion withdrew to Crombeke, where a composite reinforcement company for the 50th Division was formed under Capt. F. H. Towle, consisting of a hundred picked men fully armed and equipped.

On May 29 the 7th Battalion moved to Killem Lande, and *7 Bn* later embussed for Furnes. It had only proceeded about three *29/31 May 40* miles, however, when it was ordered to destroy all its transport. The remainder of the journey was accordingly completed on foot, and the night was spent close to the road and rail junction just north of Bulscamp.

The next morning the troops breakfasted off tinned rations and chocolate obtained from abandoned French transport, and in the afternoon moved on to Les Moeres, where they got into contact with the 5th Green Howards, who were in position along the canal. Their role was then to relieve the 5th Battalion of all manual labour, but, according to the 5th Battalion accounts, this was too much for their dignity, as, when morning came, they were no longer there ! In actual fact, they had been ordered back to Bray Dunes during the night, and arrived there at about 6 a.m. on the 31st.

At 8 a.m., however, finding that embarkation on this beach was not possible, they marched along the dunes to

Dunkirk and reached the Mole just after mid-day. Here they found the entrance full of ambulances, and for some hours performed very valuable services as stretcher-bearers. Finally, they embarked themselves and sailed for England, the last boat leaving at 7 p.m.

4 Bn
29 May 40   On arrival at its rendezvous north of Poperinghe in the early hours of May 29, the 4th Battalion took up defensive positions with " A " Company on the right, the remnants of " C " Company in the centre, " D " Company on the left and " B " Company in reserve behind Battalion Headquarters, which was situated in a farm surrounded by hop poles.

At about 4 o'clock in the afternoon two German armoured cars came up against the forward posts and captured a platoon of " A " Company. At about 9 p.m. the Battalion again received orders to withdraw, and Major Cooke-Collis set off with a reconnaissance party to Les Moeres. At the same time the enemy subjected Headquarters to rifle fire and shelling from a close support gun, which was effectively silenced by a well-aimed shot from a Boyes rifle, fired by Lt.-Col. Littleboy. The withdrawal was, however, safely accomplished without any further casualties, and the journey to Les Moeres, where the next stand was to be made, began.

5 Bn
29 May 40   The 5th Battalion passed a relatively quiet day on the 29th. A truck bringing up rations was destroyed by mortar fire, and some enemy cycle patrols supplied good targets for the machine guns. Although the enemy were very close when the Battalion withdrew at about 9 p.m., except for a little extremely confused firing, it got away safely, and took the road across the R. Yser at Stavele to Houthem, its next defensive position.

Both Battalions of the Green Howards experienced difficulties in making this journey of some fifteen miles. The drivers were worn out, and the congestion that prevailed on the roads, as the remaining transport of the B.E.F. became constricted into an ever-narrowing arc, was complete. The 5th Battalion arrived at Houthem more or less intact, except for Capt. A. A. Barber who, with the fitters truck, got lost for a while, after three hours travelling. Part, however, of the **Part of 4 Bn** convoy of the 4th Battalion, led by the padre, Capt. Elliott, **29/31 May 40** with the Medical Officer, Capt. G. R. Royston, 2/Lt. K. T. Goellnicht, R.S.M. J. Exall, and ninety other ranks went completely astray. This party never rejoined the Battalion in France, and so we will follow their remaining adventures before telling the story of the final stand of the 4th and 5th Battalions in front of Dunkirk.

When the Battalion left Poperinghe Captain Royston took Captain Elliott on board his truck behind the troop-carrying vehicles and in front of the Bren gun carriers. With the coming of darkness, the leading transport drivers had great difficulty in keeping awake at the halts, and eventually they completely lost the main body.

In the early hours of May 30 they found themselves crossing the canal just outside Dunkirk. When they got down to the beaches they found that the 50th Division had not yet arrived, and so they retraced their steps across the canal, and set off in column for Bergues, in the hopes of finding the Battalion. This was an unpleasant journey along deserted roads, with dead men and horses on either side, and after going some way they ran into a party of engineers, who were about to blow up the bridge in front of them. There was no choice but to return to Dunkirk, where the troops, under 2/Lt. Goellnicht, were billeted on some gunners, while the padre and the medical officer set off again towards Furnes to try to get into touch with the Battalion.

This trip also met with failure in the face of oncoming French troops, who did not take kindly to the British car, and started a riding off contest with it. Captain Royston, however, stoutly resisted all efforts to push him into the ditch, and, turning his truck before the faces of the enraged Frenchmen, picked up a couple of wounded men at a Casualty Clearing Station. On their way back to the rest of their party they ran into a posse of Brigadiers. None of the latter could give them much information, but one of them impressed 2/Lt. Goellnicht and his men, and carried them off to take up a defensive position along the canal. At about 5 p.m. Capt. Elliott, 2/Lt. Goellnicht, and R.S.M. Exall went down to the beach again, while Captain Royston went off in search of rations.

At the embarkation office they received orders to get the men down to the beach at once, and not to try any longer to get in touch with the 50th Division. This they proceeded to do, and spent the night on the dunes about three miles to the north of the Mole. " Our slumbers were somewhat disturbed by intermittent shelling, the shells whistling over our heads and landing on the beach beyond, but, on the whole, the night was quiet ! "

Early next morning, May 31, the embarkation officer arrived and confessed that he had forgotten them the night before, but, that if they went down to the Mole at once, they would be taken off. The march, although a fairly long one in their condition, was accomplished in record time, since they knew that the boats, already at the Mole, were to be the last

to sail that day. Eventually they got all the men aboard a
paddle steamer of the Brighton Belle class, and sailed out
across the Channel.

Meanwhile, Lt.-Col. Littleboy, together with Capt. Mansell
and three carriers, also went astray, and they found themselves
in the village of Isenberghe. Here they found Maj.-Gen.
Franklyn, who gave them some much needed refreshment
before seeing them on their right way through Houthem to
Les Moeres, where they were met by Major Cooke-Collis.

4 *Bn*
30 *May* 40

The 4th Green Howards were at first placed in Brigade
Reserve, but at 9.15 a.m. on the 30th orders were received
for the Battalion to move forward to fill a gap between the
Duke of Wellington's Regiment and the 5th Green Howards
along the Bergues-Furnes canal. The Battalion's right flank
lay exactly on the Belgian frontier, and the left flank rested on
the Houthem canal bridges. By this time the 4th Battalion
had been reduced to a strength of 15 officers and 292 men out
of a total of 25 officers and 748 men with which it had started
on May 16. With this force Lt.-Col. Littleboy had to cover a
front of nearly two miles. He placed " B " Company on the
right with " D " Company on the left, and the remainder of
" A " Company in support. " C " Company with Headquarter
Company formed his reserve, close by Battalion Headquarters
at Westmoerhoek. Each company was protected by a canal
or a ditch in front of it, but the rich arable fields all round were
rapidly becoming flooded, as it was part of the Belgian defence
system to open the dykes.

5 *Bn*
30 *May* 40

The 5th Green Howards on the left were holding a
relatively tenable position along the canal, with " B " and
" C " Companies in front, and " A " Company behind " C "
Company. There was no " D " Company left by this time.
Battalion Headquarters was established in a large white
chateau in front of which strutted a peacock, whose raucous
cries grated on the already jangled nerves of the defenders—
so much so, in fact, that Capt. F. V. Allen, R.A.M.C. shot it
with an airgun !

At about this time a situation report was received from
higher authority that " the situation is obscure, but thought to
be improving ". The Green Howards, while thoroughly
agreeing with the first statement, were soon to have their
scepticism of the second fully justified.

Two attempts were made that evening to break through
the 5th Battalion's positions, one on " B " Company's front,
which that Company dealt with effectively, and one on the

4 *Bn*
31 *May* 40

extreme left, which was also repulsed, largely due to the
initiative of Major W. Lacy. On May 31 the Germans

attacked on both sides of the 4th Battalion. The forward Companies came in for some mortaring and sniping, but the men were well dug in, and they took toll of the enemy with well-aimed rifle fire, while their own casualties were few. Most of the damage done was by enemy shell fire, particularly in the 5th Battalion sector.

5 Bn
31 May 40

The Germans had a spotting plane overhead most of the day, and were suspected of using the spire of Houthem Church as an observation post. The first serious bombardment fell on Battalion Headquarters, when R.Q.M.S. J. E. Toogood was killed, and C.Q.M.S. F. Dobson, Sgt. H. Carton and Sgt. G. Kell, stretcher-bearer sergeant, were wounded. " C " Company's Headquarters also received a direct hit which inflicted casualties, including Capt. Steede, the Company Commander, who was wounded. His place was taken by Capt. W. N. Jackson. Later in the day more shells landed on Battalion Headquarters, one of which wounded Major Guy and Lt. Lord Normanby.

Both Battalions pulled out of the line soon after midnight and withdrew to Bray Dunes, where the transport was finally abandoned, having first been burnt or rendered useless. Here they dispersed and dug themselves in as protection against the bombing and shelling. On June 1 the 5th Battalion, Green Howards, had been reduced to 17 officers and 516 men from the 30 officers and 737 men with which it had started on May 16. It was to suffer further casualties during June 1 and 2— Captain Dumville, Lt. J. M. Whittaker and 2/Lt. P. J. Spink being amongst those who were wounded on the dunes or the beaches.

5 Bn
1 June 40

Captain F. V. Allen, R.A.M.C., who had achieved wonders all through the retreat, did splendid work during these last hours, tending the wounded and performing emergency operations, although he himself was wounded in one arm. For his deeds and devotion to duty, Captain Allen was mentioned in despatches, while L/Cpl. J. R. Needham, one of his stretcher-bearers, received the Military Medal for gallantry in rescuing wounded under fire. Others of the 5th Battalion who received a mention in despatches for their services were Major Guy and Lt. (Q.M.) Evans.

During June 1 Capt. Whitehead reconnoitred a route into Dunkirk over the dunes, and several of the truck drivers volunteered to drive ambulances. The casualties of the previous day, Major Guy, Captain Steede and Lieutenant Lord Normanby had been kept with the Battalion as it was not possible to get them away. They were now taken to the Casualty Clearing Station at Rosendael in Dunkirk, where they were later joined by Lt. J. M. Whittaker, who had been wounded by a shell burst at Bray Dunes, and 2/Lt. Spink, wounded a little later on.

That night the Battalion marched into Dunkirk for embarkation. This journey of not much more than five miles took three hours to accomplish. The worn out soldiers trudged in single file, each holding on to the man in front, lest he should lose himself in the pitch darkness, sometimes through soft sand, sometimes up to their knees in the sea, only to hear the bitter words : " No more embarkation tonight ", when they reached the Mole. The men turned back to the cellars and dug-outs along the front at Dunkirk, and, when daylight came on June 2, it ushered in more bombing and shelling, and further casualties resulted.

5 Bn
2 June 40

By this time, conditions on the beach had deteriorated and organisation had almost completely broken down. The 5th Green Howards were destined to play one more part in this drama, when four officers were chosen by lot to take charge of a party to restore order, and to allow the remnants of the British Army a chance of getting away. These four officers, Capt. Dennis, Lts. H. P. Moor, W. Ramshaw and R. E. J. Lishmund, together with Major C. A. W. Pegler, R.E., carried out their task so effectively that not only did they get away all the troops who were on the beach that night, but also managed to escape themselves, a feat which seemed beyond the bounds of possibility when they started on their unenviable task. Many who were there will remember the 5th Green Howard Flag, which was hoisted on the sands as a rallying point.

One of those tragedies, directly attributable to the fog of war, occurred when many of the wounded in the Casualty Clearing Station at Rosendael, who might well have been carried down to the ships during June 2, fell into German hands. They had been told on June 1 that there was no hope of getting away, and a skeleton staff of doctors and orderlies had remained with them to await the arrival of the enemy. By the evening of June 2 the Germans had not arrived, and so three truck loads of the less badly wounded, and some walking wounded, were sent down to the beach and got away. But many were left behind to become prisoners of war, because those on the beach had known no more of the position of the wounded at Rosendael than the R.A.M.C. staff at Rosendael knew of the improved conditions on the beach—the latter largely owing to the cordon formed by the 5th Green Howards.

5 Bn
3 June 40

To quote the words of Captain Whittaker : " Those who got away sailed out into the night, the sky behind them bright with the fires of the shambles that was Dunkirk, the horizon shortly to be lit by the sun shining over the cliffs of Dover on the morning of June 3—eighteen days after we had first gone up into Belgium."

Finally we must wind up the story of the 4th Battalion, which, before moving to Dunkirk, was given one more task to perform. At 3 p.m. on June 1 Lt.-Col. Littleboy was summoned to Brigade Headquarters at Bray Dunes and told to take his Battalion to stabilize the line around Ghyvelde, and to link up, if possible, with the 1st Battalion, King's Shropshire Light Infantry, and the French. *4 Bn 1 June 40*

Accordingly, the 4th Battalion marched southwards again along roads which were rapidly becoming awash with the rising floods. " A " Company was sent forward to the cross-roads at St. Fracois, with " C " Company on its left. " B " Company was in support on the right in Ghyvelde, and " D " Company in support on the left, with orders to get in touch with the French. 2/Lt. G. G. Nuttall, with the battalion interpreter, succeeded in doing this.

Positions had barely been taken up, however, when at about 10 p.m. orders were received to withdraw to Dunkirk. In spite of the fact that one bridge was blown up while it was still on the wrong side of the canal, the Battalion reassembled and drove into Dunkirk in transport which had been salvaged by 2/Lt. G. E. R. Pendred, along roads lined with deserted transport, and beneath skies lit up by burning dumps.

It was nearly dawn on June 2 and the head of the Battalion had almost reached the boat moored to the Mole, when orders were given to turn back, as no more boats could leave that morning. At this moment four chance shells killed 2/Lt. W. M. Wilby and several other ranks, while many more were wounded around the base of the Mole. *4 Bn 2 June 40*

Wearily the 4th Battalion moved eastwards along the sands and settled down in company areas, digging holes for shelter from any " overs " as the Germans shelled Dunkirk. The day passed quietly with but one excitement : a Hurricane flew low over the troops and dropped a be-ribboned message. There was a rush for the " stop press news ", which was eventually brought to Battalion Headquarters. It was a message scribbled in pencil by the pilot : " Good luck ! we can do no more."

But the Battalion had not much longer to wait. At 9 p.m. that evening the 4th Green Howards formed up in fours at the water's edge, and passed through the regulating cordon organised by Major Pegler, R.E., and the officers of the 5th Battalion, while the flaming sun sank into a flaming sea.

CHAPTER FOUR

" INTERLUDE "

Part I. *The 1st Battalion—June* 1940——*March* 1943
The Territorial Battalions—June 1940——*June* 1941

Part II. *The Home Service, Garrison, and Home Guard Battalions—*1939——1945

Part I

AND so, by June 3, 1940, all five of the Green Howard Battalions, which had set out so hopefully such a short while ago, were back again in England. It was through no failing of theirs that all the fighting which they had experienced had consisted of defence, rear-guard action, and retreat ; but this most testing phase of warfare brought out to the full the dogged characteristics of the Northcountryman. Although some of these Green Howards were destined once again to experience the same ordeal in North Africa, and to fight to a finish, others were, in the long run—and a very long run it proved to be—to reap the reward of their labours and pursue a beaten and demoralised foe back beyond his own frontier. Some individuals were given the opportunity of showing particular courage and received rewards, some gave their lives, and some were taken prisoner, but the good name of the Regiment was safely upheld by all.

During the next eighteen months no battalion of the Green Howards was actually in touch with the enemy, but many of them stood at strategic spots around the coast of the British Isles ready to defend their homeland to the death, and, when imminent danger of invasion had passed, spent many months training themselves for the next round with the enemy.

1 *Bn*
Jun 40/
Apr 41

The 1st Battalion on arrival at Galashiels was given ten days' leave, and then spent the whole of June refitting. In July it moved to the Perth district, and in August to Hatton Castle in Aberdeenshire, when the 15th Brigade came under command of the 51st Highland Division. In October Lt.-Col. A. E. Robinson, D.S.O., was appointed to command the 115th Brigade, and the command of the Battalion devolved on Lt.-Col. A. L. Shaw.

At the end of the month the Battalion moved to Pilsworth Mills near Manchester, where it remained until April in the following year. Here the troops were billeted in an empty cotton mill, described as " grimy, dirty and cold, with a stream

58

of inky water flowing through it." However, the people of Bury and the surrounding district were most hospitable to the Green Howards and made their stay as pleasant as possible.

In April, 1941, the Battalion crossed over to Northern Ireland and took up its quarters in Omagh, county town of Co. Tyrone. Here it stayed for the remainder of the year carrying out every form of training. In October it was inspected by Lt.-Gen. Sir Harold Franklyn, K.C.B., D.S.O., M.C., Colonel of the Green Howards, and G.O.C. Northern Ireland at that time.

1 Bn Apr 41/ Mar 42

Early in 1942 the 1st Battalion moved to the vicinity of Walton Heath, where arms, equipment and transport were overhauled, the troops sent on embarkation leave, and everything prepared for a move overseas. The Battalion was inspected by H.M. The King on Epsom Downs Racecourse early in March, and on March 16 embarked at Liverpool on its way, round the Cape of Good Hope, to India, Persia, Palestine, Sicily, Italy, and finally from the south coast of France to the River Elbe.

We shall not meet the 1st Battalion again in this story until exactly a year later, when, on March 16, 1943, it arrived at Kabrit, and began its period of training for the invasion of Sicily, in which it took part. A short account, therefore, will be given here of its peregrinations during these twelve months, during which it was never in action.

The Battalion, commanded by Lt.-Col. A. L. Shaw, sailed in convoy as part of the 15th Brigade (Brigadier C. S. Rawstrorne, M.C.) from Gourock on March 25. The 15th Brigade, together with the 13th and 17th Brigades, formed the 5th Division, commanded by Major-General H. P. M. Berney Ficklin, M.C. After a short stop at Freetown, the convoy arrived at Capetown on April 23. Sailing again on the 27th, the 5th Division was now intent on an operational role, namely the capture of Madagascar. This operation was carried out successfully by the 17th and 13th Brigades, and the 15th Brigade, after stopping for a night at Mombasa, went directly on to India, arriving at Bombay on May 19. On the 21st it proceeded to Poona.

1 Bn Mar 42/ Mar 43

The threat of a Japanese advance into India was now considered serious, and the 5th Division was ordered to concentrate near Ranchi.

The remaining two brigades were still at sea on their way from Madagascar, and so the 15th Brigade was the first to arrive at Ranchi, which it did on June 4.

Conditions there were, for the first week, most uncomfortable as their camp was not ready. However, the Green Howards cheerfully overcame their difficulties, and during the next two months carried out a number of training exercises, and played a good deal of football in spite of the great heat.

On August 4 the Battalion left Ranchi, not for the jungle to the east, as had been expected, but to the west. Travelling by way of Bombay, Basra, and Khanikin, the Green Howards arrived at Kermanshah in Persia, where they pitched their camp. Here they remained until the end of November, when they moved on to Qum, about ninety miles south of Teheran.

The 5th Division now formed part of the 3rd Corps, commanded by Lt.-Gen. Sir D. Anderson, K.C.B., C.M.G., D.S.O., and its operational role was to defend the route to the Persian oilfields against a possible German advance from the Caucasus. After the intense heat of Ranchi the Battalion now experienced the bitter cold of the Persian highlands. It was, therefore, with a sense of relief that, on March 3, 1943, the Green Howards once again turned their faces to the west, and travelling by way of Bagdad, Palestine, and across the desert of Sinai, arrived at Kabrit on March 16.

4 *and* 5 *Bns*   The 4th and 5th Battalions, after their ordeal at Dunkirk,
Jun/Jul 40 landed at Folkestone and Dover respectively in the early hours of June 3, and went by train to Aldershot. On the 5th they proceeded to Knutsford and on the following day to Rugeley. Here they remained for a fortnight while stragglers came in, and parties were sent off on leave.

The threat of invasion was, however, now a serious reality, and, on June 21, the 50th Division was moved to Dorsetshire in a defensive role. The 4th and 5th Green Howards were stationed in the neighbourhood of Sherborne, and spent the remainder of June and July re-equipping and getting themselves physically fit. On July 17 the 150th Brigade gave a demonstration of de-bussing, and attack with tanks and air-
6 *and* 7 *Bns* craft before the Prime Minister, Mr. Winston Churchill. By
Jun/Jul 40 this time the Division had been allotted a third Brigade, the 69th, composed of the 5th Battalion East Yorkshire Regiment, and the 6th and 7th Green Howards. These two Green Howard Battalions had gone straight to Launceston after disembarking at Dover on June 2, and had reorganised there. At the end of June the 6th Battalion was at Hinton Admiral, and the 7th at Parkstone. The sector of coast allotted to the 50th Division for defence stretched from Lyme Regis to Christchurch, and much time was spent in digging fortifications, wiring, laying beach mines, and responding to the many

alarms of those days. During the peak period of danger of *4, 5, 6 and*
invasion, from September 12 to September 20, these four *7 Bns*
Green Howard Battalions were placed as follows : the 4th *Sept 40*
at Weymouth, the 5th at Winfrith-Newburgh, the 6th near
Studland, and the 7th at Canford Cliffs.

At the end of the month they moved into winter quarters *4, 5, 6 and*
at Weymouth, Dorchester, Swanage and Bournemouth *7 Bns*
respectively, and started intensive training. The extent of this *Oct 40*
training can best be judged by the objective laid down by
Lt.-Gen. B. L. Montgomery, C.B., D.S.O. : " The 5th Corps
must be able, by March, 1941, to fight any enemy, anywhere
and at any time. Each Battalion must be able to move from
sixty to eighty miles in Mechanical Transport, march twenty-
five miles, and fight a battle at the end of it."

At the end of November the 50th Division moved to *4, 5, 6 and*
Somerset, and the 4th Battalion found itself at Weston-super- *7 Bns*
Mare, the 5th at Cheddar, the 6th at Frome, and the 7th at *Nov 40/*
Castle Cary. On December 12, 1940, Major-General W. H. *Jun 41*
C. Ramsden, D.S.O., M.C., took over command of the 50th
Division from Major-General G. Le Q. Martel, C.B., D.S.O.,
M.C., who had been appointed to command the Royal
Armoured Corps.

Preparations for going overseas now began, and it is noted
in one war diary that on January 2, 1941, the Battalion was
inspected in tropical kit with snow on the ground. A period
of intensive training, with long route marches and tactical
exercises on Exmoor, came to an end at the beginning of April,
when the Division was judged to be at concert pitch. During
these months of training the Green Howards were frequently
visited or inspected by General Franklyn, their Colonel, now
commanding the 8th Corps.

On April 9 Major E. C. Cooke-Collis left the 4th Green
Howards to take over command of the 6th Battalion with the
rank of Lt.-Col. and, on April 7, Lt.-Col. F. E. A.MacDonnell,
took command of the 7th Battalion.

In the first week of April all units were inspected by H.M.
The King, who wished them God Speed, and, on April 23,
the first units of the Division, which included the 150th
Brigade, sailed from Liverpool to join their convoy in the
Clyde. The 69th Brigade did not sail until June 3.

Part II

Before taking the reader overseas to follow the fortunes of
the 1st and Territorial Battalions, a short account will first
be given of the Home Service, Garrison, and Home Guard
Battalions. Although the chronological sequence of the

Regimental Story is temporarily broken, the very important work, which these battalions carried out, seems worthy of a better fate than to be chronicled in a chapter at the end of the book, like an appendix. Those officers and men, who performed the essential functions of training, guards, and garrison work, tiring and often boring as they were, throughout the long years of the war, will realise that, in such a book as this, priority of space must be given to the fighting battalions. Only a brief account is therefore given of each battalion, sufficient to show that although :—

> " . . . thousands speed,
> And post o'er land and ocean without rest,
> They also serve who only stand and wait."

8 *Bn*   The 8th Battalion, designated as a Home Defence Battalion,
(13 *and* 30) was raised in the Middlesbrough area in August and September, 1939, and was commanded by Lt.-Col. J. B. W. Pennyman, late of the K.O.S.B. Composed mainly of Local Defence Force men, and of those unfit for general service, its duties were to guard vital points, with the result that the Battalion was, at this period, scattered over most of the North Riding. In its early days a somewhat unique claim was made by the 8th Battalion, to the effect that all its companies were commanded by Masters (or former Masters) of Foxhounds.

In June, 1940, the Battalion moved to Neasham near Doncaster, and shortly afterwards was split up into the 1/8th and 2/8th Battalions, commanded respectively by Lt.-Col. J. B. W. Pennyman, and Lt.-Col. V. J. Barber of the Green Howards.

In October, 1940, the 2/8th Battalion moved to Spalding in Lincolnshire, and in November was re-designated the 13th Battalion Green Howards, and the 1/8th became the 8th Battalion once again. In June, 1941, the 8th and 13th Battalions were finally amalgamated at Doncaster into the 13th Battalion, under the command of Lt.-Col. Barber, and continued to provide guards at vital points in the West Riding and Lincolnshire, until it went overseas as a Garrison Battalion in September, 1943. By this time it was known as the 30th Battalion, as all Home Service Battalions had been so re-designated in 1942.

After a short period of service in Algiers, the Battalion moved to Manouba, where it spent three months. It then crossed the sea to Italy and spent five months in Taranto, and the ensuing year in Bari. In June, 1945, Lt.-Col. Barber relinquished his command and was succeeded by Lt.-Col. E. J. Tucker, who took the Battalion back to Algiers in July.

There the Battalion was disbanded, having rendered valuable service to the Army throughout six years of comparatively monotonous duty. On more than one occasion it was congratulated upon its reliability and smartness.

The 9th Battalion came into being in March, 1940, and was formed at Grandshaft Barracks, Dover, under the command of Lt.-Col. A. E. I. Belcher, M.C., Green Howards. On April 10 the Battalion was inspected by H.M. The King in Dover Castle, and for the next seven months performed garrison duties under continuous air raids, and, from August 24 when the first German shell arrived, under intermittent shellfire. Throughout their period of service at Dover the Green Howards acquitted themselves with great distinction under aerial and artillery bombardment. For his bravery on more than one occasion C.S.M. J. Macdonald was awarded the Distinguished Conduct Medal.

9 Bn

During its time at Dover the Battalion lost one officer, Captain F. Dawson, D.S.O., M.C., and four other ranks killed, and fourteen other ranks wounded by shellfire, and dive-bombing attacks. The Battalion had originally been intended for overseas garrison duties, and had twice been under orders for France, on one occasion the transport men having actually got as far as Cherbourg. The fall of France, however, finally extinguished the hopes of overseas service, and, in November, the Battalion went to Deal to work on the defences. In March, 1941, it sailed from Aberdeen to Lerwick in the Shetland Isles. Returning in November, 1941, it was stationed at Ashington in Northumberland, at which place it ceased to exist as a Green Howard unit and became the 108th Light Anti-Aircraft Regiment, R.A., when Lt.-Col. Belcher handed over command of the unit to the Royal Artillery.

The 10th Battalion, The Green Howards, was formed on June 6, 1940, out of the 2nd line East Riding Yeomanry. Stationed at Tidworth, its first commanding officer was Lt.-Col. W. B. Moorhead of the King's Regiment, and the Battalion became part of the 206th Brigade early in 1941. In February, 1941, the 10th Battalion moved to Shorncliffe, and for the next twenty months alternated between Folkestone, Hawkinge, Shorncliffe and Hythe, mainly on defensive works. Lt.-Col. F. E. A. MacDonnell commanded the Battalion, when Lt.-Col. Moorhead was forced to retire owing to ill health, until he went to take over the 7th Battalion, Green Howards, shortly before it embarked for the Middle East. He was succeeded by Lt.-Col. N. T. Herbert.

10 Bn

In December, 1942, the Battalion moved to Truro, at which place Lt.-Col. R. G. Parker was given the command.

This officer had returned from North Russia where he had been commanding 126 Force since October, 1941. In May, 1943, the Battalion was selected for conversion into a Parachute Battalion. This conversion entailed volunteering for parachute work, and all the officers, except one, and nearly three hundred other ranks, volunteered at once.

The Battalion now became known as the 12th Battalion (Yorkshire) Parachute Regiment, commanded by Lt.-Col. Parker, and for the remainder of the war had a most distinguished career, including an air landing in France on " D " Day, a hurried sea-borne visit to the Ardennes just before Christmas, 1944, and another airborne landing across the Rhine in March, 1945. In all these operations the Yorkshire Parachute Battalion fought with great gallantry and success, and the Green Howards may well be proud of the part they played in forming the nucleus of the Battalion on its formation, and of the personnel who joined it at later dates. When the war in Europe was finished, this Battalion, now commanded by Lt.-Col. K. T. Darling, D.S.O., The Royal Fusiliers, went out to the Far East and saw service in the Dutch East Indies.

11 *Bn*   The 11th Battalion was formed in July, 1940, under the command of Lt.-Col. A. C. L. Parry, M.B.E., M.C., at Gandale Camp near Richmond. The Infantry Training Centre (Green Howards), by which name the old Regimental Depot was now known, was not unprepared for this event, and supplied the newly formed unit with its complement of officers, warrant officers and N.C.O.s at short notice.

The Battalion moved in October the same year into Northumberland, and spent sixteen months on coastal defence duties at various places on the N.E. coast including Alnwick, Warkworth, Seaton Delaval, S. Shields, Newcastle and Grimsby. In January, 1942, Lt.-Col. Parry handed over the Battalion to Lt.-Col. A. F. P. Evans. It had now moved into Lincolnshire where it remained as a mobile defence unit until the middle of 1944, being stationed at various times in Marshchapel, Skegness, Spilsby and Burgh. It then moved to Rothbury in Northumberland where it became a Holding Battalion until it was disbanded.

From 1943 onwards the 11th Battalion had assumed responsibility for administering the final polish to recruits who had completed their I.T.C. training, and, although the latter found the process, which included endurance tests on the hills, sometimes in snowstorms, very rigorous, they ultimately found that this hardening process stood them in good stead on " D " Day and after. In September, 1943, Lt.-Col. D. J. Keating, M.C., The East Yorkshire Regiment, took over from Lt.-Col. Evans. This latter officer died a heroic death in Italy when commanding a Battalion of the Royal Fusiliers, and was awarded a posthumous D.S.O.

The 12th Battalion grew out of the 50th Battalion, The Green Howards, which was stationed at Ripon in October, 1940, when it received six hundred civilian recruits. After twelve weeks' training the Battalion was re-designated the 12th Battalion, and moved to Redcar. Under the command of Lt.-Col. H. N. Bright, M.B.E., the Battalion rapidly became a well-trained and efficient unit and for the next two years moved between Redcar, Thirsk, Malton and Scarborough. In July, 1942, it was re-designated the 161st Reconnaissance Regiment (Green Howards), and in February, 1943, Lt.-Col. K. E. Savill, K.D.G., succeeded Lt.-Col. Bright as commanding officer. In March the Battalion moved to Trowbridge, where in September, the title " Green Howards," was dropped, and it became the 161st Reconnaissance Regiment. In December, 1943, this Battalion went to Ballymena in Northern Ireland, and, in July, 1944, " B " Squadron was mobilised and sent to Normandy, under the command of Major A. Graham, M.C. There it replaced " A " Squadron of the 43rd Reconnaissance Regiment, which had been practically wiped out during the fighting in June.

This squadron of the 161st Reconnaissance Regiment fought its way throughout the remainder of the campaign, and in the words of the Commanding Officer, " Later events were to show how fortunate for us it was that the Green Howard Squadron was chosen, and what a magnificent showing the Squadron made."

The 11th and 12th Battalions were both unlucky to miss active service, since there could have been few better Battalions in England in 1944. The policy, however, was at that time to use such battalions to provide replacements to existing units. And so, although many officers and men from the 11th and 12th Green Howards gained distinction in battle wearing the badges of other regiments, there is no story to tell. Many gave their lives as well, and one can be sure that, whether they returned or not, they remained Green Howards at heart.

The North Riding Home Guard

When Mr. Eden called for volunteers for local defence at the crisis of the war in May, 1940, the response throughout the North Riding was spontaneous and general and, in fact, the number of those who registered was vastly greater than could be enrolled into the new force.

In every district groups of volunteers were organised and a fervour of patriotism made these at once a formidable

F

Marginal note: 12 *Bn*

force. At the beginning their activities were confined to their own particular neighbourhood, and road-blocks and defence-posts sprang up overnight. For arms they had the strange collection of weapons that was freely handed in at all police-stations and which varied from a Purdey gun to a Malay dagger : but, by degrees, uniform and better weapons came their way ; the force became more organised and systematic training and exercises were introduced and a certain mobility achieved. Weapons continued to improve until the fire-power of the Home Guard became very great, and day after day on the ranges increased its accuracy.

As efficiency grew the Home Guard relieved the Regular Forces of more and more duties, especially in the guarding of vital points on the Coast and in the manning of observation posts in the country. New anti-aircraft rocket batteries also were most successfully operated by the Home Guard, while other detachments were trained to man the coastal batteries.

The administration of this large force threw a heavy new burden on the Territorial Association, for that body took charge of accommodation, arms, ammunition, clothing and all the other administrative details ; but the Battalion Quarter-masters and the T.A. secretary worked closely together and were brilliant at improvisation, with the result that all went very smoothly.

The Battalions centred round Middlesbrough were natur-ally the most mobile and worked continuously as Battalions, often on a Group basis. They became a highly efficient centralised force. The Country Battalions too had their full-scale exercises, but more often worked on a company or platoon basis.

In due course the operational command of the Home Guard passed over to the Military District commander and training became more systematic and co-ordinated. More courses and training cadres were organised, and the effective-ness of the Home Guard increased mightily while its keenness remained unimpaired. Indeed, throughout its life, the North Riding Home Guard had an invincible spirit, and would undoubtedly have played a vital and effective part in defending its country if an invasion had taken place. Its members would all have fought to the last man—that is absolutely certain.

The 15,000 officers and men, who sacrificed all their leisure to join the Home Guard, came from every walk of life and had served in many regiments ; but when they joined the Home Guard they became Green Howards in fact and in spirit. They became the very backbone of the Regiment and the Regimental Depot at Richmond became their home. The

Regiment, in its turn, devoted all its energies to helping to train the Home Guard and supporting its members in every possible way. The Colonel of the Regiment, Sir Harold Franklyn, as C.-in-C. Home Forces, paid many visits to our Home Guard, and keenly appreciated the value of this branch of his regiment.

The Home Guard took such a practical interest in the Regiment of its adoption that, when the Regiment launched an appeal for funds to provide comforts for Prisoners of War, it was the Home Guard that took it up and made the appeal a gigantic success ; and the fact that the Green Howards were able to look after their prisoners so well was largely due to the efforts of the Home Guard. The Green Howard Benevolent Fund also owes much of its financial success to the money raised by the Home Guard, and the strong position of that fund is a lasting and worthy memorial to this remarkable war-time force.

ORGANISATION OF THE NORTH RIDING HOME GUARD AND LIST OF BATTALIONS AFFILIATED TO THE GREEN HOWARDS

Zone Commander	1*st*	Adm. Sir Cyril Fuller, K.C.B., C.M.G., D.S.O.
	2*nd*	Col. W. T. Wilkinson, D.S.O.
	3*rd*	Col. Sir William Worsley, Bt.
Sector Commander, 3*rd*, 4*th*, 13*th Battalions*		Col. C. V. Fitton, O.B.E., M.C.
Group Commander, 5*th*, 8*th*, 9*th Battalions*		Col. J. R. McCurdy, M.C.

Battalions

Number	Headquarters	Commander
1st Bn.	Northallerton	Lt.-Col. H. Green
2nd Bn.	Whitby	Lt.-Col. F. E. Massie, M.C.
3rd Bn.	Guisborough	Lt.-Col. H. J. H. Tate
4th Bn.	Redcar	Lt.-Col. H. Emsley, M.C.
5th Bn.	Malton	Lt.-Col. G. W. Barnley, M.C.
6th Bn.	York	Lt.-Col. J. Crawford, M.C.
7th Bn.	Kirbymoorside	Lt.-Col. V. Holt, M.C.
8th Bn.	Middlesbrough	Lt.-Col. H. C. Garbutt
9th Bn.	Middlesbrough	Lt.-Col. C. B. Smith
10th Bn.	Scarborough	Lt.-Col. J. Kitching
11th Bn.	Leyburn	Lt.-Col. F. A. Heyman
12th Bn.	Richmond 1	Lt.-Col. G. Sherston, M.C.
	2	Lt.-Col. Sir Richard Pease, Bt.
13th Bn.	Loftus	Lt.-Col. S. F. Franklin

CHAPTER FIVE

" THE TERRITORIAL BATTALIONS IN THE MIDDLE EAST AND NORTH AFRICA "

" The Loss of the 150th Brigade "

April, 1941—*June,* 1942

See MAP
No. 3

WHEN the 50th Division sailed for the Middle East in the spring of 1941, the Mediterranean was closed, and all convoys, with the exception of those carrying urgent supplies to Malta, had to make the long voyage round the Cape of Good Hope. The first portion of the Division to leave consisted of Advanced Divisional Headquarters, including the G.O.C., Major-General W. H. C. Ramsden, D.S.O., M.C., and the 150th Brigade, commanded by Brigadier C. W. Haydon, D.S.O., M.C.

The 4th Green Howards (Lt.-Col. C. N. Littleboy, D.S.O., M.C., T.D.) sailed in the *Empress of Russia*, and the 5th Green Howards (Lt.-Col. W. E. Bush, D.S.O., M.C.) in the *Empress of Asia*. These ships, sailing from Liverpool, joined their convoy in the Clyde, and, on April 25, left under escort of H.M.S. *Repulse*, fourteen destroyers, and an armed merchantman.

*4 and 5 Bns
Apr/May* 41

Calling in at Freetown for the ships to coal, the convoy rounded the Cape about a week later, and reached Durban on May 27, having left behind at Capetown the *Empress of Asia*, which had been damaged in what was described as the worst storm for sixty years.

*4 and 5 Bns
Jun/Jul* 41

After four days of wonderful hospitality in Durban the convoy proceeded on its way, still without the *Empress of Asia*, and early in June the troops were disembarked into coal barges at Port Tewfik. Thence they were taken by Arab driven buses through Suez and Ismailia along the Sweet Water Canal to El Qassasin, a tented camp in the desert. Here, while the 5th Battalion was limping up the Red Sea in the *Empress of Asia*, with Lt. A. Black and a party of men below stoking the ship, owing to the desertion of some of the stokers at Capetown, the 4th Battalion began its training, while the sun blazed down on a shadeless desert.

On June 23 the 4th Battalion moved on by the single track desert railway to Fuka, where its role was aerodrome defence until the end of July. But it was not all defence—brief attachments were arranged with the " Faith ", " Hope " and

" Charity " columns of the 4th Indian Division, and some Green Howards had their first sight of the enemy holding the Halfaya escarpment.

Meanwhile the *Empress of Asia* had reached Port Tewfik and, by July 3, the 5th Green Howards had arrived in the El Daba area, and the 150th Brigade was once more united.

During the months of June and July, while the 150th Brigade was working on defence positions in the El Daba and Fuka areas, the Divisional Headquarter Staff of the 50th Division was established at Mena, and helping to plan what was to become later the historic battlefield of Alamein.

The 6th Green Howards (Lt.-Col. E. C. Cooke-Collis) and 6 *and* 7 *Bns* the 7th Green Howards (Lt.-Col. F. E. A. MacDonnell) em- 1 *June* 41 barked with the rest of the 69th Brigade (Brigadier G. W. E. J. Erskine) at Gourock on H.M.T. *Mooltan* on June 1, 1941. The convoy sailed on June 3, escorted by cruisers, destroyers, and, at times, by larger ships including an aircraft carrier. After a call at Freetown from June 16–20, during which nobody was allowed ashore, the convoy proceeded, without incident, to Durban where it arrived on July 4. Here all the troops disembarked and were accommodated in Clairwood Camp, some six miles outside the town, for the next seven days.

The stay at Durban will always be remembered by the 6th and 7th Battalions as a very pleasant interlude. The weather was perfect, there was no blackout or rationing, and the warm-hearted kindness and generosity of the people, who spared nothing in their efforts to entertain the troops, resulted in many friendships being made which still continue.

The voyage was continued in H.M.T. *Mauretania*, and 6 *and* 7 *Bns* the troops disembarked at Port Tewfik on July 21. Thence 21 *Jul* 41 they moved by train to Qassasin Camp, aptly described by one distinguished officer as " that bugbear of all British troops newly arrived in the Middle East. Existence seems to consist of sand, flies and " Gyppy Tummy ". There they remained until they sailed for Cyprus on August 7.

While the 50th Division had been circling Africa, disaster had befallen the Imperial troops, who had been sent to Greece in fulfilment of our pledge to that country, when it was invaded by the Germans in April, 1941. Driven out of Greece, they had been forced finally to evacuate Crete early in June, so that the importance of Cyprus as a further stepping stone to the Middle East was vitally increased. In those circumstances, at the beginning of August, the 50th Division was hastily despatched to Cyprus to put the island into a state of defence. Its directive was simple : " Hold the island for His Majesty's Government ".

The 6th and 7th Battalions embarked on destroyers at Port Said on August 7, and were landed at Famagusta the next day, while the 4th and 5th Battalions followed them on August 15. All Battalions now got down to the strenuous work of preparing defences—the 4th at Ailasyka, the 5th at Larnaca, where it took over from the 7th Battalion, the 6th at Limassol, and the 7th also at Limassol, after being relieved at Larnaca by the 5th. At the end of August, General Sir C. J. Auchinleck, C. in C. Middle East, Air Marshal Tedder, and Mr. Oliver Lyttleton, Resident Minister, Middle East, toured the defences, and expressed satisfaction at the work which had been done.

When " D " Company, 7th Green Howards, was being inspected by General Auchinleck, a demonstration was given of a suggested method for infantry to cross wire obstacles, which had been evolved by the company. The C. in C. was so impressed that he requested the Divisional Commander to make a platoon available to tour the Middle East. Accordingly, Lt. Walker's platoon, accompanied by Major A. C. Scott, " D " Company Commander, toured Egypt, Cyrenaica, Palestine and Syria, from Mersah Matruh to Homs, for the next two months, finally rejoining the Battalion at Acre.

As soon as the defences had taken shape, training began again. This took the form, largely, of long tactical forced marches by independent platoons up the mountain tracks, through deep and choking white dust, which reflected in glaring brightness the intense heat of the August sun. Then followed a period of all night digging, and a half hour " stand to ", as the dawn broke over the picturesque island, and heralded another sweltering day. The anti-climax then took place of filling in the trenches which had been dug, to prevent their use by the enemy should he invade the island, and the long march back to camp.

There were also many sudden moves in mechanical transport against imaginary landings af airborne troops, the chief memory of which is, again, the choking white dust.

Although the Battalions had carried out a considerable amount of training before leaving England, these three months of strenuous work in Cyprus undoubtedly smoothed out the rough edges, toughened up the soft spots, and brought them up to fighting pitch. Even more important, perhaps, than the training, was the increase in morale and discipline, with which the Battalions, particularly the 6th and 7th, became imbued at this time. Early in 1941 the Battalions had received a strong leavening of keen young regular officers, who took over most of the senior appointments, and a similar move was made with Warrant Officers and Senior N.C.Os.

It was during the Cyprus days that these regulars made their impact felt on the Battalions, and the indefinable barrier between Regulars and Territorials disappeared. It took time for the two points of view to blend. The regulars brought with them a new code of discipline, which was not, of course, at first popular. Discipline, however, needs the companion-ship of *esprit de corps*, if a first class fighting unit is to be formed, and the Territorial Battalions possessed plenty of the latter. Gradually the Regular Officers, Warrant Officers and N.C.Os. made an imprint on the Battalions, which was never lost. They trained the Territorial and National Service men to have complete confidence in themselves as real soldiers, and not merely as keen, public-spirited, and trained citizens answering the call of duty. They made no attempt to alter the special *esprit de corps* of the Territorial battalions, but added to their fighting and general efficiency.

As a result, when the days came at a later stage when the Territorials and National Service men stepped into the more responsible positions, they had a high standard to maintain ; and the story will show how this high standard brought the Battalions through the dangerous and difficult days ahead with flying colours.

Early in November, 1941, the 50th Division was with-drawn from Cyprus, being relieved by the 5th Indian Division. The move was made at night in destroyers to Haifa in Palestine and, on November 7, the 69th Brigade was in camp at Acre, and the 150th Brigade in Jalama Camp under Mount Carmel. Before leaving Cyprus all stores, equipment and transport had been handed over to the Indian Division in exchange for the latter's equipment, which was to be taken over by the 50th Division on arrival in Palestine. Unfortunately this was found to be a bad bargain, as the equipment was poor, and the motor transport practically worn out after the campaigns in Abyssinia, Eritrea, North Africa and Iraq. Replacement was slow, and had not been completed when the next move took place.

At this time the German armies were making a rapid advance along the north coast of the Black Sea and threatening the Caucasus, and preparations were hastily being made to send the 50th Division up into Persia, in order to help bar the way to a possible break through towards India or the Persian Gulf. This move was expected to be made very shortly by approximately ten German armoured divisions.

On November 28 the Division started the move to Persia. *6 and 7 Bns* The 150th Brigade, being the last in order of movement, had *28 Nov 41* exchanged all its best transport vehicles with the other two brigades, and was to follow as soon as it could get new transport.

But, in the meantime, on November 18, General Auchinleck had launched " Operation Crusader ", with the twofold objective of destroying the enemy's armoured forces in Libya and of relieving Tobruk. To support these operations the 150th Brigade was taken out of the 50th Division and placed on G.H.Q. Reserve. On November 29 the Brigade entrained at Haifa, and moved towards the Western Desert.

4 and 5 Bns
29 Nov 41

The 151st and 69th Brigades moved off from Haifa along the desert road, and arrived at Two Rivers and Kirkuk respectively on December 8. Soon after their arrival, the Caucasian plan was cancelled, but they remained at Kirkuk, spending their time training, until the second week in January, 1942, when they moved back again to Syria.

6 and 7 Bns
8 Dec 41

6 and 7 Bns
Jan 42

There is not much to relate about these moves of about seven hundred miles each way, except that, averaging as they did some one hundred miles a day, tribute must be paid to the efficiency of the drivers and maintenance men of the vehicles, which made the journey uneventful. At Kirkuk, the nights were very cold, with 10-12 degrees of frost, and an issue of the rum ration proved very acceptable.

On their arrival in Syria at the end of January, the 6th Green Howards took over from the 2/4th Australian Infantry Battalion in El Aine Camp, and formed guards at various places in the vicinity, while the 7th Battalion relieved the 2/11th Australian Infantry Battalion of similar duties at Djeideide. The Australians were going back to their own country to prepare against a possible Japanese invasion. During their short stay there of a fortnight, opportunity was taken of visits to Beirut, and the ancient city of Baalbek.

On February 12 the 69th Brigade was on the move again, and, proceeding by way of Beersheba and Moascar, arrived at Wadi El Natrun Camp near Alexandria on February 16. The next day it moved on again by way of El Daba, Sidi Barrani and Capuzzo, and on the 20th arrived in camp near Acroma, some fifteen miles south-west of Tobruk. On February 22 the Brigade went into the line, the 6th Green Howards taking over from the 2nd Mahrattas, and the 7th from the 2nd Cameron Highlanders.

6 and 7 Bns
12/22 Feb 42

During this period, while the remainder of the 50th Division had been touring the Middle East, the 150th Brigade, composed of the 4th and 5th Battalions, Green Howards, together with the 4th Battalion, East Yorkshires, had moved across from Haifa into Egypt by train, reaching Amiriya, ten

4 and 5 Bns
1/22 Dec 41

miles west of Alexandria, on December 1, 1941. On the 3rd they moved forward again to Sidi Haneish, the old headquarters of the Western Desert Force near Bagguish, and found on arrival that they were not even expected.

This move was also made by rail, and was notable for one of the " alarums and excursions " of war. Loud explosions were heard some three miles ahead of the train with the result that the Egyptian driver brought it to an abrupt halt, and at once reports began to circulate that the ubiquitous parachutists had landed and were blowing up the line. On investigation, these explosions proved to have been caused by our own engineers blowing up some unexploded German bombs, and the journey was continued, entailing a late arrival at Sidi Haneish, where the battalions were met by somewhat impatient and irate commanding officers, who had gone on ahead, and were ignorant of what had happened.

Sidi Haneish proved a good area in which to bivouac, although spoilt occasionally by sandstorms which swept down the full length of the area, reducing visibility to a hundred yards. Movement after dark was not easy, as Capt. (Q.M.) J. Corner of the 4th Battalion found out one night while hurrying in a rainstorm to his Battalion Headquarters Mess, or " Stokehold " as it was called ; he fell into an old slit trench, broke a bone in his ankle, and was seen no more. His departure to hospital made a big gap, and he was much missed. Never once had he failed the Battalion.

The next three weeks were spent in re-equipping and training for desert warfare, particularly in operations entailing movement through minefields. News from the front was scarce. All that was certain was the confused nature of the conflict south-east of Tobruk. The Brigade at this time expected a short stay, prior to an advance to Benghazi and beyond. Close liaison was established by both Green Howard Battalions with the 19th (Wellington) New Zealand Regiment and the 7th Indian Brigade, who sent officers and N.C.Os. to live with them, and many valuable lessons were picked up from these seasoned troops, and also from the Guards who were resting at El Daba.

On the 23rd the Brigade moved forward again by train *4 and 5 Bns* to the rail head at Bir Thalata, and here the troops spent *23 Dec* 41/ their first Christmas in the desert, under most adverse con- *4 Jan* 42 ditions. The camp was dispersed over an area of flat featureless desert about three miles long, and subjected to heavy sandstorms which reduced visibility often to a few yards. Digging, except with compressors, was impossible, as one foot below the sand there was nothing but solid rock. A Christmas dinner of tinned steak and kidney pudding, with beer and cigarettes, was provided, and, when the Commanding Officer toured the companies, sherry miraculously appeared, but there was no Christmas mail. The 5th Battalion postman made a valiant effort to find the Brigade Postal Unit (which was only three miles away), in a blizzard of sand, but returned some thirty-six hours later, lost, bewildered, and letterless. During the afternoon the two Regimental Padres, Elliott (4th Battalion), (who was to die later so tragically while a prisoner of war in Italy), and Jamieson (5th Battalion) toured the bivouac areas in a truck with a choral party singing carols. Wherever they stopped, men crawled out of their bivouacs and joined in. At tea-time everybody crowded round the nearest wireless and listened to H.M. The King.

While they were listening to the speech, a truck appeared from westward containing a small party of officers who had been sent forward to the battle from Sidi Haneish. They told cheering tales of the enemy in flight. Another feature of the day was a sherry party given by Lt.-Col. Littleboy and his officers, while the dance band played—with some difficulty owing to the blowing sand. In the evening 285 Battery, R.A., held an " At Home " near a derelict plane.

Training now became intensive, and the Green Howards were in fine fighting fettle when orders were at last received to
4 *and* 5 *Bns* move forward into Libya. On January 4 the Brigade was
4/25 *Jan* 42 visited by the 50th Divisional Commander, Major-General Ramsden, who had flown over from Iraq. He told them that they were shortly to rejoin the Division in Iraq, but this decision was cancelled a few hours later.

Before beginning the account of the adventures of the 4th and 5th Green Howards, which started when they crossed the Libyan frontier on January 27, and ended in tragedy when they were overrun at Got el Ualeb on June 1, when the survivors passed into captivity, it is necessary to give a brief account of the general situation at this time. The pendulum of the balance between British and Axis forces had once more swung against us. It was in December, 1940, that the British forces first crossed the Libyan frontier, and, carrying out a spectacular advance with the minimum of strength, reached Benghazi, which they captured on February 6, 1941.

On March 30 1941 the German and Italian forces launched a counter-offensive, driving the British back again behind the Libyan frontier, Tobruk being left as a bastion on the North African coast. Tobruk held out gallantly until once again the Commonwealth forces moved forward on November 18, relieved the garrison of Tobruk, and, passing once more through Benghazi, pushed as far as Agedabeia. Here they had outreached their supplies, and halted to reorganise for a further advance. But General Rommel, who was now in command of all Axis forces in North Africa, had received considerable reinforcements, and was the first commander to be ready to resume operations. On January 22, 1942, he broke through the light screen in front of the British at Agadabeia, and by February 4 had recaptured Derna.

It was to help stem this onrush that the 150th Brigade crossed into Libya on January 27, while the remainder of the 50th Division was shortly to leave Iraq on their way to join in the defence of the Libyan-Egyptian frontier, which was reached by them on February 19. At a later stage we shall find the 4th, 5th, 6th and 7th Battalions of the Green Howards once again fighting together, as they had done outside Dunkirk. In the meanwhile, we will follow the 4th and 5th Battalions into Libya.

The 150th Brigade set out on January 25 and became a competitor in what was called " The M'sus Handicap ". On the second day it ran into the most violent sandstorm which it had yet experienced, and this was followed by heavy rain which converted it into a " mud storm ". Caked with mud, or choked by swirling sand, somehow or other the battalions arrived at Libyan Scheferzen, where there was a gap in the broad wire barricade which the Italians had built from the sea down to Giarubub. There they were directed to proceed with all speed to Bir El Harmat, which they reached shortly after 8 a.m. on the 28th, having covered about a hundred and twenty miles from Bir Thalata. While they were still on the move a reconnaissance was being made of a brigade assembly area some sixty miles further west on the plateau at Garet El Auda. *4 and 5 Bns 25 Jan 42* *4 and 5 Bns 28 Jan 42*

On arrival at Bir El Harmat, the personnel to be left out of battle, and also surplus kit, were withdrawn from the battalions, and the Brigade received its first Anti-Tank guns, eight German 50 mm. weapons. At about 2 o'clock the 5th Green Howards moved off, followed by the 4th. The plan for holding the area was for two battalions to take up positions on the Garet El Auda plateau—the 4th East Yorkshires on the right round Garet El Asida and the 5th Green Howards on the left round Garet El Habib. The 4th Green Howards were to move a further fifteen miles forward and hold Bir Tengeder, with a mobile column in front of them. *See MAP No. 4*

After a nightmare journey in bitterly cold weather across a depression consisting of mud-packs, hummocks, hills,

hollows, and soft white sand, known locally as " The Bloodi-
ness ", the battalions arrived on the plateau on the morning
4 *and* 5 *Bns* of the 29th. The 4th Battalion went straight on to its positions
29 *Jan* 42 at Bir Tengeder, but, owing to the inaccuracy of the maps,
had some difficulty in locating itself. The defensive position
consisted of an area of low escarpments surrounding an area
of soft white sand, and was well sited. It was not, however,
until they had been there for two or three days that the
Intelligence Officer discovered a rickety signpost about five
miles to the north-west marked Bir Tengeder. As they were
satisfied with their defensive position, this problem was overcome by the simple expedient of removing the post, and
planting it firmly in the middle of their positions.

An interesting example of the pitfalls of desert warfare
was an order for the removal of superstructures from all
trucks in the interests of camouflage, as it was found that they
were so heightened by the mirage that the defended area
looked like a block of shimmering skyscrapers.

By this time Benghazi had fallen, and the whole Army in
front was falling back through Mekili and Tmimi towards
4 *Bn*   Gazala. Early on the morning of January 30 movement
30 *Jan*/   was seen in front of the 4th Green Howards, which proved
2 *Feb* 42   to be elements of the Royals and Hussars. There were reports
of enemy patrols some twenty miles away, and a mobile
column was formed to make a wide sweep in the vast No
Man's Land, or Playground, as this part of the desert was
known. This column, designated Licol, was under the command of Capt. E. L. Kirby, M.C., 4th Green Howards, and
consisted of " C " Company, with an artillery and engineer
section attached.

The column moved off in a south-westerly direction
making for Bir Ben Garnia, and, later in the day, joined up
with " Victor " and " Eddie " of the Royals, leaguering for
the night astride the Trigh El Abd some twenty miles south of
Tengeder. The next day, acting on information obtained from
an Armoured Car Squadron of the Royals, the column was
directed north-west towards Msus, where a concentration of
enemy Mechanised Transport was reported. At about 10 a.m.,
when some twenty miles east of Msus, " Licol " picked up a
German Volkswagen containing a Company Sergeant-Major
and one soldier, together with mail, food parcels, and a case
of brandy. These were the first prisoners to be taken by the
Battalion in the Middle East, and were brought back in
triumph by " Licol " on its return at mid-day on February 2.

5 *Bn*   At about the same time the 5th Battalion sent out a
30/31 *Jan* 42 column commanded by Capt. H. D. Whitehead. His orders

were to go out at dawn on January 30, and to sweep south and west, reporting any movement in that area. The force allotted to him consisted of two platoons of " D " Company and two field guns R.A., altogether fifteen vehicles. The column moved off at 10 p.m. on January 29, and, after proceeding twenty miles, halted until dawn. Here it carried out the instructions to dig in whenever there was a halt. This order had given rise to the song " When we debus, we dig in ! " which accompanied its fulfilment on many occasions to the tune of " Begin the Beguine ".

At 8 a.m. the column moved off again, leaving the holes which had been hacked out of the desert unfinished, and, after going for about a mile, Capt. Whitehead was surprised to see, about a thousand yards away, a large quantity of trucks of various sizes, obviously part of a bigger force. After a very cautious approach, it was discovered that this was a half Brigade column named Silverforce, which was completely lost on its retreat from Benghazi. This force, together with Goldforce, the other half Brigade (which incidentally passed through the 150th Brigade's lines on January 31), had been surrounded further to the west, and forced to make a dash through enemy tanks during the hours of darkness. They had been travelling fast for two days, and were in a very exhausted and demoralised state. They were almost out of petrol, and were in the process of arranging to drain their tanks into a few three-ton lorries, embark on these, and make for the oasis of Siwa, having first destroyed the remainder of their vehicles and equipment.

It took Capt. Whitehead a considerable time to convince the Commanding Officer that there were no enemy forces between him and the 150th Brigade. Eventually, however, he was persuaded, and Capt. Whitehead lent him his own Company Sergeant-Major to guide the force back to the 150th Brigade lines along his own wheel tracks. By this action some sixty to seventy trucks, eight anti-tank guns, a Battery of twenty-five pounders, and a few Bofors guns were saved from destruction, and a fine body of men probably saved from extinction in the desert, in their efforts to reach Siwa. Capt. Whitehead then completed his course of twenty-five miles south and twenty-five miles west without further incident, and arrived back safely at 6 a.m. on January 31.

The German advance had now reached the general line Derna-Mekili and was still moving forward. The 8th Army had been ordered to fall back and hold the line Gazala-Bir Hacheim, the 150th Brigade being allotted to the Bir Hacheim area.

4 *and* 5 *Bns*
2/12 *Feb* 42   The first unit to move was the 4th Green Howards who,
in bright moonlight at about 11 p.m. on the night of February
2, started to withdraw through the El Auda position, and next
morning arrived safely at Bir Hacheim at ten o'clock after a
journey of sixty miles. They left behind them at Tengeder a
reconstructed " Licol ", under the command of Major H.
Clapham, R.A. This column consisted of 285 Battery, a
platoon of anti-tank guns, " D " Company, 4th Green
Howards (Capt. J. B. Mansell) and an R.E. party. Its task
was to keep in touch with the enemy, and, on the evening of
the 8th, it shelled Mekili successfully, and mined some of the
tracks leading out of the village. Except for the anxiety of
operating some eighty miles away from its base, it had no
further excitements, and was relieved on February 11 by
" Bucol ", a column of the 5th Green Howards commanded
by Major Lacy.

Meanwhile, the 150th Brigade was digging feverishly on
the Bir Hacheim position under the guidance of Major F. S. S.
Lamprey, 5th Green Howards. This position consisted of an
equilateral triangle, each side about two thousand yards long,
laid out on a Hog's Back, which ran north from the Italian
fort. The fort of Bir Hacheim was reminiscent of that por-
trayed in " Beau Geste ", and it was a fitting scene for the
epic defence which was made there by the Free French Legion-
naires at a not far distant date.

The triangle was held by the 4th Green Howards at the
fort, the 5th Green Howards at the north-west apex, and the
4th East Yorkshires at the north-east apex, with Brigade
Headquarters and the Artillery in the centre. Mine fields
were laid round the perimeter, and standing patrols were sent
out some ten miles in front of each face of the triangle. The
only excitement during the short period spent at Bir Hacheim
was on February 10, when five German aircraft flew over and
machine-gunned the position in a low level attack. One
R.A.S.C. driver was killed, and one aeroplane, which was
seen to come down in the desert, was later found by the 5th
Battalion with its three occupants dead. Another casualty
was the Medical Officer of the 4th Battalion, Capt. Royston.
Hastening to an R.A.S.C. lorry which had driven into a
minefield near the fort, he was blown up and his right hand
badly injured.

4 *and* 5 *Bns*
12 *Feb* 42   On February 12, before the 150th Brigade had had time
to settle down, orders were received for it to proceed to the
area of Bir El Jeff, and take over from the Free French. The
advance parties were royally entertained at the French Headquarters in a flower-covered depression, which was a welcome

change from the sand-swept plateau of Bir Hacheim. On the 4 *Bn*
15th the 4th Battalion moved to Alem Hamza, and completed 15 *Feb* 42
taking over from the Senegalese at midnight. The 5th Battalion 5 *Bn*
moved across on the 17th and was in position at Bir El Naghia 17 *Feb* 42
by 11 p.m. The Brigade was now under the orders of the 4th
Indian Division, but, on February 22, the 151st Brigade and
69th Brigade arrived, and the 50th Division was once again
united.

The 150th Brigade's new position was laid out with the
5th Green Howards on the right round Bir El Naghia, the 4th
East Yorkshires in the centre, and the 4th Green Howards
on the left at Alem Hamza, with an outpost at the Green Post,
or Bois Sacre, as it was called by the French. Brigade Headquarters was at Bir El Jeff. The position was about four miles
long and five miles deep ; on the right of the Brigade was the
Polish Brigade, and to the left rear of the 4th Green Howards
was a Brigade of the 4th Indian Division, the latter being
relieved by the 151st Brigade on February 22.

The first undertaking of the 150th Brigade was to reorganise
the position which it had taken over from the French.
Although this constituted a defence system of sorts, it consisted merely of the old Italian defences turned the other way
round. This was not considered satisfactory ; and so the
round of digging, wiring and mine-laying began again ;
and, as the new defences grew, special tracks had to be constructed through the minefields, and to the rear defences. At
the same time patrols and columns were operating in front of
the position by day and night. Apart from the success which
these columns had in harassing the enemy, they also played
an important part in maintaining the morale of troops,
whose primary role was a defensive one, in " boxes " protected by wire and minefields.

On February 18, at dawn, Lt.-Col. Littleboy moved out 4 *Bn*
towards Bir Temrad in command of a column consisting of 18/20 *Feb* 42
" A " Company, 4th Green Howards, under Capt. Donking,
285 Battery R.A., a troop of anti-tank guns, and a troop of
Bofors guns. This force was acting as flank guard to a column
of the South African Division, which was operating in the
Eluet El Daba area. After passing through Bir Temrad, it
moved forward towards El Aleima, until it reached the line
of the Tmimi-Mekili track.

On the morning of February 20 Lt. E. W. Clay and an
armoured car were sent off on a reconnaissance to Eluet El
Daba. As they approached this area they saw some vehicles
in the distance and gave chase ; but, on being received by
shell fire, they dodged back again to the column under cover

of some friendly wadis. Apart from this minor excitement, and a few odd shells from the direction of Chechiban, which fell a long way short, there were no signs of enemy activity, and the column returned to Alem Hamza about 3 p.m. One casualty sustained in this operation was deeply felt by the 4th Battalion. Capt. W. Speke, M.C., of 285 Battery R.A., who had worked so often with the Battalion since the days at Ypres in 1940, was blown up by a mine near Bir Temrad and lost his life.

5 Bn
22 Feb 42

On the 22nd a column under Capt. Dennis, 5th Battalion, set out to harass the enemy, who had now moved forward and occupied El Aleima. This it did with success and, after Lt. J. W. W. Huntrods had led a bayonet charge against them, the enemy withdrew in confusion. After coming under shell fire from Chechiban, this column returned to Bir El Naghia.

5 Bn
27 Feb 42

On the 27th Major Lacy took out a column consisting of " A " Company, 5th Green Howards, the carrier platoon under Lt. Bateman, and supporting troops, to the El Aleima-El Eleba area. Enemy armoured car patrols were driven in, and reconnaissance parties went as far as El Ezziat during the night. This column rescued about a dozen Indian troops who had escaped from Benghazi and Martuba, and who had been brought through the enemy lines by Senussi. The latter refused to take money as a reward for their services, but asked for some tea and sugar, with which they were delighted.

5 Bn
25/30 Mar 42

During the last week in March the routine column on the Divisional front was found by the 5th Green Howards. The two enemy positions at El Eleba and El Aleima were harassed daily by artillery fire, and Lt.-Col. Bush decided to launch a minor operation against them. The 5th Battalion column was divided into three sub-columns, " L ", " M " and " N " Columns, commanded respectively by Lt.-Col. Bush, Capt. B. V. Rhodes, " C " Company, and Capt. Whitehead, " D " Company. Units of other arms were attached to each column.

At dawn on March 25 the columns moved out, and during the afternoon came into contact with some of the 11th Hussars, who reported that the enemy was busy strengthening his outposts at these positions. Reconnaissance patrols under Lts. P. L. Lindrea and N. Blunt were sent out on the night of March 26, and as a result of information obtained by them, Lt.-Col. Bush decided to attack El Eleba in the early hours of the 27th with Capt. Rhodes' column. " C " Company managed to get to the starting line undetected, but, when it went in with the bayonet, the enemy was found to be in strength. Tanks had been moved up, and there were innumerable machine-guns covering his position. After capturing half of the defended locality, and inflicting severe casualties on the enemy in hand-to-hand fighting, " C " Company was forced to withdraw under the murderous machine-gun fire. This was accomplished under cover of artillery fire, but the Company lost Capt. Rhodes, who was wounded, and twenty other ranks. That night Lt. Lindrea took out a patrol to El Eleba to observe the enemy, and, if possible, bring in any wounded men of " C " Company, but failed in his search.

The next day Lt. Blunt led a patrol to El Aleima, but did not find any concentration of the enemy there. On March 29, " N " Column (Capt. Whitehead), which was harassing El Aleima, rescued some abandoned 25 pounders, but did not come into any close contact with the enemy. All columns withdrew on March 30, and arrived at the perimeter of the 150th Brigade box at about 5 p.m.

By the beginning of March the 151st Brigade was in position south of Alem Hamza, forming a continuation on the left flank of the 150th Brigade. The 69th Brigade was situated to the left rear of the position as part of the Divisional Mobile Reserve, with the tanks of the 42nd and 44th Battalions, Royal Tank Regiment.

Spring had arrived, flowers began to bloom in the desert, and the scent of wild stocks at night was delightful. But, idyllic as the surroundings were, compared to those of Bir Hacheim, the tide of battle was rising, and on March 16 a strong enemy tank force appeared at Sidi Breghisc, only eight miles away.

Water is not easy to come by in the desert, and at Sidi Breghisc there was an excellent supply of water in a well, which, situated as it was in the Playground, was used by both sides. There is a story told of one such water expedition. A member of a Battalion water party descended the cistern-like well to facilitate the filling of tins. Unfortunately a small enemy armoured force also selected this well from which to replenish its tins at the same time, and the British water party had to beat a hasty retreat, but not before they had warned their comrade down below of coming events, urging him, like Brer Rabbit, to lie low. So enemy containers were lowered and filled. When the coast was clear once more, the party reunited and went on its way rejoicing.

On April 6 the enemy made a further advance, and 4 *Bn* established themselves on the line Bir Temrad-Sidi Breghisc. 6/16 *Apr* 42 While this move restricted the operations of the larger columns, small mobile patrols were sent out daily from first light to sunset, and played considerable havoc amongst the enemy front-line troops. They became known as the Crazy Gang.

G

Lt. E. L. Bown, 4th Green Howards, failed to return from one of these patrols on April 6, and next day his bloodstained truck was discovered abandoned. It was learnt later that Lt. Bown had been buried in the Hero's Cemetery at Derna by the Germans.

Capt. Donking, 4th Green Howards, led many such raids, and, on his last patrol on the 16th, brought back a prisoner from the enemy position near Sidi Breghisc. Shortly afterwards this gallant officer was evacuated sick, and the hospital ship, on which he had been placed at Tobruk, was bombed and sank. He, and Lt. (Q.M.) F. G. Tower, recently posted as Quartermaster of the 4th Battalion, who was also being evacuated sick, were both drowned.

Early in May Capt. J. R. Booth, M.C., 4th Battalion, was unluckily captured with his patrol, while attempting to secure a prisoner from a German post.

The 4th Battalion suffered another serious loss on April 16 when Lt.-Col. Littleboy, D.S.O., M.C., who had commanded the battalion from the beginning of the war, was withdrawn under the age limit for commanding officers in the desert. The Battalion was taken over by Lt.-Col. L. C. Cooper, who had fought as a boy at Villers Bretonneux with the Australians in 1918, and who now became a Green Howard, on transfer from the Sherwood Foresters.

5 Bn
12 Apr 42
On April 12 a mobile column, commanded by Capt. Dennis, consisting of one section of carriers of the 5th Battalion, two Anti-tank guns, one section of Machine-Guns and a troop of artillery, was engaged by enemy tanks. This column had been sent out to bring in Lt. N. Blunt, who had been lying up during the night with " sticky " bombs in an endeavour to put out of action some enemy tanks, which had been causing casualties among the South African armoured cars. During the engagement Sgt. A. E. Chapman and his driver were killed, one anti-tank gun knocked out, and a carrier damaged.

By this time the defences of the 150th Brigade were complete, and the Brigade felt that, as a result of its labours, it was in a position to repel any assault which the enemy might
4 and 5 Bns make. As so often happens in war, however, its satisfaction
20 Apr 42 was short-lived, for, on April 20, it was relieved by a South African Brigade, and moved south to take up a new position around Got El Ualeb. There it took over from the 200th Guards Brigade (later renumbered 201st Guards Brigade), which was being withdrawn to the area known as Knightsbridge.

The area to be held by the Brigade lay between the Trigh Capuzzo and the Trigh El Abd, just east of Mteifel El Chebir, where the two tracks met. This new position was the one on which the 4th and 5th Green Howards fought their final battle, between May 26 and June 1, but, before giving a detailed survey of the whole lay-out, a vital factor which affected the subsequent fighting must be recorded. The Guards Brigade, consisting of motorised infantry, had been able to cover the large area of ground between the two tracks fairly easily, but the 150th Brigade, consisting as it did of comparatively static infantry, was forced to hold the position with battalions on extended fronts, and with gaps in some places of over two thousand yards between them.

Before beginning to relate the epic story of the 150th Brigade's fight to a finish on June 1, and the events that led up to it, we must return to the 69th Brigade, which had arrived in the Gazala line a few miles south of Alem Hamza, on February 22, having left El Aine camp in Syria on February 12, and covered the long road journey of over a thousand miles in ten days. *6 and 7 Bns* *22 Feb* 42

The first task of this Brigade was to carry on the work, from where the Indian Brigade had left off, of consolidating its positions. For some weeks they dug, and constructed camouflage, observation posts, and ammunition and ration dumps. Each " box " was stocked with all necessities for withstanding a three weeks' siege. The weather at that time of the year was magnificent ; warm and sunny by day, cool and dry by night. Everybody was very fit and in good heart.

In March the Battalions began sending out " Jock " Columns, designed to patrol No Man's Land, harass enemy working parties, and prevent enemy movement taking place unobserved. During this period, until it went into Brigade Reserve on April 20 on relief by the 7th Battalion, the 6th Battalion Green Howards sent out patrols at varying intervals, and provided the infantry element of Parcol.

This column consisted of " B." Company, Captain K. Hicks, with supporting arms. Captain Hicks was later transferred to the 7th Battalion, and was killed while serving with it at Mersah Matruh. The column was out for three days, April 10/12, and during this time a fighting patrol of No. 12 platoon, commanded by Lt. A. Hill, was sent out with the object of securing a prisoner for identification purposes. This patrol came under heavy fire, and was forced to withdraw. Lt. Hill, with two of his men, was taken prisoner. With the exception of a few minor casualties from air raids, these were the first casualties sustained by the 6th Battalion in the Desert Campaign. *6 Bn* *10/12 Apr* 42

The next action carried out by the 6th Battalion was when it moved out as part of the Divisional Mobile Reserve to Bir El Aslagh, an account of which is given later, as this action formed an integral part of the 150th Brigade's final battle.

7 Bn
Mar 42 The 7th Battalion, during this period, in addition to routine patrolling, went out three times on Column. On the first occasion, in March, a column set out to capture a famous enemy outpost position, El Aleima, known as " The Pimple ", against which several unsuccessful attempts had already been made.

The moon was at its full, and the enemy were very much on the alert, when the column halted about five miles from El Aleima for a reconnaissance to be made. Some of the 25-pounders were brought into play, and made accurate shooting on the enemy's position, but meanwhile the Germans had manoeuvred a quick firing gun quite close without being spotted, and this began firing some solid shot shells. These came bouncing along the face of the desert amongst the carriers and armoured cars, and Lt.-Col. MacDonnell, commanding the column, decided to withdraw and attack The Pimple from an entirely different direction. During the night, however, a heavy thunderstorm broke, and in the morning the vehicles were immobilised until the wind and sun had dried the surface. By this time the column was due to withdraw to the Gazala Line and hand over to another column.

7 Bn
20/24 Mar 42 The next operation in which the 7th Battalion took part was known as Operation Fullsize, in which the 8th Army succeeded in diverting the Luftwaffe for a sufficiently long space of time to enable the Royal Navy to get an important relief convoy through to Malta. Three columns were sent out on the night of March 20/21 on this operation, two from the 50th Division to harass enemy landing grounds at Tmimi and Martuba, and a third column was sent to Bir Temrad to cover the assembly of the Tmimi Column. The 7th Battalion Green Howards, under Lt.-Col. MacDonnell, formed part of the Tmimi column. Its first role was to capture a ridge in sight of, and within artillery range of, El Aleima, The Pimple. This task was accomplished with a few casualties from artillery fire. The battalion held this position for two days, and on the third morning The Pimple was attacked under cover of a smoke screen by the Durham Light Infantry, supported by tanks, artillery, medium machine-guns, and anti-tank units. El Aleima was captured after a hard fight, in which over a hundred and fifty prisoners were taken, and the Durham Light Infantry force went on towards Tmimi.

The 7th Green Howards then took over the El Aleima position, and spent a very strenuous night digging in. The next afternoon, March 24, the Durham Light Infantry column broke off its engagement, and retired through the 7th Green Howards. Meanwhile the German artillery had brought down a heavy fire on The Pimple, which lasted until shortly before dark. Then there fell a stillness which was harder to bear than the shelling, and which seemed to fill the air with the gloomy foreboding of unknown events. An order was received for the Green Howards to hold on to their position for another three days, but this was cancelled within an hour, and new orders received to retire about two hours later. Just when the leading company was proceeding towards the transport vehicles, the enemy put down a heavy concentration of fire through which the men had to pass. Casualties were surprisingly small but Capt. P. W. Swift was killed by a shell.

The enemy had now, by some means, manoeuvred a force close up to the leading companies unobserved by the sentries, and this force, which included tanks, was advancing against the position. Although part of the battalion had already been evacuated, the Commanding Officer and Rear Company Company Commander were faced with the difficult task of getting the remaining troops to the transport. A troop of anti-tank guns was overrun and captured, but the Battalion managed to get safely away under cover of the rearguard, which consisted of the Carrier Platoon, and the Regimental Ambulance, since the Medical Officer insisted on being the last to leave, together with Lt.-Col. MacDonnell. Once clear of El Aleima, speed was on the side of the British force and it was soon out of range, and then out of sight, of the enemy, and returned safely to the Gazala Line.

The third column, commanded by Major T. W. G. Stansfeld, 2nd I./C. 7th Green Howards, was ordered out early in April to rescue a column of the Durham Light Infantry, which had been badly mauled by German tanks. Major Stansfeld, who was given a squadron of Matilda tanks in addition to the usual " Jock Column " component of infantry, artillery, carriers and anti-tank guns, went out about twenty-five miles until he met some of the Durham Light Infantry and a Battery Commander, the latter informing him that he had lost all his guns, and that the action had taken place about two miles away. The column proceeded to this spot and found a scene of dreadful carnage. Five British guns stood there, with their crews lying dead beside them, and also a German tank which had received a direct hit through the driving slit at point-blank range. After burying the dead and salvaging

7 Bn
Apr 42

the guns, Major Stansfeld received a wireless message from
Capt. H. J. D. Collett of the carrier platoon, to the effect that
fourteen enemy tanks were approaching from the north. No
sooner had this message been received than the column was
shot at by two German tanks from behind, one shell only just
missing Major Stansfeld's carrier. He then gave orders to withdraw and, in spite of being shot at until they were some three-
quarters of a mile clear, they escaped without casualties, and
were met on their return by the Divisional Commander, who
congratulated them on having salvaged the guns. Capt.
Collett, with his carrier platoon, displayed great initiative and
gallantry in this operation.

The Eighth Army, commanded by Lt.-Gen. N. M. Ritchie,
C.B.E., D.S.O., M.C., was now grouped in the formation in
which the battle of The Gazala Line was fought on May 26
and subsequent days. Facing the enemy, the right of the line
was held by the 1st South African Division. On its left a
Brigade of the 2nd South African Division stood on the Bir
El Jeff-Alem Hamza position. South of Alem Hamza were
the 151st Brigade and the 69th Brigade, with a gap of about
six miles between them and the 150th Brigade at Got El
Ualeb. The southern flank of the 150th Brigade rested approximately on the Trigh El Abd, with a further gap of fifteen
miles before the Bir Hacheim position was reached. The
latter position was held by the Free French Brigade. The
200th Guards Brigade was in reserve in the neighbourhood of
Knightsbridge, some twenty miles to the east, and the 2nd
South African Division, less one Brigade, was in Tobruk.
The 1st Armoured Division, consisting of the 2nd and 22nd
Armoured Brigades and a support group, was in the neighbourhood of Knightsbridge, with the 7th Armoured Division,
consisting of the 4th Armoured Brigade and a support group,
further south behind Bir Hacheim. The 50th Division was
allotted, as a mobile reserve, the 1st Army Tank Brigade,
consisting of the 44th Battalion, Royal Tank Regiment and a
squadron of the 42nd Battalion R.T.R., while the 32nd Army
Tank Brigade, consisting of the 7th and 42nd Battalions R.T.R.
(less one squadron), acted in the same capacity on the 1st
South African Divisional front. The 8th Battalion R.T.R.
was covering the coastal strip between Gazala and Tobruk,
while the 4th Battalion R.T.R. was in Tobruk itself.

The first problem which confronted the 150th Brigade in
its new position was the construction of new defences. A
continuous minefield covered the front of the 8th Army from
the sea as far as Alem Hamza, but from this point southwards,
minefields had been laid in irregular belts to allow the Guards
Brigade and the Armoured Division freedom of manoeuvre.

Orders were now received that the Ualeb position was to be regarded as a " keep ", and defended statically to the last round and the last man. Hectic digging again became the order of the day, and weapon pits, headquarters, gun positions and vehicle pits had to be prepared with all possible speed, as it was becoming increasingly evident that the enemy was building up his forces for an offensive. The work proved difficult owing to a lack of mechanical appliances to deal with the rocky ground, and there was a shortage of wire with which to strengthen the forward infantry posts. More mine-fields were laid, but they did not encircle the whole position. At the same time, constant patrolling was being carried out by mobile columns which went out for four days at a time, harassing the enemy by day and night, and gaining information as to his movements in the area of Bir Temrad, Sidi Breghisc, and Rotunda Mteifel. Liaison patrols between the 150th Brigade and the Free French, some fifteen miles to the left flank, had also to be found.

Although the primary plan was to fight a defensive battle on the Ualeb position, preparations were also made for a counter attack, and certain units were to be prepared for an advance, while all " B " Echelons of units in the line were to move up as soon as the battle started. Transport was, however, in short supply, and in the 50th Division only the 69th Brigade, which formed the Infantry Component of the Divisional Mobile Reserve, could be fully motorised, by taking over from the other brigades all reasonably serviceable vehicles. In preparation for a fairly long defensive battle, a double allowance of infantry ammunition, which included small arms ammunition, grenades, mortar, and two-pounder ammunition, was assembled, in addition to the normal reserve, and seven days' supply of food and water was also issued.

From May 22/26 a mobile column consisting of the 4th Green Howards and a battery of artillery, all under the command of Major D'A. J. D. Mander, covered the Divisional front. The Divisional Commander, Major-General Ramsden, visited this column on May 22, and gave instructions for a general reconnaissance patrol of two officers to be sent out to the area between Sidi Breghisc and El Cherima. The objectives of this patrol were to penetrate between the German strong points by night, and to lie up by day observing enemy movements, and any signs of an imminent attack. *4 Bn* 22/26 *May* 42

Lts. E. W. Clay and P. J. Howell, 4th Green Howards, volunteered for this task, and arrangements were made to drop them near Sidi Breghisc at dusk. Each officer carried two water bottles, a pistol, compass, maps and notebooks, together with hard rations and one spade between them. They decided to advance some seven miles on a bearing of 260 degrees, and then to strike north towards El Cherima, hoping to circumvent the enemy's position, and to lie up before dawn. After proceeding for about four miles, they ran into a German minefield, but found a way through it, and, in spite of being challenged by a sentry, resumed their advance unmolested. At dawn on the 23rd they found themselves in the middle of a German company, with the front line behind them and company headquarters in front. Lying doggo in their hide-out they were able to observe working parties digging from dawn to mid-day, and noted that the sentries were very slack. At mid-day the position was shelled by our 25-pounders and all work ceased. By this time both officers were feeling the strain of lying motionless in the sun. Just before dusk tanks arrived and took up positions in vehicle pits between the infantry posts, thus forming a series of pill boxes. The night arcs of the perimeter were then tested for several minutes with tracer ammunition and, as machine-gun and anti-tank fire passed over and by the two officers at heights of from two inches to four feet above the ground, they reported that the linking up was " excellent ".

As soon as it was dusk the patrol moved on to the north in an attempt to penetrate right into the position. Movement was necessarily slow, as frequent detours had to be made to avoid working parties, which were extending the minefield all night. After proceeding about three miles northward without achieving any deeper penetration, the officers were forced by the approach of daylight to lie up once more. At nightfall they moved forward again and located an ammunition dump. They then withdrew and marched due east for eight miles, then a further four miles south-east, at which point, being completely exhausted, they decided to rest until dawn. Soon after this they were picked up by Major Mander's column, and sent back to Divisional Headquarters. These two officers were sent to the rear for a short rest after their gallant effort, and did not, in fact, get back to the Battalion before it was overrun on June 1.

During this period a daring raid was made on the enemy lines by a party under Lt. N. G. Sproule, 4th Green Howards. Many casualties were inflicted on the enemy, and a prisoner was secured for identification purposes.

During the night of May 25/26 many coloured flares were seen in the enemy's night leaguer, and the rumbling of tanks and vehicles showed that they were preparing for active measures. On the morning of the 26th the enemy, despite our harassing fire, remained quiet until about 2.30 in the afternoon. At this hour our firing ceased, and Major Mander's column began to withdraw. The enemy chose this moment to advance with tanks and armoured cars under the cover of artillery fire, but halted their attack in time to allow the column to get away safely to the main position, not, however, without being bombed by six Stukas on the way back.

On the morning of the 27th a massed infantry advance, unsupported by tanks, was made against the 69th Brigade position. The enemy troops were Italian, who came over the skyline at about 10 a.m. As they slowly approached in a solid line they offered a target of which the rifleman or light automatic gunner dreams but seldom gets. Heavy toll was taken by our troops, and when the enemy reached the trip wire marking the dummy minefield, which had just been completed in front of the position, they halted, and a fire duel ensued in which the British troops, in their prepared positions, held a great advantage over the enemy in the open. The Italians withdrew after having suffered heavy casualties.

7 Bn
27 May 42

At about 2 p.m. the outpost commander to the south of the 69th Brigade Box, realising that the enemy had bypassed Fachri, and fearing that he would be cut off, evacuated his position. Although for the next few days he remained about a thousand yards outside Patrol Gap, his withdrawal had given the enemy a good Artillery Observation post near Fachri. On the 28th an artillery duel commenced which continued for several days. Little damage was done, but there were many near misses, and the troops were subjected to severe strain, pinned down, as they were, in their trenches under the hot sun.

During the next two or three days constant patrolling was carried out by the 7th Battalion. A carrier patrol operated daily on the southern flank, and, in spite of being chased from position to position by enemy tanks, succeeded in obtaining accurate and detailed information about the enemy, who had established themselves on the ridge north of the Trigh Capuzzo, between the 69th and 150th Brigades.

On May 30, the 6th Green Howards rejoined the Brigade from their operations with the Divisional Mobile Column (to be related later), and, after reorganisation, were put in to strengthen the defences.

6 Bn
30 May/
13 Jun 42

The ensuing fortnight was spent by the 6th Green Howards in moving to new positions, digging in, and moving again, and in constant patrolling. They were spasmodically shelled by the enemy and suffered severely from hot dust storms, which rendered visibility negligible and throats parched, since the water ration had been reduced to two pints a day per man for all purposes.

Fighting patrols went out each night on compass bearings for distances of from three to four miles, with the object of locating any enemy who might be attempting to infiltrate closer to the " box ". One such patrol, consisting of an officer and fourteen men, having followed the same course for several nights, as ordered, and having brought back each time a nil report, which was badly received at Battalion Headquarters, decided that the next time it would go still further into the desert—in fact as far as the darkness of the night permitted, and obtain some positive information. Having proceeded as far as they considered safe, in view of the necessity of getting back before daylight, they took up an all round defensive position. They then solemnly whistled " God Save the King " three times, and, as this evoked no response, they then fired off a magazine of bren ammunition in three directions. Receiving no reply of any sort they were satisfied that there were no enemy in the vicinity, and started for home. Unfortunately they had miscalculated the time, and only arrived back at the box an hour and a half after first light, having covered the last few thousand yards in full view of any enemy who might have been about. The reception which they received from the Commanding Officer, who had seen them come in in daylight, was explosive !

See MAPS During the night of May 26/27 the enemy were heard to Nos. 5 *and* 6 be moving across the front of the 150th Brigade in a southerly direction.

Owing to the extreme length of the front, a considerable proportion of the troops had to be used for patrolling purposes. The 4th Battalion, in addition to roving patrols north and south of Trigh Capuzzo, also maintained a standing patrol of one platoon at Rotunda Mteifel. The 5th Battalion, besides sending out patrols to connect up with the 4th Green Howards and 4th East Yorkshires, also had a standing patrol of two sections of infantry, one section of carriers and mortars, and an artillery forward observation post at Barrel 9 on the Trigh El Abd.

4 *Bn*   Early on May 27 Lt. S. P. Fawcett, commanding the stand-
27 *May* 42 ing patrol of the 4th Battalion at Rotunda Mteifel, some six miles to the west of the main position, reported several armoured cars approaching his post. A section of three carriers under Sgt. J. Leng was sent out at once to reinforce him. Soon after passing through the minefield Sgt. Leng was considerably surprised to see shell fire, and moving vehicles on the skyline to his right flank. On proceeding to investigate he met

some carriers belonging to the 7th Battalion, and learned that the vehicles which he had seen were part of the 69th Brigade column which was in contact with the enemy. He then turned south and got in touch with Lt. Fawcett, who explained that there were twelve armoured cars about a thousand yards away over the ridge, and that his 30 cwt. lorry had broken down. Sgt. Leng went off over the ridge with the object of towing in the 30 cwt. lorry, but, when he reached the top, was confronted by the enemy armoured cars approaching, and not more than a hundred yards away. Being out-gunned, Sgt. Leng quickly withdrew, but the armoured cars fanned out on top of the ridge and opened fire. Sgt. Leng's second carrier was attacked by two armoured cars and its crew captured, while his leading truck broke down. The crew of this carrier, however, succeeded in boarding the 30 cwt. lorry which had been repaired by this time, and Sgt. Leng returned safely towards dusk.

Meanwhile the noise of battle from the direction of Bir Harmat, some eleven miles due east, and to the rear of the 5th Battalion, could be heard throughout the day, and it was clear that the enemy's offensive had started in earnest. This action, in which the British armoured divisions were out-manoeuvred, and the 50th Divisional Mobile Reserve forced to withdraw, resulted in the semi-encirclement of the 150th Brigade, and led to the final disaster of June 1.

The Divisional Mobile Reserve was under command of Brigadier W. C. L. O'Carroll, D.S.O., and consisted of Brigade Headquarters, 1st Army Tank Brigade, the 44th Battalion The Royal Tank Regiment, one squadron 42nd Battalion R.T.R., one squadron armoured cars, 287 Battery, R.A., 124 Field Regiment, R.A., 6th Battalion, Green Howards, and one company of machine-guns of the 2nd Battalion, Cheshire Regiment. This force moved off soon after 10 o'clock on May 27 to occupy Bir Aslagh, and, an hour later, met a large enemy column moving northwards along the Bir Hacheim-Acroma track. At least one Panzer Regiment was halted on the track, probably refuelling, and staff cars could be seen darting in all directions. *6 Bn 27 May 42*

The 6th Battalion came under heavy shell fire, and the order was given to debus, and to advance and occupy the higher ground which lay across the Bir Hacheim-Acroma track. The Battalion went into the attack with " D " Company (Capt. F. H. Brunton) on the right, " C " Company (Capt. C. M. Hull) on the left, and " A " Company (Capt. J. L. Hughes, M.C.) in reserve.

This was the first real contact with the enemy that the Battalion had made, as a complete unit, since 1940, and the conduct of all ranks was to prove the value of the training and discipline which it had gradually built up since the return from Dunkirk. Through increasing shelling and machine-gun fire the sections and platoons advanced in perfect formation, with their bayonets at the high port. Casualties occurred, particularly in No. 14 platoon of " C " Company, which received a shell burst right in its centre, but the men never wavered, and marched straight forward, leaving the wounded to the care of the stretcher bearers.

2/Lt. B. Burn, who was so soon to lose his life in the break out from Gazala, led his anti-tank guns, with great dash and gallantry, against two enemy armoured cars which were threatening the advance. Both were knocked out and their crews taken prisoner by " D " Company.

The Battalion reached its objective, on which it proceeded to dig itself in as best it could in the hard ground. For the remaining hours of daylight there was intermittent shelling and machine-gun fire, but the Green Howards held firm.

Later, the 44th Battalion R.T.R. went into the attack, but met with little success owing to the superior fire power of the enemy. Towards evening the Panzer column attacked the 201st Guards Brigade at Knightsbridge, but was repulsed with heavy losses, and, sidestepping the Guards, moved northwards towards Bir Rigel. The night of May 27 passed quietly so far as the 6th Green Howards were concerned with the exception of the following incident. Shortly after dark a German staff car, with two others, one of which contained a fully equipped fitters' shop, drove towards No. 15 platoon of " C " Company. The platoon waited until the cars were so close that there was no chance of their getting away, before they sprang out of their trenches and effected their capture. Not a shot was fired, and hardly a sound was made.

Immediately after this Capt. Hull took out a patrol to reconnoitre the route to Knightsbridge. This he found to be clear of the enemy, and early the next morning, the Battalion moved to Knightsbridge in its transport.

4 and 5 Bns
27 May 42
Meanwhile there had been plenty of activity on the fronts of the 150th Brigade. Early on the 27th the standing patrol of the 4th East Yorkshires, two miles east of Rotunda Mteifel, had been forced to withdraw, and soon afterwards twelve enemy tanks drove into the minefield about one and a half miles south of the Ualeb gap. These were engaged by artillery fire and abandoned by their crews. The tanks were subsequently destroyed by the Engineers.

To the north of the positions, as soon as Lt. Fawcett's patrol had been driven in, Lt.-Col. Cooper established a fighting patrol of carriers, mortars, anti-tank guns, and machine-guns, under the command of Capt. A. P. Mitchell, on a ridge some three-quarters of a mile in front of his forward post in the Capuzzo Gap. This ridge became known as the Disputed Ridge, and was the scene of many encounters in the days that followed.

All through this day the enemy were moving north, trying to find a soft spot in our defences. Wherever they met the Green Howards they received a " bloody nose ", but eventually they succeeded in making a passage through the mine marsh a few miles to the north, in the gap between the 150th and 151st Brigades. This was the beginning of the other encircling movement, which resulted later in the 150th Brigade becoming completely surrounded.

At about 3 p.m. on May 27, a column under the command of Major R. Elliott, 72nd Field Regiment, R.A., was sent out from the 150th Brigade Box to give support to the Divisional Mobile Reserve in the neighbourhood of Bir Aslagh and Bir Tamar. Major P. D. H. Fox, 5th Battalion, Green Howards, was second in command, and Lt. C. G. Browning of the same Battalion, Adjutant of the column, which consisted of two troops of artillery, three sections of carriers under Capt. G. M. Bateman, one platoon of " B " Company (Lt. Gregory), one platoon " D " Company (Lt. W. Ramshaw) one section 3-in. mortars (Lt. A. E. Wheeler), and one section 150 Field Ambulance. As it advanced in an easterly direction towards Bir Harmat the column bumped into a considerable force of the enemy which it attacked. A Mark IV tank was knocked out, and five " very arrogant " prisoners were taken. In the ensuing counter-attack Lt. Gregory was killed, and Capt. Bateman was wounded. The latter was again severely wounded when the dressing station to which he had been taken was dive-bombed but, after five days in an ambulance, he reached Tobruk, and was evacuated by hospital ship before the town fell.

*5 Bn
27 May 42*

Early on the 28th this column was strengthened by the addition of " D " Company, 4th East Yorkshires, whose withdrawal from the Rotunda Ualeb was spotted by the enemy, with disastrous results as will be seen later. When this Company joined the column, the latter was in a position near Bir Aslagh overlooking the Hacheim-Acroma track, and engaging any enemy who attempted to move north from Bir Harmat. With them were all the tanks of the Divisional Mobile Reserve with the exception of " B " Squadron 42nd

*5 Bn
28 May 42*

Battalion R.T.R., which was operating independently with the 6th Green Howards at Knightsbridge. At 5 o'clock in the afternoon the enemy launched a heavy attack against Bir Aslagh, and the 150th Brigade column was forced to withdraw to a prepared position near Bir Tamar, which it reached about 10 p.m. that night.

Sgt. W. Burdett for his coolness and courage in directing the mortar fire, which helped to cover this withdrawal, was awarded the Military Medal.

6 Bn
28 May 42 Meanwhile, the 6th Battalion, with " B " Squadron, 42nd Battalion R.T.R., under Major Godwin, had established itself at Knightsbridge, and was in contact with the Guards Brigade. Although there was considerable enemy movement all round the Battalion, the day passed quietly until about 5 p.m. when it was shelled for about an hour.   The shelling was at times really heavy, but casualties were slight owing to the trenches which had been dug in the morning.

This was the first occasion, but not the last, on which the Battalion had the opportunity of watching a tank battle from the disadvantageous position of being directly between the opposing forces. Apart from ricochets, shorts, and aimed shells which landed amongst the infantry positions, an added danger came from the movement of our own tanks. Being " closed down " these were unable to see the Green Howards in their slit trenches, in spite of the latter's desperate efforts to attract their attention by visual signalling. All that the Green Howards could do was to hope for the best and, when they saw that the best was not forthcoming, to jump out of their trench, get behind the tank, and then leap back into what was left of their trench.

The anti-tank platoon inflicted considerable damage on the enemy tanks, and was especially praised for its work by Lt.-Col. Cooke-Collis.

Those who were there will remember the last shell of the day, which landed in the trench containing the brew pot, which Pte. (Pop) Rutledge had so carefully been tending throughout the latter stages of the battle. Neither will they forget the figure of " Pop " Rutledge, standing bolt upright, shaking his fist in the direction of the enemy, and bringing to bear on them all the maledictions of his vocabulary. Once again the evening menu of " C " Company read : " luke warm bully, hard biscuits and water ", when, but for this unlucky chance, it might have read : " Hot, sweet, tea ".

6 Bn
29 May 42 During the night of May 28/29 Lt.-Col. Cooke-Collis received a message : " If the Matildas (" B " Squadron, 42nd Battalion R.T.R.) are still with you, get them to escort

you to Bir Tamar ". The force set out on May 29 as soon as there was sufficient light for the tanks to move, but very soon an enemy column, which included several Mark IV tanks, was sighted directly in front. The Matildas were no match for the Mark IVs, so the Battalion Commander altered his course to the south. As the Battalion drew up for a halt on this journey, and the men were about to debus, a shell scored a direct hit on one of " D " Company's troop carriers, killing all its occupants, except one man who was sitting next to the driver. The blazing vehicle made an excellent target for the enemy gunners during this brief halt, but there were no further casualties.

Soon afterwards they met the 2nd Armoured Brigade of the 1st Armoured Division, which was moving towards Bir Tamar. The Brigade Commander ordered the 6th Green Howards to move between his two armoured regiments, the Queen's Bays and 9th Lancers, and, thus escorted, they arrived safely at Bir Tamar, only to find that the remainder of the Divisional Mobile Reserve had gone. After an unsuccessful attempt to contact Divisional Headquarters, the battalion deployed on an " all-round " position, and awaited events.

About mid-day a considerable number of small Italian tanks of the Ariete Division approached the position, apparently without artillery or infantry support. Major Godwin had moved his Matildas into a hull down position, and very quickly knocked out ten Italian tanks without loss. Several others surrendered, the tank crews shouting in broken English : " Too much bang ! Too much bang ! "

The Battalion suffered several casualties from shell fire here, mainly because the ground was rock and it was not possible to dig in, including L/Cpl. J. Clocherty of " C " Company, who was killed.

Although this engagement had been completely successful the position of the 6th Green Howards was becoming very precarious, since their supporting Tank Squadron was running short of ammunition and fuel. The Commanding Officer, therefore, decided to move at once into the 150th Brigade Box.

The journey to the 150th Brigade Box was an exciting one. The enemy were scattered all round the 150th Brigade, and the 6th Battalion was forced to run the gauntlet, being chased on one side by enemy tanks, firing as they moved parallel to the Battalion column. It was a fine sight to see all the vehicles, in perfect formation, with Lt.-Col. Cooke-Collis flying his pennant at the head, going flat out across the desert, and gradually leaving the slower moving enemy behind. On arrival outside the Box contact was made by wireless with

Divisional Headquarters, and the 6th Green Howards were ordered to rejoin the 69th Brigade, while the squadron of tanks was to remain with the 150th Brigade.

Earlier in the day a German Fiesler Storch reconnaissance machine had been shot down over the 4th Green Howards' position. The pilot was killed, but the passenger, General Kruewell, G.O.C. The Afrika Corps under Rommel, was captured uninjured by " C " Company, who were delighted to learn later of the importance of their capture. Brigadier Haydon, having no other means of evacuating him, handed over this distinguished prisoner to Lt.-Col. Cooke-Collis. On the way back to the 69th Brigade Box the truck, in which the German General was travelling, was the only one to break down. It was quickly taken in tow, however, and the Battalion reached its destination safely that evening.

Meanwhile the position on the 150th Brigade front had materially altered for the worse during May 28 and 29.

5 *Bn*
28 *May* 42

The first excitement on the 28th was the appearance of an Italian battery, which came in from the direction of Bir Harmat. The commander was captured and stated that he thought he was near Tobruk. On the southern sector the 4th East Yorkshires soon felt the loss of " D " Company, which, as will be remembered, had been sent off to reinforce Major Elliott's column. The enemy, ignoring the direct approach along the Trigh El Abd, began to infiltrate through the minefield at the spot which had been vacated by " D " Company. Large numbers of vehicles and guns came up from a south-westerly direction, and, keeping well out of the effective range of small arms fire, the enemy began lifting the mines. Artillery support was limited owing to the restrictions on ammunition, and by 7 p.m. the enemy had managed to get tanks through the minefield further south, and were attacking the post at Barrel 9, which was held by the standing patrol of the 5th Battalion under Capt. Dennis, supported by three carrier sections of the Brigade Mobile Reserve. At 11 o'clock that night this post was forced to withdraw altogether, as the enemy were pouring vehicles and guns through the gap which they had made.

4 *Bn*
28 *May* 42

On the northern flank the 4th Battalion held on to the Disputed Ridge with Capt. Mitchell's fighting patrol, but the whole position was heavily shelled all day, and Battalion Headquarters was forced to move. It was disheartening for this battalion to see the enemy working parties persistently removing the mines, which formed its northern protection in the gap between its positions and the 151st Brigade. Our artillery fire was not sufficiently intensive to stop this work going on.

SWEEPING FOR MINES UNDER FIRE IN THE DESERT.

AT REST AFTER BATTLE IN THE DESERT.

By May 28 the Battalion was running short of officers, and R.S.M. J. Exall was put in command of an important post at the Capuzzo Gap. Throughout the next two days, the enemy attacked almost continually. R.S.M. Exall, although he was wounded, continued to fight on until a relief could be effected. His courage, endurance, and the fine example which he set to his men, were largely responsible for the enemy's failure to penetrate the Battalion's lines at this point. R.S.M. Exall was awarded the Military Cross.

It was on the 28th that the ammunition situation first gave rise to real concern. Artillery expenditure was reduced to twenty-five rounds per gun per day, and, with the number of targets presented by ever increasing enemy pressure, this was absurdly inadequate. At mid-day a convoy of 3-ton lorries was sent off to Tobruk to draw ammunition for medium and field artillery and for the machine-guns. This convoy was expected to return the same evening, but it never reached the Brigade. Had it done so, the story of the next few days might have been very different.

It was, therefore, in no cheerful atmosphere that the Brigade Commander reviewed the position at 11 p.m. that night, and issued orders for the readjustment of his defences. The enemy was by this time established directly in rear of the Brigade positions ; a break had been made in the southern defences round the Rotunda Ualeb ; the enemy was obviously infiltrating to the north through the gap between the 4th Green Howards and the 151st Brigade ; ammunition was running short, and there was no news of the convoy which had gone to Tobruk for reserves of ammunition. Brigadier Haydon decided to vacate the Rotunda Ualeb, and bring the 4th East Yorkshires round behind the 5th Green Howards to a position facing east on either side of 232 Company, R.E. This move shortened the perimeter considerably, and left the 5th Battalion to cover the southern front alone. Brigade Headquarters was moved into the 4th Green Howards' area, and the Medium Battery and Field Ambulance were also brought into the centre of the defended area. At first light the 44th Battalion, Royal Tank Regiment, also moved into the Box, and was disposed in squadron groups in the defended area.

During May 29 the enemy made no advance from the East, but strengthened his position on the North, West and Southern fronts of the 150th Brigade Box. To the north, Capt. Mitchell's force on the Disputed Ridge was subjected to shelling, mortar and small arms fire, and sustained some casualties. During the morning Capt. Mitchell managed to

4 Bn
29 May 42

H

find a covered approach to the gap in the minefield, on which the enemy were working a mile or so to the north, and engaged them with Bren gun fire from three carriers. At about mid-day, the enemy could be seen from the main position to be massing tanks and infantry for an attack. Capt. Mitchell was, therefore, ordered to withdraw from the ridge, and soon afterwards the enemy put down a smoke screen in front of the Capuzzo Gap, and launched a full-scale attack with Mark IV tanks, followed by infantry in lorries, in front of " C " Company, 4th Green Howards. The 72nd Field Regiment, R.A., came into action, and the enemy column wheeled north at once, but the Mark IV tanks ran on to the minefield and were abandoned by their crews. At night 2/Lt. Sproule took out a party and destroyed them. A second attack in the afternoon was also repulsed, and the 4th Battalion still held its positions intact, although worried by the continued infiltration to the north. In these attacks some of the enemy infantry established themselves in slit-trenches in front of the gap and remained there during the night. During the next day these were subjected to effective fire from the Mortar Section, and the machine-gunners of the 2nd Cheshire Regiment.

5 *Bn*
29 *May* 42   To the south, where the 5th Green Howards now faced the Rotunda Ualeb, the enemy began to advance cautiously at about 10.30 a.m. on the 29th, against the positions vacated by the 4th East Yorkshires during the previous night. Throughout the day they kept outside effective machine-gun range, and by the evening were extended over a front of some eight hundred yards, with many guns and vehicles plainly visible. This daylight advance would not have been possible against a concentration of artillery fire, but all the artillery support available was one battery, whose ammunition was now limited to twenty rounds per gun per day. These rounds took their toll of selected targets, but could not stop the gradual infiltration of enemy troops. In the evening, the drivers and spare numbers of the Medium Battery and 72nd Field Regiment, R.A., were formed into a composite infantry platoon under Capt. Fairbrass, to assist the 5th Battalion to hold its extended front.

Throughout the day there was heavy shelling on both these fronts, as the enemy had now got the artillery of a division in position in front of both the north-west and south-west faces of the Box.

Extensive patrolling along the perimeter of the whole position, some ten miles in length, was carried out all night, but, so close had the enemy established himself, patrols of the 4th and 5th Green Howards on the western face were unable to join up.

A patrol of the 5th Battalion, under Lt. E. S. Hopkins, made a raid during the night of May 29/30 on an enemy gun position, which had been spotted during the day. As a result of skilful plotting, Lt. Hopkins reached the point at about 1.0 a.m. and found a large enemy party at work, protected by a covering force. He himself, with one man, crept forward and succeeded in killing one of the enemy with his revolver and capturing another. At the sound of a revolver shot, the remainder of the patrol opened fire and inflicted further damage on the enemy. In spite of retaliatory fire, the patrol got away without casualties, and on its way back collected an abandoned enemy lorry which contained several drums of good spring water, a valuable supplement to the rapidly diminishing stock held by the battalion.

From all reports received, it now appeared that by dawn on May 30 the position of the 150th Brigade was completely surrounded, although in places only by small forces, and the chances of the much longed for ammunition convoy getting through were very remote. R.A.F. reports came in to the effect that fifteen hundred enemy motor transport vehicles of all kinds were halted in the Cauldron area, and that the space between the 150th Brigade and the 69th Brigade was jammed with enemy transport waiting to get through the gap in the minefield. The enemy had followed up the 6th Green Howards on their withdrawal from Bir Tamar, and were now up against the eastern face of the Box.

Early on the morning of the 30th Capt. J. W. W. Huntrods, *5 Bn* of the 5th Battalion, was sent off with a patrol consisting of *30 May 42* one section of infantry, one section of carriers, two anti-tank guns, and one sub-section Royal Engineers, to contact the Free French at Bir Hacheim. In order to do this he had to find a way through the small gap between the German and Italian forces which encircled the Free French. Although shelled and chased by the enemy, and fired upon by the Free French, he arrived in their position at about 8 a.m., having lost one anti-tank gun and sustained a few casualties. Having delivered his message, Capt. Huntrods was forbidden by the French Commander to return, as the enemy had now closed the gap through which he had come. This party of the 5th Green Howards, therefore, fought with the Foreign Legion in the epic defence of Bir Hacheim, and was eventually captured when the latter fought its way out on the night of June 10. L/Sgt. L. W. Hardbattle was the only member of the patrol to escape.

Soon after dawn on May 30 the enemy launched a strong attack on Point 174 in the northern sector of the Brigade's positions, which was held by the 232nd Field Company, R.E. Getting his tanks through the minefield, he completely overran the position, capturing the entire R.E. Company and the forward observation officer of the 451st Battery, R.A. The loss of Point 174 was a very serious one, since it gave the enemy observation over a large section of the defended area. In spite of vigorous counter-attacks, the superiority of the enemy's tank guns enabled him to hold on to the position, but the gallant work of " A " and " B " Squadrons, 44th Battalion, R.T.R., and of " A " and " B " Companies, 4th East Yorkshires, who were holding this ground on each side, prevented him from making full exploitation of his success during this day.

4 *Bn*
30 *May* 42

Meanwhile, the 4th Green Howards on the northern and western fronts were being heavily attacked. Early in the day, they suffered a grievous loss when Major B. H. W. Jackson, O.C. " B " Company, was mortally wounded. One of the most senior officers in the Battalion, Major Jackson had been Staff Captain of the 150th Brigade on the outbreak of war, and had fought with it at Dunkirk. His cheerfulness in dangerous and difficult situations had always acted as a tonic on his comrades, and his loss was severely felt. Major Mander, 2nd I./C. of the Battalion, took over " B " Company's area, which was well described by the Commanding Officer as the " Achilles Heel " of his position, facing, as it did, the ever growing threat from the northern gap. " C " Company, facing the Capuzzo Gap, now had to meet the full force of the enemy attacks, since the Disputed Ridge was irretrievably lost. Nevertheless, the 4th Battalion held grimly on to its positions all day.

5 *Bn*
30 *May* 42

To the south, when dawn broke over the 5th Battalion, the enemy was seen to be in great strength on its front. In spite of the vigilance of the patrols, machine-guns and mortars had been dug in, and a great array of guns and vehicles was clearly visible. The forward platoons of " B " and " D " Companies were pinned to their slit trenches throughout the day, and the fighting spirit which they maintained, after being under heavy fire for three days, speaks well for their stamina and *esprit de corps*. All day long the mortar section under L/Sgt. R. Cass fought it out with the enemy mortars, machine-guns and artillery posts within range, until its ammunition was expended. L/Sgt. Cass was awarded the Distinguished Conduct Medal for his coolness and bravery.

A gallant action was fought during the morning by Major P. H. D. Fox, 2nd I./C. 5th Battalion, when an attack developed in front of " D " Company. Two sections of carriers were placed under his command, and, flying a blue pennant in the Commander's carrier, he set off on a circuit of the Company's position, with the object of engaging any enemy who had penetrated the minefield. On the way round he saw a company of the enemy infiltrating through the minefield, and without hesitation charged across the minefield into the middle of them. Despite heavy firing, Major Fox swept through the enemy, and firing with his pistol, the bren gun and grenades, he completely repulsed this attack. Unfortunately, on his return journey, his carrier hit a mine and caught fire, and Major Fox and his Sergeant—both badly wounded—fell into the hands of the enemy. His dashing attack, had, however, been a complete success, and no further attempt was made by the enemy on this sector of the front for the next forty-eight hours. For his gallantry on this occasion Major Fox was awarded the Distinguished Service Order.

The evening of May 30 found the Green Howard Battalions, and their comrades in arms, " bloody but unbowed ", and they were heartened by a cheering message from the Army Commander : " Well done ! Hit hard and hit again ". The will to win was there, but, alas, the wherewithal with which to hit was rapidly diminishing.

The precarious position of the 150th Brigade was now realised by the Higher Command, and plans for reinforcement and relief were being made, including the despatch of an Army Tank Unit from the Tobruk area. During the night of May 30/31 the troops of the 150th Brigade were cheered by the noise of a battle in which these relieving tanks were engaged to the north, but in the end they failed to arrive in time.

The morning of the 31st found the enemy pressure increasing on all sides. Heavy shelling from the south, east, and west began at about 8.30, and at 10.30 an attack was launched against " B " Company, 4th East Yorkshires, in the north-east corner of the Box. After a gallant fight which lasted until 4 o'clock in the afternoon, and in which the Company Commander and the Commander of the supporting battery were killed at their posts, the defenders were overwhelmed by vastly superior forces, and another breach had been made in the defences.

At mid-day another attack was made south of Point 174 at the spot where " A " Company, 4th East Yorkshires and Headquarter Company, 5th Green Howards (Captain W. N. Jackson) joined up. There was no protective minefield at this point as it had been the original site of Brigade Headquarters. The enemy attacked in armoured carriers, supported by a strong concentration of guns on the ridge above. The situation

5 Bn
31 May 42

was very serious here, and was only saved by the hurried collection of all available men from the Battalion Headquarter Staffs of the 4th East Yorkshires and 5th Green Howards, largely owing to the initiative of Lt.-Col. Bush, who took charge of these operations. Eventually " C " Company, 5th Battalion, was brought up from reserve, and the line was finally restored by nightfall. During the action Capt. W. N. Jackson and Capt. A. A. Barber were both seriously wounded. L/Cpl. W. L. Dowse and Pte. Massey were killed and Pte. J. D. L. Cowling was wounded by shrapnel.

On the south front an enemy attempt to clear a passage through the minefield in front of " B " Company was driven off, while the enemy in front of " D " Company made no serious move during the day.

4 *Bn*
31 *May* 42 Meanwhile, to the north, the 4th Battalion had been heavily shelled all day, and at about 4 o'clock in the afternoon an attack was launched against them from the north. The main attack came up against " B " Company's position, and, under cover of heavy fire from machine guns and 20 mm. guns on mobile platforms, the enemy got to within thirty yards of No. 12 platoon. Lt. Fawcett was killed while firing his revolver at point blank range at a tank commander, and, in spite of a very gallant defence, the enemy succeeded in penetrating the minefield in front of No. 12 platoon. Shortage of ammunition once again prevented artillery support, and the Germans eventually silenced the machine-gun section of the 2nd Battalion, Cheshire Regiment, after a fierce fight. By this time the enemy had had enough, and withdrew. Capt. P. B. Watson immediately took a carrier section down to the gap made by the enemy, and, under heavy fire, relaid the mines. One carrier had to be abandoned, but was recovered at night. When he returned from captivity some years later Capt. Watson was awarded the Distinguished Service Order for his rapid appreciation of this situation, and for his inspiring coolness and courage throughout the battle.

When night fell on May 31 the position of the 150th Brigade was serious in the extreme. The enemy's salient at Point 174 had been enlarged, and only the tanks prevented further penetration. The Field Artillery had only half their twenty-four guns in action with less than a hundred rounds for the regiment, while the Medium Battery was reduced to six guns with twenty rounds per gun. There were nine Bofors guns active, but stocks of small arms ammunition for machine-guns and rifles were very low, and mortar and two-pounder ammunition was almost expended. Only thirteen tanks were still serviceable. Many of the vehicles had been destroyed by enemy fire, and, although casualties among personnel had not been unduly high, all ranks were feeling the strain of continuous exposure to the hot sun and heavy enemy fire. Shortage of water was also being experienced by some units.

At 10 p.m. that night Brigadier Haydon held a conference at Battalion Headquarters of the 4th East Yorkshires. While expressing hope that relief might arrive before dawn, he made arrangements to fight it out should these hopes not be realised. Two defensive areas were formed, based on the battalion areas of the 4th and 5th Green Howards. Into the 4th Green Howard area were moved " D " Company, 4th East Yorkshires, all available tanks, and the 72nd Field Regiment, R.A., less the 451st Battery. The 5th Green Howard area contained, in addition to that battalion, the 4th East Yorkshires, less " B " and " D " Companies, and the 451st Field Battery. R.A. Brigade Headquarters was in the 4th Green Howard area. The necessary moves were made early before the moon rose, and, although flares and the rumbling of tanks and vehicles all through the night indicated intense enemy activity, the only excitement was the destruction of a German Staff car with the two officers, who were its occupants. This car, obviously lost, ran into the middle of " C " Company of the 5th Battalion and was dealt with by Bren gun fire.

At first light on June 1 the enemy attacked on all fronts. The covering fire from the enemy's guns was intense and of heavy calibre. Some 210 mm. shells were reported, and a Battery Commander stated that some of the shells were the equivalent of 11-in. The main attack first developed in front of " B " and " C " Companies, 4th Green Howards, from the north. The enemy advanced with tanks, close support guns, and 3-ton carriers packed with troops at the point where the gap had been made in the minefield in front of No. 12 platoon on the previous day. No. 12 platoon fought until its ammunition was completely exhausted, and was then forced to surrender. Three Mark III tanks, accompanied by Infantry, rushed through the gap and, securing the high ground between " B " and " C " Companies, fanned out to each flank, and by about 9 a.m. these two companies had been completely over-run.

4 Bn
1 Jun 42

The final action against the enemy on the high ground between " B " and " C " Companies was fought by Sgt. J. Leng and a section of carriers. These engaged the enemy with Bren guns from a range of about eight hundred yards, and several guns and trucks were seen to be abandoned. In the end all the ammunition was expended and, as a final gesture of defiance, Sgt. Leng filled two last magazines from his pouches and fired them at short range into a troop carrier which appeared suddenly from the rear. The Green Howard carriers were then overwhelmed, and their crews taken prisoner. Sgt. Leng subsequently escaped, as will be narrated later, and was awarded the Distinguished Conduct Medal for his outstanding courage and devotion to duty throughout the five days of battle.

A message had been received by the Brigade Commander at 6 a.m. from the Armoured Corps Commander to the effect that relief could not be expected before mid-day and, when at 8 a.m. Brigadier Haydon saw that his northern flank was crumbling, he ordered certain senior officers to attempt to escape and join the 69th Brigade. These officers, with one exception, were all captured.

At 9 o'clock, Brigadier Haydon, realising that the position was hopeless, attempted to get away according to orders previously received. After giving final instructions to Lt.-Col. Cooper, commanding the 4th Green Howards, he left in an armoured car, escorted by three tanks, making for a secret gap in the western minefield. On the way he met two of our tanks which were making for the same point. Brigadier Haydon got out of his car to speak to their commander, and was killed outright by a shell. Brigadier Haydon had commanded the Brigade since April, 1940, and had fought with it back to Dunkirk. He then trained it in England and in the Middle East, bringing it to that state of discipline and efficiency which resulted in the men of his Brigade fighting gloriously against odds, until, with their last rounds of ammunition expended, they passed into captivity.

Meanwhile, Lt.-Col. Cooper, with his northern flank completely exposed, gave instructions for the destruction of all documents and wireless, and ordered his remaining company, "D" (Capt. D. D. Mitchell), to disperse to the minefield and endeavour to escape. Very few men succeeded in doing so.

5 Bn
1 Jun 42

While these events were in progress, the 5th Green Howards to the south, after being subjected to an intensive barrage of fire from artillery and anti-tank guns along the whole two miles of their southern front, were attacked under cover of heavy machine-gun fire by enemy infantry accompanied by mobile guns. The forward companies, " D " on the right, " B " in the centre and " C " on the left, fought platoon by platoon, until, with their ammunition expended, they were overwhelmed by superior forces, supported by tanks and self-propelled guns. " B " Company, commanded by Capt. Dennis, held out the longest.

At 11 a.m. a tank and infantry attack was staved off by the gallant action of Lt. P. E. Bray, who, although twice wounded, manned the only serviceable anti-tank gun, and kept it in action until it was knocked out by a direct hit. Subsequently Lt. Bray received the Military Cross for his bravery and devotion to duty. At half past eleven No. 11 platoon was overrun, and at one o'clock, the enemy appeared in the rear of the position and overwhelmed No. 12 platoon and Company Headquarters. No. 10 platoon, with whom Capt. Dennis had made his battle headquarters, gallantly held out until 2 p.m. when it fell into the hands of the enemy. This was the final fight of the 150th Brigade and, with the exception of a handful of men who managed to escape later, the whole Brigade, with its attached troops, became prisoners of war.

The collapse of the position held by the 150th Brigade on June 1 cleared Rommel's line of communications along the Trigh Capuzzo, and within a few days he exploited this success at the great battle of Knightsbridge. Here the British Armour was to a large extent destroyed, and the German Panzers were left free to roam at will. In justice to all who fought at Gazala and Knightsbridge, it must be recorded that the enemy held at this time an overwhelming superiority in equipment. The Valentine and Crusader tanks, armed with two-pounders, were no match for the German Mark IV tanks with their 75 mm. turret guns, while the few Grant tanks which took part in the battles were severely handicapped by having their 75 mm. guns situated in the hull and not in the turret. Again, the 88 mm. anti-tank guns with which the enemy was well supplied, far outranged our six-pounders. As far as the infantry were concerned, the two-pounder was the only anti-tank gun available, as the P.I.A.T. had not yet appeared.

The result of the Knightsbridge battle was that the remainder of the Gazala position was now cut off, and the only course left for the 69th and 151st Brigades of the 50th Division was to fight their way out. Before describing how the 6th and 7th Green Howards fared in these operations, a short account must be given of what befell the survivors of the 150th Brigade and those who escaped.

Very soon after the battle ended at about 2 p.m. on June 1, Field-Marshal Rommel appeared in person on the field, and was anxious to meet the Commander. It was obvious that the capture of this position had been vital to his plans, and that he was in a great hurry to press on. Two quotations from Brigadier Desmond Young's book *Rommel* show the important

part which the 150th Brigade played in the whole scheme
of operations, and also pays a fitting tribute to all those
who gave their lives, or passed into captivity. After the war
Brigadier Young met General Bayerlein, who told him that :
" It all turned on the 150th Brigade Box at Got El Ualeb.
We never knew it was there. Our first attack on it failed. If
we had not taken it on June 1 you would have captured the
whole of the Afrika Korps. By the evening of the third day
we were surrounded and almost out of petrol. As it was, it
was indeed a miracle that we managed to get our supplies
through the minefield in time ". On another page, Brigadier
Young quotes Rommel as saying : " The attacking formation
advanced against the British 150th Brigade on the morning
of May 31. Yard by yard the German-Italian units fought
their way forward against the toughest British resistance
imaginable. The British defence was conducted with considerable skill. As usual, the British fought to the last round
of ammunition."

The dressing stations of both sides were full of wounded
and, although the enemy medical services tended some of the
more urgent cases, the majority of our wounded were bundled
into lorries, and hustled off over hundreds of miles of desert
into captivity. Many of the wounded died during this journey.
Those who were not wounded were immediately taken to an
assembly area where all weapons, knives and field dressings
were taken from them. After their ranks, names and numbers
had been entered in a ledger, they were marched off towards
the west. It was intensely hot, and several men dropped out,
while the Germans took photographs and films of the exhausted
party. During the afternoon some shells from the 69th
Brigade positions dropped close to the column, and Sgt. Leng,
4th Green Howards, attempted to escape in the confusion.
He was fired at, and had to return. After this attempt they
were all made to take off their boots and socks. At about
midnight they embussed in trucks and moved on again. An
hour later the truck in which Sgts. Leng, M. Marshall and
C. S. Kendall were travelling, broke down, and, at the same
moment, machine-gun fire and shells began bursting over
them. The Germans in the leading truck panicked and ran
off, and Sgts. Leng and Kendall at once ordered the driver,
and another German in the front of their truck, to get out.
Although there were six more Germans, including an officer,
in the back of the truck, they showed no fight and did as they
were told. Sgt. Kendall managed to restart the faulty truck
and some of our men jumped in. At this moment armoured
cars of the South African Division appeared on the scene,
and gave them an armoured car escort, with which they set off

to join their " B " Echelon. After going for about twelve miles, they were dive-bombed by five Italian planes, both vehicles were set on fire, and two men were killed. The survivors started marching, but soon their escort reappeared with more trucks, and, after handing over their prisoners to the 7th Armoured Division, they eventually arrived safely at Rear Headquarters of the 50th Division.

All that now remained of the 150th Brigade were the few 150 *Bde* officers and men who were on leave, on courses, or at the *Jul/Nov* 42 Divisional Rest Camp at Sidi Bengallad, and the handful who escaped. Major Lacy, 5th Green Howards, was in command of the Brigade details at Sidi Bengallad, together with Capt. A. G. Best, I./C. 4th Battalion details, Capt. P. L. Lindrea, I./C. 5th Battalion details, and a party of the 4th East Yorkshires. By June 15 each Battalion had built up a strength of 4 officers and 100 men, and they were moved back to El Daba. On the 23rd orders were received for each Battalion to be reduced still further to a Cadre of 3 officers and 25 other ranks, and for the remainder to be sent as reinforcements to the 50th Division. These reinforcements failed to contact the Division, and, on June 24, all the 150th Brigade details moved to Sidi Bishr outside Alexandria.

By this time the German forces were pressing on towards El Alamein, and the 150th Brigade details, together with the 1st South African Regiment and the Argyll and Sutherland Highlanders, took up a defensive position at Dekeilia under the command of the G.O.C. Australian Forces. On July 24 the Battalion Cadres and the reinforcements were picked up by motor transport, and rejoined the 50th Division at Amiyra, being attached to the 69th Brigade. During this time some of them took part in the attacks made by troops of the Division in the Alamein area, as will be recounted later. In one of these operations, 2/Lt. A. J. Taylor, 5th Green Howards, fighting with the East Yorkshires, was reported missing.

On July 30 all the personnel of the Battalion Cadres were withdrawn from the 69th Brigade, and sent down to the Infantry Base Depot, where they became part of " Z " Brigade, " Reesforce ", in the Cairo defence scheme. This Brigade took up an operational role on August 29 under command of the 154th Brigade, 51st Highland Division, which was responsible for the defence of the Delta Barrage. Although no active operations against the enemy took place here, one officer of the Green Howards, who shall be nameless, displayed great courage and coolness in the face of attack. While looking for billets he was accused of violating a harem but, on the matter being explained as a military necessity by the Egyptian Liaison Officer, he suffered in silence and with dignity while the white-bearded proprietor of the establishment embraced and kissed him in front of his troops.

Early in September the Cadres were further reduced to 2 officers and 10 other ranks for each Battalion, and on September 23 they embarked for England, arriving home on November 17, 1942.

Contrary to hopes and initial intentions, the Battalions were not reformed, and the Cadres were posted elsewhere. And so, in less than three years, the 4th and 5th Battalions of the Green Howards ceased to exist as fighting units. For nearly another three years those who survived endured the hardships and boredom of prison camps but, justly proud of the part which they had played in the fighting before Dunkirk and in the Western Desert, they kept up their spirits and morale to the end. When they were finally released and returned to their homes, they realised, even more strongly than when they set out in 1939, how comradeship and discipline can support a man through every kind of danger and hardship. The memories of those days will always remain, and the friendships made, when facing discomfort and death together under the Green Howard badge, will endure in the face of any difficulties or disasters which the future may bring.

CHAPTER SIX

" THE 6th AND 7th BATTALIONS BREAK OUT FROM THE GAZALA LINE "

" The Retreat to Alamein "

June—October 1942

THE loss of the 150th Brigade on June 1, 1942, meant, See MAP in effect, that the remainder of the 50th Division (the No. 7 69th and 151st Brigades) were virtually surrounded on two sides, to the west and to the south, and that their line of communications to the east was seriously threatened. Their position became even more precarious when the Free French at Bir Hacheim, after putting up an epic resistance, 10 *Jun* 42 were withdrawn on the night of June 10.

At about this time the Germans also delivered an attack on the 69th and 151st Brigade Boxes. This was repulsed, and the British troops, by vigorous patrolling and aggressive action outside their boxes, gradually regained the initiative. In one of these actions the 7th Battalion, Green Howards, suffered severely in an unsuccessful attack at Sidra, an account of which will be given later.

The story of the next few weeks, until, on July 4, the 50th Division was relieved and withdrawn to Mareopolis to reorganise, is so involved that it seems best to relate the adventures of the two Green Howard Battalions independently, first giving a brief account of the operations in which they played their parts.

The whole aspect of the Gazala battle was altered when, on June 13, the remainder of the British Armour was decisively defeated around Knightsbridge, and the 50th and 1st South African Divisions became isolated. Withdrawal was inevitable, but, as the coast road gave only sufficient latitude for the South African Division, the 50th Division was left to get away as best it could. The South Africans were ordered to withdraw down the coast road, and the 50th Division was ordered not to move until the former were clear of their positions, thus reducing any chance of surprise.

To the 50th Division, therefore, fell the honour of being left in splendid isolation for a short time, while the remainder of the 8th Army withdrew behind the Egyptian frontier. The Division was now surrounded on three sides, with Italian Brescia and Pavia Divisions to the west, and the 15th and 21st

Panzer Divisions, supported by the 90th German Light Division, to the east and south. Major-General Ramsden decided on a bold stroke, and ordered his two Brigades to make bridgeheads in the Italian defences to the west, break through, and, in independent columns, when once clear of the enemy, to proceed due south beyond Bir Hacheim, and then turn east, making for the Egyptian frontier at Maddalena 14/21 *Jun* 42 and Scheferzen. This manoeuvre was begun on the night of June 14/15 and was successfully accomplished, the Division reassembling its scattered forces at Bir Talatha between June 16 and June 21. Although the break out had been so brilliantly executed that casualties were comparatively small, the losses of vehicles, kit, equipment, reserve ammunition and weapons, and stores were very heavy, and the lack of vital signal stores and wireless trucks was to tell heavily in the fighting which still lay ahead.

While the Division was reorganising at Bir Talatha, an operation was planned to relieve the pressure on Tobruk, but, when the news arrived that Tobruk had fallen to the enemy on June 21, this was cancelled. A 69th Brigade Column of all arms was then formed to proceed at once to Buq Buq, where it was ordered to take up a position covering the withdrawal of the 10th Indian Division, which was at that time holding Sollum, and then to act as rear-guard back to Mersa Matruh, at which place the 8th Army was preparing to make a stand. The 6th Battalion, Green Howards, formed the infantry 21/26 *Jun* 42 component of this column, which moved off on the morning of June 21. The remainder of the Division went straight on to Mersah Matruh.

On the night of June 22/23 the 10th Indian Division passed through the 69th Brigade Column positions at Buq Buq, and on the 24th the latter began to withdraw in the face of the advancing enemy. The next position which it held was in front of Sidi Barrani, but, as soon as all dumps of food and stores, and communication and water points, had been destroyed, it retired again to a position on the coast road covering " Kilo 99 ". There information was received that enemy forces had slipped round behind them on their desert flank, and the rear-guard was forced to leave the road and follow a narrow and precipitous track along the coast. The column eventually arrived at Mersah Matruh in the early morning of June 26. There the Commander, Brigadier L. L. Hassell, D.S.O., M.C., was evacuated sick, and the command of the 69th Brigade was given to Lt.-Col. E. C. Cooke-Collis, 6th Green Howards, who, although wounded at an early stage in the proceedings, had refused to be evacuated. With his arm in a sling, he was a familiar figure wherever the fighting was hottest. For his leadership and personal bravery in the actions around Bir Aslagh from May 27/29, during the rearguard action from Buq Buq to Mersah Matruh, and during the break out from the latter place, Lt.-Col. (then Brigadier) Cooke-Collis was awarded the Distinguished Service Order, to which he subsequently added a bar at Mareth. His presence in the toughest spot, and, so often, at the most critical moment of many battles, provided a tonic and inspiration to all who saw him. The stories of " Red Ted ", as he was affectionately and yet respectfully known throughout the 50th Division, are legion, and many of them are not perhaps suitable for publication, but it is rare indeed to find one individual leader so universally admired and beloved by all ranks.

The origin of the soubriquet " Red Ted " must be recorded lest those who do not know him may think it due to a passion for blood or, in these days, possibly a sympathy for those who were then our " gallant allies " in the east. The name was given to him because, amongst all those who wore " tin helmets " or " battle bowlers ", he was conspicuous, even in the forefront of the battle, in his service dress cap with the red band of a Brigadier, which invariably he wore.

The whole Division was now reunited, and holding a defensive position south-east of Matruh, with the 10th Indian Division in the town itself. On June 26 General Auchinleck assumed command of the 8th Army and decided not to hold Mersah Matruh, but to withdraw to Alamein forthwith. As a result of this change of policy, the 50th Division was ordered to take up a rearguard position some few miles east of Mersah Matruh, to cover the withdrawal of other formations including 10th Corps H.Q. and the 10th Indian Division. The 50th Division took up this position during the afternoon and evening of June 26.

It had become known on June 27 that enemy armoured units had made their way round east of Mersah Matruh, and at 5 p.m. orders were issued for an attack against the enemy's supply lines, with the object of delaying the advance of these armoured units. On completion of the night's operation the 50th Division was to return to its positions east of Mersah Matruh. *27 Jun* 42

The 69th Brigade in this attack reached the first objective without opposition, but then ran into an enemy column. This was attacked by the 6th Green Howards, but, when it became apparent that the Brigade had met a vastly superior force, Brigadier Cooke-Collis ordered them to withdraw, as they were sustaining considerable casualties, particularly in vehicles.

By dawn on June 28 the 69th and 151st Brigades were back in their original positions. At about noon orders were received for the 50th Division to break out that night (June 28/29), and to make for Fuka. These orders were given out by Brigadier Cooke-Collis to his Battalion Commanders at about 5.30 p.m. It was known that there were considerable German forces between the Division's position and Fuka, but there was no contact. At the time the orders were given out it was hoped that it would be able to leave without interference, and that its main task would be to evade enemy columns on the way to Fuka. No movement, of course, could be contemplated before dark. Before any move could be made, however, the Germans had not only discovered their presence, but had closed in round them. The whole area was being heavily shelled, and both the 6th and 7th Green Howards were being attacked.

When, later in the evening, the break out started, the destination of the 69th Brigade was still Fuka. Fortunately at some period during the night Brigadier Cooke-Collis encountered Lt.-Gen. N. G. Holmes, C.B.E., M.C., the Corps Commander, whose car had broken down, and the latter informed him that Fuka had been in enemy hands since 4 p.m. the previous afternoon. It was impossible to do much during the hours of darkness, but most of the columns were successfully diverted next morning and, by June 30, had arrived at the fixed Alamein defences, which were held by the South African Division.

By this time the Division was so depleted that orders were received to form " Battle Groups " of any troops available in order to stop the enemy's advance. Three groups were formed out of the remnants of the 50th Division, and named respectively, Stancol, Bilcol and Ackol. " B " Company, 7th Green Howards, which, except for " B " Echelon and a few individuals who escaped on June 28, was all that was left of the Battalion, formed part of Bilcol.

The 7th Battalion had temporarily ceased to exist as such after the night of June 28/29, when Lt.-Col. MacDonnell, Major G. N. Girling, his second in command, and a large proportion of the Battalion fell into the enemy's hands while attempting to break out from Mersah Matruh. The 6th Battalion, after its gruelling experiences while fighting the series of rearguard actions back from Buq Buq, and in its attack from Matruh on the 27th, was sent straight back from Alamein to Mareopolis, where it arrived on July 2. It must be recorded, however, that the four days—July 1/4—saw one of the most critical situations in the whole war, and that these

CAPTURING A RIDGE IN N. AFRICA.

AN ADVANCE, SUPPORTED BY TANKS, IN THE DESERT.

Face page 112

50th Divisional columns fought the opening round of the first battle of Alamein, holding the key position of the Ruweisat Ridge until, on July 4, the fierce enemy attacks died down, and they were relieved by the 9th Australian Division.

The Division now reassembled at Mareopolis. Since the 1/12 *Jul* 42 opening of the Gazala battle on May 26, casualties of the 50th Division amounted to 8,875, including the loss of one complete Brigade. In the two remaining Brigades, the 69th and 151st, the average strength of battalions was only 300 men, and of their transport very little remained. On July 11 Major-General J. S. Nichols, D.S.O., M.C., assumed command of the Division from Major-General Ramsden, who had been promoted to command the 30th Corps. The latter's departure was keenly felt by all ranks. The Division was, however, only given until July 12 to reorganise, when it was ordered back to the Ruweisat Ridge.

Before continuing the story of the 50th Division any further, we must now go back to June 1 and follow the fortunes of the two Green Howard Battalions within the outline of events which has been given in the opening of this chapter.

The 7th Battalion, Lt.-Col. F. E. A. MacDonnell, was 7 *Bn* ordered on June 6 to make an attack next day at Sidra, together 6/7 *Jun* 42 with three Battalions of tanks. This attack was to be part of an operation designed to recapture the 150th Brigade positions, and was only to take place if an attack by night, to be carried out by an Indian Brigade, was successful. The night of June 6/7 was spent a short way behind the start line and, just before dawn, the tanks arrived, lining up immediately in front of the Battalion. The order of advance was two Battalions of tanks in the first wave, one Battalion of tanks in the second, and the 7th Green Howards in their transport in the third wave.

The success signal from the Indian Brigade having been received, the first wave of tanks moved forward over the crest of the hill some four hundred yards away. It was now full daylight, and soon the Green Howards were on the move. " B " Company (Major K. Pickering) was on the right, " A " Company (Lt. F. Dahl) on the left, with " C " Company (Capt. K. Gardner) following " A ", and with Battalion H.Q. echeloned behind " C " Company. The leading companies were each followed by a section of carriers and anti-tank guns. Following behind were " D " (Support) Company (Capt. D. G. Jackson) and Headquarters Company (Capt. F. Towle).

The ground fell away gently for some thousand yards beyond the crest, and then, after about five hundred yards of

I

level ground, there was an escarpment on which the enemy was firmly established. As soon as he sighted the tanks coming over the hill, the enemy put down a smoke screen and greatly increased the volume of his fire. This slowed down the advance, and the Battalion was brought to a standstill in the centre of a hail of shells, consisting of shrapnel, solid anti-tank shells and high explosive ; with the smoke, visibility was now reduced to fifty yards. Chaos reigned and, when enemy tanks appeared and opened fire with machine guns, anti-tank guns, and 88 mm. guns, the order was received : " Infantry will debus and dig in ". A quick reconnaissance was made, and positions were allotted to the support troops and companies, but the ground was such that digging without compressors was practically impossible.

Lt.-Col. MacDonnell now went up to the forward Companies, followed by his adjutant, Capt. W. Murray, who was riding in a captured German wireless truck. As he was visiting one of the support groups he came across some men of " A " Company coming back, most of them wounded, who told him that our tanks were retiring. He had hardly sent them back to their positions when he came across " B " Company in full retreat, having been ordered back by a Colonel of the tanks, who was on foot, and had received orders to retire. Lt.-Col. MacDonnell, not having received any such orders himself, was searching for " B " Company Commander to tell him to take his men back, when a Staff Officer appeared with orders for the Battalion to withdraw to a position a thousand yards in rear. He managed to pass this order on to " A " Company, but failed to find the leading platoon which was overrun. The Battalion finally extricated itself, and received fresh orders to withdraw behind the 9th Durham Light Infantry Box and reorganise. Fortunately the enemy did not follow up, but the Battalion suffered a hundred and fifty casualties in this action, and only twelve out of seventy odd tanks got back safely. A number of the Green Howard casualties were subsequently found to have been taken prisoner, and these included Capt. K. Gardner, Lts. J. B. Millington Buck and M. Williams.

Two of the regimental stretcher bearers, Pte. R. T. Ralph and Pte. D. J. Foreman, behaved with such courage during this battle that they were awarded the Military Medal. The role of stretcher bearer is one that calls for heroism of a particularly high standard, and the official accounts of the deeds, which won decorations for these two men, are recorded in full.

Of Pte. Ralph the account says : " He was a stretcher bearer attached to one of the forward companies at Sidra.

Whilst attending to the wounded he sustained a shrapnel wound in his chest during the early stages of the fighting, and was seen with blood pouring from his shirt. Regardless of this, and despite the heavy shelling and machine-gun fire, Pte. Ralph continued to render first aid and arrange for the evacuation of the wounded. Later he took some wounded men himself to the Advanced Dressing Station, and was advised by the Medical Officer that he should be evacuated himself. He insisted, however, on returning to his company and carrying on with his duties. It was not until the fighting was over that his wound was found to be severe, and he was then sent back to the Medical Dressing Station."

Of Pte. Foreman : " During the attack at Sidra the Company to which Pte. Foreman was attached, began to sustain many casualties from intense machine-gun and artillery fire. He immediately took charge of the proceedings, and carried on dressing wounds until the Company reached an intermediate position, still under heavy fire. By this time there were about fifteen casualties in one truck, and the Company Sergeant Major ordered another truck to be used. Pte. Foreman continued to dress the wounded until this truck was also full. At this point the Company was ordered to withdraw, and he took his casualties to the Regimental Aid Post. It was only then discovered that Pte. Foreman had himself been wounded in the shoulder, and had continued his work without mentioning the fact to anybody."

As a result of the battle at Sidra the Battalion was short of officers, and Capt. K. Hicks, of the 6th Green Howards, and Capt. W. Wallace, of the 5th East Yorkshires, were attached to the 7th Battalion. The former took over command of " C " Company, and the latter of " A " Company.

The Battalion was ordered almost immediately to make a new box on the right flank of the 9th Durham Light Infantry. Its new position was much better than the old one, and was ideal for anti-tank defence from all sides except the west. After a few days' hard work wiring and mining, and when the box was stocked with ammunition and rations to last out a seventeen days' siege at full scale, the Green Howards awaited attack with confidence.

On the night of June 13 orders were received to send out 7 *Bn* a patrol to locate the enemy. As the enemy withdrew at night 13 *Jun* 42 these orders entailed sending the patrol a considerable distance in order to make contact. Capt. W. Murray took out the patrol, which failed to return the next morning. The Battalion withdrew the next night, and the patrol was not seen again. Subsequently it transpired that they had all been captured.

7 Bn   As we have seen, however, the result of the armoured
14/16 Jun 42 battle around Knightsbridge on June 13 had rendered these
positions untenable, and, on the morning of June 14, the code
word for " Retire to the Egyptian frontier " was received.
Plans were immediately made for the Battalion to retire in two
columns, the first under Lt.-Col. MacDonnell, and the second
under Major Girling, 2nd I./C. Their orders were simple.
The 6th and 7th Green Howards were to pass through a
bridgehead which was to be made by the 5th East Yorkshires
(Lt.-Col. T. W. G. Stansfeld, late 2nd I./C. 7th Green Howards),
not leaving their box until after dark ; then to proceed
some thirty miles south around Bir Hacheim, and then
turn east making for the gap in the wire at Sheferzen on the
Egyptian frontier.

The first task was to destroy all the surplus stores which
had been accumulated. Rations and water for three days
only were to be taken, and the men were to wear cardigans
and light equipment only. Lt.-Col. MacDonnell's column
contained Headquarter Company, " B " Company, 1 platoon
of " A " Company, and sections of other arms, while Major
Girling had under him " C " Company, " A " Company less
one platoon, and " D " Support Company with sections
of other arms. Both columns had a carrier section as a
screen.

The actual escape through the gap, although carried out
successfully in so far as that all columns turned up eventually
at the frontier with very few losses in personnel, was a very
confused operation and soon became disorganised. When
one considers, however, the hazardous nature of the operation,
and the fact that the night of June 14/15 was one of the darkest
experienced in the desert, the greatest credit must be given
to the leaders of all the parties, big or small, into which
the Division became split up during the hours of darkness.
Even those who took part in it are unable to give a connected
story of events, and so the reader must try to piece together
a picture from the following individual accounts.

First we will take Lt.-Col. Stansfeld's account of how,
with his 5th East Yorkshire Battalion, he made the gap.
" We really knew very little about the enemy minefields,
namely, which were live and which were dummy ones. There
was no time for reconnaissance. My orders were to move out
at 8 p.m., make a gap of three thousand yards in the enemy
position and hold it until 3 a.m., by which time the whole
Brigade should have passed through. Lt.-Col. M. L. P. Jackson, also of the Green Howards, commanding a battalion
of the Durham Light Infantry, was to do the same thing **on**

my right for the 151st Brigade. In the ensuing action, Lt.-Col.
Jackson won the Distinguished Service Order. I was given
six tanks, all that were left in the Division after the Knightsbridge battle, and, having set out at 8 p.m., soon reached the
enemy lines. I saw four of my tanks go up in flames from
mines or direct hits, one very gallant crew continuing to fire
their gun, although the tank was on fire, and eventually
burnt out. It was now nearly dark, but the whole area was
lit up by tracers, shells, mortar bombs and burning vehicles.
We could have taken masses of prisoners. The Italians thought
that we were making a " push " for Benghazi. One of my
officers captured an Italian General in his silk dressing gown.
At 3 a.m., the 6th and 7th Green Howards having passed
through, we turned south and made for Bir Hacheim."

Lt.-Col. F. E. A. MacDonnell's account begins with a
reference to the intense darkness owing to which, as they were
being navigated by compass without lights, vehicles of every
sort kept running into such obstacles as slit trenches, vehicle
positions and dug-outs. Consequently there were frequent
stoppages and delays. " We struck the minefield ", he goes
on to say, " about four hundred yards north of the Divisional
Gap, not absolutely sure of our position. On reaching the
Gap, it was necessary to proceed through it by only a double
row of vehicles. It was now half an hour after midnight, and
we were not far behind time. From here onwards the route
was certainly complicated. Luckily I was able to find my way
to Patrol Gap, as I had so often lost myself in this area, but,
when I got there, there was no sign of any Brigade Reporting
Post. I continued, therefore, through the gap and halted to
reform into column when well clear of the minefield. All the
regimental troop-carrying vehicles formed up on my marker,
but nothing else made its appearance. After waiting an hour
I sent Major Girling back to see what was happening. He
came back and said he could find no one. I sent him off again,
and this time he came back saying that he could hear vehicles
moving a long way off the track in a north-easterly direction.
It was now 3 a.m., and, considering that my only hope of
getting the unarmoured vehicles through was to get well
clear of the enemy lines before dawn (about 5.30 a.m.), I
moved off shortly after 3 a.m. and drove towards the burning
vehicles in front of me. The night was so dark that vehicles
could not keep together head to tail, and I suppose that when
one ran into an obstacle it was out of sight of the one in front
before it could be salvaged. My route was directed on a
compass bearing of due south, and it was impossible to avoid
running through the enemy's rear headquarters. The tents of
their headquarters loomed larger and larger as we came

upon them, and I must have driven right through at least five of them that night. In the middle of one of them my truck ran into a slit trench. I got out to push, when there was a roar from the trench, and an Italian sentry climbed out. I took no notice of him and managed to get the truck clear. The sentry followed me. I produced my revolver but he was far too friendly, and wanted to come with me. This was no occasion, however, for taking prisoners, and he was most disappointed that I would not shake hands with him before going on my way. When dawn came I found to my horror that I had only six vehicles with me, one under tow. At about 7 a.m. we reached our southern turning point and turned east. During the morning we collected various parties, and at about 2 p.m. joined up with Major Girling, who had with him most of the missing vehicles. We reported at the collecting post at the wire with an almost complete battalion except for " D " Company, and some of the carriers under Capt. Collett, and proceeded to the Divisional Assembly Centre at Bir Thalata next day."

The story of " D " Support Company has been told by 2/Lt. A. F. Depoix, who was later killed in Sicily. This Company had been formed on May 1 and was composed of the Carrier and Mortar platoons under Capt. Collett and Lt. F. W. Lindley respectively, and the anti-tank platoon, with Lt. V. G. Taylor, 2/Lt. V. Evans, 2/Lt. P. Nicholson, sixty-three other ranks and eight anti-tank guns. " ' D ' Company," he says, " less two sections of the mortar and anti-tank platoons which were divided between the columns of the Commanding Officer and Major Girling, moved out with the Battalion at 9 p.m. on the night of June 14. Owing to mechanical breakdowns, some of the vehicles did not reach Divisional Gap until about 3 a.m." (This was, it will be remembered, some two and a half hours after Lt.-Col. MacDonnell had moved on, and the hour at which he passed through Patrol Gap.) After half-an-hour's search by Capt. J. G. Taylor and 2/Lt. Depoix, Patrol Gap was located to their right rear, and the column turned round. Led by Sgt. Sampson of the Carrier platoon, the column passed through Patrol Gap at about 4 a.m. The column, which had gathered additions in the confusion, now consisted of some South African artillery and armoured cars, some engineers and machine gunners, the 257th Battery, R.A., and the Carrier and Anti-tank platoons of the 7th Green Howards. The column advanced about four miles when it ran into barbed wire and a minefield, and was fired upon by artillery, machine-guns and anti-tank guns, with tracers and flares. It was forced to withdraw, and arrived back again at a point about a mile east of Divisional Gap at 6 a.m.

They now decided to attempt a break through to Tobruk by way of the Ageila Pass, while Capts. Collett and Taylor were to go back to the 69th Brigade Box and try to contact any missing elements. Collecting Sgt. J. Shaw with part of the Carrier platoon, they repassed Patrol Gap in broad daylight, but, finding nobody, rejoined the column some two hours later. Meanwhile, the column had joined up with the 9th Durham Light Infantry and various odd bodies of troops, mainly South African, and was being heavily shelled and machine-gunned as it was descending the Ageila Pass. After covering some fifteen miles towards the coast, they ran into enemy infantry and tanks. " D " Company took cover amongst the sand dunes, while 2/Lt. V. Evans led an attack with a party which he had collected. Some thirty-five prisoners were taken. The artillery now opened fire and a further attack was led by Capt. Taylor, with 2/Lts. Evans and Depoix, which produced another twenty-five prisoners. For his initiative and daring in these attacks 2/Lt. Evans was awarded the Military Cross. Both these attacks were supported by the Carrier platoon, which in the first one gave close support and fired over fifteen thousand rounds. Sgt. G. F. Usher, who was in charge of a section of the carriers, led it into the attack with the greatest courage and determination, forcing the enemy to withdraw, taking several prisoners, and enabling the column to proceed on its way. Sgt. Usher was later awarded the Military Medal. Capt. Collett worked tremendously hard all day, knocking out at least one tank, and stopping several counter attacks. Later in the day, while the remainder of the column went on towards Tobruk, the Green Howards reformed, and, making their way somehow across the desert, rejoined the Battalion at Bir Thalata on June 16 with approximately one hundred and ten men. Lt.-Col. MacDonnell, referring to this action, states that all the anti-tank platoon was captured with the exception of one gun and its crew. He also pays tribute to Capt. Collett's leadership and bravery, for which he recommended him for a decoration.

Lt.-Col. E. C. Cooke-Collis, commanding the 6th Green Howards says : " It was made clear that the object of this operation was to extricate the Division and that, once through the Italian lines, action against the enemy was to be avoided if possible. There were several enemy minefields to be avoided —notably around Rotunda Mteifel—no easy matter in the dark. There were patches of soft sand also to be circumvented, and this required accurate navigation. This preparatory work was carried out by Capt. C. R. Pullinger and his Intelligence Section with great thoroughness, and it was largely due to their admirable work that the losses sustained by the

6 Bn
14/16 Jun 42

Battalion in this break out were so small. The 6th Battalion began to move in the fading light, by which time the gap was under constant but not very heavy artillery fire. The Battalion was organised into several columns, each with its own navigator, and, in addition, every officer, N.C.O. and driver was thoroughly briefed in the course to be followed, in the hope that vehicles which became separated would find their own way to the Sheferzen Gap. The Battalion passed through the minefield without loss, but, a short distance beyond, the desert presented the appearance of a tremendous firework display. There were many burning vehicles, and tracer ammunition and verey lights were being fired in every direction by excitable Italians. Of course, much of the Italian fire was completely wild, causing very few casualties, and we found the disused trenches which covered this area a greater menace than Italian bullets. Once through the Italian front line fire we encountered scattered Administration Units and Rear Headquarters, the occupants of which willingly allowed us a free passage. In some cases Italian soldiers showed a considerable determination to surrender, and were much disappointed when they were not allowed to board our already overloaded vehicles. During this passage through the Italian lines in the darkness the various columns became widely separated and sub-divided, but during the following day the majority of them reached Sheferzen, and casualties proved to be far lighter than we had expected. ' D ' Company, thanks to the leadership of Capt. Brunton, did not lose a single man or vehicle. Another column, which had run into an enemy minefield, was extricated with superb coolness by Capt. R. J. L. Jackson. A party of Battalion Headquarters, however, which included R.S.M. W. Wood, failed to reach the rendezvous, and it was subsequently learned that their vehicle had run into a trench, from which it proved impossible to extricate it, and they were taken prisoners. In addition to R.S.M. Wood, Lt. E. Crossley and 2/Lt. K. Winterschladen were also missing, and Lt. H. B. Burn and 2L/t. J. P. David were killed between Gazala and Bir Thalata."

Finally, here is an extract from the story of Pte. W. P. Simpson, 6th Green Howards, which gives the view of the private soldier. " How the 69th Brigade came out was like this. It was decided that the 5th East Yorkshires were to go out first to form a three thousand yard bridgehead for the rest to pass through. They were ordered to make the gap and keep on going as we would be right behind them to pick them up as we went on. What really happened was this—as soon as the 5th East Yorkshires had started through the minefields, we were given orders to come out, and to do so without firing. Our one duty was to get through and pick up all the East Yorkshires that we could, but instead of following on their heels, our departure was delayed for nearly two hours, and what happened was that as the East Yorkshires fought their way through, the gap closed behind them, so that when we did eventually come out, all we could do was to ride through the Italian lines, which we did with many an amusing incident. For instance, in many cases we grabbed hold of bunches of Italians, and made them push our vehicles which were stuck in the sand. In another case some of our carriers were guided through the minefields by the Italians themselves. In this break through, Lt.-Col. Cooke-Collis won the admiration of all the men for his utter disregard of his own safety. He was seen to go backwards and forwards four times into the Box which we had just left, organising all the time, and making sure that everyone came out. Of course, it was impossible for us to keep any kind of contact as it was pitch dark except for the lights from burning vehicles, so the Brigade came through more by individual effort than anything else."

The last remark of Pte. Simpson gives the key to the whole operation, and although full credit must be given to the Divisional Commander for his bold conception of the plan, and to commanding officers, who, with their intelligence sections worked out the details, it appears plain that, if the individual officers, N.C.O.s and men had not been as highly trained and disciplined as they were, the Brigade would never have won through to the Egyptian frontier with so few losses. This was one of the occasions when good training, high morale and irresistible *esprit de corps* proved of greater value than any text book knowledge of tactics or strategy.

The period from June 16 to June 21 was spent at Bir *6 and 7 Bn* Thalatha with the Division reorganising. The weather was *16/21 Jun 42* extremely hot and there was no shade. Water was scarce and the troops were tired, but their morale was high, as they realised that they had come through a very daring operation with very slight losses.

It will be remembered that, on June 21, the news of the fall of Tobruk caused a change in the plans of the 50th Division, and that a 69th Brigade Column was sent off to Buq Buq to act as Rear Guard to the remainder of the 8th Army, which was preparing to make a stand at Mersah Matruh.

The 6th Green Howards set off on June 21 as the infantry *6 Bn* component of this force, and by the morning of June 22 they *21/25 Jun 42* had dug themselves in on a position astride the coast road west of Buq Buq, and were in contact with enemy ground forces. They suffered most casualties, however, from air strafing, and lost a number of vehicles. On the morning of June 24 large columns of enemy motor vehicles were observed moving along the escarpment to the south, and, to avoid being encircled, the rearguard withdrew to a position south of Sidi Barrani, where it arrived at about 1.30 p.m. While passing through Sidi Barrani it was discovered that the N.A.A.F.I. was well stocked but deserted, and all ranks were enabled to supplement their meagre water supply with any quantity of tins of excellent American beer.

During the afternoon enemy transports were seen approaching the position, and the gunners fired on them with good effect. The same evening a further withdrawal was made to a position just west of Kilo 44, which was reached at about 8 p.m. As dusk was falling large forces of enemy tanks and armoured vehicles approached the position, and were also seen moving eastwards on the southern flank. After being heavily attacked by tanks, which approached so close that the gunners were firing over open sights, the force was ordered to withdraw once more, this time to Mersah Matruh.

Considerable confusion was caused by vehicles all trying to get on to the road at the same time, and this was rendered worse by a report that the enemy had cut the road between Kilo 44 and Mersah Matruh. A number of vehicles then attempted to get round by a narrow track along the coast. Some of them got stuck in the soft sand, were intercepted by the enemy, and captured. Capt. Pullinger, the Intelligence Officer, owing to his truck breaking down, walked the whole way from Kilo 44, but arrived safe and sound at Mersah Matruh next morning. The Battalion then leaguered to the east of the town.

6 *Bn*
26 *Jun* 42

On the morning of June 26 Major T. M. S. Roberts took over the Battalion from Lt.-Col. Cooke-Collis, when the latter took command of the 69th Brigade. A reconnaissance was made at this time with a view to holding Mersah Matruh itself, but plans were changed, and the Battalion was ordered to take up a defensive position some two miles to the east. At 8 o'clock that evening, whilst moving to its new positions, the Battalion was attacked by a large force of Stukas, and Major T. M. S. Roberts, 2/Lt. P. Newman and three other ranks were severely wounded. The command of the Battalion then devolved on to Major J. L. Hughes, M.C.

6 *Bn*
26/27 *Jun* 42

During the night of June 26/27 they dug themselves in and all was quiet next morning. Later in the day, however, a large column of the enemy, estimated to contain two thousand vehicles, was seen moving to the south-east. During the afternoon Brigadier Cooke-Collis issued orders for his Brigade to attack this column. The 151st Brigade was similarly employed on the right flank. His instructions were to seek out the enemy and do as much damage to his supply lines as possible, and then return to the defensive position outside Mersah Matruh. At about 9 p.m. the 6th Green Howards, with the 5th East Yorkshires on their left, and the 7th Green Howards in reserve behind the East Yorkshires, crossed the starting line.

The Battalion at this time consisted only of two infantry companies, " A " and " C " Companies, elements of " S " Support Company, and Battalion Headquarters. " D " Company under Major Brunton had been despatched during the afternoon to try to locate and protect a battery of medium guns near Mersah Matruh. The two infantry companies were considerably depleted ; " C " Company for instance, consisted of only two platoons, a small headquarters, and only two officers, Capt. Hull, the company commander, and 2/Lt. A. H. Jackson.

The Battalion made its advance in troop carrying transport, in a series of " bounds ". The limits of the first bound were reached and found clear of the enemy. The formation of the Battalion as it started forward on its second bound was " A " Company on the left, " C " Company on the right, with sections of the carrier platoon operating on the flanks, and the Anti-tank platoon in the centre. In the rear of the Battalion column there was a Company of Vickers machine-gunners. Soon after starting on the second bound an enemy column was sighted, and Major Hughes decided to close with the enemy quickly, advancing in the transports to within about a thousand yards, then to debus and move into the attack in the same formation, except that the machine-guns were to move out to a flank, and support the attack.

Before, however, the debussing point was reached, the enemy opened up with a far heavier volume of fire than was normally to be expected from a supply column. The first salvo scored a direct hit upon one of the anti-tank guns, and also on one of " A " Company's leading troop carriers, which burst into flames. For some reason, never to be ascertained, another of the leading troop carriers turned about and made for home. The remainder followed, apparently under the impression that the leader was acting under instructions, and it can only be assumed that under the heavy fire, the R.A.S.C. drivers had only one thought in their minds, namely to save their vehicles. Some of the men of " A " Company tried to jump from the carriers, which by that time were moving at great speed, and join their Company Commander, who was making desperate efforts to stop the vehicles, but, in vain, and, for all practical purposes, " A " Company was out of the battle before it began.

The Battalion now consisted of one platoon of " C " Company, under 2/Lt. A. H. Jackson (fated to be killed the next night as a Company Commander), on the left where " A " Company should have been ; the other platoon of " C " Company under Capt. Hull on the right, and Major Hughes with his Battalion Headquarters party in the centre. After waiting for some time for the supporting machine-guns to open up, which they failed to do, this gallant band of survivors, carrying out their orders, launched themselves at the enemy, supported only by an odd round from an anti-tank gun, and some Bren fire from the carriers on the flanks. Advancing steadily in the face of heavy fire, they arrived within a hundred yards of the enemy, although they sustained considerable casualties in doing so. They then regrouped for the final assault, with close support from the automatic weapons which had by now opened up, and were returning the enemy's fire with considerable effect.

The enemy were by this time clearly visible, and made excellent targets. As several of their machine-guns had been silenced, the order was given to prepare to advance for the assault. Just at this moment, however, three enemy tanks appeared in their leaguer, and these began spraying the Green Howard positions with continuous machine-gun fire, which included incendiary ammunition. The assault order was therefore temporarily cancelled, but the fire duel continued. It was at this vital moment that Brigadier Cooke-Collis arrived in his carrier. Charging through the centre of the Green Howards he drove up to within what appeared a few yards of the enemy, firing his carrier Bren gun at point blank range. His carrier received a direct hit and only he himself and his driver survived, although both were wounded. In the meanwhile Major Hughes, unknown to Capt. Hull, had been severely wounded in the stomach, and his runner killed, his batman being the only survivor of the party.

Orders were now given to withdraw, and those who were left pulled out man by man, taking their wounded with them, and leaving the dead. The withdrawal was covered by Capt. Hull together with Pte. D. Shannon and L/Cpl. W. Anderson, Nos. 1 and 2 respectively of a Bren gun. Sgt. W. L. Pluck, who was in command of an anti-tank gun, also displayed great gallantry in helping to cover the withdrawal. Although his gun was damaged, Sgt. Pluck, on his own initiative, turned about and fired as best he could on the enemy guns and tanks. He then withdrew in short bounds, engaging the enemy at each new position until his gun finally went out of action. By his skill and coolness Sgt. Pluck succeeded in bringing his gun out of action, without a single casualty to the crew, and materially assisted the remainder of the Battalion to escape. He was awarded the Military Medal.

Major Hughes probably owes his life to his batman who, although ordered to save himself, refused to leave his officer. He bandaged his wounds, and kept him alive until daybreak, when he attracted the enemy's attention and secured proper medical attention for him. Later in the day Major Hughes travelled across the desert in a truck full of Germans, who had been wounded by the Battalion which he commanded. It subsequently transpired that the column which the 6th Battalion had attacked with such vigour and determination was not a supply line column, but an enemy motorised battalion with tanks in support.

Capt. Hull also fell into the hands of the enemy, but made his escape and rejoined the battalion late on June 29. For his outstanding example of leadership and courage throughout this action, he was awarded the Military Cross.

The remnants of this expedition joined the rest of the Brigade in their defence positions near Mersah Matruh in the early morning of June 28. While these events had been in progress " D " Company (Major Brunton), which had been sent out the day before to try to locate and protect a Battery of Medium Guns near Mersah Matruh, had failed in its mission after an all night search. When it eventually joined up again soon after mid-day on the 28th, Major Brunton found that he was now in command of the Battalion.

Orders to break out from the Matruh position were, it will be remembered, given out by Brigadier Cooke-Collis at 5.30 p.m. on the 28th. As darkness fell the 6th Green Howards were being heavily attacked, but they held on grimly until shortly after 9 p.m., when they started to make their way up the narrow track to the gap which had been made by the 5th East Yorkshires. At the top they found themselves under heavy machine-gun and anti-tank gun fire, and, to make things worse, a tank was burning furiously, which silhouetted each vehicle as it came over the skyline. It was decided that each vehicle was to cross the escarpment individually, and as quickly as possible, and that the Battalion should reassemble some distance beyond.

6 Bn 28/29 Jun 42

Capt. Pullinger, who was navigating the Battalion, got safely through, but the rest of the battalion did not fare so well. Major Brunton's truck, just as it was alongside the burning tank, got stuck, and received a direct hit from an

anti-tank shell. He, Capt. H. D. Lyttleton, his adjutant, and
the crew, had to abandon the truck, losing all their kit, but
managed to get a lift on another carrier. Once again the
Battalion was very much split up, and on reaching its re-
assembly area, only some ten vehicles could be counted. This
column, and others which formed themselves, moved on to
the south and then turned east. The morning of June 29
opened with a very heavy mist, which did not clear until about
8 a.m., when Major Brunton's column found itself close to a
large enemy force of tanks and armoured cars, which opened
fire on it immediately. An exciting chase then ensued which
resulted in the Green Howards getting away successfully,
and arriving at the Divisional reception camp near El Alamein
late the same evening. Capt. Hull rejoined the Battalion that
night.

The following story, given in his own words by Pte. W. P.
Simpson, 6th Green Howards, is a graphic example of the
type of experience which befell many individual soldiers both
in this and similar break-outs. It shows how the dogged
determination and individual initiative of all ranks brought
back to Egypt a large enough proportion of the 50th Division
to enable it, three months later, to play its part in the great
advance of the 8th Army to Tunisia.

" At about 10 p.m., when it was dark, the whole Battalion
formed up in four columns to strike out South. The column
I was with set off, and practically straight away had to run
through nearly three miles of intense cross fire, in which about
nine out of ten wagons were hit. After coming through that
we only went a short distance, and were stopped by enemy
minefields in front, and a ravine about two hundred feet deep
on the right. We could not head East from there as we would
have run into the enemy, who greatly outnumbered us, and
we knew it was impossible to go back the way we had come.
It was here that ' Every man for himself ' was ordered, and
many men set off to walk by crossing the ravine and into the
desert, and making a detour of a couple of days' march to
reach comparative safety.

My own experience of this was—I was there by the side
of this ravine quite undecided what to do, with the driver of
my old platoon truck that had been knocked out. To tell the
truth I didn't fancy the walk then at all, and the driver, who
was in the R.A.S.C., said he couldn't do it ; so we decided to
look round for a wagon we could get to go, and risk getting
it over the ravine and out. The number of men in this position
was gradually diminishing as more decided to risk walking.
At approximately 1 a.m. some senior staff officers who were

in among us were trying to think of some way to raise the minefields in front of us, and although we were given real good covering fire from the Cheshires, who were our machine-gunners, it was of no use ; but just a little later someone managed to get a 15 cwt. truck across the ravine, and, as no shots were heard from that direction, it was concluded that it was our only opening. The next thing that happened was that all the senior staff officers managed to get across in two staff cars, that managed the crossing fairly easily with being so low. This gave the R.A.S.C. man and myself some hope of not having to walk, so we searched round all the wagons left and managed to find a 3-ton truck converted into an ambulance that was not damaged at all. I was wondering at this time if it was possible for the driver to get it across, because just previously, two trucks of the same size had overturned and killed a couple of dozen men who were trying to make it. Anyhow, we decided we would try, and, at approximately 3 a.m. in the pitch black, the R.A.S.C. man got our salvaged truck across. There were very few people left when we made the crossing, and of these, not one would take the risk, so we set off on our own. I knew I could navigate our way out as I had had plenty of training with the Battalion Intelligence while in England, and also I was a trained observer, so I headed due South at once to get as far into the desert as possible. We stopped once and picked up four men who were walking, and then kept on. One of these men had been a medical orderly in some unit, and it turned out very lucky that we picked him up, as we collected some wounded during the following day, and he was able to attend to them. One of these wounded men was a Sikh, and I must say he was one of the bravest men I have met, as although he was wounded with shrapnel from head to foot, he never murmured, and I never got him to proper medical attention for nearly twelve hours, and all that time he was bumped about on a stretcher. Another fellow died with us, but we were unable to stop to bury him, as I came across an armoured car unit who let me know that Fuka, the place I was hoping to reach, was in enemy hands. When I knew this I could only head on East and hope for the best. I went on so far without seeing a sign of anyone that in the end I decided to head North to hit the coast road, and thereby hope to find a Dressing Station or something for the wounded. I did so, and when eventually I reached the coast road, it was absolutely deserted, so I headed East along the road and found that when I had hit the road I was thirty miles West of El Daba. I got them to a Dressing Station in El Daba, and it was here that I met the unit who had originally had the ambulance that we had come through on. It was the H.A.C., who generally call themselves the 11th R.H.A. They were amazed to see us in their ambulance, and asked us where the Medical Officer, Orderlies and driver were. Of course we didn't know, but they turned up in ones and twos in the next two days, and of course were astonished to find their ambulance, that they had thought was impossible to get out, had in fact landed in safety twenty-four hours before them. The men who came back in the ambulance, who were fit, found their units practically at once, and the wounded also were put in proper hands. The driver and I were made much of by all members of the H.A.C., and were invited to stay on with them for good if possible, but after a few days we found out where our Brigade was, and found that they were making for Amirya—seventeen miles from Alexandria—so we said goodbye to the H.A.C., and made our way to Amirya, arriving there a few hours before the Battalion, to whom we reported as soon as they arrived. We soon settled down here in Camp and we started the business of refitting and also had a little training to keep us active."

6 Bn
30 Jun/
4 Jul 42

Throughout the 30th small bands of troops and vehicles kept trickling in, and on July 1 the 6th Green Howards moved back to Mareopolis, arriving there next day. On calling the roll it was found that, out of a full complement of officers and men who had been at Gazala on June 14, only ten officers and three hundred other ranks remained. On July 4 the following message was received by the Divisional Commander from the Commander-in-Chief : " You have done well. You have turned a retreat by a firm stand, and stopped the enemy on the threshold of Egypt. You have done more than that ; you have wrenched the initiative from him by sheer guts and hard fighting. He has lost heavily, and is short of men, ammunition and petrol. You have borne much, but I ask you for more. You must not slacken. If we can stick it, we will break him."

7 Bn
21/26 Jun 42

We must now take up the story of the 7th Battalion, when it moved on the night of June 21/22 straight from Bir Thalata to Mersah Matruh. In view of the subsequent operations of this Battalion, it is important to note that, before leaving Bir Thalata, it handed over all its anti-tank rifles, many Bren guns, all mortars and some carriers to the 6th Battalion, to make up for the latter's battle losses before it set out for Buq Buq with the Brigade Column. It must also be remembered that the 7th Battalion had been considerably weakened by the losses sustained in the attack at Sidra, and that, although some reinforcements had been picked up at Bir Thalata, it was still considerably under strength.

On arrival on June 22 the Division, less the 69th Brigade Column, was concentrated in leaguer immediately north of an escarpment some five miles south of the Mersah Matruh, but on the 24th it moved to a new area immediately to the east of the town. On the 26th it was ordered to move up to a defensive position astride the main road a further three miles to the East. As the 7th Battalion was turning off the road onto its new positions, it was heavily bombed by Stukas, as a result of which " A " Company's Headquarters received a direct hit, and C.S.M. G. White and Pte. T. Waterworth were seriously wounded, Lt. H. Cass was killed, while two trucks were completely destroyed. By dawn on the 27th they were dug in, and mines had been laid in front of their positions.

At 6 p.m. Lt.-Col. MacDonnell was summoned to Brigade *7 Bn* Headquarters where definite orders were issued for an attack *27/28 Jun 42* on the enemy's line of communications to the South—" to seek out the enemy and destroy him wherever he was to be found." The plan was for the 69th Brigade, with the 151st Brigade co-operating on the right, to do as much damage to the enemy's supply lines as possible, and then return to its rearguard position outside Mersah Matruh. The 69th Brigade was to attack, with the 6th Green Howards on the right, the 5th East Yorkshires on the left, while the 7th Green Howards was to follow the East Yorkshires. The start line was about seven miles south of its present position, and the 7th Battalion had all it could do to get there by 8.30 p.m. After waiting for two hours for the artillery to arrive, the order was given to advance without them. The light was now failing but for the first hour the going was fairly simple. They then came to a pass which vehicles could only ascend in single file. As they were beginning to climb up through the pass, the 11th Field Regiment, R.A., gate-crashed in, and caused a certain amount of confusion, which had to be sorted out at the top of the escarpment. The advance continued until the 5th East Yorkshires came upon a nullah crossing their front, which was practically impassable for vehicles. They managed to get across, but left the gaps in an even worse state for the 7th Green Howards and the gunners, who were following, and considerable delay was caused. As soon as the East Yorkshires went over the crest they came under artillery fire—the enemy gunners, owing to the bright moonlight reflected on the windscreens, having spotted the vehicles from two miles away. The advance continued until the leading battalions came under machine-gun fire. A heavy engagement now took place in which the 6th Battalion suffered severe losses, but the 7th Battalion remained where it was awaiting the result. It was being heavily shelled, and Lt.-Col. MacDonnell, after

K

consultation with the Commanding Officer of the 11th Field
Regiment, R.A., decided that they would both move their
forces out of the shelled area by proceeding some thousand
yards to their left, then turn south again, and await further
orders. At the end of this move, Lt.-Col. MacDonnell could
find no trace of the artillery nor of a party of his battalion
which had gone with them. He sent out Major Girling with a
section of carriers to look for them, but this officer's carrier
broke down, and he eventually returned having failed to catch
up with the missing party. Shortly afterwards Lt.-Col.
MacDonnell received orders to retire northwards, and set
out with his still further depleted Battalion.

The Green Howard party which had gone off with the
gunners consisted of " B " Company (Major Pickering), the
Pioneer platoon, the Intelligence Section and three carriers.
Finding themselves completely lost, Major Pickering decided
to move forward about three-quarters of a mile to the second
objective which had been given him. He reached this point
without opposition, capturing a German patrol car with five
occupants on the way. Being unable to contact any British
formation, this party set off again at 1.45 a.m. on June 28
and, after following a circuitous track, arrived at El Daba
at 9.15 a.m. on June 30. Here the commander was informed
by the Town Major that the 50th Division was assembling at
El Alamein. At this moment " B " Echelon, under Capt.
(Q.M.) D. C. Stevenson, arrived, and they went on together to
El Alamein, where they arrived on July 1. Meanwhile the
remainder of the Battalion had, on June 28, withdrawn with
the rest of the Brigade to its previous positions.

7 Bn
28/29 Jun 42   In order to understand how it came about that the 7th
Green Howards were overrun late that night in attempting to
break out, a brief description of their position is necessary.
The Brigade was now in a comparatively small saucer-shaped
bowl, with the 7th Battalion concentrated in a similar depression about eight hundred yards to the east. This depression
was almost at the mouth of a valley which ran north. The
northern end was passable for any vehicles, but from west to
east there was only one track by which vehicles could pass.
This track led from the Brigade area to the 7th Battalion's
position, and then up over the ridge to the east. To the south,
the sides of the depression increased in steepness, and were
impassable to any vehicle except, perhaps, carriers. To get
out, therefore, there was only one route to either east or west,
good going to the north, and none at all to the south. All
day long enemy forces could be seen proceeding north towards
the coast along a ridge some two miles away to the east, and
it was very apparent that the only hope of a break through

was to go south, and then, once again, make a turning movement to the east. For the 7th Battalion any movement south
was impossible without first getting out of the depression to
the west or east. After a daylight reconnaissance a route
through the broken ground from the Brigade position to
the open desert in the south was discovered. Orders for a
break out that night were issued at 5.30 p.m. by Brigadier
Cooke-Collis at a conference at his Headquarters. Once
again, as at Gazala, the 5th East Yorkshires was to make a
gap through which the Brigade would pass.

In order to make this gap the 5th East Yorkshires had to
climb up to the top of a steep escarpment, strongly held by the
enemy, by means of a narrow track. After a storming attack
against enormous odds, they secured the top of the escarpment. Lt.-Col. T. G. W. Stansfeld was awarded an immediate
D.S.O. for his courage and leadership in this action.

This was, however, by no means the end of the affair.
The track was so narrow that vehicles could only get up one
at a time ; the top was under continuous artillery fire, and
those vehicles which were not hit here, had to run the gauntlet
under very heavy fire for a further two miles. However,
Divisional and Brigade Headquarters, the 6th Green Howards,
some of the East Yorkshires, and " B " Echelon of the 7th
Green Howards got through, and proceeded on their way to
El Alamein.

A battery of 25-pounders and a platoon of machine-
guns had been allotted to the 7th Battalion to assist it in its
withdrawal, which was timed to take place at 11.15 p.m.
Lt.-Col. MacDonnell had been told that, in the event of
the enemy attacking, no withdrawal was to take place.
Soon after he got back to his Battalion from Brigade Headquarters the positions were heavily machine-gunned and
shelled, and, by about 8.30 p.m., the enemy were attacking
from the east and south. The first attack, made before dark,
after a short artillery bombardment, was a surprising affair.
The German infantry advanced in solid formation, unsupported by other weapons, and were easily beaten off with the
assistance of the carrier platoon of the 5th East Yorkshires,
who brought fire to bear from the high ground to the rear of
the Green Howard's position. The sole anti-tank gun which
the Battalion possessed was sited in a forward position to the
right flank. Capt. D. G. Jackson established an Observation
Post in its vicinity, which proved invaluable in the later stages
of the battle. An attempt by enemy armoured vehicles to
approach the Battalion area was repulsed by this anti-tank
gun, which was fired with such accuracy that the enemy

withdrew very quickly, leaving two or three of their vehicles on fire.

Intense artillery and mortar fire was now brought down on the Battalion area, which, besides causing many casualties, caused a major disaster when the Battalion wireless truck was hit and put out of action.

Lt.-Col. MacDonnell was now left with no alternative except to guess when the remainder of the Brigade were safely away, and it was doubtless partly due to this that he naturally held on long enough to be quite certain that he had fulfilled his role, with the consequent capture of most of his command.

The next move of the enemy consisted of probing attacks against all sections of the defence. The signal platoon under Sgt. D. Nell, and the machine-gun section, were particularly hard pressed, but they beat off the attackers, and inflicted heavy losses.

Capt. Jackson, regardless of his own safety, made repeated journeys back and forth from his Observation Post to Battalion Headquarters, and gave Lt.-Col. MacDonnell valuable information about the changing situation.

Major Girling had been sent off at 2.30 that afternoon to contact Capt. (Q.M.) D. C. Stevenson, who was some seven miles away to the east, with orders for him to bring up " B " Echelon Transport. The latter officer arrived in the vicinity at about 7 p.m. with twenty-three vehicles, mainly 3-ton lorries. Leaving them a short distance away, Capt. Stevenson proceeded on foot to report to the Commanding Officer. He arrived in the middle of the battle, which by now had increased in intensity, with enemy infantry so close in position on a ridge to the north-west that orders being given in German could be heard distinctly.

At about 10 p.m. Lt.-Col. MacDonnell held a conference and decided to fight to a finish. At this conference he ordered his commanders to hold on to their positions until 10.45 p.m., and then to break off the battle and attempt to get away independently. He ordered Capt. Stevenson to take the " B " Echelon transport ut of the wadi immediately, and attach himself to the Brigade Column. This Capt. Stevenson did, and got safely away with all his vehicles. Before leaving the depression he sent a message back by Sgt. R. Sergison, " C " Company, together with a sketch showing the direction of the enemy's fire, and the position of certain tracks by which he thought the Battalion might still get out. It was, however, then too late.

The machine-gun platoon, which saved the Battalion from being overrun at a very much earlier hour than it eventually was, now ran out of ammunition, and Lt.-Col. MacDonnell ordered it to make its escape. The artillery had also been sent off at the same time as " B " Echelon. And so the 7th Battalion stood alone.

As soon as the enemy heard the transport starting up they increased their fire. They apparently knew that the only escape route lay to the west, and as the first truck, filled with men from " C " Company, including the Company Commander (Capt. Hicks), approached this track, it was hit, set on fire, and destroyed. Capt. Hicks was killed. Shortly afterwards enemy tanks broke through and overran the forward positions in the valley.

The situation was now hopeless. The Regimental Aid Post was mistaken for a defensive position by the enemy, and the wounded came under heavy fire until the Medical Officer, Capt. F. J. D. Webster, walked boldly forward carrying a Red Cross flag. Major Girling and the Padre, Capt. H. Whistler, were captured as they were attempting to lead the walking wounded over the edge of the depression to safety. Under a hail of machine-gun fire, and even solid shot, they were forced into the hands of the enemy infantry, who were pouring into the valley to " mop up ".

Eventually all was quiet and, in the strange flickering light of the burning troop carrier, the Green Howards were rounded up to await transport to take them into captivity. The officers captured were Lt.-Col. MacDonnell, Major Girling, Capt. F. Towle, Capt. D. G. Jackson, Capt. Collett and Lt. E. A. B. Dahl. Capt. V. Evans, M.C. succeeded in getting away, and, after a long and adventurous march across about a hundred miles of desert, succeeded in rejoining the Brigade, in an exhausted condition, having covered the whole distance on foot, with only the food and water with which he had started, and hiding from the enemy all the time.

Lt.-Col. MacDonnell subsequently received the Distinguished Service Order for his leadership in this action. The official despatch states that throughout the battle Lt.-Col. MacDonnell displayed outstanding devotion to duty, determination and complete disregard for personal safety. His magnificent example was an inspiration to his Battalion, and his grim determination to hold off the enemy was to a very large extent responsible for the safe withdrawal of the remainder of the Brigade.

During their long months of captivity the officers and men of the 7th Battalion were able to console themselves with the memory that they had fought an epic battle. For six hours they had stood up to vastly superior forces of the 90th Light German Division, had taken heavy toll of their attackers, and enabled the remainder of the Division to escape. Later they had the satisfaction of knowing that their Battalion came to life again, and won fresh honours at Mareth and Akarit, in Sicily, and in Normandy and Holland.

A few individual members of the 7th Battalion managed to escape in the confusion, and joined up with the party consisting of " B " Company, the Pioneer platoon, the Intelligence Section and three carriers, which, it will be remembered, had gone off with the 11th Field Regiment, R.A., on June 27, and made their way through to Alamein. These, together with " B " Echelon transport under Capt. (Q.M.) Stevenson, constituted all that was left of the 7th Battalion on June 30.

50 *Div*   During the period July 1/12 the 50th Division was busy
1/12 *Jul* 42 reorganising its depleted forces, and fitting in reinforcements as they arrived. The Division now consisted of only two Brigades, the 69th and 151st, as the 150th had not been replaced.

Before, however, these two Brigades could be made up to full strength, or had time to train the new arrivals, orders were
69 *Bde* received on July 12 to start without delay on the construction
12/19 *Jul* 42 of defence lines just east of the Ruweisat Ridge. The whole of the 69th Brigade was employed on this work, and, by the evening of July 18, the major part of the new defences was complete. There was, however, to be no rest for the 69th Brigade as it was placed under the command of the 5th Indian Division, with orders to be on the Ruweisat Ridge by dawn on the 19th. A hasty reorganisation took place, and the Brigade moved forward with only two battalions, the 5th East Yorkshires and 6th Green Howards, the latter having been made up to strength by drawing on the 7th Green Howards. The remnants of the 7th Battalion remained in the desert, working on various defence works, until they returned to Alexandria early in August.

In the following story of the 6th and 7th Battalions in their actions during the next eighteen months, it should be remembered that, as a result of the desert fighting, and the " break outs " from the Gazala position, and from Mersah Matruh, they were now but shadows of the complete, highly trained and disciplined units, which they had originally been. The lion's share of the fighting was still to come, but these Battalions never had a real opportunity for regrouping and being trained as complete units, until they returned to England after their days in Sicily. On more than one occasion Company and Platoon Commanders found themselves leading men into battle, whose names they did not even know, at such short notice had they been thrust on them as reinforcements.

Individuals, and individual units of the battalions, fought magnificently, as events will show, but, as has been said before in these pages, the great strength of a Regimental unit lies firstly in its *esprit de corps*, and secondly in the comradeship of its members, particularly when it has been tested in battle.

It speaks volumes for the spirit which had been imbued in the Battalions by all those officers, warrant officers, and N.C.O.s, who were now casualties, or lingering in prison camps, that the Battalions should have maintained the standard set by them, and covered themselves, and the name of the Green Howards, with further glory.

The 69th Brigade now received fresh orders, and on July 20 found itself under the command of the 7th Armoured Division, and heading south for an attack on the Taqa Plateau. The part played in this battle by the 6th Green Howards will be told later, but a brief account of the operation will help the reader to fit individual stories into the general framework. ^{69 *Bde* 20/29 *Jul* 42}

Brigadier Cooke-Collis, commanding the 69th Brigade, had been given orders to attack strong enemy positions in the southern sector of the Armoured Division's line. A composite battalion of the 201st Guards Brigade was placed under his orders for this operation, which was to be carried out in three stages during the night July 21/22. The first two stages—the capture of the Taqa Plateau, and the capture of Jebel Kalakn, were to be undertaken by the 69th Brigade. Stage three, dependent upon the success of the first two, was for the 4th Armoured Brigade to pass through and work behind the enemy's lines.

There was little information available about the objectives, and reconnaissance was impossible by day, as the whole area was under direct enemy observation. The force under Brigadier Cooke-Collis' command was a scratch one, consisting of composite battalions of tired troops, and the Guards Battalion was very much under strength. In fact, it was clear at the outset that the operation was going to be extremely difficult.

The plan of attack was for the Guards Battalion to attack the eastern end of the enemy's position in the hope that this would not be strongly held, and for the East Yorkshires and Green Howards to attack the Taqa Plateau from the south.

Before dark, on the evening of July 21, the latter battalions moved to the neighbourhood of Garet El Himeimat, which was as far as they could go unobserved in daylight. As soon as darkness fell they advanced to a point about six miles south of the Plateau, where they debussed, and were formed up by 1 a.m. on July 22.

At 1.30 a.m. the Green Howards on the right, and the East Yorkshires on the left, moved forward, and, when daylight came, they had reached the southern edge of the plateau. By 8.30 a.m. two companies of the Green Howards were firmly established on the plateau, but the East Yorkshires had not been able to get further than the southern edge. During the morning, therefore, the Green Howards were withdrawn to conform with the East Yorkshires, in order to consolidate the position against the counter attack which was obviously being prepared.

July 22 was a most uncomfortable day for these two battalions. In addition to being subjected to continuous artillery and mortar fire, many of the troops suffered severely from heat and exhaustion. When the expected counter attack did develop it was supported by tanks. After a bloody battle the enemy was beaten off, but patrols sent out that night reported that the enemy was getting up reinforcements, obviously with a view to further action.

Accordingly on July 23 Brigadier Cooke-Collis, seeing no hope of making any further progress, asked for permission to withdraw. This was granted, and at 9 p.m. his force started to retire under cover of darkness. This was carried out successfully, and the Brigade arrived back at a position near Garet El Himeimat early on July 24.

After a well-earned rest on the 24th, the 69th Brigade was ordered north again to Alam El Dakar to take part in an attack through the enemy's minefields in front of the South African Division near Alamein station. To compensate for losses sustained in the fighting on the Taqa Plateau, the 6th Battalion Durham Light Infantry was brought up, and put under the command of the 69th Brigade.

The 69th Brigade infantry, and a battalion of the 9th Australian Division which was co-operating with them, achieved their objectives in the face of fierce opposition, and then dug in to await the arrival of the tanks, which were to pass through the gap which they had made. Unfortunately, owing to some misunderstanding, the armoured force did not pass through, and the infantry were subjected to a very heavy counter attack in which they suffered severe casualties, and were forced to withdraw. This they did on the night of July 27 and arrived back at Mareopolis on July 29, rejoining the remainder of the 50th Division. The Division was now given the task of defending the Northern Delta, and, although remaining in the 8th Army Order of Battle, came under command of the G.O.C. British Forces in Egypt.

It was not until October 9 that the 50th Division once more took its place in the line with the 8th Army preparatory to the Battle of Alamein and the long advance to Tunisia.

We must now return to July 17 and follow the 6th Green Howards through the attacks at the Taqa Plateau, and near Alamein. During the period July 2/16 reinforcements had arrived for the 6th Battalion, many of them from other regiments, and, on the 14th, Lt.-Col. G. W. Eden took over command. When they set out for the Ruweisat Ridge on July 17, Major Brunton was 2nd I./C., and the Company Commanders were Major K. R. Fay, and Capts. D. E. Spence, C. H. Gardiner and C. M. Hull. Capt. Pullinger (in the words of his Commanding Officer : " a young officer who must have gone far had he not been killed later in Sicily "), uncomplainingly gave up command of the company which he had just been given, in order to retain his post of Intelligence Officer, since there was no junior officer available with the necessary experience. *6 Bn 17/21 Jul 42*

The Battalion was now fully equipped, complete with new vehicles, but, although up to strength, included new arrivals who had not had time to get acclimatised to desert conditions. The old hands had had a very trying time and badly needed a rest, and a portion of the Battalion consisted of 7th Battalion men lent for the occasion. Yet, in spite of being a somewhat heterogeneous body, which had had no opportunity of training together, the Battalion had a fine fighting spirit and did all that it was asked to do with credit.

After three days at Ruweisat the Battalion moved, on July 20, to a point about three miles east of Garet El Himeimat. In the afternoon of July 21 the 6th Green Howards and 5th East Yorkshires moved forward in transports to their forming up position in front of the Taqa Plateau. The going was bad, mainly soft sand, and more time seemed to have been spent in pushing vehicles than in riding in them. Each Battalion was roughly two and a half companies strong, the support companies being kept back under Brigade Control. After some four hours of this heavy going the debussing point was reached and the advance began.

The attack by the 6th Green Howards was carried out by " C " and " D " Companies, commanded respectively by Capt. Hull and Major Fay, each consisting of about seventy *6 Bn 22 Jul 42* all ranks. Charging straight on to their objective, they succeeded in securing the north eastern corner of the plateau by about 6 a.m. on July 22. Since Battalion Headquarters was tied to its wireless set in a carrier, it was unable to follow the companies in their first assault. Unfortunately this communication broke down at an early stage, and while the Battalion Commander did not know that his companies had reached their objective, equally the Company Commanders were unable to get further orders. At this juncture the enemy launched a counter attack with infantry and a small force of tanks, under a concentration of mortar and artillery fire, the latter coming from three directions.

Major Fay and Capt. Hull then decided to form a joint headquarters, and fight the battle as well they could until superior authority regained communication with them. Many casualties were now being sustained, largely from shell fire. The ground was so hard that it was almost impossible to scrape any cover, and it was found that, since a good deal of the shelling came from captured British 25 pounders, the fragmentation of British steel was superior to that of the German shells. An extempore Regimental Aid Post was formed from the Company stretcher bearers ; cardigans were used as stretchers, and towels as bandages. The work performed by the stretcher bearers, particularly Pte. F. N. Bucknall, was magnificent. One stretcher bearer completed an amputation under fire with an ordinary jack-knife. Among the casualties sustained in this action by " C " Company were L/Cpl. W. Anderson, an excellent N.C.O. who had been with the Battalion a long time, and Pte. Benson, a first class Bren gunner, and a great personality in the Company, whose loss was much felt by his comrades.

There were many instances of extreme courage, and the following instance of fortitude shows the spirit with which these Yorkshiremen were animated.

A private soldier who had been severely wounded, having lost an arm at the elbow, been hit in the right eye and also the stomach, was being carried past his Company Commander wrapped in towel bandages. Captain Hull asked the stretcher bearer who he was, but before the latter could answer, a voice from the bandages said in broad Yorkshire : "It's so and so, Sir, but I'm getting to look more like ——— Nelson every day, I know ! "

When the counter attack died down the two companies were reorganised, and shortly afterwards the Intelligence Officer, Captain Pullinger, appeared over the edge of the plateau, much to the relief of the Company Commanders.

Captain Pullinger immediately set to work getting the wounded evacuated to the Regimental Aid Post by a comparatively safe route, which he had reconnoitred. Unfortunately, soon after they got back, this Aid Post was heavily shelled, and many of these wounded men were killed. At about the same time Battalion Headquarters received some accurate mortar fire, which caused several casualties, one officer and four signallers being killed, and Lt.-Col. Eden wounded.

A little later, Brigadier Cooke-Collis, ("who", in Lt.-Col. Eden's words, "had an uncanny knack of coming forward just when his presence was most welcome"), appeared, and ordered Lt.-Col. Eden to hand over his command to Major Brunton, and go back to have his wound dressed. After a night at the Advanced Dressing Station, Lt.-Col. Eden returned to the Battalion the following afternoon.

Meanwhile the companies on the plateau had withdrawn slightly in order to conform with the 5th East Yorkshires, who had established themselves on the extreme southern edge of the plateau. On July 23 there was more shelling and considerable mortar fire, as the enemy attempted to dislodge the British troops from the plateau. During the night two sections of "C" Company, commanded by L/Cpl. F. Walpole, had established themselves well forward of the edge of the plateau. Later in the day the enemy launched another counter attack, but suffered severe casualties from the Battalion Mortar Platoon and supporting artillery. L/Cpl. Walpole and his two sections fought magnificently, and with their Bren guns took a heavy toll of the enemy who were forced to withdraw. This they did in such a hurry that they left their wounded behind. Later they came out under cover of Red Cross flags, and an unofficial truce was proclaimed for half an hour. During this period the two Company Commanders, and the Battalion Mortar officer, were able to stand up and have a good look at the enemy positions for future reference.

6 Bn
23 Jul 42

The heat was terrific, and the water ration was reduced to less than half a water-bottle per man. So desperate was their need that the radiator of a damaged carrier was drained, and inches of oil removed from the top of the water, which was used to boil a small ration of tea.

Sgt. A. E. Docherty, for his leadership and courage during this action, was awarded the Military Medal. This award came as the culmination of many occasions between May and July 1942, on which Sgt. Docherty had shown the utmost gallantry under fire, and set a magnificent example to his men.

6 Bn
24/25 Jul 42
To their great relief, orders were received for the Green Howards to withdraw that night. They left the position at midnight unnoticed by the enemy, and arrived back at Garet El Himeimat at about mid-day on July 24.

The remaining officers and men were by this time suffering a severe strain after the appalling heat on the plateau, the lack of food and water, and the exertions of pushing their vehicles through patches of soft sand during the long drive back through the night. The rifle companies, under strength to start with, had been reduced by casualties to about a third of their original strength, and one can imagine the reaction when, before they could settle down to sleep, truck loads of inexperienced reinforcements began to arrive. The rest of the day was perforce spent in reorganising, making nominal rolls, checking equipment, and generally administering the newly formed battalion. It was, indeed, incredible that the Battalion was ready to fight again thirty-six hours later. Lt.-Col. Eden writes : " We were now all ready for a clean-up, food and a good sleep. Everyone was looking forward to this, but in good spirits after our little action which seemed to have gone well and had blooded the new reinforcements. It was therefore a disappointment to be told to move again the same evening. We moved off and made our way over some heavy going. Orders came when it was dark to halt and rest, but we resumed our march at first light and reached our destination, Alam El Dakar, at about 10 a.m. on the 25th." Here they dug in, and had twenty-four hours respite before going into the attack at Alamein.

6 Bn
26/27 Jul 42
At 10 p.m. on the night of July 26 the Battalion advanced behind the 5th East Yorkshires, and the composite Durham Light Infantry Battalion, through the gap in the minefield, which was subjected to heavy artillery fire. At first light the Battalion arrived at its position, which was outside the gap in the enemy minefields, and, at that time, only sufficiently wide for the passage of infantry and light vehicles. " C " Company, Captain Hull, and a troop of the Battalion's anti-tank guns, were the most forward troops in the area of the gap. The first task which they undertook was the enlargment of the gap for the passage of the tanks. Later they regretted this, as the only tanks to use the gap were enemy ones. Our own tanks arrived at about mid-day but, instead of passing through the gap, they settled down in the middle of, and to the rear of, " C " Company's area. The result was that they attracted considerable attention from dive bombers and artillery. One forward platoon, under 2/Lt. R. V. Mather, did a considerable amount of execution amongst the enemy with its Bren guns during the

afternoon. Sgt. Docherty was particularly noticeable by the coolness with which he gave his fire orders, and observed the results.

In the early evening enemy tanks appeared in force, outnumbering and outgunning our own tanks. A tank battle commenced, once again with the Battalion between the opposing forces as at Knightsbridge, and the Green Howard anti-tank gunners were unable to fire. When our tanks began to withdraw, they put down a thick smoke screen which, in the evening breeze, was unfortunately blown towards the west, and formed an excellent blanket under which the enemy tanks advanced. Orders for a general withdrawal had, however, now been received, and the Battalion managed to get away platoon by platoon. Great credit must be given to No. 14 Platoon, under 2/Lt. R. F. B. Evans, and the anti-tank platoon under Sgt. T. Dean, who covered the withdrawal.

This appears to have been a very confused operation, which was not perhaps surprising when one reads that the 69th Brigade went into it on a "paper" plan, and never saw the ground beforehand. Lt.-Col. Eden's chief recollections of those two days were :—" The difficulty of getting one's bearings in the desert at first light, when one has advanced in the dark over ground that one has not had the chance to look at previously :—holding positions all day without being able to make a reply :—tanks unable to keep up because of enemy mines, and so, from our point of view, merely drawing more fire ;—the spectacular effects of enemy dive-bombing attacks ;—the wonderful refreshment a cup of tea provides under such circumstances and, lastly, the steadiness of our companies when the orders came to withdraw."

During the withdrawal from this position Sgt. A. Huggins won the Military Medal, to which he was to add the Distinguished Conduct Medal in the following November at the Munassib Depression. On this occasion there was a heavy ground mist, and when it lifted the column found itself extremely close to a large enemy force. Heavy shelling started in the area, and in the path of the column. The column turned south and moved away with great speed, but Sgt. Huggins noticed that one carrier had fallen behind. Under heavy fire he returned, and managed to bring the carrier back to the column.

After this action, the 69th Brigade went back to Alexandria and joined the remainder of the Division.

For his outstanding leadership and courage throughout the period from May to the end of July, Major F. H. Brunton was awarded the Military Cross. In the official citation which accompanied the award four separate occasions are mentioned on which he distinguished himself, namely during the fighting near Knightsbridge on May 27/29, at the break out from the Gazala line, at the break out from Mersah Matruh, and at the attack on the Taqa plateau. On the last two occasions, Major Brunton succeeded to the command of the Battalion at crucial moments, when the Commanding Officer became a casualty, and as a result of his energy, devotion to duty and forceful leadership, in each case a critical situation was speedily restored.

Colour Sgt. J. G. Oliver received the Military Medal for his gallantry on two occasions. At the break out from the Gazala line C/Sgt. Oliver found himself leading one of the escaping columns. Under intense artillery and machine-gun fire he led the way through the Italian defences. He set a magnificent example to the rest of the column, and had it not been for his presence of mind a great number of vehicles would have been lost. Again, at the break out from Mersah Matruh on June 28, C/Sgt. Oliver jumped from his truck under heavy machine-gun fire, and rescued a wounded officer. During the whole of this period C/Sgt. Oliver set a splendid example to the men of his Company.

6 *Bn*
1 *Aug/*
14 *Oct* 42
During the first week of August every man had three or four days' leave either in Alexandria or Cairo, and for many it was their first leave since their arrival in the Middle East. Lt.-Col. Eden had to go into hospital again on August 14, handing over to Major Brunton, but returned to resume his command three weeks later.

During Lt.-Col. Eden's absence the Battalion was put under the command of the 7th Armoured Division. Its first role was to lay minefields along the famous " Barrel Track ", which was used by Rommel as the axis of his advance, when he made his final attempt to break through to the Nile on August 31. When this work was complete the Battalion took up defensive positions overlooking this track. They were now without their anti-tank guns and other supporting weapons, as these had been taken away when they were back at Alexandria. At this juncture, General Montgomery, newly arrived from England, appeared on the scene, inspecting the positions. When he, in company with the Armoured Division Commander, visited the Green Howards and found how ill-equipped they were, he said to the Army Commander : " I will not have any men put into action without proper equipment. Remember, if you cannot equip them, then my orders are that they are to be sent away from the battlefield ! "

Every effort to secure equipment was made, but without

success, and, to the great regret of the 7th Armoured Division, General Montgomery's orders were complied with, and in the early evening of August 30, the Green Howards withdrew, and on September 1 rejoined the 69th Brigade near Alexandria. Later they were to have the satisfaction of knowing that a few days after their departure, when Rommel was extricating his beaten forces, his transport blocked itself in the gaps which had been made in the Green Howards minefields. This transport provided a magnificent target for the Desert Air Force, and hundreds of vehicles were later discovered to have foundered on these minefields, in an attempt to escape the attention of the attacking aircraft.

The Battalion now attempted once more to start serious training for the next round, but this attempt met with a further set-back. The 151st Brigade had been sent up to the line again, and the 6th Green Howards had to send two out of their three rifle companies, namely "A" and "C" Companies, to one of the Durham Light Infantry Battalions to make it up to strength. During this period "A" and "C" Companies sent out many successful patrols, gaining information which was most valuable later in the battle of Alamein, one of which received special praise from the Brigade Commander.

Early in October the Battalion moved up to an area behind the front for battalion and brigade training, but, when it arrived, it was ordered to move next day into the New Zealand Box. After some ten days there, spent in digging more defensive positions, the Battalion regained its two missing companies on October 6 and, after a few days of company training, the 6th Green Howards, on October 14, relieved the 5th Queens Regiment in a position some fifteen hundred yards from the enemy, on what was to become in nine days' time the historic field of El Alamein. On the previous day, October 13, Lt.-Col. G. C. P. Lance (Somerset Light Infantry), had taken over command of the Battalion from Lt.-Col. Eden.

There is not much to relate about the 7th Battalion, which, as will be remembered, withdrew to Alexandria early in August after sending reinforcements to the 5th East York- *7 Bn 1 Aug/ 14 Oct 42* shires and 6th Green Howards. The command of the Battalion had been given to Lt.-Col. A. W. Gibbon (Argyll and Sutherland Highlanders), on July 6, 1942. At that time it consisted of some three hundred officers and men, including some survivors of the 150th Brigade. In the previous two months' fighting it had suffered about five hundred casualties, and lost most of its equipment. Lt.-Col. Gibbon had no opportunity of getting the Battalion organised during his period of command. He was left in doubt for a long time as to whether the personnel of the 150th Brigade were to remain with the Battalion, he had to supply drafts to other units, and the rest of his troops were employed for the greater part of the time on work on defensive areas, and were scattered in detachments over a wide area. Towards the end of September a draft arrived, and, with the return of some of the officers and men who had been lent, the Battalion was almost up to strength, although still short of equipment. On October 4 Lt.-Col. D. A. Seagrim took command of the Battalion, and on October 14 he led it into the line on the Alamein position. And so the 50th Division once again took the field as part of the 13th Corps, 8th Army.

The story to date has shown that, having been fighting in the Western Desert for seven months on end, and suffered severe casualties in its retreat from Gazala, the Division was denied anything but the most limited facilities for training between July and October. The New Zealand Division, and the fresh 51st Highland Division, had spent most of this period in the most intensive preparations and rehearsals, and so it is to the greater credit and glory of those men from Yorkshire, Durham and Northumberland, that they played their full part in the advance into Tunisia, and, in particular, gained great honours at Mareth and El Akarit.

CHAPTER SEVEN

" THE 6th AND 7th BATTALIONS AT THE BATTLE OF ALAMEIN "

" The Pursuit to Mareth "

October 1942—*March* 1943

See MAP No. 7

A LTHOUGH the 50th Division did not play a spectacular part in the Battle of Alamein, the 69th Brigade, with whom we are concerned, made a subsidiary attack on October 25/26 against strongly held positions around the Munassib Depression, and later, on November 7, mobile columns of the Brigade made a spirited dash forward, which took them as far as the track leading from Mersah Matruh to Siwa. Before describing in detail the part played by the Green Howards in these operations, a brief description of the general plan and dispositions of the 8th Army is necessary, in order to bring it into the right perspective.

Before the battle of Alamein began the opposing forces were entrenched facing each other on a line from El Alamein to the Qattara Depression, with both flanks secured by natural obstacles. The British were disposed with the 30th Corps holding the line from the sea roughly as far as the Ruweisat Ridge, the 13th Corps from Ruweisat to the Qattara Depression, and the 10th Armoured Corps in reserve, astride the Alexandria-Cairo road. The enemy, consisting of both German and Italian troops, faced them in a series of strongly fortified positions, covered and connected by deep and elaborate minefields. Their reserves, which consisted chiefly of the 15th and 21st Panzer Divisions, and the 90th Light Division, all seasoned troops, were stationed within deep minefields, approximately behind the centre of their line, and so able to move to either flank if threatened.

In simple words, General Montgomery's plan was to make a sufficiently strong attack in the south with the 13th Corps to draw off the enemy's reserves, while the 30th Corps, in the north, was to pierce the enemy's defences on a sufficiently broad front to allow the 10th Armoured Corps to pass through. In order to deceive the enemy, the 10th Armoured Corps was at first kept well back, and then brought up behind the 13th Corps. Only at the last moment was it switched across to the north, and, as is now well known, it broke

L

right through the enemy's defences, and started the great advance of the 8th Army, which was to end in the complete defeat of the German and Italian forces in Tunisia six months later.

23 Oct 42   The battle was timed to begin on October 23, and the main attack on the 13th Corps front was to be made by the 44th Division, between Himeimat and the Munassib Depression, where the enemy's defences were considered to be weakest. As soon as a gap had been made there, the 7th Armoured Division was to pass through, and roll up the enemy defences behind the Munassib area. The role of the 50th Division was to attack the Munassib position frontally, with, as its first objective, a penetration of some fifteen hundred yards. It had originally been decided by the 13th Corps Commander (Lt.-Gen. B. G. Horrocks), that the attack of the 50th Division should take place on the night subsequent to that of the 44th Division, and not until the 7th Armoured Division had broken through. As it turned out, however, the 44th Division failed to pierce the enemy defences and suffered heavy casualties, and so the 50th Division was ordered to attack on the night *25/26 Oct 42* of October 25, with the object of relieving the pressure in front of the 44th Division.

See **MAP**   The plan of the 50th Divisional Commander was that *No.* 8   the main attack should be made by the 69th Brigade, supported by the divisional artillery of both divisions, and of the 7th Armoured Division. The objectives given to the 69th Brigade were firstly the " Moor " and the " Cape " ; and secondly a line of defences some three hundred yards behind these strong points. The 69th Brigade orders were that the attack was to be carried out by the 6th Green Howards on the right, and the 5th East Yorkshires on the left. The 151st Brigade was to assist this attack on the right, and further to the north the 1st Greek Brigade was to make a diversionary raid.

It was planned that the 50th Division should then hold its positions as a firm base for any future operations of the 13th Corps, and it was not anticipated that it would be used for follow-up operations.

As will be seen later in the account of this battle, the Green Howards, after severe fighting, advanced to within a few hundred yards of their final objective, but were then pinned down by very heavy shelling and mortar fire. The East Yorkshires on their left, after three separate attempts, also failed to get through, and were held up some four hundred yards short of the " Cape ". Late in the afternoon of October 26 the Divisional Commander decided to break off the battle, and for the next few days the 69th Brigade had to content itself with an intensive programme of harassing the enemy with mortar and small arms fire.

Meanwhile the 30th Corps in the north, although it had made a number of indentations in the enemy defences, had so far failed to make a gap sufficiently broad for the 10th Armoured Corps to pass through.

On the night of October 28, therefore, the 151st Brigade 28/29 *Oct* 42 was taken out of the Munassib line, and sent north to reinforce the 30th Corps, with which it took part in the culminating phase of the battle of Alamein, which resulted in the break through on November 3, after the great tank battle of El Aqqaqir. In the first days of November the 7th Armoured Division also moved north, and the 13th Corps was left with only two Divisions, the 44th and 50th, the latter being without the 151st Brigade and, at this stage, composed of the 69th Brigade, the 1st Greek Brigade, and the 2nd Free French Brigade. On October 29 the 69th Brigade was relieved in the Munassib position by the French, and moved north to take over positions on the Ruweisat Ridge from troops of the 4th Indian Division. There it was faced by a very strong locality on the western edge of the ridge, with Deir El Shein immediately to the north.

On the night of November 3/4 patrols all along this front 3/12 *Nov* 42 reported signs of enemy withdrawal, and on the morning of November 4 the forward movement began. But, much to the disappointment of the 50th Division, its orders were to hand over its second line transport to the 44th Division, and to make only a limited advance on foot as far as the Rahman Track.

The 69th Brigade, by the night of November 4, had secured the western edge of the Ruweisat Ridge, and set out next day to force a way through the minefields in front of it, to strike direct for the Rahman Track, and to seize a commanding feature some twelve miles east of the Ruweisat Ridge. After a very slow advance through minefields, some of which were two thousand feet in extent, the Brigade reached its objective before dark on November 6. The Brigade was, however, to receive its reward for this dogged progress, as additional orders were received for the 50th Division to form mobile Brigade columns, to strike hard due west with the utmost speed, and to cross the Rahman Track at 8 a.m. on November 7.

The Divisional Commander ordered every available vehicle to be sent to the 69th Brigade during the night, and, thanks to its past experiences in mobile operations, and in quick organisation, the Brigade was ready to start in the early hours of the next morning. The orders given to Brigadier Cooke-Collis by Major-General Nichols were short and to the point. " Advance as fast as possible ; accept big risks and attack the enemy with the utmost dash." A better man than Brigadier Cooke-Collis to carry out these orders could not be imagined and, with the greatest enthusiasm inspiring all ranks, the 69th Brigade started off in three mobile columns, each consisting of one company and the carriers of each battalion, and supporting arms.

After proceeding only six miles a small enemy defensive position was encountered. With anti-tank guns firing at point blank range, the infantry charged in their motor transport, firing from their vehicles. The result was that the position was taken without any casualties being sustained, and the captures included the Headquarters of the Italian Brescia Division, together with the Divisional Commander and his staff. During the next three days thousands of prisoners were taken and despatched on foot to the rear. Eventually the Brigade columns crossed the Matruh-Siwa track level with the leading troops of the 10th Armoured Corps. However, since during the last twenty-four hours no prisoners had been collected, and no enemy encountered, they were ordered to withdraw on November 9, and rejoined the Division three days later. At about the same time the 151st Brigade also rejoined, and for the next fortnight the 50th Division was employed in clearing the battlefield of Alamein.

6 and 7 Bns
13/14 Oct 42

See MAP
No. 8

At 7 p.m. on October 13, 1942, the 6th Green Howards, under the command of Lt.-Col. G. C. A. Lance (The Somerset Light Infantry), who had that day taken over from Lt.-Col. Eden, moved off in column behind the 5th East Yorkshires towards their new positions. They arrived at their dispersal point at about 10 p.m. and from there marched to the forward positions, in which they relieved the 5th Battalion, the Queen's Regiment. By 3 a.m. on the 14th the relief was completed, and the battalion was established in defensive fortifications some fifteen hundred yards from the enemy, who were holding the high ground of the " Moor " and the " Cape ", which fringed the southern side of the Munassib Depression. On the same day the 7th Green Howards, commanded by Lt.-Col. D. A. Seagrim, who had taken over from Lt.-Col. Gibbon ten days before, moved into positions overlooking the Munassib Depression from the north. The two Green Howard Battalions remained in this sector of the line for the next fortnight. The enemy facing them consisted of the Italian Folgore Division, a force of volunteer parachutists ; these were determined fighters, and, occupying strong defensive positions as they were, they put up a redoubtable resistance.

The 6th Battalion made a full scale attack on the Moor on October 25 and 26, in which it sustained many casualties, earned several decorations, and much glory. Before describing this attack in detail we will chronicle the operations of the 7th Battalion, which carried out a good deal of preliminary patrolling, and supported the attack of the 6th Battalion on the 25th and 26th with cross fire.

The 7th Battalion was disposed in a rough semi-circle 7 *Bn* with " A " and " B " Companies entrenched on the northern 13/29 *Oct* 42 escarpment of the Munassib Depression. The carrier platoon was stationed between and slightly in rear of these companies. " C " Company, on the right of " B " Company, faced east, and had in front of it, a little less than a mile away, two features, Pts 94 and 98, known as the " Twins ", which were held by the enemy.

As soon as it was dark, " A " Company sent forward a listening post to a pimple some four hundred yards in front of its position, but soon after 9 p.m. this post was compelled to withdraw on the approach of a strong enemy patrol. Fire was opened by light machine-guns, and the enemy patrol withdrew. Early the next morning the Green Howards announced their presence by engaging all the enemy positions in front of them with mortar and machine-gun fire. Much activity was observed on and around the Moor, and the enemy landed about twenty mortar bombs in the area occupied by No. 12 platoon of " B " Company, fortunately without causing any casualties. On the 16th " A " Company received a salvo of mortar bombs, which wounded five men, and a little later, two Fiesler Storch reconnaissance planes, with Red Cross markings, flew down the depression, and, having circled round the area of the Twins, flew off to the west. In the afternoon a severe sandstorm blew across the locality, followed by heavy rain, and this made conditions very uncomfortable. Just before midnight, the enemy put down a curtain of heavy shell, mortar and machine-gun fire on the battalion area. A general " stand to " was ordered, but the expected attack failed to materialise.

The story of the next few days is one of shelling, mortaring, and repeated sandstorms.

On the 19th a patrol sent out from " B " Company located an unfenced minefield, through which it proceeded until it heard a small enemy working party. The latter withdrew, and the patrol returned, locating on its way back a new signal wire running to the north west.

On the same day a report came in from No. 13 platoon of "C" Company that the enemy were playing football. An attempt to join in the game with mortar bombs failed, as the distance was too great.

On October 21 a patrol of one N.C.O. and ten men, commanded by Lt. E. J. Moss, was sent out to harass an enemy post near Pt. 94 of the Twins, and to obtain an identification. After proceeding for about six hundred yards they came upon an enemy platoon position, on which there was a working party. Making their way to the north of this position, they found a trip wire, which they were about to cut when they were challenged. Their reply to this was to throw two hand grenades and fire several bursts from a tommy gun. In the ensuing fight two Italians were discovered in a slit trench, of whom one was killed, and the other captured. They also threw hand grenades into another trench, almost certainly killing the occupants. Unfortunately, on their way back, they stumbled over a trip wire which set off an anti-personnel mine, and six men of the patrol were wounded, one seriously. However, they had successfully carried out their mission, and the prisoner was identified as belonging to the 5th Company, 2nd Battalion, 185th Regiment of the Folgore Division.

On October 24 considerable activity was observed both on the Cape and the Moor, and the mortaring and shelling of the 7th Green Howards positions increased ; so much so that the War Diary mentions a morning, mid-day, and evening "hate". On the 26th they had a grandstand view of the attack made on the Moor by the 6th Green Howards, and assisted them by keeping up an almost continuous fire on the enemy positions. When the 6th Battalion had to withdraw from Pt. 92 on the Moor in the afternoon of the 26th, the enemy put down a heavy concentration of shell fire on to the Depression, but little damage was done.

During the 28th and 29th the Battalion was relieved by a battalion of the Free French, and withdrew to positions just north of the Munafid Depression.

6 Bn
13/25 Oct 42 As soon as the 6th Green Howards had settled down in their new positions, patrols went out, and contacted enemy working parties behind defensive wire some two to three hundred yards east of Pt. 94 on the Moor. For the next ten days fighting and reconnaissance patrols, commanded by, amongst others, Lts. M. R. W. Gray, R. M. Dimond and P. Delf, went out by night, harassing the enemy and gaining information about the ground over which the Battalion was to fight on the 25th and 26th. In particular, information was

vitally needed about the defences in front of the enemy's forward localities, such as wire obstacles, booby traps on the wire,
and anti-tank and anti-personnel mines.

Great determination and courage was shown by these
patrols, who persistently reconnoitred inside the minefield
itself under the very noses of the enemy. The minefield, which
lay between two lines of wire hung with booby traps, was
somewhat of a mystery. Enemy working parties had been
previously reported working between the wires, and yet no
anti-personnel mines were encountered, neither did the mine
detectors give any evidence of anti-tank mines. As a final
effort to solve this mystery on the night of the 24th, a special
patrol went out, accompanied by a party of Engineers with
the very latest form of mine detector. The patrol was led by
Lt. C. A. Lawrence, who succeeded in getting his covering
party right through what appeared to be a minefield as far as
the wire on the enemy's side. The Engineers worked hard
behind them, but without any success in detecting mines. Unfortunately, after a little time, the party was discovered and had
to fight a rearguard action, in which Lt. Lawrence was killed
and several of his men wounded. The remainder returned in
good order, bringing their wounded with them, and supplying
information which materially affected the plans for the attack
on the following night.

While these reconnaissances had been taking place, orders
had been received for the Battalion to make an attack on the
" Moor " starting at 11.5 p.m. on the night of October 25.
On the 22nd the Battalion had been strengthened by a draft
of four officers and sixty men, and Major K. R. Fay took over
the duties of second-in-command from Major Brunton, who
had gone to Palestine on a tour of duty.

Throughout the day of October 25 the enemy positions   6 *Bn*
on the Moor were subjected to heavy artillery fire, and at   25 *Oct* 42
10.30 p.m. an artillery smoke screen was put down in front
of them. Under cover of this screen, the 6th Green Howards
advanced to the starting line, which they crossed punctually
at 11.5 p.m. The leading companies of the Battalion were
" B " Company (Major Pullinger) on the left, and " C "
Company (Major Hull) on the right. " A " Company (Capt.
G. H. Walker), and the carriers (Capt. F. Edwards) were held
in reserve.

Both the leading companies advanced with two platoons
forward, and the third in reserve. As the four leading platoons
approached the wire, one man from each platoon ran forward
and attached a grappling iron on a long length of rope to the
wire, and, on a pre-arranged signal between the two Company

Commanders, the ropes were pulled together, tearing up the wire, and setting off the booby traps. The enemy then put down a heavy curtain of mortar and machine gun fire, but the Green Howards, cheering, and with their bayonets at the ready, charged across the minefield and assaulted the forward enemy machine guns.

The two leading platoons of " C " Company, No. 13 (Lt. H. L. Cull) on the left, and No. 15 (Lt. R. M. Dimond) on the right, continued their advance over the crest but, as they did so, they were met by intense fire from a second line of machine-guns. No. 13 platoon received the full brunt of it, and Lt. Cull was killed instantaneously, while several of his men were also killed or wounded. No. 15 platoon, on the extreme right of the Battalion, missed the bulk of the fire, which had struck down No. 13 platoon. Lt. Dimond immediately swung his platoon back off the escarpment and, moving forward along the depression itself, managed to make considerable progress. Unfortunately, in the bright full light of the " Alamein " moon, he was spotted by the enemy and, in the ensuing fire fight, he himself was wounded, and his platoon suffered very heavy casualties.

By this time Major Hull, with his batman and two runners, was working his way round to the right flank of his Company. They, however, were spotted by an enemy machine-gun post, and fired upon. One runner was killed, Major Hull and the other runner wounded, and the batman was the only one of this small party left standing.

Lt. R. C. Mitchell, commanding No. 14, the reserve platoon, was now the only officer left of " C " Company, and was still lying back behind No. 13 platoon, which was pinned down on the top of the Moor on the left flank.

" B " Company, ably and gallantly led by Major Pullinger, reached the high ground at Pt. 94, at which point it was held up from further progress by heavy machine-gun fire from both flanks. This was soon intensified by mortar and artillery fire, and the position looked critical. At this stage Major Pullinger was to be seen walking about among his men and encouraging them. Having steadied his company, he personally led them in a bayonet charge on to the final objective. He himself killed four of the enemy with his revolver, and another two with a hand grenade.

6 *Bn*
26 *Oct* 42   Soon after midnight " B " Company began to consolidate its position, and Major Pullinger, under heavy shell fire, went off to try to make contact with " C " Company on his right. He found No. 13 platoon lying pinned to the ground, with their commander dead, and so, taking command of them

himself, he led them successfully in the assault of their objective. Later he personally called on the enemy to surrender, and more than seventy prisoners were collected. For his coolness, courage and leadership, Major Pullinger was awarded the Military Cross.

While this desperate fighting had been in progress, advanced Battalion Headquarters had received several direct hits from shell fire, as a result of which Major Fay, the second-in-command, Capt. G. S. Piper, the adjutant, and several of the headquarters staff were badly wounded. Lt. F. H. Honeyman, who was acting as Intelligence Officer, did magnificent work on this occasion, extricating the wounded, supervising their removal, and taking over control, since Lt.-Col. Lance had gone up to the forward area.

By this time the Royal Engineers had finally checked up a path through the minefield, and Lt.-Col. Lance ordered up a section of the Battalion Bren Carriers. The first carrier to enter the marked gap was immediately blown up on a mine, and burst into flames. The mystery of the minefield deepened, and the Engineers once again went into the minefield, with their detectors, to clear another gap. This time they entered the area which had already been passed over by " B " and " C " Companies, but they had not gone far before they themselves were blown up. At the time, so heavy was the shelling and mortaring, it was thought at first that they had received a direct hit, but, nevertheless, the mine detectors were dispensed with, and resort was made to the old method of careful prodding with a bayonet. This method produced immediate results, as a wooden cased mine was unearthed. This was a new type of mine, which, of course, did not react to the mine detectors, which were only attracted by metal. It was later discovered that the area between the two belts of wire was thick with these mines, and it was a stroke of fortune that they had failed to explode when " B " and " C " Companies charged over them.

When Lt.-Col. Lance arrived in the front line, the first person he met was Lt. Mitchell, who told him the perilous position of " C " Company as far as he knew it. Lt.-Col. Lance ordered Lt. Mitchell to remain where he was with his platoon, until he had got the complete picture. He then went on to " B " Company. A little later on No. 14 platoon took part in the final assault on Pt. 94 under the command of " B " Company, in the course of which, Lt. Mitchell was wounded and his platoon sergeant Sgt. G. Chambers was killed.

By 1.30 a.m. on the 26th Lt.-Col. Lance had established

his advanced Headquarters within the enemy's defence works south-east of Pt. 94, and had called up " A " Company, his reserve, and the carriers. At 1.40 he launched " A " Company (Capt. G. H. Walker) and the carriers (Capt. F. Edwards), against the enemy strong points which were still holding out on the Moor. A great deal of hand to hand fighting took place, in the course of which the Green Howards sustained many casualties, including Capt. Edwards, who was killed. The positions were, however, eventually taken, and some thirty-five prisoners, many of whom were badly wounded, were captured. Two anti-tank guns were also captured intact.

When Capt. Edwards was mortally wounded, leading his carriers with great dash against a very strong machine-gun position, Sgt. A. Huggins, M.M., was left in command. Without hesitation he marshalled two carriers, and, while under heavy fire, organised another attack. He rushed over to a nearby platoon, which was pinned to the ground by enemy fire, and ordered the platoon commander to fire Verey lights and flares. This exposed Sgt. Huggins to great danger, but he got back to his carrier, remounted, and advanced. When within five yards of a machine-gun post, he threw a grenade into it, and the enemy surrendered. This action was carried out under intense machine-gun and small arms fire, and his carrier was spattered with bullet marks. Sgt. Huggins, by his prompt action and complete disregard of his own safety, was largely responsible for the final capture of the position, together with some forty prisoners. Sgt. Huggins was awarded the Distinguished Conduct Medal.

Capt. G. H. Walker won the Military Cross for the conspicuous gallantry with which he led " A " Company into this assault, and also in a further attack later in the day. He was to be seen going from section to section under intense fire, encouraging his men, and finally leading a charge against an enemy machine-gun post.

" A " Company's success in this operation was also largely due to the bravery of Sgt. J. R. Rodgers, who was acting as Company Sergeant-Major. When Capt. Walker was preparing for his final assault, he ordered Sgt. Rodgers to organise the supporting fire of the company. With resolute determination Sgt. Rodgers collected the bren guns from neighbouring sections, and, with complete disregard for his own safety, grouped them on one flank, and enabled the company to advance. For his courage in this action, and also later in the day, Sgt. Rodgers was awarded the Military Medal.

One of these bren gunners, Pte. C. Mackinnon, acted with great gallantry, and also won a Military Medal. Not being satisfied with his position, he took his gun forward, and silenced at least two enemy posts. Later, when his Section Commander was wounded, although he was not the senior soldier, he took complete control, organising the unit, and rallying the other men. The initiative and daring of Pte. Mackinnon, under intense fire of every kind, had a marked effect on all those in his vicinity, and contributed in no small degree to the success of the Company.

Pte. J. Armstrong, in a battle in which so many brave deeds were accomplished, showed such continuous dash and courage through the night and all next day, that he received the Distinguished Conduct Medal. On more than one occasion he went forward single handed and destroyed enemy posts which were holding up the advance of his platoon, and later in the day, when the company was being heavily mortared in the positions which they had won, he personally engaged an enemy sniper post, killing at least one sniper, and eventually forcing the enemy to vacate the post.

By 2.30 a.m. on October 26 the 6th Green Howards were established on Pt. 94, with " B " Company on the left, " A " Company on the right, and " C " Company in reserve. At this juncture the Battalion position was strengthened by the arrival of two machine-gun sections, and a troop of anti-tank guns.

The remaining hours of darkness were spent in consolidating the positions under heavy shell and mortar fire. At about 10 a.m. Lt.-Col. Lance and Capt. Walker made a reconnaissance for a further attack across the " Moor " on Pt. 92. At 2.30 p.m. an artillery barrage and mortar smoke screen was put down on Pt. 92, and at 3 p.m. " A " Company went into the attack.

Advancing steadily across the bullet-swept and open plateau, the company had almost reached its objective when the enemy put down a tremendously heavy artillery concentration. The company was now reduced to approximately a third of its original strength, and orders were sent to Capt. Walker to retire. Under this heavy fire Capt. Walker inspired his men, until he was severely wounded, his leg and arm being shattered by shell fire. He was rescued, together with several other severely wounded men, by Sgt. Rodgers, but refused aid until his men were attended to. Even when his wound was forcibly dressed and he was lifted back, he complained that he was past aid, and that others should come first.

So ended another gallant failure, in which " A " Company, 6th Green Howards, lost some sixty men, but added further lustre to the regimental record.

Many of the wounded had to be left behind on Pt. 92, as it was found impossible to get them away. The total casualties sustained by the Battalion in the battle of Alamein, in which this action at Munassib played an important part in deceiving the enemy as to where the main blow would fall, were approximately one hundred and fifty. These included some well-trained old stagers, whose loss was seriously felt. Of the officers, Capt. Edwards, Lts. Cull and Lawrence were killed, and Majors Fay and Hull, Capts. Walker, Piper, Merson Davies, and Meek (the Regiment's Medical Officer), and Lts. Delf, Dimond, Mitchell and Gray were wounded.

Lt.-Col. Lance was awarded the Distinguished Service Order for his courage and leadership.

6 *Bn*
28/29 *Oct* 42

During the night of October 28/29, the Battalion was relieved by the Free French, and moved to new positions just north-west of the Munafid Depression.

6 *Bn*
2/3 *Nov* 42

On November 2 the 6th Green Howards moved up to the Ruweisat Ridge, where they relieved two Companies of the Sussex Regiment and one Company of Punjaubis, in forward positions facing a group of German paratroops of the Burck-hardt Battalion. On the next day a carrier patrol went forward as far as Deir El Shein, and reported signs of enemy withdrawal. Large columns of smoke were seen behind the enemy lines during the afternoon.

6 *Bn*
4/13 *Nov* 42

At 10 a.m. on November 4 the Battalion moved forward in a column which included artillery, anti-tank and machine-guns, and a Field Ambulance, all under the command of Lt.-Col. Lance. Progress was slow owing to enemy minefields, but the column arrived at Mungar Wahla at 10 a.m. on the 5th. Here orders were received to proceed forward at once in order to intercept an enemy column which was moving north-east. During the day the carrier sections, which were patrolling in front of the Battalion, captured over fifteen hundred Italians from the Brescia Division, who were despatched to the rear.

On November 6 the Column passed through the 4th Indian Division, but its further progress was halted by orders received at about 5 p.m. These orders were to the effect that the Battalion would return next day to the area around Deir El Mireir to take part in salvaging operations, with the exception of " C " Company, and the carriers, which were to form part of a mobile 69th Brigade Column under command of Major Mellor, 2nd Battalion Cheshire Regiment. " C " Company rejoined the Battalion on November 13, after having pursued the enemy as far as the Mersah Matruh-Siwa track. On the way back the carriers ran out of petrol, but returned a few days later.

The remainder of November, when the salvage operations   6 *Bn*
were completed, was devoted to training and reorganisation. 14/30 *Nov* 42
On the 18th " A " Company was sent back for five days to a
Rest Camp at Imayid and, on its return on the 23rd, " B "
Company took its place.   On November 15 Major Brunton
and Capt. D. E. Spence returned from Palestine, and, on the
21st, Major Hull and Lt. Mitchell rejoined from Hospital.
On the 25th, a draft of reinforcements arrived, consisting of
6 officers and 107 other ranks.

At 8 a.m. on November 4 the 7th Green Howards left   7 *Bn*
their positions north of the Munafid Depression and pro- 4/12 *Nov* 42
ceeded in a westerly direction through the minefields. After
having covered about eight miles, in the course of which a
carrier and an anti-tank carrier were lost on scattered mines,
the Battalion was held up by another minefield at about
11.30 a.m. It was not until 3 p.m. that the hard worked
sappers succeeded in clearing a gap, and during this time the
column was somewhat heavily and accurately shelled by the
enemy. Luckily there were only two minor casualties. During
the next two days the Battalion made better progress, although
held up at times by more minefields, and on the evening of
November 6, it was on the heels of the retreating enemy.
A number of prisoners were collected, culminating in the
capture by " A " Company and the carriers, in the early
hours of November 7, of the Divisional Commander of the
Pavia Division, and his staff. Later in the day, however, as
in the case of the 6th Battalion, hopes of further pursuit were
dashed when orders were received for the Battalion, less " B "
Company and the carriers, to return to Deir El Mireir for
salvaging operations.

Meanwhile the mobile column, of which " B " Company
formed the nucleus, drove forward to the west, and early
on November 7 made contact with the enemy. Some sixty
officers and seven hundred men from the Brescia, Pavia and
Folgore Divisions, and two Germans of the Burckhardt
battalion were captured at Deir El Sheka, and sent back
under a small escort.

On November 8 the column reached Minqar Abu
Mukhaiyet without incident, and, early the following evening,
arrived at Minqar Falma on the Mersah Matruh-Siwa track.
Here, to the great disappointment of everybody, orders were
received to return. On the homeward journey a truck and
two carriers had to be abandoned, but were recovered later,
and " B " Company rejoined the Battalion at Deir El Mireir
on the evening of November 12.

The remainder of November was spent in reorganising
and training.

On November 7 Capt. W. Warrener, who had fought many battles with the 6th Battalion, won a Military Cross, when serving the with 8th Army Headquarters Staff. At the tank barricade on the Smuggler's Cove road at the entrance to Mersah Matruh, an officer of the Seaforth Highlanders was seriously wounded by a mortar bomb, and lay helpless on the road, while the enemy mortars continued to fire. Heedless of the falling bombs, and of machine-gun fire which was opened upon him, Capt. Warrener ran forward, lifted the wounded officer, and carried him to safety.

While the 69th Brigade had been carrying out these operations, great events had been in progress to the north. The major portion of the Italian African Army had been destroyed or taken prisoner, and the 10th British Corps had chased the German Afrika Corps across the Egyptian frontier, and beyond Mersah Matruh. The latter, although considerably weakened, was still able to contest the advance of the 8th Army, and early in December, the 30th Corps took over the pursuit from the 10th Corps, the latter being withdrawn into reserve.

The 10th Corps was now under the command of Lt.-Gen. B. G. Horrocks, who had commanded the 13th Corps at Alamein, and the 50th Division now formed part of it. The 151st Brigade had rejoined the Division, and the Greek and Free French units, which had fought with the Division at Alamein, had gone elsewhere.

On December 1 the 50th Division moved forward as far as El Adem, south of Tobruk, where it remained for about a fortnight. Meanwhile, the enemy, who had been chased as far as Agheila, made a further withdrawal to Buerat, at the western end of the Gulf of Sirte. The 50th Division was then ordered to make a big jump forward, and to take part in the attack on the Buerat positions. Its first halt was to be at Agedabia.

While, however, it was crossing the desert, near Msus, a violent storm severely damaged the harbour installations and ships lying at anchor in Benghazi. As a result, it was found impossible, for the time being, to maintain any additional troops in the forward positions in front of Buerat, and the 50th Division was ordered to go direct to Benghazi, where it could be maintained from the port by its own transport.

6 *and* 7 *Bns*   The Green Howards arrived in Benghazi about December
Dec 42/   12, and immediately set to work in helping to restore the
Mar 43   damage in the harbour. The 6th Battalion had to find about one hundred and fifty men daily for guard duties, while every

other available man was employed unloading supplies at the docks. So intensive were the supply problems, they had to work on Christmas Day, and had to postpone their Christmas dinner until the evening. The Battalion at this time was billetted in " spacious, if somewhat dirty " buildings, and it is noteworthy that this was the first occasion on which the majority had had a roof over their heads since leaving England.

All the companies had worked hard decorating their dining rooms, rations were good, with plenty of poultry, and a certain amount of beer and spirits was available. This Christmas Day was a welcome contrast to their previous one in the bitterly cold camp at Kirkuk.

Towards the end of the year it was found possible to take one company off working party duties for training. In the course of this training Lt.-Col. Lance received some shrapnel in his knee, and, after trying to carry on for a day or so, was evacuated to hospital. Major Brunton took over the command, which he retained until Lt.-Col. Lance rejoined the Battalion in Tripoli some ten days before the battle of Mareth.

On January 6, 1943, the Green Howards moved out from Benghazi, and settled down in bivouacs in the hills near Regima, some fifteen miles to the east. Training now began in earnest, but it was somewhat handicapped by the fact that the carrier platoons of all battalions were absent, as they had continued their journey to Sirte, when the Division had been diverted, and had not returned. The Divisional Engineers had also gone forward to assist in the work of opening up ports, and improving communications. Nevertheless, the Battalions worked very hard, practising, amongst other activities, the laying of mines, the breaching of minefields, and a very dangerous three-day course of street fighting in Benghazi. Great attention was also paid to physical fitness ; cross-country running, football and drill competitions were held, and, by February 28, when they moved forward again, they were as fit and ready to fight as they had ever been.

On March 7 the Battalions arrived at Tripoli, and moved on the next day to Zarzis, where they arrived on March 9. On March 11 Lt.-Col. Lance, with a selected party of officers and N.C.O.s, and a similar party from the 7th Battalion, visited the Headquarters of the 30th Corps, to listen to an address given by General Montgomery.

On March 12 both battalions moved up into positions facing the outposts of the Mareth line, on which naturally strong and artificially fortified position Field-Marshal Rommel was preparing to make a desperate stand.

CHAPTER EIGHT

"THE 6th AND 7th BATTALIONS AT MARETH AND AKARIT"

March—May 1943

See MAP
No. 9

THE Mareth defences, in front of which the 8th Army had now arrived, were manned by German and Italian infantry divisions, with supporting arms, but Field-Marshal Rommel was keeping the main portion of the armour of the Afrika Corps in reserve in the neighbourhood of Gabes.

General Montgomery's plan for dealing with this situation was simple and straightforward. It was for the 50th Division to make a frontal attack on the Mareth defences between the sea, and the strong point of Zarat Sud Est, some three miles inland, while the New Zealand Division and the 8th Armoured Brigade made a left hook attack round the Matmata hills, with the object of cutting off the enemy's line of retreat through Gabes.

The Mareth line stretched from the sea inland to a point beyond the main Mareth-Medenine road, about two miles south-east of the town of Mareth, but we are only concerned in this story with the sector from the sea to Zarat Sud Est. The defences of this sector were held by the Italian Young Fascist Division, and the 164th German Infantry Division. The whole defensive position was based on the Wadi Zigzaou, a natural obstacle with steep banks. At the seaward end, where it is tidal, there was a muddy stream some fifteen feet in width in the bed of the wadi. This line had been heavily fortified by the French in 1939, with concrete pill boxes, and gun emplacements, and a system of deep trenches ; these were skilfully sited so that fire of all calibres could be brought to bear on the bed of the wadi, and on the gradual slopes which led down to its edge. The main redoubts of this defensive system, as it was faced by the 50th Division were, from right to left, Ksiba Est, Ksiba Ouest, Ouerzi, Zarat Sud Est, and the Bastion. Behind this line, and between it and the village of Zarat, there were other strong points, the chief of which were Ouerzi Est and Ouerzi Ouest. The Bastion was not one of the original redoubts, but had been built by the Germans on the eastern side of the Wadi Zigzaou. It was well forward of Zarat Sud Est, and from it the approaches to the wadi in front of Ouerzi and Ksiba Ouest were dominated by enfilade fire.

ASSAULTING THE MARETH LINE.

ON GUARD OVER PRISONERS AT MARETH.

Face page 160

The Germans had also constructed an anti-tank ditch which ran along the western side of the wadi covering Ksiba Est, Ksiba Ouest and Ouerzi, and thence to Zarat Sud Est, and beyond. At Ouerzi a further anti-tank ditch had been thrown out to the south-east which, encircling the Bastion, led away to the south beyond Garact Djedla. The whole line had also been strengthened by wiring, the laying of minefields, and steepening of the banks of the wadi at certain points. This main position was covered by a line of outposts which were placed between two and three miles in front of the Wadi Zigzaou. These outposts were protected by unmarked minefields, and lay just on the western side of another wadi— the Wadi El Zeuss, which widened out into a bog as it neared the sea. Situated as they were on comparatively high ground, these outposts effectively prevented observation of the main positions from the ground, and any preliminary reconnaissance.

Such briefly was the formidable series of defences which the 50th Division was ordered to breach, and then to establish a bridgehead, through which the remainder of the 8th Army, less the New Zealand Division and the armoured brigade, could pass. The operation was, naturally, divided into two phases, firstly the capture of the outpost line, in order to gain observation and the opportunity of reconnoitring the main positions, and secondly the frontal assault of the Wadi Zigzaou.

The preliminary phase of securing the outposts was 16/19 *Mar* 43 entrusted to the 69th Brigade under Brigadier Cooke-Collis, and was successfully completed by March 18, but not without severe fighting as will be told later.

On that morning the forward troops of the 69th Brigade were within a thousand yards of the main defences, and, during the two following nights, a series of very daring reconnaissances were made right up to the Wadi Zigzaou, in the course of which many of the enemy's positions and minefields were located, and the most suitable crossing place for the main assault was marked down.

Meanwhile the 151st Brigade, which was to make this assault, had been busily training for its tremendous task in a rear area. The sector which had been selected for the main attack lay between Ksiba Ouest and Ouerzi. The chief reason for this selection was that this part of the enemy positions was not covered by any advanced main position, as at Zarat Sud Est. There was, however, one great disadvantage, in that it was dominated by the Bastion, on the left flank.

It was obvious that the Bastion would have to be eliminated before the 151st Brigade could advance across its flank. This

M

20 *Mar* 43 supremely important, in fact vital, task was entrusted to the 7th Green Howards, who went into the attack at 10.30 p.m. on the night of March 20, half an hour in advance of the 151st Brigade on their right. How successfully they fulfilled their mission, and how Lt.-Col. Seagrim, leading his forward troops, won the Victoria Cross, will be related when we take up the story of the battalions.

Meanwhile the men of Durham had moved over the ridge, and down into the wadi under a stream of shells, mortar bombs, and machine-gun fire. Keeping steadfastly on, they crossed the water, and were faced with great mounds of earth, thrown out from the anti-tank ditch in front of them. Swarming over this they fanned out to the right and left, and stormed the redoubts of Ksiba Ouest and Ouerzi with the bayonet.

21 *Mar* 43 When daylight came on March 21 the situation was that the Bastion was securely in the hands of the 7th Green Howards, who held it throughout the day in the face of fierce counter-attacks, until they handed over their positions to the Gordon Highlanders during the night of March 21/22. The two leading battalions of the Durham Light Infantry were established in Ksiba Ouest and Ouerzi, having taken a considerable number of prisoners, and inflicted heavy casualties on the enemy. Only four tanks, however, had succeeded in crossing the wadi, and, although the men of the 2nd Cheshire Regiment had gallantly manhandled their guns across the very rudimentary crossing, which had been constructed during the night, the British forces on the far side of the wadi were not strong enough to withstand any counter-attack in force.

The immediate problem facing the Divisional Commander, therefore, was to improve and strengthen the crossing place, in order that the troops who were across could be supplied and reinforced. Fortunately the enemy had been so shaken by the fury of the assault that he did not stage any counter-attack during the 21st. He did, however, concentrate a terrific curtain of fire upon the crossing place, and on the troops in the bridgehead, throughout the day, which grew in intensity as night approached. In spite of this, the working parties in the wadi worked so heroically that, during the day, forty-two more tanks crossed into the bridgehead. These, however, had so damaged the crossing in their passage, that it was found impossible to get anti-tank guns across, or to replenish the infantry with adequate supplies of ammunition.

Meanwhile plans had been made to enlarge the bridgehead during the night of March 21/22. Orders were given for the 151st Brigade to take the second line of defences at Ouerzi Est and Ouerzi Ouest, and also Zarat Sud Est on the left flank. All these attacks achieved success, but, on the morning of March 22, after hours of severe hand to hand fighting, the Durhams were exhausted, and had suffered such severe casualties that they were in no shape to repel a determined counter-attack, while the crossing place behind them was still inadequate for the supply of ammunition and reinforcements.

As daylight came on the 22nd the Royal Air Force reported a considerable concentration of artillery, tanks, and vehicles amongst the palm groves around Zarat. The enemy had clearly moved up, during the night, part of his mobile reserve from Gabes, and was preparing to launch a counter-attack. Throughout the morning all his attempts to move forward were stopped by the British guns, but then it rained. This not only caused the water in the wadi to rise, but also temporarily grounded the R.A.F. planes, and the enemy was thus enabled to move his tanks out into the open and stage his counter-attack. *22 Mar 43*

This was delivered soon after mid-day, and was supported by heavy artillery concentrations, and some aircraft. Three columns, each containing Mark IV tanks, anti-tank guns, and large numbers of infantry, advanced on Ouerzi Est, between Ouerzi Est and Ouerzi Ouest, and along a shallow valley between Ouerzi Ouest and Ouerzi. By 5 p.m. some thirty of the forty-five tanks of the 50th Royal Tank Regiment had been knocked out, and the ammunition of the infantry companies was running very low. When darkness fell the infantry had been pushed back to the anti-tank ditch, and were hanging on by the skin of their teeth. The 69th Brigade was then ordered up to support the 151st Brigade on the line of the anti-tank ditch.

Soon after midnight on March 22/23 the Divisional Commander withdrew the 151st Brigade to reorganise and refit, leaving the 5th East Yorkshires alone on the west side of the Wadi Zigzaou to hold Ksiba Ouest, as a pivot on which to renew a possible further attack later in the day or evening. The remainder of the front was held throughout the 23rd by the 6th and 7th Green Howards on the east bank of the wadi. Throughout the day the East Yorkshires were repeatedly attacked, but the enemy failed to shift them from their positions. Soon after dark they were withdrawn, and, during the night of March 23/24, the 69th Brigade was relieved by troops of the Highland Division, and the 50th Division went into reserve. *23 Mar 43* *24 Mar 43*

Meanwhile General Montgomery had seized the opportunity presented to him when Field-Marshal Rommel moved up part of his reserve to counter-attack the 50th Division on March 22. This move seriously weakened the southern flank of the enemy's positions at Gabes, and General Montgomery immediately reinforced the New Zealand Division, sending forward the 4th Indian Division to form a link between that mobile force, and the main body of the 8th Army on the coastal plain. The result of these moves was that the enemy, in order to escape complete destruction, was forced to make a hurried retreat, and, on March 28, the town of Mareth was entered by the 69th Brigade without opposition.

28 Mar 43

Such briefly is the picture of the Mareth battle in which the 50th Division, at tremendous cost, was indirectly responsible for the enemy's withdrawal one step further towards his final defeat. Had there been a fresh Brigade available on March 22, the 50th Division would, in all probability, have been able to complete its heroic assault of the Mareth line, and overrun the enemy in the area around Zarat, and, incidentally, have saved many casualties to itself.

6 and 7 Bns
12 Mar 43

We must now go back to March 12, on which date, just before midnight, the 69th Brigade took over positions from the 51st Highland Division, facing the Wadi Zeuss. The Brigade was disposed with the 5th East Yorkshires on the right, the 6th Green Howards in the centre, and the 7th Green Howards on the left. The order of battle of the two battalions at this time was :

	6th Battalion.	7th Battalion.
Commanding Officer	Lt.-Col. G. C. A. Lance, D.S.O.	Lt.-Col. D. A. Seagrim
Second in Command	Maj. F. H. Brunton, M.C.	Maj. A. W. Edgar, M.C.
Adjutant	Capt. P. J. Carr, M.C.	Lt. E. J. Moss
O.C. "A" Coy	Maj. C. H. Gardiner	Capt. R. T. C. Waters
O.C. "B" Coy	Maj. R. J. L. Jackson	Capt. I. T. R. Hay
O.C. "C" Coy	Capt. C. M. Hull,	Capt. J. B. Mansell
O.C. "D" Coy	Maj. C. R. Pullinger, M.C.	Maj. W. K. Pickering
O.C. H.Q. Coy	Capt. D. E. Spence	Capt. R. A. Mason
O.C. Carriers	Capt. P. R. Delf	Capt. W. O. Stobo
O.C. Mortars	Capt. C. H. Stephens	Capt. R. H. E. Hudson
O.C. Anti-tank platoon	Capt. S. Wheeler	Capt. V. Evans, M.C.
Intelligence Officer	Lt. J. Isaacs	Lt. A. F. Depoix (Mar. 16/17) Lt. G. V. Richley (Main actions)
Signals Officer	Lt. L. A. K. Levine	
Transport Officer	Capt. G. L. Carmichael	
Q.M.	Lt. C. McAuley	Lt. D. C. Stevenson

At this time the Battalions were organised on a three rifle company basis. In the 6th Battalion " B " Company, and in the 7th Battalion " D " Company, were the Support Companies.

During the next four days, while the Battalions prepared themselves for the attack due to take place on the night of March 16, a number of reconnaissance patrols were sent out to investigate the enemy positions, and minefield and wire defences, and also the best lines of approach across the Wadi Zeuss. The general plan for the attack was for the 6th Green Howards to assault the main enemy positions around Pt. 26, with the East Yorkshires attacking on their right, while the 7th Green Howards were to make an attack with one company on another Pt. 26 (some seven hundred yards south-east of Pt. 27), and then advance in conformity with the rest of the Brigade. The main work of reconnaissance was carried out by patrols from the 6th and 7th Green Howards, and these ranged right across the Brigade front during the three nights previous to the attack.

It is not possible to give anything more than a general account of these patrols, which, with great daring, covered the whole front, and, at times, penetrated right up to the enemy's defences. The result of their efforts contributed in no small measure to the success of the operation. The officers who led the 7th Battalion's patrols, each of them going out on several occasions, were Lts. R. N. Cockburn, D. A. Hone, G. D. Wing and E. J. Hudson. The following extracts from the reports of some of these patrols will give an idea of the hazardous nature of their work and the valuable information which they obtained.

7 *Bn* 13/16 *Mar* 43

" Lt. Hone, with three men and three sappers, went out from the Battalion H.Q. of the East Yorkshires to reconnoitre enemy positions at Pt. 26. When within some four hundred yards of Pt. 26, they encountered the bed of the wadi, which was at that point about sixty yards broad, with a five foot drop into it, and considered impassable for all vehicles. The patrol got across, and, after proceeding another two hundred yards, encountered trip wires, and found mines attached by a green cord to the bushes. Further investigations discovered a recently laid Italian minefield about eighty yards deep. The patrol then returned, having been out for five hours."

" Lt. Hudson, with three men, went out to reconnoitre the extent of an enemy minefield west of Pt. 12. When they had proceeded about a quarter of a mile they came upon a minefield which extended for two hundred and fifty yards, and consisted of four rows of B4 and anti-personnel mines to a depth of about twenty yards. This minefield thinned out towards the road, and was laid with trip wires fixed to posts about one foot in height. The patrol reported that a machine-gun was firing down the road at Pt. 12 at fairly frequent intervals."

" Lt. Wing took a patrol of " B " Company out from Pt. 20, and worked his way up the Wadi Zeuss in a northerly direction, finding slit trenches in the bed of the wadi. They soon came under fire, but continued to advance some two hundred yards north east, only to be fired upon whenever they attempted to cross. After having searched for more than two hours for a crossing place, they returned to Pt. 20, reporting that the wadi banks in that area were some fifteen to twenty feet in height, and that there was a stream of water in the bed, which was twenty yards across."

" Lt. Cockburn, with three men and three sappers, went out from the Battalion H.Q. of the East Yorkshires to recon-noitre enemy positions north of Pt. 26. After covering about a mile they crossed the wadi at a ford, which was wet and muddy. On the other side the going was firmer, and, getting quite close to the enemy's lines, they were able to take a bearing on a machine-gun, which was firing on a fixed line. On their way back they located a minefield bounding the wadi, with trip wires to some B4 mines on the edge of the track. The sappers disarmed these, and then replaced them. The patrol had, during these operations, approached within a hundred yards of the enemy and stayed there for half an hour. They could hear Italian being spoken, and intensive digging in progress."

6 *Bn*
13/16 *Mar* 43

A most successful series of patrols was led by Lt. R. F. B. Evans, of the 6th Battalion, during the three nights of March 13/16. These culminated, on the night of March 16/17, in the successful capture of an enemy position in front of the 5th East Yorkshires, which was instrumental in enabling that Battalion to secure its objectives practically unscathed. This had an important bearing on later events, when the 69th Brigade went over the Wadi Zigzaou on the night of March 22/23. At that vital moment in the battle both the Green Howard Battalions had been seriously reduced in numbers after their attacks on the Wadi Zeuss outposts, and the 7th Battalion's attack on the Bastion, and it was fortunate that the 5th East Yorkshires were comparatively at full strength, and able to play the gallant and important part which they did in holding on in Ksiba Ouest all through March 23.

Lt. Evans' patrol was formed of men from " C " Company, all volunteers, and consisted of fourteen men in addition to himself, with Sgt. P. C. Bawcombe as second in command. In his preliminary reconnaissances he did not take the full patrol out, but, in the final assault on the night of March 16/17, when he went out in full strength, he was supported by a second patrol from " A " Company, commanded by Lt. W. D. Jones. So successful was Lt. Evans' party that Lt. Jones' patrol was not used until after the objective had been taken, when it came up in case of a quick counter-attack before the East Yorkshires passed through.

On March 13 Lt. Evans, together with Sgt. Bawcombe, L/Sgt. J. Pearson, L/Sgt. G. Moore, L/Sgt. C. Webb, Pte. H. Yates and Pte. F. E. Breckon, went off to the forward trenches of the East Yorkshires, where they established themselves for the next three nights, being joined by the remainder of the patrol on March 16. The feature which it was their duty to reconnoitre, and finally assault, lay some two thousand yards ahead, across a flat salt marsh with some low bush and scrub at scattered intervals. It was about two hundred yards in length, with a small re-entrant in the centre. After spending the first day scanning the ground through field-glasses, the small party moved out as soon as it was dark, accompanied by two sappers to deal with mines. The moon was rising as they neared their objective, and they moved forward very cautiously until they heard voices. They then lay still for some considerable time watching figures moving over the hillside, and listening to pickets being driven into the ground. After a while Lt. Evans signalled that he was going forward alone with L/Sgt. Pearson, and, after two hours had elapsed, Sgt. Bawcombe led back the remainder of the patrol to the defence lines. There he found Lt. Evans, who had got back only a few minutes previously. L/Sgt. Pearson was missing, and it was discovered later, when the position was taken, that he had lost himself, and fallen into the hands of the enemy. On the following night the party went out again with the dual object of gaining more information and of searching for L/Sgt. Pearson. During his solitary patrol on the previous night Lt. Evans had located a single strand of barbed wire, some fifty yards from the nearest enemy position, and leading away to the north-east. A further investigation of this wire was made on the second night, and it was followed to a point at which it ended. It was presumed that this wire marked a minefield running parallel to the enemy's position, and, as the ground at this point was broken, and ideal as a starting point for an attack, it was decided that on the night of March 16/17 the main patrol should make its assault from this point, out-flanking the enemy's position from the north-east.

At 8 p.m. on the night of March 16 Lt. Evans and Lt. Jones, with their patrols of fourteen men each, set off for their starting point where the wire ended. Passing through a line of twelve Vickers machine-guns, whose crews wished them good luck, and promised to give the enemy hell, they moved slowly and silently across the salt marsh, and arrived at their position soon after 9 p.m. At 9.30 p.m. the artillery and machine-gun barrage came down, and soon the whole objective was screened by the dust and smoke of exploding shells and the strike of bullets. Verey lights were going up from the enemy lines every half minute, and the signal " Prepare to move " was circulated. As soon as the guns ceased firing, Lt. Evans' party rushed forward, leaving Lt. Jones with his men, and the accompanying sappers, at the starting point. So quickly did they arrive amongst the enemy, there was practically no resistance. Six prisoners were taken in the first dugout which they came to, and, in a very short space of time, one officer and twenty-three prisoners were in the hands of the Green Howards. Within half an hour the leading Company of the East Yorkshires came up, and the Green Howards began to withdraw. As they went back they found that there was a minefield some three hundred yards in depth, which had been marked by the strand of wire on the enemy side. How they had escaped being blown up on their previous recon-naissances was a miracle. The engineers had, however, by this time, taped a line through the minefield, and they pro-ceeded to shepherd their prisoners along the tapes. Unluckily someone stepped over the tape at one point and there was a terrific explosion. The engineers came up with mine detectors, and cleared an area round them, uncovering a quantity of Teller and " S " mines. In this tragic accident Ptes. Goodwill and Duckworth were killed, and L/Sgts. Moore and Webb and Ptes. J. Morse, Breckon and Yates were wounded, while, of Lt. Jones' party, one man was killed and three men were wounded. In the darkness and confusion it was four hours before all the injured could be removed from the minefield, and taken back to the Regimental Aid Post.

This was a most disappointing finish to a brilliantly planned and successfully executed operation, for the planning of which, and for his courage and leadership, Lt. Evans was awarded the Military Cross.

6 and 7 Bns   By the time that the attack was due to be launched,
16 Mar 43 namely at 9.30 p.m. on March 16, the Brigade Staff and
Commanding Officers had a fairly complete picture of the

enemy's dispositions and defences. It was decided that, since the 7th Battalion patrols had so familiarised themselves with the ground, two strong fighting patrols, named " thug patrols ", from the 7th Battalion, should precede the leading companies of the 6th Battalion in its assault.

These two " thug patrols " were commanded by Lts. Cockburn and Hone, and they started moving forward towards the edge of the minefields at 8.15 p.m., in front of " A " and " B " Companies of the 6th Battalion. At 9.30 p.m. the artillery barrage came down, and parties of engineers began to clear gaps in the minefields, closely followed by the thug patrols.

The attack started badly, as the enemy opposition was stronger than had been anticipated. Both Lt. Cockburn and Lt. Hone were wounded in the initial assault, but their men carried on with the utmost bravery, and, although suffering very heavy casualties, the survivors fought their way through to the objective, in company with " A " and " B " Companies.

Both Lt. Cockburn and Lt. Hone were awarded the Military Cross for their personal courage and leadership, whilst Sgt. H. J. Blackmore and L/Sgt. N. Collins won the Distinguished Conduct Medal, and Cpl. R. Cooper, Cpl. W. H. Bell and Pte. C. Hare were awarded the Military Medal. Such a high percentage of awards for gallantry to those who took part in these fighting patrols is a gauge of the intensity of the battle, and a brief record of the deeds, for which they were given, will serve to show how well deserved they were.

Lt. Cockburn, as he entered the field of anti-personnel mines, with great deliberation and heedless of the enemy's heavy fire, led his men, picking up the mines as he went along, thereby making a safe passage for those who followed him. When he reached the far edge of the minefield he was confronted by a machine-gun firing at him from a range of thirty yards. Coolly and deliberately he opened fire on the crew with his revolver, but a bullet from the machine-gun hit his right hand, knocking the revolver out of it. With great presence of mind, and regardless of his wound, he picked up the revolver with his left hand, and continued to fire. He killed most of the crew, and the remainder fled in confusion.

Sgt. Blackmore, who was a platoon sergeant, proved, by his coolness in the face of very heavy fire, an inspiration to all his men. The deliberate and cheerful manner in which he moved about put fresh heart into the patrol, when they were suffering severe casualties. He was invaluable to his commander in helping to keep the patrol together, and, when the latter was wounded, he unhesitatingly assumed command. Personally leading his men in the final assault and completely disregarding his own safety, he charged the enemy with all the dash and determination of a real leader, firing his tommy-gun continuously, and inflicting heavy casualties upon the enemy.

L/Sgt. Collins, despite intense enemy fire from a flank, led his command with supreme courage and calmness. Firing his tommy-gun he personally charged an enemy machine-gun, killing or capturing the whole of the crew. Later he assaulted another post, single handed, and, throwing grenades, captured the post. The great bravery and initiative of L/Sgt. Collins so inspired those who followed him, that he was largely responsible for the capture of the position.

Cpl. Cooper displayed great coolness in the early stages of the attack in neutralising many mines and booby traps, in the face of heavy machine-gun and mortar fire. In the final assault he led his section with the greatest dash and gallantry, firing from the hip, and inflicting heavy casualties upon the enemy. Although he was wounded, Cpl. Cooper refused to leave the battlefield until the operation had been brought to a successful conclusion.

Cpl. Bell led his section throughout with great dash and eagerness. There were no bounds to his energy, and, paying no heed to the machine-gun bullets and mortar bombs, he time and again rallied his men, finally leading them into the assault, killing many of the enemy and putting the remainder to flight. On his own initiative he outflanked an enemy machine-gun post which was holding up the main portion of the patrol, and, by his quick appreciation of the situation and his own gallantry, contributed largely to the success of the patrol.

Pte. Hare was pacer to one of the patrols. In the face of intense small arms fire he charged an enemy post single handed with the bayonet, killing some of the enemy and capturing one prisoner. By this courageous action he saved the patrol from being attacked from the rear. Later on Pte. Hare was badly wounded by a shrapnel mine, and, although in great pain, he refused immediate assistance, ordering those who attended him to look after others first. When he was finally evacuated, he had suffered considerably from exposure, but had set a wonderful example of devotion to duty and to his comrades.

6 *Bn*
16 *Mar* 43   When it was found that the " thug patrols " had run into such strong opposition, and would obviously be unable to capture the objectives unaided, as had been somewhat

optimistically expected, " A " and " B " Companies, 6th Green Howards, were committed to battle.

During the interval of twenty minutes, when the artillery barrage was coming down in front of them, both these companies, and also " C " Company and Battalion Advanced Headquarters, came under heavy counter fire from the enemy's guns and mortars, and several casualties were sustained. At 9.50 p.m. the barrage lifted and the companies advanced in the face of considerable small arms and mortar fire. No. 10 platoon of " B " Company joined up with the " thug patrols " and pushed on through the gap in the minefield towards Pt. 26, the objective. No. 11 platoon was held up near the gap, but No. 12 platoon passed through it and gained its objective. The company then proceeded to consolidate on and around Pt. 26. Many Italians were killed and taken prisoner, but " B " Company had paid a heavy price. Lt. Smith and Lt. L. H. Peers had been killed, and there had been forty casualties among the other ranks.

Meanwhile " A " Company on the right, led by No. 7 platoon and Company Headquarters, and followed by No. 8 platoon, passed through their gap in the minefield soon after 10 p.m. The sapper party attached to the company suffered many casualties in its attempts to make a gap, as, on this sector, there were a great many scattered mines. Major Gardiner was wounded early on by one of these and Capt. Metcalfe assumed command. Soon after midnight " A " Company was established on a feature north of and slightly to the rear of Pt. 26. In addition to Major Gardiner " A " Company suffered forty other casualties in this advance.

At dawn the company was moved across to join " B " Company on Pt. 26.

Sgt. L. Blackham of " A " Company, for his courage, dash, and leadership, during this attack was awarded the Distinguished Conduct Medal. In the early stages he gave the sappers considerable personal assistance in the dangerous work of lifting the mines. Soon after getting clear of the minefield he was wounded, and lost one finger, but continued to organise his platoon despite intense machine-gun and mortar fire. When a mortar bomb wounded all the men with him at platoon headquarters, he picked up an anti-tank rifle, and charged an enemy machine-gun post single handed. Having captured this post, he assaulted another post with grenades causing its surviving occupants to surrender.

Sgt. J. Clayton, who was the Battalion Intelligence Sergeant, showed great coolness and devotion to duty. During the assault he guided " A " Company through heavy mine-fields, under intense artillery, mortar and machine-gun fire. Later, on the 22/23rd, Sgt. Clayton went out alone, and, under heavy fire, reconnoitred enemy positions in the Wadi Zigzaou. For his exceptionable activities in this battle, and a similar display of courage a fortnight later at Akarit, Sgt. Clayton was awarded the Military Medal.

Sgt. Clayton, at the conclusion of this campaign, after a course of training, was given a commission, and later served as Intelligence Officer with the 7th Battalion in Sicily.

Pte. F. W. Vickers, a No. 1 bren gunner, of " B " Company, behaved with great gallantry and was awarded the Military Medal. Most of his section had been wounded by a mortar bomb, and the enemy fire was intense. Pte. Vickers, on his own initiative, worked his way around the flank of a strong machine-gun post, and charged it by himself, killing or wounding most of the crew and capturing one prisoner. By this action the remainder of his platoon were enabled to capture the position. His courage and dash proved a great inspiration to his comrades.

7 *Bn*
16/17 *Mar*43 While the 6th Battalion was making this successful but costly attack on the main outpost positions around Pt. 26, the 7th Battalion launched an attack with one company on Pt. 26, on the left flank. At 9.25 p.m. " A " Company formed up behind Pt. 12, and, following the artillery barrage from 9.30 to 9.50, advanced towards Pt. 26. In this advance Capt. Waters was wounded, and Lt. W. H. Coles took command of the company. By 10.30 " A " Company reported that it was on Pt. 26 and consolidating.

Lt. G. W. Nosotti then took out a patrol, whose task it was to cover a party of sappers who were lifting mines from the road, which ran from west to east between Pt. 26 and Pt. 27. Very heavy shelling delayed this work considerably, and it was not completed until 4 a.m. on the 17th. Lt. Nosotti then started to return to Pt. 12, but met Capt. Mansell, who was on his way up to Pt. 27. He was then given fresh orders to take out a reconnaissance patrol to try to make contact with the enemy, but after an hour and a half he returned to Pt. 27, without having got in touch.

In the advance of " A " Company, Pte. T. G. Patterson, who was in charge of the stretcher bearers, showed great calmness and contempt for danger. He frequently entered anti-personnel minefields to rescue the wounded, and tended them under intense fire. There can be no doubt that, as a result of his devotion to duty, many lives were saved. He was awarded the Military Medal.

As soon as " A " Company had started its attack, Lt.-Col. Seagrim brought up his command post to Pt. 12. On receiving a report from " A " Company that no contact had been made with the 6th Green Howards on the right, he called up Capt. Mansell, and ordered him to take " C " Company across the road, and occupy Pt. 27. This order emanated from Brigadier Cooke-Collis, who, when the position was still somewhat obscure, and realising that the 6th Battalion was having a tough battle and making slow progress, decided to assist it by tackling Pt. 27, from the left flank, with the 7th Battalion. It was still dark when Capt. Mansell set forth, but, soon after first light, he arrived at Pt. 27, and occupied positions there.

Meanwhile, to return to the 6th Battalion, soon after midnight on March 16/17 Lt.-Col. Lance had come up to Pt. 26, and, having given orders regarding the dispositions of " A " and " B " Companies, and ordered up the support groups, he sent Capt. Hull forward with " C " Company to make his way to Pt. 27, and safeguard his left flank, being unaware, at this juncture, that the 7th Battalion now included Pt. 27 in its objective. When " C " Company started to move forward it was still dark, but, when day broke, they found themselves in thick smoke, which was drifting across the front from the east and which lasted for some time. The position at which they had arrived was a series of entrenchments, probably an Italian headquarters, and three prisoners were taken. When the visibility improved Capt. Hull found that his range of view extended well over the whole front, and decided to stay where he was for the time being. As his wireless set had broken down Capt. Hull went back to report his position personally to Lt.-Col. Lance. After consultation, they both went up to Pt. 27 to visit Capt. Mansell, and the decision was then taken to move Capt. Hull's Company. Later in the day " C " Company, 6th Green Howards, took over from " C " Company, 7th Green Howards, on Pt. 27, and Capt. Mansell took his company back to join the remainder of the Battalion, just behind the Wadi Zeuss.

6 Bn
17 Mar 43

At about mid-day on March 18 the 7th Battalion marched to new positions near Chet Meskine, some two thousand yards in front of the main Mareth defences. During the 17th Lt. Depoix went over a Teller mine in his jeep. He was lucky to escape being killed, but was badly concussed and had to be evacuated. Lt. Richley took over the duties of Intelligence Officer.

7 Bn
17/18 Mar 43

Throughout the night of March 16/17, and the following day, the staff of the 6th Battalion Regimental Aid Post worked unceasingly, dealing not only with their own casualties, but also with those of the 7th Battalion patrols. Sgt. Galbraith,

6 Bn
17/19 Mar 43

in particular, was untiring in his efforts to alleviate the suffering of his comrades.

The 6th Battalion remained in its positions on Pts. 26 and 27 throughout the 17th and 18th, being sporadically shelled, and was relieved by the 9th Gurkha Regiment soon after midnight on March 19. It then marched to new positions on the left flank of the 7th Battalion near Chet Meskine.

And so, on March 18, the 69th Brigade had completed its task of driving in the outposts with complete success, and the stage was set for the final assault of the Mareth Line. The ridge which overlooked the Wadi Zigzaou was in its hands, and, for the first time, it was possible for reconnaissances to be made of the enemy's main positions. Time was short, and the nights of the 18/19th and 19/20th were ones of great activity. Patrols from the 151st Brigade came forward from the rear, and examined the bed of the wadi, reconnoitred the anti-tank ditch, and located enemy minefields.

7 Bn
19/21 Mar 43   In front of the 7th Green Howards, Lts. Nosotti and Wing took out patrols on the two nights previous to the attack on the Bastion, making very thorough reconnaissances of the ground in front of that section of the anti-tank ditch which the Battalion was going to assault on the night of March 20/21.

Lt. Nosotti's own description of his adventures on the nights of March 19/20 and 20/21 give a clear picture of the hazards which he and his men overcame, and of the courage, endurance and determination which they displayed.

"The patrol which I took out on March 19/20 consisted of two members of my platoon and two sappers, equipped with a Polish mine detector. My orders were to discover if mine laying was taking place and to see if a copse, and another position on our side of the anti-tank ditch, were occupied. We went out at 8 p.m. and returned at about 4 a.m. next morning, having located a new but unfinished minefield of Italian " box mines ", and discovered that the copse was not occupied by the enemy. At one point I left the patrol, and went forward to examine a position. I found myself on the edge of the anti-tank ditch, and rolled down into it. I was able to take some rough measurements. I could see the enemy against the skyline, and could hear a lot of talking and the noise of transport moving behind their lines. Torrential rain made it very difficult to see anything clearly, and also put the mine detector out of action. Cpl. Surtees, however, said that he could locate the mines without the detector, and this he proceeded to do, the remainder of the patrol following him in single file.

On the night of the 20/21st I was given permission to choose any men I liked from " C " Company for the ' thug patrol '. I took them all from my own platoon, and also my platoon sergeant, Sgt. Crooks. We were accompanied by sappers who were equipped with detectors, and angle irons and tapes, with which to mark the cleared path. We also carried scaling ladders, with which to get over the anti-tank ditch.

Our task was to move up as far as possible before the artillery barrage began, and then to follow it at about two hundred yards distance. We were to clear a path through the minefield, and wipe out any machine-gun posts, which we might encounter.

We moved forward at 10.15 p.m., some five hundred yards ahead of the Battalion, but, owing to the very heavy fire, we could not advance very far until we had the cover of the barrage. Once that had come down we were able to clear a path and, having scaled the anti-tank ditch, we moved through the enemy ground unmolested, until I wheeled the patrol to the left. We then came up against an enemy machine-gun post, which we wiped out. No prisoners were taken.

Having secured our first objective, I decided to move on to another position from which more machine-guns were holding up the advance of the battalion. Passing through another minefield, we attacked the flank of this position, and captured between thirty and forty Germans and Italians. There was still one machine-gun firing, and, without waiting for orders, Cpl. H. E. Bevan went round on the flank, and wiped it out. This was a very gallant performance, and deserved the highest praise. Unfortunately Cpl. Bevan was killed later in the battle.

When the fighting at this point had died down, I took my patrol back to where Lt.-Col. Seagrim was directing the Battalion. I and my patrol then went forward again with " A " Company, and helped it to secure its objective. In this engagement we killed many of the enemy with grenades and automatic fire, and only suffered one casualty, Cpl. H. Woodall being wounded by a grenade splinter."

At 10.15 p.m. on March 20 the 7th Green Howards *7 Bn* moved up to their start line, some five hundred yards from *20 Mar* 43 the anti-tank ditch. The Battalion advanced in three waves, with " B " Company, Major Hay, leading, followed by " C " Company, Capt. Mansell, and " A " Company, Lt. Coles. During this advance from their forming up positions to the start line, they came under very heavy shell fire, and a certain number of casualties were sustained.

At 10.30 p.m. the assault began, preceded by " thug patrols " under Lt. Nosotti and Lt. Wing, and a party of sappers, whose task it was to lift the mines and lay tapes to guide the companies who were following. Lt.-Col. Seagrim's plan was for " B " Company, as soon as it had got across the ditch, to proceed straight through the enemy's positions within the Bastion towards the Wadi Zigzaou. " C " Company, once across the ditch, was to wheel to the left, followed by " A " Company, and the latter company was finally to pass through " C " Company, and establish itself on the Battalion's left flank. When the companies arrived in the ditch they found scaling ladders already set up by the leading sections, and, although no enemy had been met as yet, the mortar and shell fire, which was being brought to bear on the ditch, was terrific. In the midst of this tornado of fire, at the centre of the crossing point, Lt.-Col. Seagrim stood calmly waving on his men, and, by his own enthusiasm and coolness, inspiring them for the grim work which lay ahead. " B " Company crossed the ditch first, and disappeared into the labyrinth of trenches and emplacements of the Bastion. The leading platoon of " C " Company, commanded by Lt. J. P. L. Haslam, as it left the scaling ladders, was met by a withering fire, and suffered severe casualties, Lt. Haslam being amongst those killed.

Capt. Mansell, who was at the head of his men to lead them in their left wheel, was then temporarily knocked out by a shell splinter, and " C " Company was for the moment in a state of some confusion. At this juncture Lt.-Col. Seagrim took charge, and, with " C " Company Headquarters and elements of Lt. Nosotti's " thug party ", rushed the enemy's positions. The deeds which Lt.-Col. Seagrim performed that night have become legendary, and no one who was there will forget the sight of their commanding officer charging ahead of them, tackling machine-gun posts single handed with his revolver, completely ignoring the hail of fire, and shouting, " Come on, Green Howards, we must not let the New Zealanders down ! " He was never to know that he won the Victoria Cross for that night's work, as he died of wounds at Akarit two weeks later, but, such was his modesty and affection for his Battalion and Regiment, the greatest pleasure which he would have got from the knowledge of the award, would surely have been that he had added further glory to the record of the Green Howards. The full story of his actions are given in the following citation, which accompanied the award.

" On the night of the 20/21st March, 1943, the task of a battalion of the Green Howards was to attack and capture

ENTERING LETOJANNI GALLODORO.

ADVANCING TOWARDS TAORMINA.

an important feature on the left flank of the main attack on the Mareth Line. The defence of this feature was very strong and it was protected by an anti-tank ditch twelve feet wide and eight feet deep with minefields on both sides. It formed a new part of the main defences of the Mareth Line and the successful capture of this feature was vital to the success of the main attack.

From the time the attack was launched the battalion was subjected to the most intense fire from artillery, machine-guns and mortars, and it appeared more than probable that the battalion would be held up, entailing failure of the main attack.

Realising the seriousness of the situation, Lt.-Col. Seagrim placed himself at the head of his battalion, which was at the time suffering heavy casualties, and led it through the hail of fire. He personally helped the team which was placing the scaling ladder over the anti-tank ditch and was himself the first to cross it. He led the assault firing his pistol, throwing grenades, and personally assaulting two machine-gun posts which were holding up the advance of one of his companies. It is estimated that in this phase he killed or captured twenty Germans. This display of leadership and personal courage led directly to the capture of the objective. When dawn broke the battalion was firmly established on the position, which was of obvious importance to the enemy who immediately made every effort to regain it. Every post was mortared and machine-gunned unmercifully and movement became practically impossible, but Lt.-Col. Seagrim was quite undeterred. He moved from post to post organising and directing the fire until the attackers were wiped out to a man.

By his valour, disregard for personal safety and out-standing example, he so inspired his men that the battalion successfully took and held its objective, thereby allowing the attack to proceed."

Before following the companies into the defences of the Bastion, some account must be given of the great dash and courage of the " thug parties ", who cleared the minefields and made the first bridgehead across the anti-tank ditch, thus paving the way for the assault on the main defences. It must be remembered that all through the preliminary advance they were subjected to very heavy shell and mortar fire, and then took the first shock of the enemy's automatic and small arms fire.

Lts. Nosotti and Wing both received the Military Cross, while Sgt. J. Yarrow and Sgt. C. Craddock received the Distinguished Conduct Medal and Military Medal respectively.

N

Lt. Nosotti led the assault on the enemy posts covering the forward obstacles, and silenced them with his own grenades. Still under heavy fire from positions further on, he organised the clearing of gaps in the minefield with great speed and efficiency. Then, acting on his own initiative, he led his patrol off to a flank, and, using grenades at close range, put out of action a machine-gun post which was enfilading the remainder of the battalion, and holding up its advance. His rapid appreciation of situations as they arose, and the vigour with which he led his men to deal with them, were largely responsible for the success of the entire operation. Throughout the whole action, including the enemy's counter-attack the next day, Lt. Nosotti displayed the most conspicuous gallantry, and his coolness and cheerfulness were an inspiration to all around him.

The fearless leadership of Lt. Wing enabled his patrol to make a gap in the minefield, and establish a bridgehead across the ditch in the face of a hail of machine-gun and shell fire. Once the ditch was crossed the patrol ran into a smoke screen, which added to the confusion of the darkness, and caused the patrol to split into two parties. Lt. Wing led his party through wire and mines, and knocked out a machine-gun and mortar position which was holding up the main advance. Later in the day Lt. Wing rescued a wounded man from a blazing vehicle, and, although he was wounded himself, succeeded in bringing him back to safety.

Sgt. Yarrow, whose initial task was to cover a party of sappers working on the minefield, on being informed that the mine detector had failed to work, immediately went forward, and took on the hazardous job of detecting the mines, since he knew that the leading company was close behind and that any delay would imperil the operation. When his patrol got broken up in the smoke screen, which the enemy had put down, Sgt. Yarrow collected a handful of men and charged and captured an enemy mortar post. He then went on, and knocked out a machine-gun. Finally he led his men on to the objective, and then rejoined his company, with which he fought for the remainder of the action, proving by his complete disregard for his own safety, a great source of inspiration to his men.

Sgt. Craddock, whose platoon was, at the beginning, advancing very cautiously amongst the numerous mines and booby traps, moved about amongst his men with the greatest coolness, helping each member in turn. He was tireless in his efforts to hearten and cheer his men. Towards the end of the advance his patrol commander was wounded, and Sgt.

Craddock took over command. He displayed a very high standard of leadership, reorganising his patrol, and directing the evacuation of casualties. His personal courage and cheerful devotion to duty played a large part in the ultimate success of the attack.

During the next few hours, in the darkness of the night, which was intensified by smoke, and with all hell let loose, the fighting was necessarily of a very confused nature, entailing a great deal of hand to hand fighting, as the companies worked their way through the labyrinth of trenches and defence works, of which the Bastion was composed. Many deeds of valour were performed unseen, but the story of those who received recognition for their bravery is equally applicable to many others who died, or fought their battles alone.

Capt. Mansell was awarded the Military Cross for the unsurpassable dash and determination with which he led his company, both on this occasion, and, as will be related, a fortnight later at Akarit. Recovering from the blow which had knocked him out in the anti-tank ditch, Capt. Mansell was soon back at the head of his men, working his way along the enemy trenches, and clearing the way with hand grenades.

Lt. G. V. Richley, who had recently taken over the duties of Intelligence Officer, was the first casualty in this attack, as he was slightly wounded by a shell splinter, when laying out the start line. He then accompanied Lt.-Col. Seagrim into the battle, and displayed the greatest courage and initiative in directing individual platoons on to their objectives. He personally knocked out one enemy machine-gun post single handed. During March 21, when the enemy delivered a strong counter attack on the Battalion, he organised a section of light machine-guns to fire across the enemy's line of advance. Under very heavy shell fire he kept his three guns in action, causing many casualties to the enemy, and, after an hour or so, forcing them to withdraw. Lt. Richley's personal bravery and initiative played an important part both in the capture and holding of the Bastion, and he was awarded the Military Cross.

C.S.M. M. McLoughlin of " B " Company was an outstanding figure of courage and inspiration. In the early stages of the advance, while the company was waiting for the minefield to be cleared, and shells and mortar bombs were dropping all round them, C.S.M. McLoughlin was to be seen moving here and there amongst his men, rallying them, and imbuing them with his own indomitable spirit. Later, when they ran into a storm of machine-gun fire, he shepherded his party through on to the objective, and urged them on to greater effort. All through the 21st, when, as daylight came, they found themselves in a position exposed to heavy shelling and machine-gun fire, he continued to inspire all around him with cheerfulness and confidence. He was awarded the Distinguished Conduct Medal.

L/Cpl. A. Dixon, of " C " Company, displayed great courage and initiative throughout the battle. At one period, when an enemy machine-gun post opened fire suddenly at close range, L/Cpl. Dixon without hesitation, worked his way round to the back of the position, and, dropping a grenade into the gun pit, silenced the gun. Throughout the attack he preceded the signallers to cut wires and look out for mines, and, when the Battalion was consolidating its gains, L/Cpl. Dixon, by carrying many messages and leading sections to new positions, materially assisted in the Battalion's reorganisation. He was awarded the Military Medal.

7 *Bn*   When daylight came, the Bastion was firmly in the hands
21 *Mar* 43 of the Green Howards. " B " Company, driving those of the enemy who survived, across the Wadi Zigzaou, had wheeled to the left, and taken up exposed positions between " C " Company, who had come through on the left, and the wadi. " A " Company, having passed through " C " Company, was consolidating on the somewhat higher ground on the left flank of the Battalion and facing south-west. Almost without a pause, the companies were subjected to heavy shell and mortar bombardment, and, at about 8 a.m., the enemy launched a counter-attack mainly against " A " Company.

During the day, a direct hit from a mortar bomb killed Ptes. Barwick, Payne, Rogers and Dawson, all belonging to Lt. Nosotti's platoon of " C " Company. When the counter-attack was launched, R.S.M. Jaye, Sgt. Blackmore and Cpl. Bevan were manning two captured spandaus. Lt. Nosotti was acting as loader to Cpl. Bevan, and went off to get some more ammunition. When he returned two minutes later he found that all three had been shot by a sniper from the rear. R.S.M. Jaye was dead, Sgt. Blackmore had been hit in the neck and Cpl. Bevan in the back. The latter died later in the day. Cpl. J. M. Carver, of " C " Company, was also killed by a bullet through the head.

This attack was eventually driven off, and the enemy suffered heavy casualties.

Throughout the 21st the Battalion was virtually imprisoned in the Bastion, and cut off from outside communication, as wireless services had broken down. Capt. W. O. Stobo, who was in command of the carriers, made a very gallant attempt to reach the Battalion by crossing the anti-tank ditch in his carrier. On his first attempt his carrier was knocked out, but, nothing daunted, he mounted another carrier, and, passing through heavy fire, he finally penetrated into the Bastion.

For the remainder of the day, the enemy contented himself with shelling and mortaring, which was almost continuous, and at midnight the Battalion was relieved by the Gordon Highlanders.

The withdrawal from the Bastion was not easy, as the whole position, and particularly the anti-tank ditch, was under heavy fire. As the Green Howards had been led in, so they were led out again by Lt. Nosotti, who reconnoitred a crossing place over the anti-tank ditch, across which they passed in single file, crawling on their hands and knees for about fifty yards. Once again, in the words of one who was there : " Lt.-Col. Seagrim was very cheerful during this somewhat trying withdrawal and, by his encouraging presence, helped his exhausted men to make a final effort."

Casualties had been heavy and, in addition to those already mentioned, included Lt. Moss, the adjutant, who was killed, and Capt. G. W. Thrift and C.S.M. A. R. Rayner both of " C " Company, wounded.

With so many wounded being brought back, Capt. W. Marsden, R.A.M.C., and his small staff at the Regimental Aid Post, were kept working without a pause throughout the battle, under conditions of great strain, as they were under continual shell fire. Cpl. J. A. Muir, one of the staff, displayed a particularly high standard of courage, and devotion to duty, for which he was awarded the Military Medal. Throughout a period of three days Cpl. Muir never allowed the shell fire to interfere with his quick, methodical and accurate treatment of casualties, and was always the first to dash out from cover to bring in those who were wounded, and who fell in the immediate vicinity of his position.

By 3 a.m. on March 22 the Battalion was back in the positions from which it had started on the 20th ; but was given little respite, as, at four o'clock in the afternoon, it was rushed forward in reserve to positions within a few hundred yards of the Wadi Zigzaou. *7 Bn 22/23 Mar 43*

This proved to be a very unhealthy spot when the tanks of the 7th Armoured Division moved into the area. The enemy reacted violently to their presence, and put down a heavy concentration of shell fire. Lt. L. W. Smith and his runner were buried by a shell which landed near to their trench, and were only extricated in the nick of time. Although suffering from shock and concussion, Lt. Smith refused to be evacuated.

He remained with the Battalion until he was killed in Sicily, when in command of the anti-tank platoon.

Orders were now received for a new attack across the Wadi Zigzaou, but these were cancelled later in the evening, and the Battalion remained stationary, in a centre of enemy shell fire, until it was relieved just before midnight on March 23, by the Black Watch, and moved back to Bou Ghara.

6 *Bn*
20/21 *Mar* 43

Returning to the 6th Battalion, which on March 19 had moved up to positions near Chet Meskine, there is little to relate about its activities on March 20, beyond the fact that orders were received during the afternoon for the Battalion to make an attack, in conjunction with the 50th Royal Tank Regiment, to consolidate any gains made during the night by the 151st Brigade. These orders were, however, cancelled later, and the Battalion remained where it was until the late afternoon of March 22. Throughout this time its positions were being shelled, with an increasing ferocity as the 151st Brigade progressed across the Wadi, and the enemy's counter-attack developed.

6 *Bn*
22 *Mar* 43

At about 5 p.m. the Battalion moved forward and occupied positions astride the track leading to the crossing place in the Wadi Zigzaou. From the moment when it arrived in these positions the Battalion came under heavy artillery and machine-gun fire. It was dark and raining slightly when Lt.-Col. Lance called together his Company Commanders and gave out his orders for an attack to recapture the positions which had been lost by the 151st Brigade during the afternoon. During this period of waiting Lt. P. F. B. Evans, M.C., was badly wounded in the chest by a machine-gun bullet.

The information available at this time was that the Durham Light Infantry battalions were still holding positions well forward of the anti-tank ditch. Lt.-Col. Lance therefore gave orders to the effect that the anti-tank ditch itself would be used as the Battalion's forming up line, and that the start line for the attack would be some three hundred yards in front.

At about 11 p.m. the Battalion moved down to the crossing-place in single file, led by " C " Company, Capt. Hull. As they moved forward along the track they met a steady stream of wounded men from the 151st Brigade, none of whom seemed to have any clear idea of what was happening in front. As the Green Howards approached the ditch they met a scene of great devastation. Knocked out tanks and burnt out vehicles littered the area, and, of a palm tree grove beside the track, all that remained were a few blasted stumps. The ditch itself was about ten feet deep, and only wide enough at the bottom for one man to walk in single file. The far bank rose in an almost sheer slope.

No. 14 platoon of " C " Company, commanded by Sgt. Bawcombe, since Lt. Evans had been wounded, led the Battalion into the ditch, its task being to proceed straight along the ditch, and make contact with the 5th East Yorkshires on the right.

As the remainder of the Battalion was entering the ditch, " C " Company was attacked by a German patrol on top of the far bank. Lt. E. S. Corbett, commanding No. 13 platoon, was killed instantly, and several of his men were wounded, including L/Cpl. Mills, who, although badly hurt, refused to go back until ordered to do so by his Company Commander.

Led by C.S.M. W. Freeman, Capt. Hull, and Lt.-Col. Lance, the men of " C " Company clambered up the slippery clay bank, and attacked the German patrol. C.S.M. Freeman accounted for three spandau gunners with his rifle, while three grenade throwers, who were lying a few yards away on the very edge of the embankment, were thrown bodily into the ditch into the midst of some very bewildered men of the Battalion who were wondering what was happening.

Meanwhile two sections of Sgt. Bawcombe's platoon, commanded by L/Sgt. A. Longstaff and L/Cpl. Laidler, M.M., having failed to get in touch with the East Yorkshires, had worked their way forward well out in front of the Battalion's right flank, where they remained throughout the action, and were instrumental later on in preventing enemy troops, who were trying to infiltrate round that flank.

After the German patrol had been eliminated it was discovered that there were three enemy tanks some two hundred yards directly to the front of the Battalion, that is to say between the Battalion and its proposed start line. These tanks immediately opened fire, spraying the top of the ditch with small arms fire, interspersed with high velocity and armour piercing shells. Lt.-Col. Lance ordered up an anti-tank gun, which had to be manhandled across the ditch, and, when it was in position, he fired white verey lights towards the tanks, to assist the anti-tank gunners in taking their aim. Although no hits were scored, the firing of the verey lights had the desired effect, as the tanks stopped firing and moved their position each time a light was sent up.

Under the lights enemy infantry could be seen moving in the vicinity of the tanks, and it was quite apparent that the enemy was also staging an attack. It became a question of who would start first.

By this time the anti-tank ditch had perforce become the Battalion's start line, and, as the men waited on the fire step for the supporting artillery barrage to open up, they were subjected to an aerial attack of bombing and machine-gun fire.

6 *Bn*   There followed a nerve wracking period as the " zero "
23 *Mar* 43 hour for the attack approached, and there was still no sign of the artillery support, which had been promised. Lt.-Col. Lance decided that, in view of the situation in front, he could not launch his Battalion into an attack with any hope of success, unless he had artillery support. He therefore postponed the attack for one hour to enable a revised artillery programme to be laid on. It was typical of the confidence which the men placed in their leaders when one private soldier was heard to say, during this period of waiting under heavy fire : " Don't you worry, lads. Monty and Red Ted have got this show laid on, and they won't move us from here until everything is properly organised."

After an hour's wait the artillery support again failed to materialise, and the Battalion then began to reorganise the anti-tank ditch from a starting line into a defensive position, as it was clear that the enemy were about to launch an attack. However, at about 3 a.m., orders were received to withdraw to the positions which had been left a few hours previously.

Sgt. Bawcombe's platoon, as it had been first into the ditch, was the last to leave. It was only with difficulty that L/Sgt. Longstaff's and L/Cpl. Laidler's sections were extricated. As Sgt. Bawcombe was waiting for his last man, Pte. G. Mangham, he saw the enemy swarming over the top of the ditch, and engulf Pte. Mangham, who was captured. Sgt. Bawcombe and L/Cpl. Laidler were picked up by Lt.-Col. Lance, who was waiting in his carrier to see all his men out.

When the Battalion was back in its old positions an enemy patrol, which included a spandau team, attacked L/Cpl. J. R. Pritchard's section of No. 15 platoon, " C " Company. A spirited action between Brens and spandaus ensued, at the conclusion of which the enemy withdrew leaving three dead and a spandau behind them.

Just before dawn tanks from the 7th Armoured Division took up positions covering the exhausted battalion, and, except for occasional shelling, the Green Howards were unmolested until they were relieved shortly before midnight by the Seaforth Highlanders, and marched back to Bou Ghara.

6 *and* 7 *Bns*   On March 25 both Battalions went into the line again,
25/28 *Mar* 43 occupying positions in a quiet sector to the south of Mareth.

Extensive patrolling was still carried out, and reconnaissance parties went out each night. On the 27th the enemy began to withdraw, and, on the 28th, the Green Howards had the satisfaction of entering the town of Mareth unopposed. The famous Mareth Line had melted away, and the 6th and 7th Battalions, Green Howards, had, at great cost but with great glory, fought with tremendous courage and determination a grim battle, with which their name will always be associated.

During the eleven days, since they launched their first attack upon the outposts, a Green Howard, who was there, estimates that they only had between twenty-five and thirty hours sleep all told. They had been constantly on the move, and practically continuously under shell, mortar and machine-gun fire. The losses suffered by the 6th Battalion consisted of two officers killed, five officers wounded, and a hundred and twenty other casualties. The 7th Battalion lost two officers killed, eight officers wounded, and a high proportion of other casualties.

The next few days were spent in cleaning up the battlefield in and around Zarat, in reorganising, and fitting in the reinforcements which had arrived. Both Battalions were at this time reorganised on a four rifle company basis. In the 6th Battalion " B " Company became a rifle company under the command of Captain H. T. Fairclough, while in the 7th Battalion a new " D " Company was formed under the command of Capt. S. N. Roberts, with Capt. H. L. Howard as second in command.

Just, however, as the 50th Division was settling down *See* MAP for a well-earned rest, orders were received that it was to take No. 10 part in an attack on positions covering the Wadi Akarit, on which the enemy was making his next stand.

On April 3, therefore, the Green Howards were on the 6 *and* 7 *Bns* move again and, having made a rapid advance of about sixty 3/5 *Apr* 43 miles, and, having passed through Gabes, the 6th Battalion arrived at Oudref at approximately 4 p.m. It had been a nightmare of a journey, as the one main road was packed tight with transport, and, at places, vehicles seemed to be turning up from four different directions at once. Just as it was getting dark the Commanding Officer and Company Commanders, who had gone on ahead to reconnoitre the new positions, arrived back at Oudref. The Battalion now moved forward again, and in the words of one observer : " . . . after struggling along the road for about three miles, we turned off along a badly laid and ill-defined track, and bumped our way along, nose to tail, for what seemed like hours and hours. Just when I had decided that we must be lost, our guide told us that we were there, and the companies swanned off into the night into their respective positions. It was getting very near first light, but we managed to get rid of all the vehicles and, when dawn broke, we found ourselves completely in the open with the Boche sitting on the hills overlooking us from about five thousand yards away. Our administration problems were not easy, as all food had to be brought up at night, and no cooking whatsoever could be done by day."

Prior to April 3 approximately half of the 7th Battalion had been moved up to Gabes to off-load ammunition and stores, which were being landed on an improvised break-water. It was surmised, probably correctly, that some of the twenty-five pounder ammunition, which they had been handling, was used for the barrage behind which they advanced at Wadi Akarit, and some caustic comments about the role of Infantry were made.

Having played their part as scene shifters, they rejoined the remainder of the Battalion, which was in the assembly area in front of Akarit, and prepared to make their entry as star performers on the stage.

Before proceeding further with the story of the Battalions we must give a brief outline of the situation, and a description of the 30th Corps plan for the battle of Akarit, and of the terrain over which the attacks took place on April 6/7.

The position taken up by the Afrika Corps at Akarit was a naturally strong one. The Wadi Akarit penetrated inland for some five thousand yards into the foothills of the Jebel Romana, a prominent feature some five hundred feet in height. There was then a gap between the Jebel Romana and the Fatnassa hills, in which the ground level was some two hundred and fifty feet. The ground then sloped up steeply to the Hachana Ridge, and to Mesreb El Alig, the highest point, which was some eight to nine hundred feet high. The gap between these two hills was only about a thousand yards across. The right flank of the enemy's position was secured by the impassable salt marshes of the Sebket El Hamma. Covering the gap between the two hill features, and slightly in front of Jebel Romana, an anti-tank ditch had been dug, which in its turn was protected by the usual wire obstacles and minefields, and by an outpost on Pt. 85, a prominent feature some distance in front of the main position.

The Corps Commander's original plan for overcoming this defensive position was to attack it with two divisions, the 51st Highland Division on the right, and the 4th Indian

Division on the left. After further consideration, however, it was decided that there might not be enough troops on the ground to clear such widely spaced and intricate positions, and that one Brigade of the 50th Division should attack in the centre. The final order given out on April 2 was that the 51st Division would attack the Jebel Romana, and any enemy positions there might be between this feature and the sea ; the 4th Indian Division was to make a silent advance, without artillery support, into the Fatnassa Hills, and the 69th Brigade was to make a frontal assault on the gap in the centre.

As soon as it was dark on April 5 the 4th Indian Division moved off into the hills on the left. At 3.30 a.m. on April 6 " C " Company of the 7th Green Howards, led by Capt. Mansell, launched an attack on Pt. 85, one hour in advance of the main attacks, which were made by the Highland Division against the Jebel Romana, and by the 5th East York-shires and the 7th Green Howards against the enemy's main positions behind the anti-tank ditch. It was essential that Pt. 85 should be dealt with before the main attack, as it lay on the flank of the 7th Green Howards' line of attack, and, in order to give " C " Company the artillery support which Brigadier Cooke-Collis considered necessary, an early start had to be made, as all the artillery was fully committed to support the main attack, which was launched at 4.30 a.m. The 6th Green Howards followed closely behind the 7th Battalion.

The 69th Brigade ran into trouble straight away. " C " Company, in a very spirited attack, captured Pt. 85 successfully, but " A " and " B " Companies, of the 7th Battalion, became completely pinned down in front of the ditch. The artillery barrage had not been of sufficient density to subdue the enemy forward positions, and the anti-tank ditch was found to be sited on the reverse slope of a hill, a fact which had not been appreciated from reconnaissance. In addition, neither of the flanking divisions had as yet cleared the hill tops, and the leading troops of the East Yorkshires and the 7th Green Howards were pinned down in the open under a withering frontal fire from the enemy's forward defences, and long range enfilade fire from the high ground.

However, at about 9 a.m., both the Indian Division and the Highland Division began to appear on their respective hill tops, and, at about the same time, a squadron of tanks belonging to the 3rd County of London Yeomanry managed to get across the anti-tank ditch on the right flank. The East Yorkshires and 7th Green Howards were then able to make some further progress, and the 6th Green Howards passed round to the east of Pt. 85 towards their final objective, some thousand yards beyond the anti-tank ditch. Soon after 11 a.m. it was clear that the enemy's resistance had been broken, and, with the exception of a threatened counter-attack against the 6th Green Howards late in the afternoon, this proved to be the case. At first light on April 7, the tanks of the 8th Armoured Brigade passed through the gap, and soon the remainder of the 10th Corps was pouring through on to the Tunisian plain.

We must now take up the story of the 6th and 7th Green Howards, who moved up to their forming up points just before midnight on April 5. Very little reconnaissance of the ground had been possible, but a patrol commanded by Lt. Nosotti from the 7th Battalion on the night of the 4/5th had approached near enough to Pt. 85 to be able to report that it was held by the enemy.

In his patrols, both at Mareth and Akarit, Lt. Nosotti was accompanied by Cpl. Surtees, a young sapper, who showed great courage and coolness. His skill and determination in detecting and removing mines contributed largely to the success of the patrols. During the night of the attack on the Bastion, after the engineers' task had been completed, Cpl. Surtees expressed a wish to join in the fighting, and accompanied the Green Howards into the Bastion. He was later awarded the Military Medal.

7 Bn
6 Apr 43   At 2 a.m. on April 6 Lt. Richley, with three men and a covering party from " D " Company, moved forward to lay the start line for the 7th Battalion. At 3 a.m. " C " Company, commanded by Capt. Mansell, moved to the start line, and at 3.30 advanced on Pt. 85 one hour in advance of the remainder of the Battalion. The front face of Pt. 85 was very steep, and Capt. Mansell decided to attack the feature from the left flank, as this gave the easiest line of approach. The leading platoon, commanded by Lt. F. W. M. Underhay, was preceeded by a party of sappers, who laid tapes through the minefield, while a section under Sgt. Topcliffe gave them covering fire. When this platoon made its assault it was met by very heavy rifle and machine-gun fire, and also grenades. Sgt. Topcliffe was killed, Lt. Underhay wounded, and the platoon suffered heavy casualties. At the same time Capt. Mansell himself led Sgt. Dixon's platoon round behind the feature, and, throwing grenades, they rushed the enemy positions.

Meanwhile Lt. Nosotti, with the rear platoon, had scaled the front edge of Pt. 85, and many of the enemy, caught between Sgt. Dixon's and Lt. Nosotti's platoons, surrendered. These two platoons then, under Capt Mansell, jointly cleared the position.

Lt. Nosotti's platoon, having climbed up the face of Pt. 85 on their hands and knees, found themselves close up to the enemy, who were established behind a sangar. A grenade was thrown at them which, slightly wounding Lt. Nosotti and Pte. Brennan, blew off the foot of Pte. Priest. Pte. Priest, who had accompanied Lt. Nosotti on most of his patrols, showed great fortitude, and in the words of his officer : " He was a calm soldier, who always showed the greatest courage."

In this heroic and highly successful action " C " Company had suffered severe losses, and, when dawn came, only Capt. Mansell, Lt. Nosotti, wounded but remaining at duty, and twenty-two other ranks remained. About eighty prisoners had been taken, many enemy killed or wounded, and Pt. 85, which was to prove an invaluable reconnaissance point, was securely in the hands of the Green Howards.

Of the many brave men who followed Capt. Mansell on to Pt. 85, L/Cpl. Bradford, a stretcher bearer, was particularly noticeable for the unselfish devotion with which he tended his comrades.

While this action had been going on " A " and " B " Companies, commanded by Lt. Coles and Capt. Hay respectively, had come up to the start line, and at 4.30 a.m. began their advance on the anti-tank ditch. Their objective lay some two hundred yards beyond it. As they approached the ditch, however, they ran into an anti-personnel minefield, which delayed their progress. As daylight came they found themselves in the open, exposed to very heavy fire from the enemy, and unable to make headway. Lt.-Col. Seagrim, with his Intelligence Officer, Lt. Richley, then went forward, and, with the same inspiring dash and contempt for danger which he had displayed at Mareth, started to lead his men down into the anti-tank ditch. This time, however, he was wounded, and so was Lt. Richley. Lt.-Col. Seagrim died the following day, to the great grief of his men, and all who knew him.

Lt. Depoix, who had recovered from the concussion which he had sustained on the first day of the Mareth attacks, resumed the duties of Intelligence Officer when Lt. Richley was wounded.

Meanwhile " D " Company of the 7th Battalion, under Capt. Roberts, had gone up to Pt. 85 and reinforced " C " Company. During this advance Capt. Howard, second-in-command of the company, together with several others, was wounded. A platoon of the Cheshire Regiment's machine-guns also arrived at about this time to strengthen the defences of Pt. 85.

" A " and " B " Companies had fought magnificently, and it was through no fault of theirs that they had failed to reach their final objective. Their casualties had been very heavy.

Capt. Hay was awarded the Military Cross for his courage, determination and untiring energy in this action. When " B " Company was caught in an extremely exposed position, and pinned down by the most intense and accurate machine-gun and mortar fire at short range, Capt. Hay never lost control of his company, and was continually moving from one position to another, looking for opportunities to get forward. When, at last, withdrawal was ordered, he personally remained for a considerable time with a few automatic weapons, snatching every chance to hit back at the enemy, and materially assisting the advance of the leading companies of the 6th Battalion.

Sgt. C. Craddock gained a bar to the Military Medal which he had won only two weeks previously at Mareth. Sgt. Craddock was in charge of the ladder carrying party of " A " Company for scaling the anti-tank ditch. During the advance to the ditch he displayed much initiative, and disregard for danger, and, when the ditch was reached, he directed covering fire at very close range with the greatest coolness. He then led his party with the ladders into the ditch, and was the last man to leave it. Throughout the whole of the action Sgt. Craddock set a wonderful example of fearlessness, and, when the withdrawal took place, he assisted in carrying many of the wounded back under very heavy fire.

Cpl. J. O'Rourke, who was a member of a fighting patrol which preceded the leading companies, assumed command of it when his officer was wounded at an early stage. He led his patrol into the anti-tank ditch in the face of heavy machine-gun fire. As soon as they got into the ditch they were enfiladed by a machine-gun firing along the ditch from a position about two hundred yards away. Without hesitation Cpl. O'Rourke led a charge against this post, firing his tommy gun, and floundering through the thick mud which filled the bottom of the ditch. He succeeded in knocking out the post and taking six prisoners. He then organised his party to give covering fire for the leading companies, materially assisting their advance. Finally, on the withdrawal, he carried back many wounded men to safety.

At about 5.30 p.m. Major A. W. Edgar, M.C., who had taken over command of the Battalion, received orders to withdraw " A " and " B " Companies back to the positions on

which they had originally formed up. " C " and " D " Companies remained on Pt. 85 during the night of April 6/7, and
rejoined the remainder of the Battalion during the afternoon of
the 7th.

On April 8 the command of the Battalion was taken over
by Lt.-Col. D. G. Jebb, D.S.O., of the Cameronians.

The 6th Battalion, which was following up the 7th Battalion,   6 *Bn*
found itself, when daylight came, lying in an exposed position   6 *Apr* 43
in open ground. The enemy artillery spotted them, and, as
they were unable to move forward owing to the 7th Battalion
being hung up, they suffered severe casualties, amongst them
being R.S.M. D. Carter, who was killed by shell fire, and Lt.
Levine, who was wounded.

When Pt. 85 had been finally cleared, Lt.-Col. Lance
led " A " Company (Capt. Honeyman) and " C " Company
(Major Hull) up to a position in the lee of the hill, and
Major Brunton followed some ten minutes later leading " B "
Company (Capt. Fairclough) and " D " Company (Major
Pullinger). They had not been there long before a salvo
of mortar bombs fell amongst " C " Company, fatally
wounding Lt. J. Dimond and Pte. J. Fellows, Major Hull's
batman.

Soon after their arrival at Pt. 85 Brigadier Cooke-Collis
came up, and, having made a reconnaissance from the top
of it, gave his orders to Lt.-Col. Lance. Lt.-Col. Lance then
took Major Hull and Capt. Honeyman to a small feature near
to Pt. 85, from which a gap in the enemy minefield was clearly
visible. It was through this gap that two tanks of the County
of London Yeomanry had penetrated, but one tank had been
knocked out, and lay in the centre of the gap. Lt.-Col.
Lance's orders were for " A " and " C " Companies to move
through the gap together in single file, cross the anti-tank
ditch as quickly as possible, and then fan out and advance
with all speed on to the plateau beyond. " A " Company
was to be on the right, " C " Company on the left, and the
axis of the advance was to be parallel to the track which led
north-north-west. The only support to be given to the
companies was from the two County of London Yeomanry
tanks, firing from a hull down position, as it was not considered
desirable to draw the enemy's attention to the gap by an
artillery barrage put down in front of it.

This was a bold plan, when it is remembered that only
a short distance away on the left, the East Yorkshires and 7th
Green Howards were still fighting hard in front of the anti-
tank ditch. The very boldness of the move, however, brought
success, and " A " and " C " Companies, with Lt.-Col.
Lance at their head, were through the gap before the enemy

woke up to what was happening. They then brought down a heavy concentration on the gap, and the rear companies suffered considerable casualties as they passed through.

" A " and " C " Companies made good progress, and many Italians gave themselves up as successive positions were overrun. When " A " Company, however, came up against the lower slopes of the Jebel Romana, they came under heavy fire concentrated against them and were pinned down. " C " Company, not meeting such strong opposition, was meanwhile advancing with No. 13 platoon (Sgt. A. E. Docherty, M.M.) on the left, No. 14 platoon (Lt. Lee) on the right, and No. 15 platoon (Lt. T. T. Macadam) in reserve. No. 14 platoon, however, eventually came under the same fire as was holding up " A " Company, and Lt.-Col. Lance sent off Lt. Macadam with his platoon, with instructions to advance well round the right flank of " A " Company, and outflank the enemy. At the same time, he called up " D " Company (Major Pullinger), and put it into the attack on the left of " C " Company. " D " Company continued to advance, and made a great haul of prisoners.

Lt. Macadam made some progress with his platoon, and took a number of prisoners, but they suffered several casualties, including Lt. Macadam who was wounded. On receiving a report of this, Lt.-Col. Lance sent off Major Hull to clear up the position on the right flank. Major Hull rallied the remainder of No. 15 platoon and led them in a successful assault, in the course of which L/Cpl. L. Coughlan, of the Battalion Intelligence Section, who had been attached to " C " Company both at Mareth and in this battle, was killed instantaneously by machine-gun fire. L/Cpl. Coughlan had done magnificent work with " C " Company, and was displaying great courage at the moment when he was killed.

The pressure on " A " Company, and on " C " Company's right hand platoon, having now been relieved by Major Hull's action, Lt.-Col. Lance ordered Lt. Lee to advance with Nos. 13 and 14 platoons across the plain towards an enemy vehicle, which was visible some thousand to fifteen hundred yards ahead. Sgt. Bawcombe took over command of No. 14 platoon.

Advancing in a series of bounds, these two platoons, in conformity with " D " Company on their left, advanced without meeting any opposition for about a thousand yards, until they reached a small wadi lying across their front. Much to their surprise, they found the leading edge of the wadi all prepared for defence, with a string of machine-gun positions, and an excellent field of fire covering the ground across which they had advanced. Below the edge of a small re-entrant were some mortar positions dug to a depth of twelve feet. Much greater surprise, however, was experienced by the German and Italian troops who were supposed to be manning these weapons. The Green Howards found them sitting at the bottom of the wadi resting and eating, and, in the space of a few minutes, captured the lot. Some two hundred prisoners fell into their hands, and a position, which might have seriously held up the advance, had been taken without loss. Sgt. Docherty was then ordered by Lt. Lee to take his platoon forward another two hundred yards to a point where there were visible signs of earthworks. No enemy were found there, and Sgt. Docherty remained on this position until the counter-attack was threatened later in the evening.

Meanwhile Sgt. Bawcombe, with two sections of his platoon, commanded by L/Cpl. C. Bull and L/Sgt. Laidler, M.M., moved down the wadi towards the right, and overran four high velocity anti-tank guns, which had been holding up the advance of any vehicles along the track. Sgt. Bawcombe and a Bren-gun team stayed with the captured guns, while L/Sgt. Laidler and L/Cpl. Bull proceeded further up the wadi. There they captured four Italian officers, including one of general's rank. The Italian general, having packed a suitcase, asked L/Sgt. Laidler to take him to his Commanding Officer. The four officers got into the general's cream and yellow car, the general driving himself with L/Sgt. Laidler sitting beside him, and covering him with his automatic. Much to L/Sgt. Laidler's annoyance, as he was proud of his distinguished captive, one of Sgt. Bawcombe's men fired at the strange car and killed the general outright. The remaining officers decided to walk the rest of the way.

Meanwhile, Major Hull had rejoined his Company, and Sgt. Bawcombe had brought his two sections back to the sector of the wadi occupied by Lt. Lee.

While " C " Company had been establishing itself in the wadi, Major Pullinger's company had come under some very heavy fire from tanks and high velocity guns. The company sustained severe casualties, including C.S.M. J. G. Oliver, M.M., who was killed, and Sgt. S. Moffitt, who was wounded. The company wireless set was also put out of action, and both signallers wounded.

Major Pullinger was, in fact, at this moment, the only one of his company headquarters group still left in the battle. He himself then went across to find Major Hull. In view of increasing enemy activity, " D " Company's lack of the means of communication, and the sadly diminished strength of their

o

companies, these officers decided to establish a joint head-quarters, and take up the best possible defensive position.

While " D " Company was making a hazardous journey across the front to join up with " C " Company, further casualties were sustained, including Ptes. R. MacMillan and D. Jardine, both of whom were wounded. Amongst those who lost their lives with " C " Company at about this time were Pte. J. Hall, an original member of the 6th Battalion and a fearless Bren gunner, Pte. G. Challenger, a stretcher bearer who was doing magnificent work at the time, and Ptes. G. Weir and W. J. Williams, both of whom had always given of their best when things were at their worst.

The two depleted companies were now some fifteen hundred yards in front of any friendly troops, and completely cut off from communication with them. Thanks, however, to the action of Sgt. Bawcombe and his party, in capturing the anti-tank guns, five or six tanks of the County of London Regiment were able to move round to the lower edge of the plateau on the right flank, and take up a hull down position some thousand yards behind the Green Howard companies. As the enemy's fire increased in intensity it was found impossible to get anti-tank guns or an artillery forward observation officer up to the front line.

As dusk was approaching, enemy infantry, supported by tanks, were seen advancing some eight hundred to a thousand yards in front. In the absence of an artillery officer, Major Pullinger himself spotted for the guns and with great success. The enemy came on for about five hundred yards, supported by small arms fire, high velocity fire from their tanks, and also artillery fire. But the fire from the British tanks and artillery was so intense that their advance was halted some four hundred yards in front of the Green Howard companies. Their casualties must have been very heavy, but their sacrifices were in vain, as the survivors fell into the hands of the Armoured Brigade, when it passed through at first light next morning. When darkness fell all enemy activity in front of the Green Howards ceased, except that continual movement of transport could be heard behind his lines. Nevertheless, every eye and ear of the tired troops was strained, with the enemy only a few hundred yards away.

6 *Bn*
7 *Apr* 43　　Late that night the 6th Battalion, Durham Light Infantry, moved up into position on the right flank of the two companies, and, at about 3 a.m. on April 7, they were relieved by " A " Company, with the Battalion anti-tank gun.

When daylight came on April 7 it became clear that the enemy had fled during the night, and at 7 a.m. the 8th

Armoured Brigade, followed by the New Zealand Division, and later by the 7th Armoured Division, began to pass through along the track which led into Tunisia, while the Green Howards, justly well pleased with themselves, sat on the high ground watching the procession go by.

When Major Hull went round the right flank of " A " Company and took command of No. 15 platoon after Lt. Macadam had been wounded, he displayed such gallantry, that he was awarded a bar to the Military Cross, which he had won at Mersah Matruh. After proceeding a short way the party was fired upon by three machine-gun posts. Major Hull immediately took four of his men round to a flank, and managed to silence one post with grenades and a Bren gun. In this action one of his men was killed. Major Hull then charged the other two posts with his remaining three men, putting them out of action and taking forty prisoners, including ten Germans. By his determined action he so inspired his men that nothing could stop them, and his fearless élan enabled the Battalion to continue its advance.

L/Cpl. A. Winterbottom, of " C " Company, led his section with such gallantry that he was awarded the Military Medal. On more than one occasion, he charged enemy machine-gun posts, killing or capturing the crews. Although he was eventually wounded, he led the final charge well ahead of his men.

Pte. H. Harper, of " A " Company, No. 1 of a Bren gun, on two occasions assaulted machine-gun posts single handed. firing his gun from the hip. These individual actions, in which he exposed himself to great danger, and by which he drew the enemy's fire away from his comrades, were a source of great encouragement to all who saw him. He was awarded the Military Medal.

L/Cpl. R. W. Smith showed the greatest bravery and devotion to duty throughout the battle. As a stretcher bearer attached to " C " Company, he was to be seen tending the wounded under heavy fire. He himself was wounded in the hand, but continued his work of rescue. He was finally the only stretcher bearer left with the company but, owing to his determination, all the casualties were successfully evacuated. For his coolness and courage L/Cpl. Smith was awarded the Military Medal.

Throughout this battle, and the battle of Mareth, the work performed by the signallers was of the highest importance, and of an extremely hazardous nature. This was recognised by the award of the Military Medal to Sgt. L. Smith of the 6th Battalion, who, throughout both actions, carried out his duties of repairing equipment or cable lines, under very heavy fire, with complete disregard of his own safety. He was always cheerful, and it was greatly due to his untiring efforts that communications were maintained.

The battle of Akarit was one of the most successful fought by the 8th Army. The enemy's defences had been broken through in twenty-four hours, and the 69th Brigade was entitled to a major share of the credit for this feat. Between them the two Green Howard Battalions and the East York-shires captured or killed practically the whole of the Italian Spezia Division, as well as taking all their weapons. The casualties had, however, been very heavy. The 6th Battalion lost Capt. Wheeler, and Lts. Dimond and Pratt, killed, Lts. Macadam, Whitworth, Redfern, Levine and Priestley wounded, and over a hundred and twenty casualties among the other ranks, including R.S.M. Carter and C.S.M. Oliver, killed, and Sgt. Moffitt, wounded. The 7th Battalion lost Lt.-Col. Seagrim, died of wounds, Capt. Howard, Lts. Richley, Nosotti and Underhay, wounded, and more than a hundred casualties among the other ranks.

No account of these two battles would be complete without a reference to Brigadier Cooke-Collis, who was awarded a bar to his D.S.O. Not only did he plan a series of brilliant operations, but he took a personal part in many of the reconnaissances, and was always to be found in the forward positions at times when the commanders on the spot were most in need of his advice and encouragement. From colonel to private, all who served under him bear witness to the great inspiration which they received whenever " Red Ted " appeared amongst them.

Throughout the two battles of Mareth and Akarit the Green Howard Battalions received invaluable support from the 124th Field Regiment, R.A., commanded by Lt.-Col. C. F. Todd, the 233rd Field Company, R.E., commanded by Major K. Osborn, M.C., and " C " Company of the Cheshire Regiment (Machine Guns), commanded by Major A. Mellor. The successes gained were due, to a large extent, to the close and happy co-operation extended by these units and their commanding officers.

In these two battles, within three weeks of each other, the Green Howards added to their Roll of Honour, 1 Victoria Cross, 1 Bar to a Distinguished Service Order, 1 Bar to a Military Cross, 8 Military Crosses, 4 Distinguished Conduct Medals, 1 Bar to a Military Medal, and 15 Military Medals. Their losses in the same period had been very heavy, and it is no wonder that they were now given a week's rest, in which to reorganise. Although reinforcements arrived, both Battalions were feeling an acute shortage of N.C.O.s.

On April 9 Major Pullinger left the 6th Battalion to take *6 and 7 Bns* over duties of second-in-command of the 7th Battalion, and *9/25 Apr* 43 Capt. R. Lofthouse assumed command of " D " Company.

Meanwhile, the pursuit of the Afrika Corps had been continuing, and Field-Marshal Rommel was making a final stand just south of Enfidaville.

On April 14 the 50th Division took to the road again, and, on April 17, arrived at a concentration area north of Sousse. On the night of April 19/20, the New Zealand and the 4th Indian Divisions made a night attack, and on the 20th, the Guards Brigade attacked Enfidaville.

The 69th Brigade went forward on the 20th and took over reserve positions, which had been vacated by the Guards, in some olive groves on the right of the road about a thousand yards south of Enfidaville. Later in the day, the Green Howards followed up the Guards through the town, and took up positions a short way to the north—again in reserve.

On the 21st and 22nd the Battalion areas received a certain amount of shelling, and they could see the New Zealanders having a stiff battle on their left flank.

On April 23 they were relieved by troops from the 56th Division, and moved in mechanised transport back to the 50th Divisional concentration area about twelve miles north of Sfax.

On the 25th they set out for Tripoli, and began the long trek back of nearly two thousand miles to Alexandria, where they were, after a short rest, to start reorganising and training for their next adventure—the invasion of Sicily.

CHAPTER NINE

" THE GREEN HOWARDS IN SICILY "

July—October 1943

See MAP
No. 11

AS an introduction to the part played by the Green Howards in the capture of Sicily, it is well to give first a brief outline of the general plan of campaign, in so far as it affected the 13th Corps.

In this Corps commanded by Lt.-Gen. Sir Miles Dempsey, were the 1st Battalion, Green Howards, forming part of the 15th Brigade of the 5th Division, and the 6th and 7th Battalions, Green Howards, forming part of the 69th Brigade of the 50th Division. The primary objective of the 13th Corps, after landing on the south-east coast of the island around Avola, was the capture of the port of Syracuse, whilst the 30th Corps, landing some ten miles on its left flank, was to capture aerodromes in the vicinity of Pacchino.

Broadly speaking, the landings and the initial stages of the advance towards Messina were accomplished successfully, and such good progress was made by the forward troops, despite inadequate transport facilities, that it was not until the Catania plain was reached, some five days after the landing on July 10, that the enemy was able to regroup his forces and put up an organised resistance.

The second stage of the operations now began. This lasted until the first days of August when the enemy, having lost Adrano, the key point of his lateral communications in front of Mt. Etna, to the 30th Corps, began a general withdrawal to Messina and across the straits to Italy. During the middle of July fierce engagements took place on the Catania plain in which the Green Howards played their part.

The final stage consisted of the pursuit of the enemy up the coast to Messina, in the course of which skilfully handled German rearguards, making use of extensive demolitions and of favourable terrain, made the task of the British forces a slow and arduous undertaking.

The immediate plan of the 13th Corps was for the 5th Division to land in the Cassibile area, then to turn due north and capture Syracuse, while the 50th Division was to land near Avola and protect the left flank and rear of the 5th Division. Since the paths of the 1st Battalion and the 6th and 7th Battalions crossed each other on more than one occasion on the road from the beaches to Messina, their stories will be told, as far as possible, conjointly in the three stages of the campaign, namely, the landings and initial advance, the fighting on the Catania plain, and the pursuit.

Before entering, however, on a detailed account of these adventures we must return to Egypt, and say a few words about the preliminary concentration and training. The 1st Battalion, commanded by Lt.-Col. A. L. Shaw, arrived at *1 Bn* Kabrit, on the shores of the Bitter Lakes in the Suez Canal *16 Mar 43* area on March 16, 1943, having left Qum in the highlands of Persia on March 3. At the latter place it had spent a bitterly cold winter, rendered more so by contrast with the intense heat of Ranchi in the eastern provinces of India, where it had passed the previous summer. The 2nd i/c of the Battalion at this time was Major P. G. Bulfin, Capt. J. M. Barwick was Adjutant, Capt. J. Gundrill, Intelligence Officer, and the Company Commanders—Major B. N. O. Gosden, " A " Company,—Capt. H. Verity, " B " Company—Capt. A. R. M. Tanner, " C " Company,—and Capt. A. T. Parkinson, " D " Company. For the next three weeks training exercises in assault landings and combined operations were carried out on the lakes.

On April 11, this phase of their training being finished, *1 Bn* the Battalion left Kabrit, the personnel by rail and the trans- *11 Apr/* port by road, and arrived at Qatana, some ten miles south of *2 June 43* Damascus on the 14th. Here it went into a good camp of timbered huts, the nearest approach to permanent structures which it had experienced since landing in India a year before. The camp was situated in typical hill country, fresh and green, with the towering snow-clad height of Mount Hermon across the valley, and, although the ground was very stony, the general surroundings were a pleasant contrast to the bare plains of India, the freezing tablelands of Persia, and the scorching sands of the desert.

Here the next phases of training were carried out. The transport drivers practised driving on and off close-packed " mock up " landing craft, and water-proofing their vehicles. Extensive landing trials were carried out and loads were checked. At the same time the Brigade Commander, Brigadier G. S. Rawstrorne, who had been informed where the landings would take place, explained his plan of operations to Battalion Commanders only, but did not give them any date. An operations room was set up complete with maps, aerial photographs and plastic models of the beaches and hinterland, but these contained no place names, and the grid lines on the maps were not numbered. Every officer and man had the opportunity of studying these maps and models, and the Commanding Officer carried out various exercises based upon them, and upon the knowledge which only he in the Battalion possessed at that time.

During the last week in May the motor transport and carriers were loaded operationally and sent off to unknown destinations. Capt. M. R. Newman and Lt. N. W. S. Tolson left with the Carrier and Mortar platoons respectively. It is interesting to record that Lt.-Col. Shaw gave these officers detailed operation orders at Damascus on May 28, which were to be carried out at a time and place, which they did not know, and at a time which he did not know. These orders were fulfilled to the letter six weeks later on July 10 on the Sicilian beaches. The transport had travelled by way of Benghazi and Malta, and Lt.-Col. Shaw's own carrier waddled up to him within an hour of his landing.

All surplus kit was dumped and left behind at Damascus when the Battalion, less transport, left by train on June 2. After an uneventful journey it went into camp at El Shatt on the east bank of the Suez Canal.

1 *Bn*
8/16 *Jun* 43

On June 8 the Battalion embarked at Suez in H.M.T. *Tegelberg*, which was to be its Landing Ship (Infantry) for the forthcoming operations, and, on the 10th, the whole of the 13th Corps sailed for a full dress rehearsal of the landing operations in the Gulf of Akaba. The 1st Battalion, York and Lancaster Regiment, was also on board the *Tegelberg*. On arrival in the Gulf, the ship stood about seven miles off shore, and for several nights all lights were switched off, while in the inky blackness the troops practised getting up in full battledress from their mess decks to the sally ports, and then going over the side into the assault craft. This disembarkation from the ship to the small craft was repeated over and over again until all ranks became thoroughly conversant with the route they had to take, and with the feel of the ship in the darkness.

1 *Bn*
16 *Jun*/
4 *Jul* 43

They returned to El Shatt on June 16, and on the 28th all officers of the 8th Army taking part in the operations were addressed by General Montgomery. In the words of one of the officers present :—" I think it is true to say that he got it across all right—that magic personality and ability to inspire us all with confidence, and to make us feel that he had the whole thing taped—which indeed he had ! "

All preparations were now complete, and during the period of waiting a cricket match was played between the 1st Battalion and a strong side got up by Major N. S. Pope of the K.O.Y.L.I., whose ambition it had always been to defeat the Green Howards. On this occasion he failed to do so by a narrow margin with a side composed of, amongst others, the Corps Commander, General Dempsey, Rear Admiral Troubridge, Brigadier G. S. Rawstrorne, and several useful South African Cricketers. This match is worthy of record, as in it Hedley Verity made his last appearance on the cricket field. He bowled as well as ever and took six wickets for thirty-seven runs—including that of his Corps Commander.

This seems to be a fitting place to include a few words about Hedley Verity, who was to die some three weeks later, a prisoner in enemy hands, having been wounded when gallantly leading his company against a strong enemy position on the Catania plain. Verity will always be remembered by the world at large as a great cricketer, but, by those who served with him, he will also be remembered as a man of high qualities, a charming personality, and a loyal Green Howard. It is a remarkable tribute to his character that at the time of Munich, when he held an assured position in the world of cricket, he should have approached Lt.-Col. Shaw in the pavilion at Headingley, and asked his advice as to how he might best prepare himself for war, should it come. The constant travelling entailed by his profession prevented him from being able to fulfil his obligations should he join the Territorials or Civil Defence Services, and the best that Lt.-Col. Shaw could do was to give him a collection of military books to study.

How many of those thousands of cricket lovers, who watched Verity going from triumph to triumph on the field throughout those summer days of 1939, realised that here was a serious-minded patriot, who, in his spare time, was industriously preparing himself for the profession of arms ;—a profession to which he did not belong, and which was foreign to his gentle nature ? The time, however, was not wasted, and a few months after war broke out he obtained a commission, and was later posted to the 1st Battalion, at that time commanded by Lt.-Col. Shaw. As the Battalion was then at home in Northern Ireland, his services as a cricketer were naturally in demand, but he did not only play, he also spent many hours in laying out pitches, and in coaching others less proficient than himself.

During all this time he studied and worked at his new profession with all the thoroughness and thoughtfulness which he applied to his cricket. He had a natural aptitude for tactics, as one would expect from one who had so often and so successfully appreciated the situation when playing for Yorkshire or England. His death was a tragedy. England lost a great cricketer, and the Green Howards lost a fine officer and a true friend.

At last the great day arrived, and on June 30 the Battalion once again embarked at Suez on the *Tegelberg*, and, sailing up the canal, reached Port Said on July 4. Here it found the harbour, basins, and quaysides crammed with shipping of every description including H.M.T. *Orontes* with the 6th Battalion Green Howards on board, and H.M.T. *Devonshire* with the 7th Battalion Green Howards.

6 and 7 Bns
6 May/
4 Jul 43

These two battalions were commanded respectively by Lt.-Col. D. J. M. Smith, D.S.O., The Essex Regiment, and Lt.-Col. D. G. Jebb, D.S.O., The Cameronians. After the severe fighting at Mareth and Akarit, they had been taken out of the line near Enfidaville on April 22. By May 6 they had reached Sidi Bishr, where they spent the next five weeks reorganising and re-equipping for their next operational role. After a weeks' training in combined operations at Kabrit, they marched thirty miles in intense heat along the banks of the Suez Canal to a camp just south of the Atara oil refineries After a final ten days training they embarked at Suez on their transports and sailed to Port Said.

1, 6, and 7
Bns
5/9 Jul 43

Early in the morning of July 5 the convoys moved off, and. after an uneventful voyage, except for a rising sea, Mount Etna appeared standing out on the horizon against the setting sun late in the evening of July 9. The transports anchored about seven miles off shore just before midnight, and the leading assault troops began to embark on their assault craft soon after midnight. The first Green Howards to land were the 1st Battalion, as the 69th Brigade had been allotted the role of " follow up " Brigade to the 50th Division and was not ordered to land until 8 a.m. The stretch of coast line allotted to the 13th Corps for assault was approximately twelve thousand yards in extent, with the small town of Avola as its southern boundary. This stretch was divided into three sectors of about four thousand yards each. The most southerly of these, Jig Beach, was allotted to the 50th Division, the centre, How Beach, to the 15th Brigade, 5th Division, while the northern sector, George Beach, was tackled by the 17th Brigade, and No. 4 Commando. The 13th Brigade was in reserve to the 5th Division.

The first objective of the 13th Corps was the capture of Syracuse, and, to assist in this operation, an Airborne Brigade was launched to land, just before dawn, west of Syracuse, with the object of creating a diversion, and seizing an important bridge, Ponte Grande, near Cassibile. This airborne venture was, however, to some extent, unlucky, many of the gliders

missing their mark and landing in the sea or amongst the
mountains inland. Only a very small part of the force reached
the bridge, but those who did fought a gallant battle, and
prevented its destruction by the Italians for a sufficient length
of time to enable the 17th Brigade to pass across it on its way
to Syracuse.

At 1.25 a.m. on July 10 all ranks of the 1st Battalion
were standing to on their mess decks, but the two landing
craft, which were to take them ashore, were late in arriving.
Eventually one L.C.I. turned up on the port side of the ship,
and, as this was the weather side, took a long time to make
fast owing to the swell. As there was no sign of the second
L.C.I., Lt.-Col. Shaw, being behind his time schedule, decided
to disembark his leading companies, " A " and " B ", together
with Battalion Tactical Headquarters. These, according to
the plan, should have disembarked on the starboard side.
While this was taking place, the second L.C.I. arrived, and
" D " Company, part of " C " Company, and main battalion
Headquarters disembarked into it, all under the command of
Major Worthington. Both craft left at about the same time,
well after 4 a.m., and the battalion was faced with a landing
in broad daylight instead of one in darkness as had been
originally intended.

To add to the difficulties of the situation no success
signals, as arranged, had been received from either the 1st
Battalion K.O.Y.L.I. or 1st Battalion York and Lancasters,
and Lt.-Col. Shaw did not know whether he was approaching
a beach held by our own troops or by those of the enemy.
Eventually he decided to make two landings instead of one
in order to minimise losses from shell fire, since, on getting
within two miles of the shore in broad daylight, it could be
seen that the beaches were in our hands, and being fairly
heavily shelled.

The Commanding Officer's party landed on How Beach
just before 7 a.m., and was greatly relieved when the battery
which had been shelling the beach was almost immediately
knocked out by the guns of a British Cruiser.

Major Worthington's L.C.I. was within half a mile of
How Beach when the landing craft in front, which was about
to land, received a direct hit from a shell. On the suggestion
of the naval officer commanding the L.C.I., Major Worthington agreed to alter course to Jig Beach, which appeared to be
free from troops landing, and was not at that time under fire.
Here they landed successfully, and, after a march of about
five miles, rejoined the rest of the battalion.

By 9.30 a.m. the Battalion had assembled in its concentration area, and soon afterwards orders were received to

1 *Bn*
10 *Jul* 43

seize the enemy positions on the Hyblean Plateau, a mile or so
inland, in order to prevent any counter-attack against the left
flank of the 17th Brigade, which was moving up towards
Syracuse after the capture of Cassibile. At 10 a.m., the
Battalion moved off with " A " Company as vanguard,
followed by Battalion Tactical Headquarters, " B ", " C ",
and " D " Companies in that order. Lt. R. Bell, with No. 12
Platoon, was sent off on an independent mission to mop up
some pill boxes on the left flank at the foot of the escarpment
above the Cassibile River. These were in action and threatened
the advance.

The country consisted of a coastal plain rising gently from
the sea for about a mile to a steep escarpment some fifteen
hundred feet in height. The plain was thickly wooded with
olive groves and vineyards, and the roads and fields were
enclosed by very strong dry walls similar to those found in the
North Riding. These walls, characteristic of the whole
country, had a marked effect on operations throughout the
campaign, as they made it impossible for vehicles to move off
the roads at short notice.

At the foot of the escarpment the vanguard encountered
a strong position which, had it been stubbornly defended,
might have held up the advance for some time. The troops
of the Italian Coastal Division, however, had other views, and
when Lt. J. J. Quinn, commanding the leading platoon, fired
a P.I.A.T. bomb into one of the pill boxes shouting :—" Come
out you blackguards or we will blow you to blazes ! ", a
white flag immediately appeared, accompanied by the reply
in a strong American accent : " For Gahd's sake, mister,
don't do that ! " These heartfelt words came from an American paratrooper, who had been captured earlier in the day.
Some thirty Italian prisoners were taken and despatched to
the rear.

Meanwhile Lt. Bell with his platoon had also encountered
some opposition, but after a short fight they silenced the pill
boxes on the left flank, capturing some prisoners, with a loss
to themselves of two men killed and two wounded.

As soon as the opposition at the foot of the escarpment
had been overcome, a carrier and mortar group under Capt.
Newman preceded the Battalion up the winding road which
led to the plateau. They met with little opposition—only a
few snipers—and by half-past-two in the afternoon, the
Battalion was safely esconced in its predetermined positions,
and the initial stage had been successfully accomplished.
Patrols were sent out along all roads, but the only contact
made with the enemy was by a carrier patrol, which captured

eight Italians near Canicattini-Bagni. Contact was established with the K.O.Y.L.I. on the right, but there was no sign yet of the 50th Division on the left.

The landing of the 50th Division, although delayed partly 6 *and* 7 *Bns* by weather and partly owing to the fact that the transports 10 *Jul* 43 anchored much further off shore than had been arranged, was eventually successfully accomplished in daylight, and the 69th Brigade received orders at 8 a.m. to proceed ashore. Within two hours the troops were in positions to the west of Avola astride the road leading to the interior. At about mid-day original plans were changed, in view of the lack of opposition, and orders were received for the 69th Brigade to move north, and to relieve troops of the 17th Brigade in the vicinity of Floridia. This march of about twenty miles was completed by 10 p.m., and the 6th and 7th Green Howards found themselves occupying a defensive position facing west, and covering a very wide front. No enemy had been encountered, but the men were very tired, having had very little sleep the night before, and having accomplished a long march in great heat and with wet boots.

The night of July 10/11 passed quietly on the 50th Divisional front, and patrols which had been sent out made no contact with the enemy. At dawn carrier patrols went out, and reported all clear as far as Canicattini Bagni.

As a result of a visit from General Dempsey to the 50th Division's Headquarters at 7 a.m. on the morning of July 11, the 15th Brigade, which had been placed under the orders of the 50th Division the previous afternoon, was ordered to revert to the 5th Division. Accordingly at 2.15 p.m. the 1st   1 *Bn* Battalion Green Howards set off down the hill, which it had 11 *Jul* 43 climbed the previous day, and took the road leading north to Floridia. On the way orders were received to bivouac for the night on the roadside some two miles east of this town. After covering some eighteen miles, and being " strafed " by Messerschmits on the way, it arrived at its bivouacs at 11 p.m.

In the meanwhile arrangements had been made for the 51st Highland Division of the 30th Corps to relieve the 50th Division. When this relief was completed the 50th Division was ordered to relieve the 13th Brigade of the 5th Division in the Floridia-Solarino area, and to be prepared to push on to Lentini.

Early in the morning of July 11 the 69th Brigade was 6 *and* 7 *Bns* ordered to advance about three miles into the foothills, and 11 *Jul* 43 take up a more advantageous position. Just before this advance began, the 7th Battalion, Green Howards, suffered a grievous tragedy. A chance shell landed in the middle of a small quarry in which the command group was located. Major C. R. Pullinger, M.C., the second in command, and R.S.M. S. Wilson were both severely wounded in the head, and succumbed to their injuries a few days later. Major H. R. D. Oldman, M.C., was appointed second in command, and Capt. R. H. E. Hudson took over " D " Company.

The Battalion occupied its new positions by 3 p.m., and was strengthened by the arrival of the carrier, anti-tank and mortar platoons.

The 6th Battalion had sent out two carrier sections under Capt. P. R. Delf early in the morning, and at 6 p.m. this patrol returned to the new positions with fifty Italian prisoners and a number of horses. Another carrier patrol under Lt. A. T. Semple went out towards Pallazolo, and reported having been fired upon, and having one motor-cycle damaged, on its return.

After a quiet night the 69th Brigade withdrew the next afternoon to an assembly area near Floridia, preparatory to starting its advance to Lentini by way of Sortino.

Before, however, continuing the narrative of this advance, we will follow the 1st Battalion Green Howards to the end of the first phase of the campaign, when it arrived on the Catania plain prior to crossing the R. Simeto. This Battalion, it will be remembered, had arrived near Floridia at 11 p.m. on July 11, and at 4 a.m. on the 12th, it moved off again to a concentration area just south of Priolo where it arrived at 7 a.m.

1 Bn
12 Jul 43

New objectives had now been given to the 5th Division. These were, Augusta for the 17th Brigade, and Mellili for the 15th Brigade, while the 13th Brigade was to hold a firm base at Floridia. The first move was the capture of Priolo, which was cleared by the 17th Brigade at mid-day on July 12, by which time " C " Company, which formed the vanguard of the Green Howards, the leading battalion of the 15th Brigade, was in the town and in contact with the Seaforth Highlanders. As the Battalion passed through Priolo, the exits were being shelled, and Sgt. J. B. Dixon was killed.

There was stiff resistance in the woods north of the town, and it was apparent that the enemy were no longer Italian, but German troops. This resistance was overcome by the 17th Brigade, which then took the right fork towards Augusta, while the Green Howards, as vanguard to the 15th Brigade, moved on, just after 2 p.m., towards Mellili. In the fighting at Priolo troops of the Hermann Goering Division were identified, but they must have withdrawn well to the north, for when the Green Howards approached Mellili they found it held by Italians, and had little difficulty in capturing it by 7 p.m. that night.

Capt. L. H. Wilson, who was commanding a leading platoon in this attack, gives the following account of his adventures :—" Our next job was to climb another mountain and take Mellili, a small town perched high up above us. I took my platoon across a tomato field into a wood at the foot of the slope and started the climb. We passed some scared civilians hiding in a cave half way up, and captured a very frightened Italian soldier who was drawing water at a farm near the top. We could then see the main position, which was based on a very strong looking pill box about three fields away, and standing high over the town. The men were pretty winded, and the attack was ragged, but as soon as the Bren guns opened up, the Italians came running out with white flags, and gave themselves up, laughing and giggling like a lot of school-girls. We sent about two hundred of them back, under escort, and occupied the post ourselves ".

Mellili had been badly knocked about by naval gun fire, and there had been many civilian casualties. There was no water or light, and the streets were blocked with rubble, but the battalion spent a quiet night there, except for a " stand to " from 8.30 to 11 p.m. Casualties had been slight, and, by the time it moved on again late next night, it was ready to tackle the Germans, who proved to be a very different propostion from the flag-waving Italians. While at Mellili various patrols 1 *Bn* were sent out towards Sortino in an endeavour to contact 13 *Jul* 43 the 50th Division, and one of them succeeded in joining up with the 6th Green Howards near Sortino at 10 a.m. on July 13. Some three hundred more Italians were captured in odd parties during the day.

At half-past four that afternoon the Green Howards were relieved in Mellili by the 2nd Battalion, Wiltshire Regiment, and moved forward about two miles up the road leading north to Villasmundo. About a mile further on the remainder of the 15th Brigade was meeting very strong resistance from a Battle Group of the Hermann Goering Division, which was holding the far side of a deep ravine across which ran the road to Villasmundo. Both the K.O.Y.L.I. and the York and Lancasters made gallant frontal attacks, only to be pinned down by enemy fire. It was now about half-past-five, and the Brigadier took Lt.-Col. Shaw and his Intelligence Officer up to the south bank of the ravine to reconnoitre a possible line of attack by which the Green Howards might outflank the position. Here they had an unpleasant five minutes, as they were spotted by the enemy, and received a salvo from every weapon which he possessed.

At about 7 p.m., however, the enemy started to withdraw, and it was decided that the Green Howards should make a direct night advance on Villasmundo, passing through the K.O.Y.L.I., who were to hold the bridgehead across the ravine. Accordingly, just before midnight, the Battalion set off, with " D " Company as Advance Guard, and, advancing against only slight opposition, the Green Howards entered Villasmundo at 2.40 a.m. on July 14, capturing forty prisoners in the town.

1 Bn
14/17 Jul 43

The next four days were spent in Villasmundo, with Battalion Headquarters and " A " Company in the village, " B " and " D " Companies holding the outpost line, and " C " Company in reserve behind " D " Company. On the 14th the carrier platoon went out about mid-day to reconnoitre the high ground overlooking Carlentini, and, after a minor brush with the enemy, returned with one Italian and two German prisoners. On July 15 Major Bulfin took two companies to mop up some of the neighbouring villages, and they returned after about four hours with thirty-one officers and five hundred and seventy-five other rank prisoners. During the night of the 15/16th a stick of bombs was dropped on Villasmundo and caused a few casualties.

1 Bn
18/19 Jul 43

At 4 a.m. on the 18th the Green Howards marched forward again to a concentration area some three miles north of Lentini. Here they halted for some time while the 13th Brigade was making a reconnaissance in force across the R. Gornalunga. Late in the day the Battalion was ordered forward to support the 13th Brigade, which had run into strong enemy opposition on the banks of the R. Simeto. It finally bivouacked just south of the R. Gornalunga, having marched twenty miles without meeting the enemy.

Early next morning the Green Howards were placed under the command of the 13th Brigade to form a base, while the latter attacked across the R. Simeto. The Battalion moved forward a short way across the Gornalunga, and deployed onto its positions, but apart from a certain amount of mortar fire, it spent a comparatively peaceful day.

While the 1st Battalion had been pursuing its march to Villasmundo, with very little opposition, from July 12 to the 17th, the 6th and 7th Battalions had been advancing towards Lentini some twenty miles on the left flank, and had encountered strong opposition between Sortino and Lentini on July 13.

69 Bde
12 Jul 43

At 11.45 a.m. on July 12 the G.O.C., 50th Division, received orders by wireless not to wait to be relieved in his positions around Floridia, but to press on with all speed to

ADVANCING FROM TAORMINA.

Face page 208

Sortino and Lentini. Italian troops facing the 151st Brigade
in front of Solarino formed a potential threat to the line of
communications, and, in view of the successful advance of the
5th Division on the right, it was essential that the high ground
overlooking the Catania plain beyond Lentini should be
occupied as rapidly as possible, before the enemy had a chance
to co-ordinate any serious opposition. Accordingly orders
were given for the 69th Brigade to send one battalion with
one battery to capture Sortino, if possible before dark.

During this advance a squadron of Sherman tanks, and
the carrier platoon of the 7th Green Howards, under Capt.
Stobo, circumvented the Italian position, and entered their
transport lines. A good many prisoners were captured, and
taken aboard the carriers. An 88 mm. gun then fired on the
party, and three of the carriers were knocked out, the prisoners
being killed, but the crews being untouched. These crews then
drove away some Italian lorries, and several score of mules,
the lorries proving a valuable addition to the battalion transport. An amusing incident then occurred when Capt. Stobo,
wishing to warn the tanks of the presence of the 88 mm. gun,
was unable to attract the attention of the Tank Commander.
Running alongside the tank, he eventually succeeded in lobbing
a fair sized rock through the open turret, a procedure which
produced a very quick result in the appearance of the indignant
and astonished face of the Tank Commander.

The Brigade was led by the 5th Battalion East Yorkshires,
followed by the 6th Green Howards, with the 7th Green
Howards in reserve. By 6.20 p.m. the East Yorkshires reported
that they were in sight of Sortino having met only slight
opposition, but, when one mile south of the village, they came
under heavy fire and were pinned down. At about midnight,
however, the enemy began a partial withdrawal, and the
East Yorkshires were able to occupy all the high ground on
each side of the village. Some prisoners had been taken,
from whom it was discovered that they were part of a German
battle group, which had been rushed forward to support the
Italian Napoli Division.

The 6th Green Howards started advancing through
Solarino at about 6 p.m. and were mortared on entering the
town. The Commanding Officer, Lt.-Col. Smith, went
forward with his Intelligence Officer, Capt. J. Isaacs, to make a
reconnaissance, and found the East Yorkshires held up in
front of Sortino. The Battalion was then ordered to pass
through them and capture the village. The order of march
was " A " Company, one section of carriers, one section of
mortars, Battalion Headquarters, and " B " Company. The

P

remainder of the Battalion under Major Brunton followed in
reserve. After a stiff climb, Sortino was captured soon after
10 a.m. on July 13, and the troops received an enthusiastic
welcome from the population.

The 151st Brigade was still engaged in mopping up around
Solarino, and so the 69th Brigade was ordered to continue the
advance at once on to Lentini, leaving one Battalion behind to
hold Sortino until relieved by the 151st Brigade. The 7th
Green Howards had now moved up, and, leaving the East
Yorkshires to hold Sortino, the 6th Green Howards went on
towards Lentini as the spearhead of the advance, followed by
the 7th Battalion.

6 *Bn*
13 *Jul* 43

The 6th Battalion moved off at 1.30 p.m. with the carrier
and mortar platoons as a screen, followed in order by " C ",
Capt. Hull, " D ", Major Lofthouse, " A ", Capt. Honeyman,
and " B ", Capt. Fairclough, Companies. After going for half
an hour the carriers were held up by an armoured car, and a
" Semovente " (a 75 mm. gun mounted on a Mark III Chassis).
The mortars went into action and blew up the Semovente,
which blocked the road. A few Germans armed with spandaus
appeared, but quickly took refuge in a cave. The carriers
then advanced and cleared the obstacle, capturing at the
same time three Germans and two spandaus.

At about this time the Divisional Commander received
fresh orders from the Army Commander, which rendered a
speedy advance more necessary than ever. In the first place
the Division was ordered to capture Carlentini and Lentini
that night, and secondly to take over the Primosole Bridge—
some seventeen miles ahead—next day from an Airborne
Brigade, which was being dropped to capture it during the
night of July 13/14.

The road having been cleared, the 6th Green Howards
continued their advance at 5 p.m., but almost immediately
came under machine-gun fire from the hills in front of them.
Capt. Delf took out one section of carriers on patrol in order
to draw the enemy's fire, and a considerable number of
machine-guns opened up, interspersed with solid shot from
high velocity guns. The enemy fire was found to be coming
mainly from a ridge on the far side of a shallow valley. As an
attack against this feature would entail an advance down an
exposed slope, across a few hundred yards of country with
very little cover, and a final assault uphill, it was decided to
postpone the Battalion attack until darkness fell.

Accordingly at 9.15 p.m. the assault was launched. " C "
Company advanced on the right flank, with its objective a
farmhouse on the ridge, and " D " Company on the left.

" A " Company was held in reserve. The attack was supported by 124 Field Regiment, R.A., and " D " Company of the 2nd Cheshire Machine Gun Battalion. The ridge was captured successfully ; twelve Germans were taken prisoner, but many more escaped, running madly in the direction of Mt. Pancali across the road, as the leading companies of the Green Howards swarmed over their objective. Two high velocity guns, several machine-guns, and two half-track vehicles fell into the hands of the Battalion. Casualties had been light, but included Lt.-Col. Smith, D.S.O., who was wounded in the leg.

The Battalion was reorganised under Major Brunton. Capt. Hull became 2nd i/c, and Capt. Young took over " C " Company from him. The Battalion now moved back onto the road, and attempted to advance round Mt. Pancali, and so on to Lentini. The two forward companies, however, could make no progress against strong opposition in front, and a withering machine-gun enfilade fire from Mt. Pancali. After making *6 Bn* repeated efforts, orders were received at 4 a.m. on July 14 for *14 Jul 43* the 6th Battalion to withdraw to the ridge which it had captured the previous night, and to hold a firm base there.

Meanwhile it had become clear to the higher command that the chances of capturing Lentini that night, as ordered, were remote, but that it was too late to suggest any postponement of the plan. The hill on the left of the road, against which the 6th Battalion had failed to make any progress was called Mt. Pancali, and formed a considerable feature of the landscape. It was afterwards learnt that it was held by about a hundred Germans with thirty machine-guns, one troop of self-propelled guns, and some tanks. It was of vital importance that this feature should be captured at the earliest possible moment if the advance was to continue, and if the parachute landings ahead were to be reinforced in time.

Accordingly the 7th Green Howards were brought up, *7 Bn* and ordered to attack at 8 a.m. on July 14, two hours after *14 Jul 43* receipt of orders. Their attack was supported by two Field Regiments R.A. (the 98th and 124th) and all available machine-guns of the 2nd Cheshire Regiment, but it was plain that this support fire could not be very effective, as details of the enemy's dispositions were unknown. Zero hour was put off half an hour at the request of the Gunners, but at 8.30 a.m. " A " Company (Capt. Waters) and " B " Company (Capt. Hay) started off against the hill, followed by " C " Company (Major Mansell) and " D " Company (Capt. Hudson), with the carrier platoon covering the exposed left flank. The leading companies moved rapidly under excellent control, and, although at the foot of the hill they came under very heavy artillery, mortar, and machine-gun fire, they climbed the hill and ejected the enemy. By 10 a.m., Mt. Pancali was in their hands, and the way was open to Lentini and beyond.

An observer, who had a grand stand view of this attack from the Headquarters of the 6th Battalion, wrote :— " Watching the attack from a good vantage point was an experience not to be missed, and the " show " put in the shade any demonstration which an Infantry School could produce. The planning was masterful, and the execution, under intense fire, was brilliant. When it is considered that thirty German machine-guns under excellent cover, and cunningly concealed, swept the entire area continuously, and that the climbing of the hill would have been unpleasant under peace conditions, some idea of the stupendous task which was undertaken can be imagined ".

What finer tribute could be paid to the officers and men of the Battalion than the words of a German desert veteran captured on Pancali ?—" Since Britain started this war against my Fatherland, (or words to that effect), I have been against many British attacks, but that was the finest I have ever seen. I congratulate you ! "

An account exists, written by Capt. K. A. Nash, who took part in this attack, and the following extracts will give an insight into the mind of a soldier in action. So vividly is it written, the reader will, for a moment, almost see himself playing the part. Those who have experienced it themselves will, we feel sure, agree as to the reality of the description.

05.30. We are to attack Mt. Pancali, a high hill on our left, alive with machine-guns. "A" Company goes left, and we make a frontal assault. I can see the objective rising suddenly about two thousand yards away, with a flat plain between us. H. hour is 08.00.

07.45. Hell ! Start time altered to 08.30—gunners not ready yet. This waiting before an attack is bloody, especially when shelling is on. The men don't like it—neither do I. " Pedestrian " Smith seems quite cheery, and is telling his platoon it will be dead easy. He and I found out some time ago that the best way to spend this last hour is to joke with the men—its good for them and good for you. I pick out the Company " funny man " and he gets cracking about his " Missus ", who, according to him, gets all his money and weighs fifteen stone.

08.30. The guns open up, and we move forward into the
open. 6th Battalion on our right are going to
have a grand-stand view of the attack.

09.00. At the foot of the hill at last. Looks bloody steep
from here. I stop the artillery over the wireless ;
we're not going to get into our own barrage. There
are big boulders as we climb. The men are splendid,
climbing up grimly not knowing what to expect at
the top. I move over to the right to search for
Nigel's (Lt. N. Mounsey) platoon but cannot see
them. We reach a ledge just before the summit, and
pause for breath, and then I hear " Pedestrian "
shout : " Follow me, 11 platoon ",—and I find
myself on the top.

We have been covered during the climb by steep
sides and boulders, but now machine-guns open up
all round. The ground now is flat but covered with
rocks. A miserable Boche crawls from behind a
boulder about ten yards in front shouting the
inevitable " Kamerad ". He could have killed me
twenty times over as I stood there, but he is too
shaken to press the trigger. I run past him—gosh,
this is great fun now ! Bullets are whining everywhere, but our blood is up—we are shouting,
swearing, cheering—it's easy, they're giving themselves up—they've had it ! Except that on the
right there's no sign of Nigel, and a lot of fire is
coming from behind that wall. I see Boche moving,
but now away—they're advancing in the copse
where I think Nigel's crowd is—three spandaus
open up on us, and I drop just in time. I look
round. Gosh, I've only one section with me ! The
rest of the Company has swept forward. I can hear
the C.S.M. yelling encouragement to them. Geoff is
quiet, and looks bad, he was hit in the thigh, but
staggered on to the top to collapse in a hail of
bullets.

I am as excited as hell, and get a Bren to open up
towards the copse, and Jerry quietens down. I
must be excited now as I do a damned silly thing—I
zig-zag forward under cover of the Bren—only half
a dozen Boches there at the most I should think—
two blokes say " Good luck, Sir ", and a voice says
" I am coming with you, Sir ". Grand troops !—its'
Cpl. Kendrick. We dash forward amongst the
spandau lead, our Bren silences one machine-gun.

Another twenty yards, then more spandau, and a dash for cover behind a big boulder—I turn round to see Kendrick shot clean through the throat. I grab his tommy and loose off the magazine. Poor Kendrick ! Courage evaporates. I hug the ground and pray ; then Jerry starts shelling us. I shout back for a smoke screen on the copse. The first smoke bomb lands nearer to me than to the copse, and I shout a correction, only to find that the mortar crews have been knocked out. I lay there nearly half an hour sweating. Presently the Boche get browned off and come out with their hands up— about thirty of them, armed to the teeth. What a morning ! "

Lt. C. G. Smith, referred to in the foregoing account, as the leader of No. 11 Platoon, was later awarded the Military Cross for the great courage and resolution with which he led his men into the attack. Although hit in the thigh at an early stage, Lt. Smith still ran on ahead of his men, until a burst of spandau fire smashed his knee. In the words of the official citation accompanying his award. " There is no doubt that the resolute leadership shown by this officer was largely responsible for the success of the operation, which cleared the way for the 8th Army on this sector ".

As soon as it was clear to Lt.-Col. Jebb that he would not need to use his reserve companies, he ordered " D " Company to move forward astride the road, to cover the reorganisation of the Battalion. He had received orders to continue the advance as soon as possible. " D " Company soon came under heavy fire, and suffered several casualties, including Lt. D. A. Hone, M.C., who was mortally wounded.

It was not until 1 p.m. that they were able to make any headway. The Battalion then advanced towards Lentini with the Carrier Platoon in the lead, followed by " C " Company. By 3 p.m. Carlentini and Lentini were reported clear of the enemy, and the Battalion passed through on to the Catania road, capturing eight Germans who were trying to make their escape.

The 7th Battalion was now well ahead of any other formation, and dropped off detachments of the Anti-Tank platoon to block the lateral roads as it went along. Some three miles north of Lentini the leading elements of the carrier platoon ran into an ambush of three German tanks, which, after knocking out the leading carrier, withdrew rapidly. Unfortunately Capt. W. O. Stobo was killed, and two other ranks wounded, by a direct hit from an anti-tank shell. Capt. H. T. Caden took over command of the carrier platoon.

Throughout the day the Battalion was subjected to dive-bombing attacks, and received several casualties, including Capt. L. W. Smith who was killed. Some vehicles were also lost.

In the late afternoon the 8th and 9th Battalions of the Durham Light Infantry, and part of the 4th Armoured Brigade passed through the Battalion. These units were attempting to reach the Primosole Bridge, and relieve the airborne troops, before dark.

The Green Howards then took up a defensive position some four miles north of Lentini, their role being to form a firm base, and protect the western flank of the main advance. After dark, they received their first hot meal of the day. In the words of the commanding officer :—" It had been a hard but satisfactory day, and the Battalion had acquitted itself well ".

Meanwhile, the 6th Green Howards had remained in their positions until 5 p.m. when they advanced to Lentini, and took up a defensive position to the west of the village.   **6 Bn**
14 Jul 43

During the next three days, July 15, 16 and 17, there was very severe fighting to secure the Primosole Bridgehead, the brunt of which was borne by the Durham Light Infantry Battalions of the 151st Brigade. During the night of the 16th a small bridgehead was established by the 8th Battalion Durham Light Infantry, and on the following night, this was enlarged by the 6th and 9th Battalions Durham Light Infantry. While this battle was being fought the 6th and 7th Green Howards remained comparatively static in their positions, but had a certain amount of excitement.

The 6th Battalion accepted the surrender of thirty-five Italians and four Germans on the 15th, and, at about mid-day on the 16th, a report was received that a party of Germans had looted a farm to the west of Lentini, and then made off in the direction of Mt. Pancali. A strong patrol under Major Hull went out in search of them, but returned in the evening, without having seen any enemy. On the 17th, the Battalion moved forward, prior to taking part in another attack at Primosole on the 18th.   **6 Bn**
15/17 Jul 43

Early on the morning of the 15th the 7th Battalion moved forward about a mile to a stronger position on the high ground overlooking the Catania plain. It covered here a frontage of two thousand yards, with its left flank completely open. " B " Echelon was left behind at the previous position. In the evening thirty-two prisoners surrendered to " A " Company. It was known that considerable parties of the enemy were still roaming the countryside to the west and south, and, at 3 a.m. on the 16th, the left hand platoon of   **7 Bn**
15/17 Jul 43

" A " Company, which was on the railway line, was attacked by a small party of the enemy. The attack was driven off, but the platoon suffered two casualties. Soon after this, Lt. F. A. Goodenough, who had gone forward on patrol, was reported missing.

At about 9 p.m., in brilliant moonlight, a force of about two hundred Germans approached " B " Echelon area. Two parties under Capt. D. C. Stevenson, M.B.E., the Quarter Master, and Capt. R. A. Mason, the Transport Officer, respectively, attacked them. In some confused fighting, they were driven off. One man was killed and one wounded, while Capt. Mason was captured.

Great credit must be given to the men of " B " Echelon, who, while keeping their flanks intact, managed to save all the transport, and disperse the vehicles to safer surroundings. As soon as the position was cleared up Capt. Stevenson took out a small patrol to search for Capt. Mason. Having returned without success, Capt. Stevenson was snatching an hour's sleep, when he was awakened by Capt. Mason in person. Greatly surprised he asked what had happened : to which Capt. Mason's only reply was :—" They set off with me down the railway line, but it was the wrong way for me, so I came back ! "

Capt. Mason had however collected information from his captors that a number of the enemy were hiding in a railway tunnel north west of Lentini. Accordingly two platoons of " B " Company went to the north end of the tunnel, while an anti-tank gun fired up the south end. The resultant bag was twelve prisoners from the north end and twenty from the south end, and some useful identifications of both German and Italian formations were obtained.

In the early hours of the morning of July 17 an officer of a German Parachute Regiment gave himself up to " A " Company. Later in the day, the Battalion moved forward and arrived in its assembly area south of the Primosole Bridge at about 4.30 p.m.

See MAP No. 12   The position at Primosole on the morning of July 17 was that the 151st Brigade was stabilised on the positions which it had taken up after its second attack on the night of July 16/17. The 9th Battalion Durham Light Infantry was on the right of the road to Catania, and the 6th Battalion Durham Light Infantry on the left, both Battalions being entrenched some fifteen hundred yards to the north of the R. Simeto. The 8th Battalion Durham Light Infantry was established just north of the Primosole Bridge for its close defence. The enemy, consisting largely of élite German parachute troops, who were still landing on Catania airfield, were holding the line of the river on either side of the bridgehead, and were facing our forward troops. The Corps Commander, General Dempsey, visited the 50th Division's Headquarters at 10 a.m. on July 17, and gave orders for the Division to deepen the bridgehead by some two thousand yards up to the Bottaceto ditch on the southern edge of the aerodrome. The orders issued by the 50th Division for this attack were for the 168th Brigade to pass through the 151st Brigade, with its centre on the main road, and its objective the Bottaceto ditch. The 69th Brigade was then to pass through, swing to the west and capture the railway, and so screen the left flank of the 168th Brigade.

The leading Battalions of the 168th Brigade, the London Scottish on the right and London Irish on the left, started their advance at 10 p.m. on the 17th. At first all went well, but, as a result of a faulty reconnaissance made during the morning, and owing to the fact that the enemy had been reinforced by more paratroops during the evening, the resistance was more formidable than had been anticipated. This was the first attack which the 168th Brigade had made, and the unexpectedly strong opposition created a great deal of confusion. Eventually, at some time about 3 a.m. on the 18th, the G.O.C. 50th Division ordered the 168th Brigade to fall back slightly, and to take up a defensive position on the general line of a ditch some thousand yards short of the original objective.

Meanwhile, despite the confusion in front of them, the *7 Bn* Green Howards had proceeded to carry out their orders. *17 Jul 43* Lt.-Col. Jebb led the 7th Battalion across the Primosole bridge at 10.30 p.m., and proceeded straight up the Catania road. Soon after crossing the bridge, sounds of a considerable battle ahead made it clear that the enemy were contesting the advance of the 168th Brigade much more strongly than had been anticipated. It had been originally planned that the 7th Green Howards, following up the 168th Brigade, should, when a few hundred yards short of the Bottaceto ditch, turn westwards and advance towards the railway line, their objective being the western end of the ditch. As they advanced up the road, however, they came across troops of the 168th Brigade, who had been pushed back to a point short of that from which they were to begin their turning movement. Nevertheless, having received no orders to the contrary, the *7 Bn* 7th Battalion passed through, and, at 1.30 a.m. on July 18, *18 Jul 43* started its advance westwards according to plan.

It was a moonless night, although only moderately dark, and the flat country over which they had to pass was intersected by high banks and deep ditches. It had not been possible for the Company and Platoon commanders to get a closer look at the ground over which they were going to pass than could be obtained from the higher ground immediately south of the Primosole bridge. Consequently the Battalion entered upon an operation, which transgressed most of the recognised canons of warfare, in so far as they were making a night advance, across ground which had not been reconnoitred, parallel to the enemy's front at a distance of only about four hundred yards.

The plan was for " A " Company and " C " Company to lead, followed respectively by " B " Company and " D " Company. When they came level with their objectives, in their case the western end of the Bottaceto ditch, " A " and " B " companies were to wheel to their right, and make a frontal attack. " C " Company was to veer off to the right, and make for the railway bridge which crossed the ditch, whilst " D " Company was to proceed straight on to the railway line, on the immediate right of the 6th Battalion's objective.

The enemy remained in ignorance of the Battalion's movements until " A " and " B " Companies started wheeling to the right. The latter were then immediately detected, and very heavy machine-gun fire was opened upon them. This set numerous haystacks on fire, against which they were silhouetted, and these companies suffered severe casualties. The enemy were found to be strongly entrenched, and making full use of the permanent forward defences of the Catania aerodrome. Major Hay was killed almost immediately, and the command of " B " Company was taken over by Lt. Coles. In spite of the most courageous efforts to come to grips with the enemy across the ditches and banks, both companies were finally pinned down within about a hundred and fifty yards of the ditch.

During this action L/Sgt. E. A. Hood behaved with conspicuous gallantry when his platoon commander had been killed, and was awarded the Military Medal.

At about 3.30 a.m. orders were received for the Battalion to reorganise around the positions on which " A " and " B " Companies were held up, and not to press the attack any further. This order involved the withdrawal of " C " and " D " Companies, who had proceeded some considerable distance to the west. " C " Company, in particular, was by this time practically isolated, and fighting a stubborn battle in the vicinity of the railway bridge. The company was, however, skilfully extricated by Major Mansell, and, by first light, Lt.-Col. Jebb had got his battalion together again, but

found that his own Headquarters were in a farm only a
hundred and fifty yards away from the enemy, and in front
of his forward troops. Fortunately the enemy were surprisingly
inactive, and, although the Battalion was in very close contact
with them, the day passed without any counter-attack being
launched. As soon as darkness fell a slight withdrawal was
made on instructions from the Brigadier, and more suitable
dispositions were taken up, in which the Battalion conformed
with the 6th Green Howards on the left, and the London Irish
on the right.

The Battalion was by this time very depleted, the strengths   7 *Bn*
of the companies being :—" A " Company—30 ;   " B " 19/21 *Jul* 43
Company—10 ; " C " Company—45, and " D " Company—
30. Nevertheless the 7th Green Howards clung on to these
positions until relieved by the 8th Battalion, Durham
Light Infantry at midnight on July 21. From the 19th to the
21st enemy activity was confined to intermittent mortar fire
and some sniping. The battalion, however, gained virtual
domination of " No Man's Land " by vigorous patrolling at
night, and by periodical harassing of the enemy's positions
with all available weapons.

During one of the exchanges of mortar fire an enemy
bomb landed in one of the Battalion's mortar pits, killing the
whole of the crew, with the exception of two men who were
wounded, smashing the mortar, and setting the bombs on fire.
Pte. J. McCurry, one of the wounded men, realising that the
bombs in the pit might explode at any moment, limped out to
fetch a shovel, and, returning at all speed, proceeded to put
out the fire. For his courage and quick action he was awarded
the Military Medal.

The 6th Battalion, following the road which led along the   6 *Bn*
north bank of the R. Simeto from the Primosole bridge,   18 *Jul* 43
reached its objective, the railway bridge over the road, soon
after first light on July 18, without opposition. The delay,
however, caused by the obscurity of the general situation on
the front of the 168th Brigade, prevented them from reaching
their objectives unobserved. Immediately on arrival " C "
Company was taken by surprise and attacked by a strong
enemy fighting patrol, some fifty men in strength, and a hand
to hand struggle ensued. Two of the enemy were killed, and
one wounded and captured, while the remainder scattered and
fled. The main body withdrew straight back up the railway
line, while the remainder ran in the direction of the Red House.
During this skirmish C.S.M. Hollis threw a grenade at one
German which hit him full on the chest. It did not explode,
but was sufficient to send him dashing off down the railway
line like a " scalded cat ".

At about 10.30 a.m. some Sherman tanks arrived, and took up a position to the left rear of the Battalion. Throughout the remainder of the day the Battalion positions were intermittently but accurately shelled, and considerable trouble was experienced by the left forward company, caused by enemy machine-guns in the vicinity of the Red House.

The Red House was obviously a serious threat to the Battalion's positions, and, after a preliminary reconnaissance had been made, a strong fighting patrol from " B " Company, under Lt. A. R. Smith, was sent out to deal with it on the night of July 18. The attack was successful, and the enemy was driven out, but the patrol lost two men killed, and seven wounded, the latter including Lt. Smith and Sgt. W. Dawson, his second in command.

Lt. Smith was wounded at the start of the action, and Sgt. Dawson took command. Although he was himself hit, he continued to lead his men with great coolness and gallantry, and it was solely due to his personal courage that the attack was successful. Sgt. Dawson was awarded the Military Medal. In the following year Sgt. Dawson, although he had lost the sight of one eye, gallantly insisted on accompanying his battalion to Normandy, and was killed in the action near Oristot on July 11, 1944.

As a result of the elimination of this menacing stronghold " C " Company was able to advance across the railway line, and take up positions further to the north-west, while " A " and " D " Companies also infiltrated to the north, and the whole front of the Battalion was extended on to considerably improved positions.

6 *Bn*
19 *Jul* 43   In this advance from the Primosole bridge the 6th Battalion was commanded by Major Brunton, who now received orders to make a further attack on the night of July 19. Shortly before midnight the Battalion moved forward under an artillery barrage. Three companies, " A ", " C " and " D " made the attack, in which " A " Company occupied its objective without casualties. " C " Company also was successful, but " D " Company ran into a hail of machine-gun fire, and sustained fairly heavy casualties. Lt. A. H. Davidson was wounded and missing, and his platoon was forced to retire. Nevertheless, " D " Company had managed to advance about three hundred yards, and the Battalion had, in the main, accomplished its task.

This attack, which took place simultaneously with that launched by the 1st Battalion Green Howards on the left, to be recounted later, was to some extent affected by the failure of the latter Battalion to gain its objectives. The left hand company of the 6th Battalion, having achieved an initially successful advance, was forced to make a considerable withdrawal when it came under heavy fire from its exposed left flank.

Later in the morning quite a number of men from Capt. Verity's company of the 1st Battalion withdrew through the 6th Battalion.

6 *Bn*
20/21 *Jul* 43

At midnight on July 21 it was relieved by the 6th Battalion, Durham Light Infantry.

During this attack Pte. L. Snowdon, a stretcher bearer attached to " D " Company, attended the wounded under very heavy machine-gun and mortar fire, and for his devotion to duty and disregard of his personal safety, was awarded the Military Medal.

These attacks by the 6th and 7th Green Howards between July 18 and July 21 had been designed to strengthen and secure the bridgehead at Primosole, and had achieved their object. The question of any further advance by the 50th Division for the time being had been ruled out by General Montgomery's decision, on July 18, to switch his attack to the 5th Division on the 50th Division's left. It had become apparent that the coastal route to Catania was blocked by strong enemy forces based on the permanent defences of the aerodrome, which had been built long before the invasion took place, and which consisted of concrete fortifications, belts of wire and minefields. The Army Commander therefore ordered the 5th Division to attempt to break through into the foothills of Mount Etna further inland and so turn the aerodrome defences.

The 1st Battalion Green Howards took part in these operations, as will be related, but the 5th Division was eventually held up on a defensive line which the enemy had established, with the aid of reinforcements from the mainland, as a continuation westwards of the Catania defences. It was left to the 30th Corps finally to break this line at Adrano, the key point of the enemy's lateral line of communications. Troops of the 30th Corps entered Adrano on August 6, but some days before this the enemy had foreseen the danger of being split in two, and had started to withdraw on August 4, on which day the whole of the 13th Corps started forward on the chase to Messina.

Leaving the 69th Brigade, with the 6th and 7th Green Howards, having just been relieved in their defensive positions north of the Primolsole bridge, we will now follow the 1st Green Howards in their attack with the 5th Division, and subsequent pursuit of the enemy.

We left them, it will be remembered, waiting, on the morning of July 19, just across the R. Gornalunga to assist in the attack of the 13th Brigade across the R. Simeto.

The enemy now had their backs to the wall, but were holding a very strong position on the high ground, which rises to the north of the railway line crossing the Catania plain. This position was guarded by forward machine-gun posts, dug every twenty yards into the side of the railway embankment, and was held by troops of the Hermann Goering Division.

At 5 p.m. on July 19 orders were issued for the 15th Brigade to make a night attack under an artillery barrage against this position. As darkness was approaching, it was not possible to make a ground reconnaissance before the attack, and this, together with the difficult nature of the terrain, helped to contribute to its ultimate failure.

The line of battle of the 15th Brigade was the Green Howards on the right, and the York and Lancasters on the left, and the K.O.Y.L.I. in reserve. The attack was launched at 12.45 a.m. on the 20th, with " A " Company on the right, and " D " Company on the left, followed by " B " and " C " Companies respectively. All went well until the leading companies were within a few hundred yards of the railway line. Here they encountered unexpectedly deep fosses which held up their rate of advance to such an extent that the barrage ran away from them. The result was that when they approached the forward defence line, the Germans had emerged from their dugouts and were manning their machine-guns. The leading Companies then came under a withering fire from machine-guns and mortars. In the face of this they pressed on right up to the German posts but were unable to break through. In the confusion " B " Company had lost its position, and; working round the right flank, had overtaken " A " Company in the darkness. It had therefore become a leading company, and met the full volume of the enemy's fire. It was eventually forced to retire down the fosses, leaving many of its wounded in enemy hands, including Capts. H. Verity and L. J. Hesmond-halgh. These two officers were so severely wounded that they died later as prisoners of war. Lt. A. R. Johnson was also mortally wounded in this gallant but unsuccessful attack.

Lt. R. Bell particularly distinguished himself in this action, and was awarded the Military Cross. He was commanding a platoon of " B " Company, which penetrated the enemy defences in the face of very heavy machine-gun fire. A fierce hand-to-hand encounter ensued, in the course of which Capt. Verity, his second in command, and the senior subaltern of the Company, all became casualties. The C.S.M. and two of the platoon sergeants were also put *hors de combat*. At this point the wounded senior officer ordered Lt. Bell to extricate the company, and take it back some five hundred yards. Under very heavy fire Lt. Bell carried out this order and established the remnants of the company in a defensive position. He then returned in broad daylight, and rescued the wounded subaltern. Once again he went back under fire for his Company Commander and 2nd i/c, but failed to find them. Throughout the battle Lt. Bell showed courage and determination of the highest order, which were an inspiration to all who saw him.

When day broke on the 20th the Battalion found itself pinned down and overlooked by the enemy at close range. Any movement immediately drew fire, and, in addition, it was mortared and machine-gunned from a strong German post on the flank which had been bypassed in the darkness. During the night of July 20/21 the Battalion withdrew from contact with the enemy and moved a mile to the rear, where the Brigade was forming up for another night attack. This was, however, cancelled at the last minute, as it had been decided to withdraw the 5th Division to the line of the R. Simeto, and allow the 30th Corps to make its encircling advance on Adrano.

1 Bn
21 Jul 43

At 3 p.m. the Green Howards took up a rearguard position just north of the bridgehead at Basso del Fico, the remainder of the Brigade passing through them. During the night of July 21/22 the 17th Brigade arrived to relieve the 15th Brigade, and, at 3 a.m. on the 22nd, the Green Howards withdrew to a rest area around Massa Valle Paola.

1 Bn
22/25 Jul 43

The next two days were spent resting and refitting, until, at 3.30 a.m. on July 25, the Battalion moved forward once again to the R. Simeto, and took over positions from the K.O.Y.L.I., who had been left there under command of the 17th Brigade. These positions were strung out along the river westwards from the bridge at Basso del Fico, for a distance of about two miles, and were held by the Battalion until relieved by the York and Lancasters during the night of July 28/29. During this period there was considerable patrolling activity, and " B " Company made a particularly successful raid on Massa Passiti and Massa Francesca, capturing some prisoners.

1 Bn
25/28 Jul 43

On July 29 the Battalion was again relieved and moved back to a new rest area near Massa Bonierno, bivouacking in olive groves, where it remained until August 3. Whilst in this rest area it received a draft of a hundred men from the Royal Sussex Regiment.

1 Bn
29 Jul/
3 Aug 43

1 *Bn*
3 *Aug* 43   At 11 p.m. on the night of the 3rd the Green Howards set
out to attack two hill features on the western flank of the main
German position, and after a four-hour cross country night
1 *Bn* march, which included wading across the R. Simeto, arrived
4 *Aug* 43 at the start line at 3.15 in the morning of August 4. They
captured their objectives by 5 a.m. without opposition, but
suffered some casualties from mines and booby traps. Since
the enemy had evacuated this position, orders for the next
advance were issued at once. The first objective was Motta St.
Anastasia, and at 2 p.m. the Battalion advanced, with the
York and Lancasters on its right, and the K.O.Y.L.I. in
reserve. " D " Company, under Capt. Parkinson, led the
battalion as vanguard.

See MAP
No. 11   Motta was captured by the Green Howards at half past
eight on the evening of August 4, to the accompaniment of
much clapping and " vivas " from the inhabitants, despite the
fact that their town had been severely shelled by the 92nd
Field Regiment, R.A., during the attack. A certain amount of
opposition had been encountered by " D " Company in front
of the town, and, before its final capture, a troop of tanks,
together with " C " Company, under Capt. Tanner, had had
to be utilised.

The following account by Capt. H. L. Wilson, who commanded the leading platoon of " D " Company, gives a typical
picture of a vanguard in action. " All seemed peaceful
enough until, just as we rounded a bend, a Boche machine-gun
opened up. We flung ourselves down, and I wriggled forward
round the bend. I could not see where it was, but got a Bren
gun up and opened fire on a house, just for effect. Leaving
the Bren there, I got back and took my platoon off the road
to the right. I got two more Bren guns over into the vineyard
and spread the sections. Then, firing from the hip, we went
forward. Norman Yardley, meanwhile, had got his platoon
down on the left, and put a couple of well-aimed mortar
bombs on the spot. The Boche then fled, leaving his guns and
one man dead. We continued the advance, picking bunches of
grapes off the vines as we went along, and climbed up into the
village without any further opposition ".

In less than twenty-four hours the Battalion had completed
a fourteen mile march across country, crossing three rivers;
made a successful night attack, and consolidated the captured
positions; carried out a further five mile advance against the
defended town of Motta, and captured it.

1 *Bn*
5 *Aug* 43   Early next morning, the Green Howards were visited
by General Dempsey, G.O.C. 13th Corps, who congratulated
them on the progress which they had made so far, and sym-
pathised with them on their losses.

MULES TAKING UP SUPPLIES IN FRONT OF LANCIANO.

ADVANCING TO POSITIONS NORTH OF LANCIANO.

Face page 224

At 11 a.m. on August 5 orders were received to continue the advance, and capture Belpasso, some five miles further to the north. The Green Howards were on the left, the K.O.Y.L.I. on the right, and the York and Lancasters in reserve.

The advance proceeded unmolested until " Hell Fire Corner ", the name given to a crossroads at Fondaco, about one third of the way to Belpasso, was reached. The Germans had a strong post there, including a Tiger tank, and, owing to the stone walls and impenetrable country, it was very difficult to manoeuvre. One section of carriers and two anti-tank guns were sent up, but it was not until artillery fire was brought to bear on the Tiger tank that the way could be cleared. Eventually at about 4 p.m. the Commanding Officer was able to order the advance to continue.

He himself, with " A " and " B " Companies, took the road leading north-east, and made contact with the K.O.Y.L.I. an hour later, while a force under Major Worthington, consisting of "C" Company, one section of carriers, and one section of mortars, took the track leading due north to Belpasso. The advance from Hell Fire Corner to Belpasso was made under great difficulties. " The country was very rough, with sharp pointed lava like black glass, and immediately to the front was a dense forest of cactus. The prickles of the cactus became embedded in the men's clothing, and eventually in their skin, causing festering sores."

Both Major Worthington's party and the remainder of the Battalion spent the night some two miles south of Belpasso, and about a mile apart. It was a very dark night, and it was a noteworthy feat by C.Q.M.S. M. Durkin of " C " Company to find his way across the cactus and lava covered country to Battalion Headquarters. He had been sent by Capt. Tanner for orders, as the company wireless set had broken down.

Soon after midnight Lt.-Col. Shaw issued orders for the final advance on Belpasso to take place on a three company front at 5 a.m. This attack was rendered difficult owing to the very close nature of the country, and by German Tiger tanks which commanded the roads and tracks. However, in face of all opposition, the Green Howards were in the outskirts of the town shortly before 9 a.m. on August 6. Here they halted while an artillery barrage was put down on the exits and entrances. At 9.15, when this was lifted, they entered the town unopposed to the usual friendly demonstration from the inhabitants. Forty-eight casualties were sustained in this operation, including C.S.M. W. H. B. Askew, D.C.M., of Headquarters Company, who was killed. The Battalion

1 Bn
6/9 Aug **43**

Q

established itself in Belpasso for the next four days, and, except for a small mopping-up operation by "C" Company at Nicolosi and Pedara on the 7th, no contact was made with the enemy.

1 *Bn*
10 *Aug* 43
By August 10 the enemy in retreat was some miles ahead, and the Green Howards moved on to Mascalucia, where they received orders at 4 p.m. to attack Milo.

1 *Bn*
11 *Aug* 43
Milo was entered by the Battalion on the heels of the enemy at half past five in the morning of August 11 and positions were quickly taken up in the front edge of the town. Soon after the Battalion entered the town, the Germans started shelling it and there were some casualties, particularly in " A " Company, which was situated in the vicinity of the Church. This formed a prominent landmark, and the first shell to arrive knocked down the spire. It seemed probable that the enemy were going to counter-attack, but this did not materialise, and, as soon as it was dark, the companies moved clear of the town, and took up new positions.

1 *Bn*
12 *Aug* 43
On the evening of the 12th the enemy put down a heavy fire from all weapons, a sure sign that he was preparing to withdraw. The following morning the Battalion advanced without meeting any opposition, and established a bridgehead across the R. Nigro. Later in the day the 51st Highland Division took up the advance, and passed through the Green
1 *Bn*
16/23 *Aug* 43
Howards' bridgehead, while the latter moved back to a rest area near Sferro. On August 16 they moved to the Paterno area to rest and refit for the next operations.

This was the end of the fighting in Sicily as far as the 1st Battalion Green Howards was concerned. On August 23 Lt.-Col. Shaw handed over his command to Major Bulfin, as he was leaving the Battalion on promotion to Brigadier. For his leadership of the 1st Green Howards throughout the Sicilian campaign, Lt.-Col. Shaw was awarded the Distinguished Service Order. His citation reads as follows :—
" Throughout the Sicilian campaign he has commanded his battalion with marked skill, gallantry and determination. On July 12 he carried out a Battalion attack on Mellili, which resulted in the occupation of that town the same evening. Again, on August 4, his Battalion made a successful attack and captured the town of Motta St. Anastasia, taking a number of prisoners. On August 5 his Battalion was the left battalion of the Brigade in the advance on Belpasso. He conducted a skilful advance over extremely difficult country, and his Battalion captured Belpasso by mid-day on August 6. The ability and leadership shown by Lt.-Col. Shaw during the campaign have contributed largely to the success of the operations carried out by his Battalion and the Brigade ".

Returning to the 50th Division, which had assumed 6 *and* 7 *Bns*
a defensive role in front of the Primosole Bridge on July 19, 22/25 *Jul* 43
we had brought the story of the 6th and 7th Green Howards
up to the point where they were relieved in the line at midnight
on July 21. Both Battalions reached their rest areas at about
3.30 a.m., and the 7th Battalion appears to have been luckier
in its positions than the 6th, as the only entry in the former's
diary for the next four days is " Resting ", while the 6th
Battalion, on the other hand, were shelled on the evening of
the 22nd, and " B " Company had two casualties. Later in
the evening " D " Company suffered the indignity of being
fired upon by an Italian boy. This small aggressor had the
honour of being caught by the Commanding Officer and the
second in command, and was handed over by them, for some
unexplained reason, to the gunners.

On the next day, the 23rd, the area was shelled again, but
the troops managed to get some sea-bathing, and the battalion
rested and generally tidied itself up. During the afternoon
Lt.-Col. R. H. W. S. Hastings, M.C., The Rifle Brigade,
arrived to take command of the Battalion. Lt.-Col. Hastings
was destined to take the Battalion home after the Sicilian
campaign, and it was due largely to his training and leadership
that the Battalion achieved distinction in the landings in
Normandy nearly a year later. Having led the Battalion on to
the beaches, and throughout the first three weeks of fierce
fighting, Lt.-Col. Hastings was wounded and evacuated back
to England. He was a great loss to the Battalion and his
name will always be remembered by the Green Howards.

On July 24 there was more shelling, and the Battalion was
ordered to move to a quieter area. During the day a welcome
draft of fifty reinforcements arrived.

At midnight on July 25 the Battalion relieved the 8th   6 *Bn*
Battalion, Durham Light Infantry, in the line, where it was 25/26 *Jul* 43
subjected to intermittent shell fire. On the 26th the Regimental
Aid Post received a direct hit and Capt. L. Herbert, the
Medical Officer, Capt. C. G. Wallace, the Padre, and Pte.
Willson, stretcher bearer, were killed. The next day " B "
Company was mortared, and Lt. Jackson and his batman
were killed. Despite the shelling, however, conditions were
not too bad, as the war diary states : " The Battalion has
been able to obtain plenty of wine, tomatoes, potatoes and
grapes in this area. There are also melons, peaches and
some chickens to be had ".

The 7th Battalion relieved the 9th Battalion, Durham   7 *Bn*
Light Infantry, at midnight on the 26th, and during the next 26 *Jul* 43
seven days experienced occasional sniping, shelling and

mortaring. Patrols were sent out at frequent intervals to harass the enemy, and keep an eye on his movements.

The total casualties which this Battalion had suffered since the landings were, up to August 1, 92 killed and wounded, 21 missing, and during this period they captured 100 enemy prisoners. The country in which they had been operating for the last fortnight was very malarial, and both Battalions lost a number of men from this cause.

On August 4 the 50th Division advanced across the Bottaceto Ditch, the enemy having withdrawn the previous night, and began the pursuit of his rearguards, which was to take it almost to the gates of Messina.

The 30th Corps had captured Centuripe, five miles south-west of Adrano, on the 3rd, and it was on this day that there were obvious signs on the Primosole front, that the enemy were about to withdraw.

Before beginning to relate the actions in which the Green Howards took part in their advance during the next fortnight, a brief description of the country over which they fought will help the reader to realise the arduous nature of the fighting. As soon as they passed through Catania, they left the plains, and traversed the roads between Mount Etna and the sea, which cut across ground falling away sharply to the sea from the lower slopes of the mountain. These roads were intersected at frequent intervals by deep river beds, which, although mainly dry at that time of year, presented impassable obstacles to both tracked and wheeled vehicles. The enemy had taken full advantage of this difficult country and succeeded in blowing up all the bridges on the main roads, and at least half of them on the secondary ones. The whole countryside between Mount Etna and the sea is intensively cultivated except where covered with lava. The land is terraced by lava walls, and the roads are enclosed by similar walls varying from four to twelve feet high. These were, in many places, unscalable, and formed a death-trap if the road was covered by machine-gun fire. From Riposto to Taormina the country opens out again into a coastal plain, but, from Taormina on to Messina, the road is dominated for thirty-five miles by precipitous hills rising to three thousand feet—so steep that in places the road is cut into the rock.

In addition to blowing up the bridges, the enemy had laid mines freely on the roads, in the fields on either side, and in the farms. As he withdrew he held rearguard positions, usually about a day's march apart, in which, owing to the nature of the country, he was able to conceal his troops and support them with mortars and artillery. Our troops, on the other hand, being practically confined to the roads, had to advance in the open, often without artillery support, as gun positions were hard to find. It was difficult for the forward troops to avoid being surprised, and casualties were fairly heavy. The enemy never stayed long enough in one position for a brigade to launch a deliberate attack, and most of the fighting was done by individual companies operating on their own.

The 50th Division started its advance at 7.30 a.m. on 6 and 7 Bns August 4, with the 151st Brigade on the right, the 69th Brigade 4/8 *Aug* 43 on the left, and the 168th Brigade in reserve. The 69th Brigade moved with the 7th Green Howards in the van, followed by the 6th Green Howards and the 5th East Yorkshires.

On the first day progress was much hindered by minefields, craters, and mortar and machine-gun fire, and, after advancing some six thousand yards, both forward brigades were held up by determined resistance close in front of Catania. The 7th Green Howards reached the heavily wooded foothills of Mount Etna by 9 a.m., and the leading companies, " A " and " B ", were well across the road which runs south-west from Catania, before they were pinned down by mortar and machine-gun fire.

" C " Company, which was following " A " Company, had several casualties from artillery fire, including Major J. B. Mansell and 2/Lt. J. Neild, who were both wounded.

Towards evening the Brigadier came up and ordered the 6th Green Howards to pass through, and take up the attack at dawn next day. When morning came, however, the enemy had gone, and the 6th Battalion, Durham Light Infantry, having entered Catania at 8.30 a.m., had received its unconditional surrender from the Mayor. The 168th Brigade now passed through the 69th Brigade, and took up the advance along the inland road, while the 151st Brigade proceeded up the coastal road.

During the next seven days the forward troops of the 50th Division consisted of the 151st and 168th Brigades, and there is not much to relate about the Green Howards. Progress, though slow, was steady, and, by August 12, both the forward Brigades were in contact with the enemy on the line of the R. Macchia, north of Giarre and Riposto. The 151st Brigade was held up in the northern outskirts of these two towns, and the 168th Brigade had some of their forward troops in Macchia and on the Mascarello ridge.

The 6th and 7th Green Howards were following the 168th Brigade up the inland road, and, on August 6, assistance was given by both battalions to an attack made by the London Irish near San Giovanni.

In this action, L/Cpl. H. Heatley of the 6th Battalion, behaved with the greatest courage and resource, and was awarded the Military Medal. L/Cpl. Heatley was a volunteer member of a patrol which went into close enemy controlled country in search of two wounded men. The enemy opened fire on the patrol at very short range, killing three members of the patrol, and wounding one. The remainder crawled back for help, but L/Cpl. Heatley stayed with a wounded man, within a hundred yards of the enemy. For more than ten hours he looked after his comrade, dressing his wounds, and, when dusk fell, he carried him back for a distance of about half a mile. When he returned to his company, he was able to give accurate information about the enemy posts.

Lt. W. Pinkney, 2nd i/c of the 6th Battalion's carrier platoon, was killed in his carrier by a high velocity shell, when trying to contact the 8th Battalion Durham Light Infantry on the Battalion's right flank.

Capt. A. W. Hull, who was adjutant of the 7th Battalion, was evacuated to hospital, and his duties were taken over by Lt. Cockburn, M.C.

On August 8 the Battalions were near San Antonio, but, on August 12, the 69th Brigade moved across to the coastal road to take over from the 151st Brigade. The 6th Battalion Green Howards took over from the 8th Battalion Durham Light Infantry, and the 7th Battalion from the 6th Battalion Durham Light Infantry—the reliefs being completed at 3 p.m. and 10 p.m. respectively.

At about this time Capt. C. M. Hull, M.C., of the 6th Battalion, went sick. It is not surprising that Capt. Hull should have at last succumbed to the strain and fatigue of more than a year's continuous fighting. With the exception of a few hours spent in the enemy's hands near Mersah Matruh, he had fought with the Battalion in all its battles, Gravelines, Dunkirk, Gazala, Mersah Matruh, the Taqua plateau, Alamein, the Munassib depression, Mareth, Akarit, and Primosole. A wonderful record of continuous service, during which he had been wounded more than once, and been awarded the Military Cross and bar. He made a speedy recovery, and in 1944 landed with the Battalion on " D " Day, and served with it through to Holland.

7 Bn
13 *Aug* 43
During the night of August 12/13 the enemy withdrew once more, and the advance was continued at dawn. The 7th Battalion, in the lead, covered about seven miles on the 13th, but failed to make contact with the enemy by the time darkness

7 Bn
14 *Aug* 43
fell. Towards evening artillery activity increased, and continued throughout the night. At dawn the next morning the

Battalion continued its advance along the coastal road, with
" D " Company as advance guard. It had been planned to
move " A " and " B " Companies across country between
the main road and the coast, but it was found that the orchards
were thickly sown with anti-personnel mines, and, after
several casualties had been sustained, including the Company
Commanders of " A " and " B " Companies, Major Waters
and Lt. Coles, who were wounded, the whole Battalion
moved on along the road.

The 7th Green Howards then made good progress, until
a halt was called at about 5 p.m. just short of Taormina.
There were now two demolished bridges behind them, and
they were isolated from their transport. A patrol was sent
into Taormina, which reported that the enemy had left, and
that the local authorities were anxious to surrender the
town. Arrangements had now been made for supplies to be
sent up to the Battalion by sea, as it was going to take some
time to open up the road. However, it was not until 3 a.m. on   7 Bn
August 15 that the landing craft, carrying food for the   15 Aug 43
Battalion, arrived on the beach, having been guided in by large
fires lit on the shore. In the meanwhile, " D " Company had
gone forward at 2 a.m. and occupied Taormina. Soon after
the arrival of the landing craft, the road was opened and
" B " Echelon transport and some tanks came up.

At 6.30 a.m. the remainder of the Battalion moved forward,
but, a short distance from Taormina, they found the road
badly blocked at a spot where a large part of the cliff face
had fallen across it as a result of demolition. Making a
detour over the hills the Battalion rejoined the road a mile
beyond the block, but only the rifle companies succeeded
in getting through. These continued their advance without
any supporting weapons.

After proceeding for about six miles northwards of
Taormina without making contact with the enemy, at about
3 p.m. they ran into a strongly held rearguard position on a
knife-edge ridge running down to the sea. For several hours
the leading companies, " A " and " C ", were pinned down
by heavy artillery, machine-gun and mortar fire. Without
artillery support further progress was impossible. At 7.15
p.m., the enemy launched a counter-attack which overran
" C " Company, and the Battalion was forced to withdraw
about a mile, when it took up a position for the night.

During the withdrawal of the forward companies Pte
A. N. Dale, displayed great initiative and courage. Taking
up a position by himself with his Bren gun, he opened fire
on some enemy machine-gun posts, thus drawing fire upon

himself. Pte. Dale remained in this position until he had exhausted his ammunition, and then rejoined his Company. By his action he certainly prevented the casualties from being more numerous. He himself was wounded in the leg, and was evacuated through the Regimental Aid Post. Later he was awarded the Military Medal for his bravery and devotion to duty.

In this action Capt. Depoix, the Intelligence Officer, was killed. In addition four other ranks were killed, seven wounded and twenty-one missing. The counter-attack was not pressed home, having been made to cover the withdrawal of the main body, and the enemy withdrew altogether during the night.

**7 Bn
16/26 Aug 43** At dawn on the 16th the 6th Green Howards passed through and took up the pursuit. Soon after this the first food which the 7th Battalion had had for twenty-four hours arrived by mule transport, and in the afternoon it went back to a rest area south-west of Taormina. This marked the end of the Sicilian campaign for the 7th Battalion. Since landing at Avola, thirty-seven days before, the Battalion had lost, (either killed or wounded) the second in command, all Company Commanders, the Carrier platoon Commander, the Intelligence and Medical Officers, the R.S.M., and, in addition, a number of experienced platoon commanders. In all, the Battalion's casualties amounted to about two hundred, apart from those who were evacuated sick from malaria and other causes.

On August 18 Lt.-Col. D. G. Jebb, D.S.O. left the 7th Battalion to take over the appointment of G.S.O. I of the 50th Division, and Major H. R. D. Oldman, M.C., took over command. A week later, on August 26, Lt.-Col. P. H. Richardson, the Queen's Regiment, was appointed to command the 7th Green Howards, which Battalion he was to train for the Normandy invasion, and which he led until he was wounded and missing on June 18, 1944.

While the 7th Battalion was moving up the coast road on August 13, the 6th Battalion had moved towards Piedmonte, between the 7th Battalion, and the 168th Brigade on their left. During August 12 the 231st Brigade, which formed part of the 30th Corps operating on the left of the 50th Division, was placed under command of the 50th Division, and the Division itself was placed under the command of the 30th Corps.

On August 13 the G.O.C., 50th Division, decided to rest the 168th Brigade, which had completed a most arduous advance through the lava country on the slopes of Mount Etna, and ordered the 231st Brigade to take over its sector, including that portion held by the 6th Green Howards on the Piedmonte road.

The 6th Battalion had made rapid progress during August 13 and, in spite of being held up by blown bridges, mines and other demolitions, and towards evening coming under heavy shell fire, " A " Company, under Capt. Honeyman, had reached Piedmonte by dusk, where it was welcomed by the village priest, who rang the church bells in their honour. Later in the evening, contact was made with the 2nd Battalion, Hampshire Regiment, of the 231st Brigade, and with the 7th Green Howards in Fiume Freddo. Just before midnight Battalion Headquarters was heavily shelled. At this juncture, the Brigadier arrived and congratulated them on the speed of their advance.

6 Bn
13 Aug 43

The next day, August 14, saw a further advance to Giardini, which was unopposed. That evening the 6th Battalion entertained three Canadian war correspondents to dinner, and regaled them with Sicilian champagne.

6 Bn
14 Aug 43

On August 15 the Battalion was ordered to be prepared to make a landing by sea, leap-frogging the 7th Battalion, and to continue the advance. Arrangements were being made to supply them with mule transport, owing to the frequent demolitions which were being encountered. This plan, however, was cancelled, and, at 1 a.m. on the 16th, they received the order to move as soon as possible after daybreak, pass through the 7th Battalion, and advance to Messina.

6 Bn
15 Aug 43

6 Bn
16 Aug 43

During the night of the 15/16th No. 2 Commando, with supporting troops, sailed from Augusta with the intention of landing near Marina D'Ali, and preventing the enemy blocking the road at a place where it could easily be blown away from the cliff face. It was hoped that the 69th Brigade would be able to join up with this independent force early on the 16th. The landing was made successfully at about 3 a.m., but took place further north than had been intended. The force, realising that it was impracticable for the 69th Brigade to join up that day, made an attempt to advance alone towards Messina, but was held up.

A second force, consisting of the 5th East Yorkshires and supporting troops, was landed before dawn on the 17th, and, finding that the enemy had gone, speeded up the advance. The leading troops of the 50th Division entered Messina at 10 a.m. on August 17, and established touch with American patrols, who claimed to have entered the town at 10 p.m. the previous night.

Meanwhile the 6th Battalion passed through the 7th Battalion at 9 a.m. on the 16th near Forza d'Agro, with the enemy in retreat about an hour's march ahead. When evening fell, the Battalion, held up as usual by mines and demolitions, was still five miles short of Capo D'Ali. At about 7 p.m. the mule column arrived, with R.S.M. G. Dixon riding the leading mule, and blankets and rations were sent out to the companies.

6 Bn
17 Aug 43
The next morning a patrol of " B " Company under Capt. J. C. Linn went forward at 6.30 a.m. to make contact with the Commandos ahead. The Battalion followed soon afterwards and reached Marina D'Ali at 10 a.m. At mid-day, it arrived at Capo D'Ali and was greeted by Brigadier Cooke-Collis, who had landed from a motor launch, with the news that Messina had fallen, and that the campaign was at an end. The troops then bathed, and at 4 p.m., the mules arrived with rations.

6 Bn
18/25 Aug 43
The next day the Battalion marched back as far as Forza D'Agro, and was then taken by motor transport to Letojanni Gallodoro. After a day's rest Lt.-Col. Hastings, on August 20, held a training conference at which he gave some instructions which may well be taken as a model, at a time when the inevitable reaction from strenuous fighting to peaceful conditions set in.

"All ranks will remember that the British people and the British Army will be judged by the inhabitants by your behaviour. A reputation won in fighting can easily be lost in a lull. I have placed the tasks of the Battalion in order of importance—welfare, administration, training. Welfare and sound administration form the basis upon which morale is built. It is training that wins battles and saves casualties. The Battalion has now an unrivalled opportunity of putting into effect the lessons gained in recent active operations. On this basis will be built up the best Battalion the Green Howards has ever had. The great danger is boredom, and it is up to every officer to see that his training is made interesting and alive."

The transition from war conditions to those of peace had been sudden, but the Green Howards quickly adapted themselves, and found amusements as well as training. On the 21st Lt.-Col. Hastings, we read, acquired a horse and groom, and, although there is no record, he doubtless jumped every obstacle in the vicinity ! On the 25th " A " Company's football team defeated a local Italian team from San Alessio, and three days later the Battalion football team defeated the 7th Green Howards by three goals to one.

At the beginning of September the 6th Battalion was temporarily broken up, one company being sent to Catania, and two companies to Syracuse to construct convalescent camps.

And so, after a further six weeks on the island, these two 6 *and* 7 *Bns*
Green Howard Battalions embarked at Augusta on H.M.T.   17 *Oct*/
Otranto on October 17, and docked at Liverpool on November 5 *Nov* 43
5, 1943, after nearly two and a half years' campaigning. On
the long and arduous road from Gazala to Egypt, from
Alamein to Enfidaville and back, and from Avola to Capo
D'Ali, they had acquitted themselves with honour, and
maintained the name of the Green Howards in the face of
every danger and discomfort. Nevertheless, although war
weary, they were destined to add another glorious chapter to
their history when, in June 1944, they sailed with the great
Armada to the beaches of Normandy.

CHAPTER TEN

THE INVASION OF ITALY

" The 1st Battalion Advance to the R. Sangro "

" The Battles of Minturno and Trimonsuoli "

September 1943—*March* 1944

See MAP
No. 13

THE conquest of Sicily having been completed on August 15, 1943, the plan for the invasion of Italy, which had been originally fixed at the Casablanca Conference to take place on December 15, 1943, was hurriedly advanced.

In the ensuing operations the 1st Battalion, Green Howards, played an important part, until it was withdrawn to Egypt in June, 1944.

Following the method hitherto observed, a brief outline of the campaign, in so far as it affected the Green Howards, will be given, and we will then follow the individual fortunes of the Battalion within its framework.

3/9 Sep 43   In the initial assault on the mainland, three landings were made. On September 3 the 13th Corps of the British 8th Army landed on the toe of Italy near Reggio, and, on September 9, the United States 5th Army, which included the British 10th Corps, made the chief landing at Salerno. On the same day the 5th Corps of the 8th Army captured Taranto, with its fine harbour almost undamaged.

The assault by the 13th Corps, commanded by General Sir Miles Dempsey, was made with the Canadian Division on the right, and the 5th Division on the left. After landing, the 5th Division advanced by the coastal road, through Scilla and Gioia, to Nicastro, while the Canadians took the road, through St. Stefano and Cittanova, to Catanzaro.

10 Sep 43   By September 10 the 13th Corps had reached the line Nicastro-Catanzaro, having encountered very little opposition.

At this point the 8th Army Commander found it necessary to call a halt for a short time. The 5th Division had then advanced a hundred miles in seven days, and it was becoming increasingly difficult to maintain it owing to the heavily damaged roads, and also to the fact that there were not sufficient transport vehicles being landed at the Reggio base to keep up this rate of progress. Both the 5th and Canadian

236

Divisions sent forward strong reconnaissance parties ; those from the latter having the particular object of reporting on the situation at the port of Crotone, and its neighbouring airfields.

General Montgomery considered the capture of Crotone of vital importance in order to ease the strain on the supply line from Reggio, and also to secure aerodromes from which the Desert Air Force could act against the Germans at Salerno, or against any German forces which the 13th Corps might encounter in a subsequent advance.

Crotone was captured intact on September 11, and, on 11/18 *Sep* 43 September 14, the 5th Division was ordered forward to the line Belvedere-Spezzano, while the Canadians came up into line with them on their right flank two days later.

Meanwhile, the 5th U.S. Army at Salerno was being hard pressed. On September 11 and 12 the Germans delivered a heavy counter-attack, which very nearly succeeded in driving the allied troops back into the sea. General Mark Clark called on General Montgomery to send up his 13th Corps with all possible speed to protect the 5th Army's right flank, and to relieve the pressure. The latter, as we have seen, was at this time reorganising his supply routes, and was not able to move the 13th Corps forward until September 14. The 5th Army, however, had received some reinforcements by sea, and, aided by powerful support from naval vessels and allied aircraft, held grimly on, until, on September 16, it struck back at the enemy in force. By September 18 the Salerno battle had been won, and the enemy withdrew towards Naples.

As part of the reserves which they had brought up for the counter-attack at Salerno, the Germans had called on their 1st Parachute Division, which had hitherto been facing the 13th Corps, so that when the 5th Division was ordered, on September 14, to press forward to Sapri, and up the Agropoli road to join up with the right flank of the 5th Army, it was able to make a rapid advance. Forward troops of the 5th Division met American patrols near Vallo on September 16, while, on the same day, Canadian patrols on their right made contact with troops of the 5th Corps, 8th Army, which had advanced from Taranto.

Although the progress of the 5th Division had not been strongly opposed by the enemy, it had been rendered difficult and arduous by various obstructions and demolitions, to which the country lent itself. The Germans had taken every advantage of the natural features of the terrain, and had made skilful use of the opportunities presented to them.

On September 17 rearguards of the 26th Panzer Division were driven out of Lagonegro, and the 13th Corps swept on

19 *Sep* 43   as far as Auletta and Potenza, which were occupied on September 19.

The 13th Corps had now advanced nearly three hundred miles in seventeen days in spite of many administrative difficulties, and across country most favourable to rearguard action.

22 *Sep*/   On the night of September 22/23 the 78th Division and
9 *Oct* 43   the 4th Armoured Brigade landed at Bari, and the remainder of the 5th Corps was moving up from Taranto. On September 27 the 5th Corps made a further thrust forward and captured Foggia, and all the important airfields in its vicinity.

During this period, from September 22 to October 8, the 5th Division, having been squeezed out of the battle, remained quietly in an area around Brienza and Picerno, and it was not until October 9 that it moved across to Lucera, behind the 5th Corps front, which was by that time moving forward north of the R. Biferno.

15 *Oct* 43   On October 15 the 5th Army secured the passage of the R. Volturno, some twenty miles north of Naples, and moved on towards the R. Garigliano, along which river, and the R. Rapido, the Germans had entrenched themselves on the Gustav Line, intended to guard the approaches to Rome by way of the valley of the R. Sacco.

It was to the seaward end of the Gustav Line that the Green Howards crossed over from the Adriatic early in 1944, and took part there in the fighting round Minturno and Trimonsuoli during January and February of that year.

When the 5th Division arrived in the Foggia area on October 9, the 8th Army was advancing towards the R. Trigno. The crossings over the R. Biferno at its seaward end had been forced by the 5th Corps after fierce fighting which lasted for four days. On October 3 a force had been landed behind the river at Termoli, and at the same time a frontal attack had been launched against the river positions. The initial frontal attack failed, and the Germans delivered a strong counter-attack with a Panzer Division brought up from their right flank. After four days of bitter fighting, however, they were driven back, and a junction was effected with the sea-borne force at Termoli.

The 8th Army's advance now continued, with the 5th Corps on the right, and with the 13th Corps pressing its way through the mountains toward Isernia, where contact was eventually established with the right wing of the 5th Army in front of the R. Rapido.

The 15th Brigade of the 5th Division took part in this 11/27 *Nov* 43
advance, and by November 11 had reached the neighbourhood of Castel Di Sangro, overlooking the Sangro River.
Here it remained until November 27, by which time the 5th
Corps on the Adriatic coast had crossed the R. Sangro on a
five-mile front, and was attacking the Lanciano ridge, between
the Rivers Sangro and Moro.

This position was captured on November 30, and, on
December 5, Canadian troops forced the crossing of the R.
Moro ; but it was not until December 27 that, after severe
fighting, they occupied the town of Ortona.

On December 20 the 5th Division moved across from the 20 *Dec* 43/
left flank, and on the 21st went into the line on the R. Moro, 4 *Jan* 44
where it remained until January 4, 1944, when it went back
into reserve at Lanciano.

The 1st Battalion, Green Howards, now commanded by 1 *Bn*
Lt.-Col. Bulfin, left Paterno, in Sicily, where it had been 30 *Aug* 43
resting, on August 30, 1943, and arrived at Forci on the 31st.

At about mid-day on September 3 the Battalion embarked 3 *Sep* 43
on landing craft, and, some two hours later, disembarked at
Gallico Marina on the Italian mainland after an uneventful
passage across the Straits of Messina. There was no opposition
at first on land, and the Battalion proceeded to advance up
the coastal road through Rosali, Villa San Giovanni, and
Scilla as far as Favazinna, which was reached at about 4 p.m. 4 *Sep* 43
on September 4.

During the day a small force had been landed from the
sea near Bagnara, and the 15th Brigade was moving forward
as rapidly as possible to effect a junction with it. The 1st
Battalion York and Lancaster Regiment was leading the
Brigade along the coast road, with the 1st Battalion, King's
Own Yorkshire Light Infantry, moving on the high ground
inland. There was a very steep rise up to this high ground, and
there were only a few valleys giving access to it. By the time
Favazinna was reached the York and Lancasters were in
touch with enemy rearguards, who were between them and the
seaborne force. The Green Howards were now sent up one
of the valleys to join the K.O.Y.L.I., and both battalions took
up hastily constructed defensive positions for the night.

On the morning of September 5 the York and Lancasters 5 *Sep* 43
were still held up on the coastal road, and the Brigade Commander, Brigadier Martin, came up to the high ground, and
ordered the two battalions to advance, with the object of
turning the enemy's left flank. The K.O.Y.L.I. acted as vanguard, followed by the Green Howards. During the advance,
which was without incident, the two Commanding Officers

moved with the Brigadier, and the latter remarked how illogical it seemed that he, and his three commanding officers, at the head of the leading troops in the invasion of Europe, should all come from a professedly neutral country. Once again in history the wild geese were flighting !

The Green Howards reached the road from Bagnara to Euphemia at noon, and were then ordered to move across country to secure the high ground east of Cerimido. During the afternoon " D " Company was sent off on patrol, and made the Battalion's first contact with the enemy in Italy at the entrance to Cerimido.

Without any loss to itself, " D " Company (Capt. A. T. Parkinson) captured three Italian officers and fifty-two other ranks, together with three machine-guns, and a quantity of other weapons and ammunition. During this action L/Sgt. J. W. Parkin commanded the leading section, which ran into heavy machine-gun fire. He immediately went forward himself, followed by his section, and attacked the enemy with hand grenades, killing one of them and causing the remainder to surrender. This determined leadership quickly cleared a strong point which was delaying the forward advance of the Brigade. For his courage and leadership he was awarded the Military Medal.

This skirmish marked the last fighting against Italian troops by the Green Howards.

It was obvious that the Italians were not going to put up much resistance and, although it was not known at the time, an Armistice between the Allies and Italy had already been signed on September 3. It had been a condition of the Armistice terms that they should be kept secret for five days, that is until September 8, but this condition of secrecy was not observed.

6/11 *Sep* 43   On September 6 the Battalion moved on as far as Barretieri, in the neighbourhood of which it remained until September 11.

Meanwhile the 17th Brigade had landed at Gioia, and taken up the advance, while on September 8, the 231st Brigade had made a landing at Pizzo against strong opposition.

11/13 *Sep* 43   On September 11 the Green Howards took to the water again, embarking at Gioia at mid-day. After an hour at sea, they came ashore again north of Pizzo, and, by 9 p.m. that night, were established at Gizziera, about six miles west of Nicastro.

September 11 and 12, it will be remembered, were the days on which the situation at Salerno was critical, and help had been called for by the Commander of the 5th Army.

ADVANCING NEAR MONTESANO.

ADVANCING NEAR FORLI.

Face page 240

On September 14 the Green Howards made an advance 14/16 *Sep* 43 of between fifty and sixty miles to St. Agata, and, on the 16th, proceeding by way of Praia A Mare, arrived in the vicinity of Lagonegro at about 7 p.m. A small German force was still in occupation of Lagonegro, and the bridge at the southern entrance to the town had been blown up. Orders were given for the Green Howards to advance across country to the west of the town, and to secure the high ground and approaches from the north-west.

This advance was carried out successfully, and Lagonegro 17/18 *Sep* 43 was occupied by the 1st Battalion, York and Lancaster Regiment, early on September 17.

The Green Howards then pushed forward across the R. Noce, and arrived at Casalbuono in the afternoon of September 18. At 9 p.m. Lt.-Col. Bulfin received orders to move forward in transport at 2 a.m. on September 19, and 19/20 *Sep* 43 to seize and hold Montesano. After going a short distance, the vanguard of the Battalion, the Carrier Platoon, came up against a bridge, which had not been repaired, and the road was soon jammed with transport. The Carriers, however, managed to clear a diversionary route, and at 6 a.m. on September 19 the Green Howards entered Montesano without opposition. At about 11 a.m. a patrol was sent off to reconnoitre the road to Moliterno. This patrol returned about three hours later with a report that the road was impassable for all vehicles owing to demolitions, but that a party had entered Moliterno on foot, and found it clear of the enemy. Orders were then received for the Battalion to make contact with the Canadians at Corleto, some twenty-five miles beyond Moliterno ; but before repairs to the road made this possible, fresh orders were received to move forward along the northern road to Brienza.

The Battalion left Montesano in troop carriers at 1 p.m. 21/22 *Sep* 43 on September 21, and arrived at Brienza at about 4.30 a.m. on the 22nd. At 7.30 a.m. fresh orders were received to proceed by march route to Picerno, and the Battalion moved on again, arriving at Picerno about mid-day.

On September 23 orders were received for the Battalion 23 *Sep* 43 to advance next day through the K.O.Y.L.I. to Bargiano, and to seize and hold Bella Muro Station, together with the high ground to the north-west. In order to get there, it was necessary to advance along the railway line which, for a great part of the way, ran through a very long tunnel. At 6 a.m. next morning pack mules arrived, which were loaded with three-inch mortars and ammunition, and the Battalion moved off at 7 a.m. After an eerie journey in the darkness it arrived

R

at Bargiano Station at 11 o'clock, where it found a platoon of the K.O.Y.L.I. in occupation. Moving on to Muro Station, contact was made with a reconnaissance unit of the 45th U.S. Division, and reports were received that the 5th Reconnaissance Battalion was being fired on by enemy mortars south of Castel-Grande. Before the Green Howards could make any further advance, the enemy rearguard withdrew, and the Battalion was ordered back to Picerno, where it arrived just before midnight.

23 *Sep*/
8 *Oct* 43 Here it remained until October 8, resting and training. The only incident worthy of note during this period was the despatch of a small party, commanded by Lt. P. L. Saulet, to Maschito to put down civil disorder. Accompanied by a representative of A.M.G.O.T., two stretcher bearers, and a platoon of " C " Company, Lt. Saulet set out in the early hours of October 5, and was able to report by the evening that his show of force had been sufficient to restore order without bloodshed.

When still at Picerno the 15th Brigade was placed under command of the 5th Corps, and, when the 5th Division arrived in the Foggia area on October 9/10, this Brigade immediately moved up into the line overlooking the R. Biferno, between the Canadian Division on the left and an Indian Division on the right. The remainder of the 5th Division remained near Foggia for some time resting and training.

8/11 *Oct* 43 On October 8 the Battalion moved off in two columns, a slow one commanded by Capt. Bade, and a fast one commanded by Major Radcliffe, leaving " D " Company behind at Picerno, owing to lack of sufficient troop carrying transport. Both columns united at Minervino during the afternoon, and moved on next day to the neighbourhood of Lucera, where " D " Company rejoined in the evening.

On October 11 a further advance was made under most difficult conditions to Montelongo. In heavy rain and mist the Battalion set forth, and, just when it was getting dark, found that a river crossing had been washed away. Part of the Battalion had got across, but some were left stranded on the Bonefro side, while the cooks' three-ton lorry was well and truly bogged in mid stream. However all was well in the end, and the Battalion was established in Montelongo before midnight. Throughout the previous days the Green Howards had been passing through the wine country, a pleasant change from the mountains. It was the grape pressing season, and, although some of the vineyards possessed modern presses, in many cases " filthy little urchins were treading the juice with their bare feet in old fashioned troughs ". Some officers slept on the wine press in their billets, and were nearly intoxicated with the fumes, but it is not stated whether the memory of the little urchins prevented them from enjoying the wine out of the bottle.

On October 12 the Battalion arrived in the front line and 12/18 *Oct* 43 took over positions held by the York and Lancasters. On the 13th, a further advance was made to the high ground over-looking Providenti. During the night of the 13th/14th, a fighting patrol of " D " Company, which had been sent forward to Morrone, encountered strong opposition from the enemy who were situated on a dominating ridge above the town, and who were strongly armed with machine-guns. After silencing four of these guns, the company broke off the engagement soon after 1 a.m. Several men were wounded, and they estimated that they had inflicted about a dozen casualties on the enemy. At 6 p.m. on October 14, " D " Company, supported by a company of the Cheshire machine-gunners, occupied Morrone, which had been evacuated during the day.

The following vivid account of this action, given by Capt. H. L. Wilson, who was second-in-command of " D " Company, gives a good picture of the country in which the Green Howards were now fighting.

" Just through Providenti was Morrone, a veritable fortress of a place towering high on a conical hill overlooking the R. Biferno. The only road up to the town lay along a ridge which connected the hill with the main massif of the mountains. Apart from this one line of approach the ground fell sheer away from the walls of the town, leaving it perched like a medieval fortress on an apparently inaccessible position. From Providenti there was a rough track which wound round the side of the mountain, and eventually climbed up this same ridge.

It was a fine night, with bright moonlight, as we made our way up this mule track. When we rounded the last bend, and came in view of the ridge, we stopped and took a long look through our field glasses. There was a small farm on the top and I could see someone moving about. I thought it was a local inhabitant, but Archie (Capt. A. T. Parkinson, com-manding ' D ' Company) had a hunch that it was a Boche sentry. We decided to push on while keeping one eye on the ridge. I was with Company Headquarters. The first platoon was right below the farm and about fifty yards past it, when a machine gun opened up from the farm. We could see the frantic sentry in the moonlight turning out his men, and they

soon had four machine-guns spraying tracer all over the place
in a panicky way. Rockets and flares went up—evidently
a signal—as about fifteen machine-guns now opened up from
the walls of the town, firing tracer into us.

The Company swung into action. The leading platoon
was too far advanced to do much, but No. 16 platoon
deployed on the slopes of the ridge, and our Brens came into
action. The bullets were cracking past unpleasantly close.
I was lying behind a slight bump in the ground, with tracer
bullets passing only two to three feet above my head.

Sergeant W. C. Lambert got a section right up on to the
ridge, and the Boches packed up and faded into the night,
leaving everything behind them. We only had two casualties
in this spirited engagement. Sergeant Lambert was in terrific
form and stormed right into the Boche post—a deed for which
he was later awarded the Military Medal.

Our task was accomplished, as we had spotted all the
enemy positions, and so we withdrew down the track by which
we had approached.

The most frightened man was a civilian from Providenti
who had volunteered to guide us up the track. At the first
burst of fire he leapt down the mountain like a goat, turned
at least six somersaults, and never stopped running until he
was back in Providenti, four miles away. I saw him several
times afterwards, and we had a good laugh together over a
bottle of ' Vino '."

" D " Company, after occupying Morrone on October 14,
remained there until it was relieved by a company of the
K.O.Y.L.I. on the 18th, and then rejoined the Battalion.
Meanwhile the remainder of the Battalion moved to the
left flank through Ripabottoni towards Petrella, with the
object of joining up with the Canadians.

There was only one lateral road, and this was heavily
mined. This took some little time to clear, but eventually the
Green Howards arrived at Petrella on October 18, and took
up a defensive position. A period of active patrolling now
commenced, with the object not only of doing as much
damage as possible to the enemy, but also to give the impression
that the whole of the 5th Division was in the line, when, in
fact, it was not.

18 *Oct* 43   On the 18th a fighting patrol under Lt. Ambler reported
the road to St. Elia clear, and a patrol under Capt. E. S.
Roberts was sent forward to Lucito. This patrol came under
machine-gun fire on reaching the R. Biferno, and withdrew,
keeping the enemy under observation. It was on this day also
that the Green Howards made contact with patrols from the
Canadian Division on their left flank.

At about 8 p.m. on October 18 " B " Company, commanded by Capt. Bade, was sent forward to seize the high ground at Pt. 330 to the east of Lucito, and crossed the R. Biferno just before midnight. Soon after 1 a.m. on the 19th, however, they were fired upon by machine-guns from the rear, and after sustaining some casualties, were ordered to withdraw. Lt. Ambler and Lt. A. I. Arnott were wounded. During this attack Cpl. T. Pears behaved with great gallantry and was awarded the Military Medal. He was commanding a section of No. 10 platoon when one of his men was wounded, and lay exposed within twenty-five yards of the enemy. Under heavy automatic fire Cpl. Pears dashed forward and dragged him back to a place of comparative safety. Throughout the engagement he showed a fine fighting spirit, which acted as an inspiration to all who saw him.

Early in the morning of October 20 " C " Company, 20 *Oct* 43 commanded by Major D. St. J. Radcliffe, M.C., went forward as a fighting patrol, with the village of Lucito as its objective. When within sight of Lucito the Company took up a covering position, while Lt. Saulet went forward with a small reconnaissance patrol. This party ran into machine-gun fire about four hundred yards south-east of the village, and was ordered back into dead ground. When it finally rejoined the Company seven of its members were missing.

At 10 a.m. Lt. D. M. D. O'Driscoll went forward with two platoons of " A " Company, with orders to occupy Pt. 620, on the high ground south-west of Lucito, and, if successful, to penetrate into the village itself.

This patrol soon became pinned down by heavy machine-gun fire from Pt. 620, and returned at about 2 p.m. with two men wounded and one missing.

Throughout the 20th patrols, reconnoitring between the R. Biferno and the high ground on either side of Lucito, encountered enemy fire, but, on the 21st, the enemy started to withdraw, and on the 22nd Major Radcliffe was able to lead " C " Company through Lucito as far as Castelbottacio, which was reported clear at 3 p.m. In the evening the Battalion was relieved by a Canadian unit, and went back to Petrella and Providenti.

During this period a number of allied prisoners of war made their way into the Green Howard lines, as many as seventeen being received during the course of one night. In addition there were, at intervals, queer characters in the form of guides and agents, both male and female, whose bona-fides required careful examination. One of the nocturnal visitors was an Italian Chief of Staff, who spoke excellent English, and was most scornful of the southern Italians.

21/31 *Oct* 43   Here the Battalion remained until October 31. Several changes took place at this juncture. Capt. J. M. Barwick left the Battalion to take up the duties of Staff Captain of the 15th Brigade, and Capt. H. L. Wilson succeeded him as Adjutant. Lt. I. S. Pope took over the Signals in place of Lt. H. I. Dessain, the latter officer going to 5th Divisional Headquarters in place of Lt. M. R. Newman.

31 *Oct*/   On October 31 the Battalion moved to San Guiliano,
11 *Nov* 43 where it spent a week, and, on November 7, it advanced further to Miranda by way of Pesche.

The first part of this journey was accomplished in motor transport, and numerous Bailey Bridges, which had been thrown across the demolitions, were crossed. As the Green Howards approached the front, however, this form of progress became impracticable, and they had to take to their feet. Leaving the valley, they climbed up a rough mule track for some five miles to the village of Miranda, perched up amongst the hills. There was no method of getting wheeled transport into the village, and everything had to be carried by man or mule. The enemy had only just left but, although patrols were sent forward in all directions, no contact with them was made.

Accordingly, after three days in Miranda, the Battalion descended into the valley again and pressed on to Rionero, stopping for one night on the way at " a small collection of miserable houses " called Canali. " D " Company had been sent on as advance guard to Rionero, and the remainder of
11/25 *Nov* 43 the Battalion joined it there on November 11. From this date until November 25 the Green Howards held Rionero, and the positions in front of it, and, although no definite action was fought, they had a very uncomfortable time and suffered some casualties from shelling and in patrolling activity.

The following general account of this fortnight, based on Capt. Wilson's story, gives a picture of the conditions under which the Battalion was now fighting.

Rionero was another typical Apennine village, high up in the hills, situated on the central road which led to Rome, and overlooking the valley of the R. Sangro towards Castel Di Sangro. On either side of the town the mountains towered up to a height of approximately four thousand feet.

For the first few days things were strangely quiet, while battery after battery of British guns passed through the village, and gun positions were being excavated in the mountain side, covered by the forward companies.

The Green Howards were now the most forward infantry troops, and the leading companies were patrolling towards the R. Sangro. The battalion was spread out on a front of approximately five thousand yards, covering the Divisional artillery, and was intended to make a demonstration in force. The Germans, it was felt, would be bound to react to a threat at this point, and so weaken their forces further to the east, where the main attack was to be made.

The weather had become really bad ; it was bitterly cold, and the rain came down in torrents, pouring down the narrow streets of the village and into the trenches of the forward companies.

The only means of reaching the men in the front line was by mule transport, and this meant a journey of from two to three hours. It was not possible to cook in the forward positions, as they were all very exposed, without an inch of cover, and all food and drink had to be taken up to them in six-gallon containers by mule pack. The result was that the men never got a really hot meal or drink, as the journey took several hours.

The exposure was so severe that a hot room with braziers was organised in the village, to which those men who succumbed were brought back and revived.

After six days the Battalion was relieved by the K.O.Y.L.I. and went back into billets at Forli. On November 19 it returned to the same sector, and took over positions from the York and Lancasters. By this time shelling and counter shelling had started in earnest, and there were a number of casualties.

An instance of the constant dangers, even behind the lines, is exemplified in the fate of Provost Sergeant R. Crookston, who was directing a truck back on to a " pull in ", which had been in use for a week, when it went up on a mine. Sgt. Crookston was killed instantaneously.

Soon after this the mule transport broke down through overwork, and the Battalion had to organise its own pack train. This was composed of the Anti-tank platoon, loaded with Alpine Everest packs and rucksacks, and a collection of ponies, horses, and donkeys impressed from the local inhabitants. Some of the latter were knock-kneed, and little bigger than alsatian dogs. Somehow or another the supplies, and some blankets, were got up to the forward troops.

Throughout this period patrols were constantly going out, in some cases on quite long reconnaissances, and, owing to the difficult nature of the country, these were very arduous performances.

On November 25 the Green Howards were again relieved and went right back to Castelpetroso, where they found good billets waiting for them, and were once more able to get dry, warm, and clean. 25 Nov/ 2 Dec 43

2/12 *Dec* 43   After a week's rest in Castelpetroso the Battalion moved off in trucks on December 2 to Capracotta, a small town high up on a saddle in the mountains. Caprocotta was some miles to the east and slightly north of Rionero, and overlooked the R. Sangro which ran some three to four miles to the north. Here it remained until December 12 when it was relieved by the 56th Reconnaissance Regiment.

The story of these ten days is mainly one of constant patrolling, probing the enemy's lines, marking down his dispositions, and reconnoitring the possible river crossings.

The rain turned to snow, it was bitterly cold, and the Sangro rose rapidly and became impassable ; although, on December 8, when it had subsided a little, a patrol of " B " Company under the command of Sgt. J. Kerridge did manage to get across near Castel Di Guidice.

12/20 *Dec* 43   On December 12 the Battalion moved by motor transport to Castiglione, where it remained for a week, resting and reorganising.

It will be remembered that the 5th Corps had crossed the R. Sangro at its seaward end late in November, and that the Canadians had forced a crossing of the R. Moro on December 5. The New Zealanders and the 9th Indian Division were, however, encountering stiff opposition between the latter river and the towns of Orsogna and Ortona.

The 5th Division was now ordered across to this front, and on December 19 the Green Howards left Castiglione, and arrived in Lanciano at about 7 a.m. They found Lanciano a less primitive town than those which they had been occupying during the past weeks, but it was under shell fire and close to the front line. However their stay was of short duration, as orders were received for the Battalion to relieve the Royal Scots Fusiliers on the banks of the River Moro.

21/31 *Dec* 43   The Battalion accordingly moved forward on December 21 to a small plateau on which were a few houses ; these were given the name of Colli.

The Green Howards managed somehow to cram themselves for the night into these houses, and established Battalion Headquarters in the village, when the forward companies went up into the line next day.

The approach to the trenches consisted of a steep descent to the river, and then a climb up on the other side, through mud that was so thick and sticky that it almost sucked the boots off the men's feet.

After a time Headquarters moved forward from Colli into a gully, in the banks of which the pioneers excavated dug-outs, which, well shored up with timber, proved dry, and a good defence against shell fire and bombing, which went on fairly continuously.

The Battalion spent the next fortnight in these positions, including a miserable Christmas Day, since it was impossible to get the extra rations up, and the Christmas dinner consisted of cold bully beef, biscuits, and tea. Soon after Christmas snow began to fall, and after two days, it lay from three to four feet deep and, in the drifts, up to ten feet.

This snow-fall broke down the temporary covers which the men had put up over their slit trenches with gas capes or old sacking, and they were left exposed to the elements, and to the enemy.

The signallers, in their successful efforts to keep communications alive, suffered particularly severely. The signal exchange trench at Headquarters became flooded when the snow began to thaw, and the men on duty had to sit at the switchboard with water up to their knees.

The linesmen were out continuously day and night repairing lines which had been broken by shell fire, and lost four men killed and two wounded at this work.

L/Cpl. A. Hill was one of these, and was awarded the Military Medal. On December 30, under almost continuous shell fire, he mended fourteen breaks in the line, and carried on until he was wounded and ordered back.

Meanwhile, the enemy were showing increased activity, and Lt.-Col. Bulfin was anxious about his positions, as they were very extended and lightly held. He gave orders, therefore, for some of the anti-tank guns to be taken up into the front line.

This entailed taking the guns to pieces, as it required ten men to lift the barrel alone. Staggering a few yards at a time, they got the guns into position eventually. An attempt was also made to get some tanks up on to the positions, but the ground and the weather defeated them, and two were blown up on hidden minefields.

Throughout this period patrols went out by day and night, harassing the enemy and marking down his dispositions.

One such patrol, commanded by Lt. H. A. Ransom, with Sgt. Lambert, M.M., went out early in the morning of December 28 towards Le Piane. The patrol proceeded in two parties, and the section under Lt. Ransom, as it approached the first houses of the village, was engaged by automatic fire and grenades. Lt. Ransom was wounded and unable to get back. Sgt. Lambert, who was working up a neighbouring nullah, on hearing the firing, went across to investigate. He found the remainder of Lt. Ransom's section, but no trace of the officer, and so, at about mid-day, he brought the whole patrol back.

3/6 *Jan* 44   On January 3, 1944 the Battalion was relieved by troops from the 6th Airborne Division, and was withdrawn to Lanciano. During the relief Lt.-Col. Bulfin was slightly wounded, but was soon able to rejoin the Battalion.

After three days in Lanciano orders were received for a move, which was shrouded in mystery, as all number plates and signs were taken off the vehicles.

6/9 *Jan* 44   When, on January 6, the Battalion set off towards Naples, the troops, with their incorrigible optimism, were convinced that they were on their way home. Little did they know that the bloody battles of Minturno, Trimonsuoli and Anzio lay ahead of them.

The whole of the 5th Division had now been taken out of the 8th Army, and put under command of the 5th U.S. Army, which at that time was held up facing the Gustav Line beyond the R. Garigliano.

9/18 *Jan* 44   On January 9 the Battalion arrived at Carinola near Naples, and immediately started to train for the forthcoming attack on the Gustav Line. This training included a practice crossing of the R. Volturno in assault boats.

On January 18 the Battalion moved forward in motor transport, and arrived behind a pontoon bridge, which crossed the Garigliano, at about 9 p.m.

19 *Jan* 44   At 1 a.m. on January 19 the Green Howards crossed the Garigliano, and three hours later were established in the positions from which they were to launch their attack on Minturno, their first objective, about four miles ahead.

Lt.-Col. Bulfin's orders for the attack were for " C " Company (Major Radcliffe) to lead, and capture the southern end of the town. " A " Company (Major B. N. O. Gosden) was to follow close behind, and seize the north-eastern portion, while " B " Company (Major Tanner) was to pass through them and capture Pt. 141. " D " Company (Capt. Parkinson) was to be held in reserve.

At 10 a.m. "C" Company advanced on Minturno behind a strong artillery barrage, and secured a footing in the town half an hour later. " A " Company then passed through, and completed the capture of the town. At 11 a.m. " B " Company passed through on its way to Pt. 141, but soon ran into strong opposition.

One platoon eventually succeeded in establishing itself on the position, but the remainder of the Company was held up by machine-gun and mortar fire, and was pinned down short of the objective.

The ultimate capture of Pt. 141, which was vital to the consolidation of the main position covering the town, was largely due to the extreme determination and outstanding courage of Capt. E. S. Roberts, who was second-in-command of " B " Company. When the leading platoon faltered on coming under heavy fire, this officer immediately assumed command of it, and by his own energy and example urged on the platoon across a further three hundred yards of open ground, in the face of heavy machine-gun and mortar fire. He finally reached his objective with fourteen men, with whom he held the position for the next four hours, driving off two counter attacks, until they were reinforced under cover of darkness. For this action Capt. Roberts was awarded the Military Cross.

L/Sgt. J. R. Maddox of " C " Company also displayed great courage in this action and was awarded the Military Medal.

When his company was enfiladed by machine-gun fire from the flank, L/Sgt. Maddox detached his section and, with great dash and utter fearlessness, led them into the assault. He personally accounted for two machine-gun posts, killing or wounding twelve of the enemy with grenades. Later in the day L/Sgt. Maddox was wounded in the leg, his platoon commander had been killed, and the remainder of the platoon were pinned down by heavy fire. Despite his wound, he immediately took over the platoon Bren gun and, by his accurate fire, enabled the platoon to extricate themselves in daylight, while he subsequently led out his own section two hours later at dusk.

The positions were finally consolidated with " C " and " D " Companies holding the forward edge of the town, two platoons of " A " Company on the north-west edge of the town, and two platoons of " B " Company at Battalion Headquarters as a mobile reserve.

The operation had been a success, and between forty 20 *Jan* 44 and fifty prisoners were taken. During the night there was intermittent shelling and machine-gun fire, and, at 7 a.m. on January 20, Lt.-Col. Bulfin went forward to make a reconnaissance for an attack on Trimonsuoli, which had been ordered to take place that morning.

On his return he issued his orders for the attack. " B " Company was to lead on the left flank with the objective of capturing the town and securing the south-western approaches. " C " Company was to advance on the right, and capture

Pt. 110, " D " Company was to take over Pt. 141 from " A " Company, and the latter company was to come into immediate reserve.

At 11 a.m., behind a barrage which lifted a hundred yards every three minutes, the Green Howards began to descend from Minturno into the valley in front, and then to climb up the next ridge to Trimonsuoli. By mid-day the forward companies had reached their objectives, and the supporting companies, " A " and " D ", had moved up to positions on the high ground behind them.

Success, however, had not been won without cost, and the citation accompanying the award of the Military Cross to Major A. R. M. Tanner, who commanded " B " Company, shows that it was only grim determination that won the day at Trimonsuoli.

" Major Tanner," the citation states, " throughout the action showed exceptionally high standards of leadership in controlling and directing his company, cleaning up opposition, and ensuring the immediate mopping up, and consolidation of the objective. During the whole operation the village was under heavy enemy artillery and machine-gun fire, and his Company was in close contact with the enemy on the lower slopes.

Major Tanner moved continuously from platoon to platoon, directing operations wherever the fire was heaviest, and, by his coolness and untiring energy, set a magnificent example which was an inspiration to his men."

As the Green Howards began to consolidate their positions, their natural elation at their success was somewhat damped by the news that the troops on either side of them had failed to secure their objectives, and that they were therefore left holding a salient.

There was little rest that night, as the village and the battalion positions were subjected to almost continuous shell and mortar fire. A good many casualties were sustained, among them being Capt. H. L. Wilson and Lt. N. W. D. Yardley, both of whom were wounded by shell splinters.

21 *Jan* 44　　　At mid-day on January 21 the Battalion was relieved by the Coldstream Guards, but was not given much respite, as, late the same evening, " A " and " C " Companies were sent up the line again to support the York and Lancasters.

Major Radcliffe was ordered by the Commanding Officer of the York and Lancasters to carry out a counter-attack with " C " Company, and to regain a feature, which had been lost to the enemy during the previous night. While he was giving out his orders, a direct hit knocked out the majority of his party. The attack was then postponed, and finally cancelled owing to the deterioration of the situation. After some rather confused fighting during the morning of January 22, " A " and " C " Companies were withdrawn, and took up positions just north of Minturno. They were now once more under Lt.-Col. Bulfin's command, the latter having brought up the remainder of the Battalion, with a view to launching an attack on Pt. 172 later in the afternoon. This attack was made at 5 p.m. led by " C " Company, which was now reduced to thirty-three all ranks. This Company's objective was a cemetery to the north-west of Pt. 172. " B " Company was ordered to attack on the left, and " D " Company on the right. " C " Company's orders were, after delivering the assault, to withdraw through " B " Company, and take up position in reserve on the reverse slope of Pt. 172. " C " Company made some progress, but was held up on the near edge of the cemetery, mainly by two German tanks. The Company took several prisoners, and, after a certain amount of confused fighting, withdrew at the appointed time.

By 7 p.m. " D " Company reported that it had reached its objective, and was consolidating the position, but " B " Company had been forced to withdraw. A portion of the carrier platoon was sent up to reinforce " B " Company, and the Battalion consolidated on the positions which it had gained.

During the night and early hours of the next morning the whole of the Battalion area was exposed to heavy shell fire, but the Green Howards held on to their hardly won positions, until they were relieved by the K.O.Y.L.I. on the evening of January 24.

The Battalion moved back by motor transport to Carinola, arriving about midnight, and there it remained until January 30.

For deeds of gallantry on January 22 the 1st Battalion, Green Howards, received no less than seven decorations, namely a bar to a Military Medal and five Military Medals, while, for his leadership and courage throughout the attacks on Minturno and Trimonsuoli, Lt.-Col. Bulfin was awarded the Distinguished Service Order.

The words of the citations of these awards will help to give a picture of the severity of the fighting in these actions.

Of Lt.-Col. Bulfin it is stated that he pressed the attacks on Minturno and Trimonsuoli with great vigour and determination, despite intense enemy fire of all kinds.

His personal influence was most marked, and his presence at points of danger throughout the action were an encouragement and inspiration to all ranks under his command. Despite

22 Jan 44

23/30 Jan 44

great physical exertion, Lt.-Col. Bulfin's efforts never flagged, and he roused his tired battalion to great efforts. His cool judgement under fire, his skill in directing his battalion, and his own example of fearlessness, showed qualities of leadership which were quite outstanding.

Sgt. F. M. Roche, who had won the Military Medal at Otta nearly four years previously, now gained a bar to his decoration. On January 22 he found himself commanding a platoon in the area of the Minturno cemetery. His orders were to hold on at all costs. Soon after 6 a.m. his position was attacked by a Mark IV tank, and his platoon suffered several casualties. Ten minutes later the enemy infantry came on in force, and the situation became critical, when his position was outflanked and completely surrounded. At this juncture, Sgt. Roche and Cpl. J. Murphy collected all available grenades and went out alone to attack the enemy. By superb courage and offensive action of the highest order they overcame great odds, killing or wounding several of the enemy, and causing the remainder to break up and run away. Cpl. Murphy killed six Germans himself, and was awarded the Military Medal.

In the same vicinity that day L/Cpl. H. C. Archer won his Military Medal. His platoon was ordered forward to try to destroy one of three German tanks, and to break up the infantry covering party which threatened the left flank of the position. The attack with P.I.A.T. guns failed, but L/Cpl. Archer, undaunted, rushed forward without hesitation in the face of heavy machine-gun fire, and got within thirty yards of one tank. Throwing grenades amongst the enemy, he killed or wounded several of them, and caused great confusion. The platoon then moved to a flank, but was again pinned down by heavy fire. In spite of this L/Cpl. Archer crawled forward, and personally accounted for another six Germans. Throughout this action L/Cpl. Archer showed an extremely high example of bravery and coolness under heavy fire.

Cpl. R. Peel was a member of " B " Company, which led the advance on Pt. 172. He soon found himself, owing to casualties, taking over the duties of Platoon Sergeant. Although under heavy fire he ran from section to section urging his men forward. Shortly after darkness fell he and part of his platoon were surrounded and taken prisoner. His courage undaunted, he escaped and rejoined his Company, bringing back with him valuable information as to the enemy's strength and positions, which enabled the artillery to be used effectively against them.

He then manned the platoon P.I.A.T. gun, and was largely responsible for breaking up a party of Germans who were assembling for a counter attack. Cpl. Peel's actions on this night were worthy of the highest traditions of his Regiment and the British Army. He was awarded the Military Medal.

Sgt. H. Sissons took over No. 1 platoon, on his Platoon Commander becoming a casualty, early in the operations near the Minturno Cemetery. Although wounded in the shoulder, he refused to be evacuated and remained controlling and directing the fire of his men until, on receiving orders to withdraw, he brought them safely back. He was awarded the Military Medal.

Finally, Pte. E. Gilbert received the Military Medal for his work as a stretcher bearer with " C " Company. Time and time again he crossed and recrossed the bullet swept ground, tending casualties in the open, and carrying them back to the Regimental Aid Post. His devotion to duty, and great fortitude in spite of fatigue, were magnificent.

After six days of rest and reorganisation at Carinola *30 Jan/* the Battalion was placed under the command of the 17th *10 Feb* 44 Brigade, and, on the evening of January 30, proceeded up to the front line, where it took over positions from the 6th Battalion, Seaforth Highlanders, in front of Minturno. The relief was completed soon after dark.

The Green Howards remained in these positions until February 10, and, although no major action with the enemy took place, the forward companies sent out constant patrols by day and night, and the Battalion positions came under a certain amount of shelling and harassing fire.

During this period considerable trouble was caused by a party of the enemy who were established on a feature, Pt. 165, in front of " C " Company. On February 2 " C " Company was ordered to attack and hold Pt. 165 for three hours, making sufficient noise to give the impression of a Battalion attack.

The object was to force the enemy to counter attack, thereby getting them out of their trenches, and so into the open where they could be dealt with. " C " Company successfully occupied the position for the three hours, meeting only slight opposition. They captured three prisoners, who gave valuable identification, but, unfortunately, the counter attack failed to materialise, as the enemy lay low.

On February 4 a fighting patrol of " B " Company was sent out with instructions to go to St. Maria Infante and return by Pt. 165, with the object of securing information and identifications. This patrol ran into heavy mortar and machine-gun fire, and Lt. Berny, together with six of his men, failed to return.

The next evening, Lt. W. A. Metcalf went out alone after

dark to reconnoitre the best route to St. Maria Infante, but failed to return.

On the night of February 7/8 another patrol was sent out from " D " Company to Pt. 165. This patrol consisted of L/Sgt. M. Robinson and two men. While they were moving up the southern slopes of the feature a German grenade, thrown from above, burst in front of L/Sgt. Robinson, severely wounding him in the face and eyes, and inflicting deep cuts in his shoulder and legs. At the same time the enemy opened fire with two machine-guns from the ridge in front. Undeterred by the intense pain which he was suffering, L/Sgt. Robinson, after sending back one of his men to give immediate information, remained to complete his task of pin-pointing the position of the machine-guns. He continued making his reconnaissance until the effect of the blast on his face completely closed his eyes. It was not until fifteen hours later that he was observed, staggering about, and was brought in by Cpl. Pears, who went out to his rescue. Before being taken down to the Regimental Aid Post L/Sgt. Robinson personally gave his detailed information to his Company Commander. For his courage and tenacity of purpose he was awarded the Distinguished Conduct Medal.

10/13 *Feb* 44   On February 10 the Battalion was relieved by the 6th Battalion, Royal Scots Fusiliers, and moved back into reserve at Sobello.

During this tour of duty in the line Lt.-Col. Bulfin was evacuated to hospital, and Lt.-Col. J. M. Perreau, North Staffordshire Regiment, who had been second-in-command, assumed Command of the Battalion.

Capt. Parker, the adjutant, also became a casualty, and his place was taken by Lt. G. R. Hovington.

After three days' rest the Battalion went into the line again in front of Trimonsuoli, taking over positions from the Grenadier Guards.

14/26 *Feb* 44   From February 14 to the 26th the Green Howards spent their time improving their defences, and constant patrols went out to harass the enemy. There was a good deal of mortar and counter mortar activity, and Trimonsuoli and the roads leading from it came under spasmodic shell fire during the whole period.

On February 23 Lt.-Col. Bulfin rejoined from hospital, but two days later was personally ordered by the Brigade Commander to return, as he was unfit. Lt.-Col. Perreau again assumed command of the Battalion.

28 *Feb* 44   Back again at Sobello, the Commanding Officer, on the last day of February, gave out the news that the Battalion was going to Anzio, and outlined his general plans for the move.

In the Wadis at Anzio.

Bren carriers coming ashore at La Riviere.

CHAPTER ELEVEN

" THE 1st BATTALION AT ANZIO "

" The Crossing of the Moletta "

March—June 1944

T HE Green Howards now entered upon their last *See* MAP period of fighting in Italy, during which they were to No. 14 play their part in the break out from the Anzio beachhead, which opened the way to Rome.

On March 3 the Battalion left Sobello, and moved to 1 *Bn* Pozzuoli, its embarkation port, spending a most unpleasant 3 *Mar* 44 night on the way at a camp, where few tents were available, and the rain converted the ground into a morass of mud.

At 8 p.m. on March 5 the four L.C.I. carrying the Green 5 *Mar* 44 Howards sailed from Pozzuoli in rough weather, and many of the troops were sick. Early next morning they arrived in 6 *Mar* 44 Nettuno bay, which was alive with D.U.K.W.s unloading the ships, which were standing off shore in the deeper water. In front of them lay the flat coast line, which formed the base of the Anzio beachhead, looking very peaceful in the early sunshine, until one noticed the white shell bursts on the perimeter inland, and heard the inevitable orchestral accompaniment of the guns.

Greeted by two or three shells from " Anzio Annie ", the usual large long range gun which harasses the back areas in static warfare, the Battalion went ashore soon after 7 a.m., and proceeded to its " B " Echelon area, which was only a few hundred yards from the coast, and some ten miles south of Ardea. Here the companies and other sub-units were well dispersed amongst trees, the vehicles were dug in, and the troops slept and lived below ground level in holes covered with bivouac tents.

This spot was to be their base for the next three months, to which they returned after each tour of duty in the line, and after the battle of the Moletta River crossing. From here also they set forth for their final battle in Italy north-east of Ardea.

The following time table may help the reader to follow the events of the next three months, particularly if it is read in conjunction with Map No. 14.

S

March 6	.. ..	At " B " Echelon
March 6/15	..	In the line near " The Fortress "
March 15/20	..	At " B " Echelon
March 20/22	..	In the line in Reserve
March 22/23	..	At " B " Echelon
March 23/April 15		In the line near San Lorenzo on the south bank of the Moletta River
April 16/20	..	At " B " Echelon
April 20/28	..	In the line near the Fortress
April 28/May 6	..	At " B " Echelon
May 6/15	.. ..	In the line just south-east of the Fortress
May 15/21	.. ..	At " B " Echelon
May 22/24	.. ..	Crossing of the Moletta River
May 25/28	.. ..	At " B " Echelon
May 29/June 1	..	Action north-east of Ardea
June 2/7	..	Resting near Ardea
June 7/13	..	Resting near Castel Porziano
June 13/19	.. ..	Resting near Pignataro
June 20	.. ..	Sail from Naples to Egypt.

On arrival at " B " Echelon the Battalion received orders to proceed up to the front line on the perimeter the same evening, and relieve the 7th Battalion, Oxfordshire and Buckinghamshire Light Infantry. As luck would have it, the sector of the line concerned was that known as " The Fortress " and was reputed to be the worst position in the " wadis ", which formed the main part of that section of the perimeter extending from the mouth of the R. Moletta to Carroceto. These wadis all followed the same pattern, deep and steep sided, covered with trees and undergrowth, and, at times, very very muddy.

The Fortress, called for obvious reasons by the Germans the " Swallows' Nest ", consisted of a tongue of high ground, which split the end of a large wadi, thereby forming on each side, a small subsidiary wadi. The Germans held the tip of this tongue of land, but, about half way up there was a small plateau, which was held by one of the forward British platoons. The remaining platoons held positions slightly lower down, clinging (like swallows) to the sides of the subsidiary wadis. The enemy held the heads of these subsidiary wadis, dominated the high ground on the right, and were in possession of the main wadi on the left flank. In fact, except for the main artery of the large wadi, the position was almost entirely surrounded.

Although, as a defensive post, the Fortress position was unsound, its retention was vital, as it was the key point of the surrounding, and somewhat precarious positions in the maze of the Moletta wadis.

It will be easy to understand that under such conditions casualties were bound to be heavy for a defensive position, and that the troops holding the Fortress were exposed to continuous tension, and were able to get little or no sleep.

Soon after midnight on March 6 the relief was completed, **7/15 *Mar* 44** and the Fortress was occupied by " C " and " D " Companies, under the command of Major A. T. Parkinson. The ensuing ten days were occupied with the usual routine of trench warfare. A certain amount of sniping and machine-gun fire took place at intervals, patrols went out, and every now and then the Battalion's positions were subjected to concentrations of shell fire, which caused casualties, including C.S.M. S. Oakley, who was killed, together with three others, when the Headquarters of the Support Company received a direct hit from a shell on March 11.

The Battalion was relieved by the 2nd Battalion, Cameronians, on March 15 and returned to "B" Echelon area.

On March 20 the Battalion relieved the 2nd Royal Scots **20/22 *Mar* 44** Fusiliers in reserve positions south of the Fortress, but on the 22nd, was brought back again to " B " Echelon, preparatory to moving up the coast to take over a sector of the line from the 36th Battalion, United States Engineers.

At this juncture Capt. P. J. Howell took over command of " B " Company from Major Tanner, who left the Battalion for another appointment.

On March 23 the Green Howards moved, and completed **23 *Mar* 44** the relief by the early hours of the 24th. They were now in close touch with the enemy, and overlooking that portion of the Moletta river, in the crossing of which they were to play so distinguished a part two months later.

Their new positions more or less encircled the little village of San Lorenzo. Here there was a road junction, which had been aptly named " Stonk Corner ", and which proved itself a worthy successor of the " Windy Corners " of 1914/1918. The first entry in the War Diary for March 24 states that " three heavy shells, probably 17 cm., fell near Stonk Corner ", and further references to this unhealthy spot lead one to believe that it is probably the best remembered feature of that sector of the line.

The Battalion took up its positions with " B " Company on the left, near the coast " D " Company a few hundred yards north of Stonk Corner, and " C " Company on the right, just east of San Lorenzo.

During this tour of duty " B " Company was somewhat isolated from the remainder of the Battalion, well forward of the spit of land leading to the mouth of the Moletta, from which there was excellent observation over the flank of the German positions. The Company was, in fact, approximately on the same ground as that which formed the jumping off point for the crossing of the Moletta on May 23. As a result of its observation, and the knowledge obtained by the reconnaissance patrols, which covered the " no-man's land " in front of the Moletta, " B " Company was able to supply much useful information, when the time came for planning the break out attack.

28 *Mar* 44   The Green Howards now settled down to a period of patrolling, and improving their defences.   On March 28 " D " Company was approached by an enemy patrol, and succeeded in killing one of the enemy, thus securing an identification that the patrol came from the 2nd Company of the 10th Parachute Regiment.

Later the same evening " B " Company sent out a patrol, with the object of securing a further identification. This patrol, on reaching its objective, was fired on very heavily from the flank, and four men were hit by the first burst of automatic fire. L/Cpl. S. Gibson was ordered to get the wounded back, while the rest of the patrol endeavoured to out-flank the enemy position. L/Cpl. Gibson succeeded in bringing three of the men back out of danger and then went back for the fourth and most badly wounded man, Pte. Middleton. In the darkness he failed in his search, so he then assisted the two men who could walk back to his company positions. He immediately returned to guard the third man, who was lying on the river bank within fifty yards of the enemy, until the stretcher bearers arrived. When the latter had got the wounded man on to a stretcher, L/Cpl. Gibson remained behind to cover them until they reached safety. For his courage and cool handling of the situation L/Cpl. Gibson received the Military Medal.

1/2 *Apr* 44   On the night of April 1/2 another patrol went out on the same mission. This time it was successful, but some hours of suspense were spent by the Company Commander without any news or sounds of action, before, without any warning, a rather terrified Lance Corporal of the 10th Parachute Regiment descended the steps of his dug-out, being prodded from behind by an exultant private soldier.

The prisoner turned out to be the Post Corporal, who had

been intercepted on his round of the enemy positions, and still had his company's mail in his possession. Early next morning a shower of leaflets, fired from a shell, fell on to " B " Company's positions, begging for the return of the mail, as the company had not had any letters for some time.

It was obvious that the enemy were busily engaged in strengthening their positions, as the night patrols reported sounds of wiring parties and of heavy stakes being driven into the ground. For the remainder of this period there was no offensive action by either side, except patrolling, but there was constant shelling and mortaring.

During the first fortnight in this position the Battalion fired off four thousand mortar bombs, and continually harassed the enemy by every means available.

On April 15, the Green Howards were relieved by the 15/19 *Apr* 44 2nd Battalion, Wiltshire Regiment, and returned to " B " Echelon area in the early hours of the 16th.

After three days' rest the Battalion returned to the Fortress sector of the front, and took over positions from the 6th Battalion, Seaforth Highlanders, during the night of the 19th and early hours of the 20th.

During this tour of duty the Fortress was held by " C " 20/24 *Apr* 44 Company and " B " Company (Capt. P. J. Howell), less two platoons, all under the command of Major D. G. St T Radcliffe. " D " Company occupied a less exposed position in the main wadi as reserve, where Lt.-Col. Perreau also had his tactical Headquarters.

Major Radcliffe and Capt. Howell shared a dug-out as their headquarters on the edge of the lower spur formed by the left hand wadi, which they took over from their predecessors. This wadi, which lay between " C " and " D " Companies, was unoccupied, and full of British and German mines. At " stand to " on the 20th voices were heard calling in German from this ravine. Two of the enemy eventually appeared, and were challenged. They were a German and a Pole from a parachute regiment, which was in the line opposing the Green Howards at this point, and who had decided to desert. They were disarmed and sent back to Battalion Headquarters. As Company Headquarters was the first post which these enemy deserters had reached, Major Radcliffe decided to move his headquarters to a more secure position, well within the Company perimeter, instead of on the right edge of it.

The exposed forward position on the central plateau was held at first by a platoon of " C " Company, commanded by Lt. C. B. H. Ryrie. On the night of April 21 the enemy

launched an attack against this position. The platoon suffered
heavily from mortar and small arms fire, and fron grenades
thrown at close range. However, with the aid of artillery support and the gallant leadership of Lt. Ryrie, who was later
awarded the Military Cross, the position was held. The slit
trench, in which Lt. Ryrie was stationed, received a direct hit
from a mortar bomb and, although his comrades were killed,
and he himself buried for a while, he managed to extricate
himself and continued to fight the battle.

The next night was comparatively quiet, and on the
night of April 23/24 the badly battered platoon of " C "
Company was relieved by a platoon of " B " Company.

25 *Apr* 44   The following night this platoon beat off another enemy
attack but unfortunately its commander, who had already
distinguished himself in carrying out patrols in the Moletta
area, trod on a " pencil " mine, when attempting to bring in
a wounded German for purposes of identification. With
some difficulty, he was rescued, and taken safely away to the
Regimental Aid Post that night. Sgt. J. Kerridge, later to be
wounded at the Moletta crossing, then took over the platoon
for the remainder of the time, during which two further
attacks were beaten off. The platoon acquitted itself magnificently, and no words can be good enough to describe the
leadership and personal bravery of Sgt. Kerridge.

During this period Pte. V. Oldham distinguished himself
and gained the Military Medal.

On the night of April 23/24 the platoon in which he was a
Bren gunner was sent up to relieve another platoon in a forward
position. The route was under continuous fire from machine-
guns, mortars, and grenades. Owing to the intensity of the
fire, only one section succeeded in making the relief that
night. The following night another attempt was made, but it
was still only possible to do so by sending one man up at a
time. Pte. Oldham spent four hours guiding men into the
position, and was in the open all the time, showing complete
disregard for his own safety.

On the next morning his trench received a direct hit, which
killed one man and wounded three others. It was impossible
to evacuate the wounded during the day, and Pte. Oldham
gave every assistance to them, although still being subjected
to very heavy fire.

During the following night ammunition in the area was
set alight by enemy mortar fire, which greatly endangered the
position. Pte. Oldham jumped out of his trench, and, in spite
of grenades and bombs exploding all round him, extinguished
the fire with sandbags. All this time he was silhouetted against

the flames, and provided an easy target for enemy machine-guns only fifty yards away.

On April 26 the platoon had nine seriously wounded men in their trenches. Pte. Oldham volunteered to go back over ground covered by enemy fire to fetch the stretcher bearers. This he succeeded in doing, and the lives were saved. Throughout the three days he spent in this position, Pte. Oldham showed complete disregard for his own safety, and his courage and selfless devotion to duty was an outstanding example and inspiration to all who saw him.

The enemy positions were very close, and such action as there was consisted mainly of mortaring and counter mortaring, with intermittent shelling. These caused a certain number of casualties, and it was with relief that the Battalion handed over its positions to the 2nd Battalion, Northamptonshire 28 *Apr* 44 Regiment, on April 28, and returned once more to " B " Echelon area.

During this relief Cpl. J. Tierney behaved with great gallantry, and won for himself the Military Medal. His section had, for the previous forty-eight hours, been mortared and shelled by day, and harassed by enemy patrols at night. Cpl. Tierney, who had already engaged the enemy in grenade battles at close range, and killed at least two of them, observed an enemy patrol trying to infiltrate into his position just as the relief was due to begin. Appreciating the fact that this patrol would probably encounter the relieving troops, he went forward alone with a Bren gun, and in a spirited action drove the enemy off.

Under heavy fire he remained in the open for forty minutes, until he was sure that the enemy patrol had dispersed. Throughout the whole period Cpl. Tierney was a source of encouragement and example to his men.

After so many months of rapid movement, to which they had become accustomed, the troops found the inactivity of trench warfare particularly galling. Unlike their predecessors of 1914/1918, they had not become inured to the boring and dispiriting experience of sitting in trenches under more or less constant bombardment, and at times suffering discomfort from cold and rain.

There occurred, however, even in their grim and unpleasant surroundings, some incidents of light relief, which are perhaps worth recording, and will doubtless be remembered by those who were there. The first concerns Lt. Whitehead, who commanded the mortar platoon with such energy and daring that his appearance was not always popular with the Companies, owing to the retaliation which his activities generally brought down on the area from which he operated. On the other hand, all ranks were loud in his praise, when, as he so often did, and particularly at the withdrawal from the Moletta, he provided covering fire which saved them many casualties.

It was his habit, after his platoon had fired their salvoes on to an enemy position, to turn up in the front line and ask each section commander whether his section was all right, usually to receive the reply, " Yes, Mr. Whitehead ". After one particularly severe bombardment in the Fortress area, he appeared in the front line to be greeted by a voice calling out in impeccable English, " Are you all right, Mr. White-head ", followed by considerable laughter from the German platoon, which was almost within hand shaking distance.

Some, too, will remember how their spirits were cheered when listening in their dug-outs on their wireless set to Lt. C. Newton, later to die so gallantly at L'Americano, giving a running commentary, in imitation of Howard Marshall, on some Germans who were rolling grenades down on to his platoon from the slopes above.

The Green Howards, however, after a week's rest at " B " Echelon, were destined to spend one more period under these conditions before they took up the advance once again. When they did so, although they were faced with tenacious opposition, and had to fight hard, they had the satisfaction of breaking into the enemy lines, and helping to bring this phase of the Italian operations to a successful conclusion.

6/15 *May* 44   On May 6 the Battalion returned to the Fortress area, and took over a sector of the line immediately south-east of the Fortress from the 2nd Battalion, Royal Scots Fusiliers. A week was spent in these positions, and once again the story is mainly of mortar and shell concentrations. " C " Company had a minor clash with the enemy on May 9, when a fighting patrol, which had been sent out to search a group of houses, ran into an enemy patrol. Grenades and rifle fire were exchanged, but our patrol sustained no casualties, and the enemy withdrew.

" B " Company sustained heavy casualties from mortar and shell fire during these nine days. The first blow was when Cpl. Murphy, M.M., was killed outright by a shell, when talking to Capt. D. M. D. O'Driscoll, the second-in-command. Cpl. Murphy, who won his Military Medal at Minturno in January, had been a tower of strength in many an engagement, and his loss was a grievous one to " B " Company. The following night a mortar bomb penetrated the dug-out in which Lt. G. Whittaker had his headquarters. Although it failed to explode, the fins wounded Lt. Whittaker in the back and he had to be evacuated. Then came the final tragedy when Sgt. J. Gott, who had taken over the platoon, was killed, together with two other N.C.O.s, in the same dug-out by a mortar bomb which, on this occasion, penetrated and exploded.

The Company had, however, one piece of luck when the dug-out, in which both Capt. Howell and Capt. O'Driscoll were living, received a direct hit on the roof. Luckily it was strongly built, and the bomb failed to penetrate.

On the 15th the Green Howards were back once more in " B " Echelon area.

The time was now approaching for a general move forward towards Rome, and General Mark Clark issued orders for the break-out from the Anzio beachhead to take place at 6.30 a.m. on May 23.

The main attack was to be made by the 34th and 45th American Divisions from the centre of the beachhead with the primary objective of Cisterna, followed by a swing north towards Valmonte. On the immediate left of the Americans was the 1st British Division, while the 5th British Division held the extreme left of the line down to the sea, facing the 4th German Parachute Division. As part of the plan, the British troops were ordered to make diversionary attacks on their sectors of the front before the main attack started, with the object of drawing off the enemy reserves.

Accordingly the 3rd Brigade, 1st Division, made a thrust towards Pantoni on May 22, and the Green Howards made an assault crossing of the River Moletta some two hours before the main attack was launched on May 23.

It is not necessary in this book to give an account of the main attack, except to state that it was successful, and that the main body of the 5th American Army forced its way through to Rome, which fell into its hands on June 5.

The part played by the British troops will not receive much mention in history, as their role was a subsidiary one, but it must be recorded that they contributed their share to the success of the whole operation.

At any rate, as far as the Green Howards were concerned, they fought so gallantly, and against such fierce opposition, both on the Moletta, and near Ardea a few days later, that their numbers were so reduced as to make their reinforcement and reorganisation essential. They were, therefore, withdrawn from the battle on June 1, and were unable to partake in the pursuit of the enemy whom they had helped to put to rout.

22 *May* 44 On May 22 the Battalion, under command of Lt.-Col. M. J. Perreau, moved forward from " B " Echelon area, and by *See* MAP No. 15 7 p.m. was established a few hundred yards short of the Moletta River, with Headquarters close to the sea shore. The Battalion was organised into Headquarters Company (Major A. T. Parkinson), three rifle companies, all slightly below full war establishment, " B " Company (Major C. S. Scrope), " C " Company (Capt. E. Roberts, M.C.) and " D " Company (Major R. G. Hewitt, The East Yorkshire Regiment), and the 3-inch Mortar and Anti-tank platoons.

The line at this point was being held by troops of the Northamptonshire Regiment, and the Green Howards occupied slit trenches, which had already been dug for them, immediately behind the forward positions. At 11 p.m. a heavy bombardment of the enemy position by the 5th Divisional artillery, intensified by supporting fire from the 1st Divisional and American Corps artillery and naval gunfire, began, and was continued throughout the night. The sound of the shells whistling over their heads encouraged the Green Howards as they crouched in their trenches, and wondered what the morrow held in store.

The general orders for the Battalion were to capture and hold the area of the sandhills between the Moletta River and the Fosse Dell' Incastro.

The carrying out of these orders was to be divided into three stages. The first stage was the preliminary one of taping the route to the river, erecting scaling ladders against the banks, and making gaps in the enemy wire. This task was to be undertaken by three parties of Royal Engineers, protected by No. 12 platoon of " B " Company, commanded by Lt. J. Storey. The latter party was also to carry the scaling ladders. Pioneers of the Green Howards were to lay the tapes, and the engineers were to make three gaps in the wire at fifty yard intervals.

These parties were to move forward at 3.15 a.m. on May 23, and to withdraw when their task was completed, leaving one section of No. 12 platoon to guide the assaulting company to the scaling ladders.

The second stage was the assault by " D " Company of the enemy positions from Pt. 10 to the beach. Having captured these positions, " D " Company was ordered to consolidate them, and push one platoon slightly forward on its left flank to cover any approach by the enemy along the beach. " D " Company was ordered to launch its attack at 4.45 a.m.

The final stage was to be carried out by " C " Company, as soon as news was received that " D " Company had gained its objective. " C " Company was then to pass through, and capture the enemy positions in and around the group of houses which went by the name of L'Americano. These were some seven hundred yards ahead, on the southern bank of the Fosse Dell' Incastro.

" B " Company was to be kept in reserve, and a troop of tanks was to be held ready to go up on to the objectives as soon as the Engineers had constructed a bridge across the Moletta. It was hoped that these would be in action about two hours after the initial assault had been launched.

Within a quarter of an hour of starting No. 12 platoon 23 *May* 44 and one of the R.E. parties met with disaster, when they ran into a new and unknown minefield. The Engineer Officer was killed, and all his men wounded, while of No. 12 platoon, one man was killed, and eight wounded, including the platoon commander. At the same time the Germans opened a heavy fire, and raked the minefields with machine-gun fire.

Cpl. E. Arbuthnot now found himself the senior surviving N.C.O., and rose gallantly to the occasion. Realising how supremely important it was that the scaling ladders, which they carried with them, should be placed in position against the far bank of the Moletta, he rallied his few remaining men, and led them forward in the face of heavy fire across the river. Eventually he succeeded in placing two or three ladders, which were all the small party could carry, in position, in time to enable " D " Company to make use of them. Cpl. Arbuthnot was wounded twice during this exploit, but later on in the day volunteered to go forward and take over a section at a critical stage in the action.

For his bravery and leadership Cpl. Arbuthnot was awarded the Distinguished Conduct Medal.

Punctually, at 4.45 a.m., " D " Company crossed the starting line, and soon entered the minefield which was under heavy fire. This minefield had been reconnoitred three nights previously by Major Hewitt, who led a patrol of one platoon commanded by Lt. R. Trevelyan, together with an Engineer officer and corporal. They had found the thickest anti-personnel minefield they had yet seen, some forty yards in depth, and extending laterally further than they were able to penetrate. During the preliminary bombardment over two thousand shells had been fired into the minefield but, owing to the casualties suffered by the Royal Engineer Gapping parties, they found that the mines had not been completely cleared, and they suffered a number of casualties from anti-personnel mines. The actual crossing of the river (which at this point was about twelve yards across, two feet deep, and

with very steep banks about twelve feet high), had also been
more difficult than had been anticipated, but they pressed
forward with great dash and determination, and were able
to report, about an hour after starting, that they had captured
their objective, with the exception of one machine-gun post
on their left flank. This post was eventually knocked out by
No. 18 platoon, and by 7 a.m. they were able to report that
the whole position was in their hands. The Company was,
however, sadly depleted by this time, the right hand platoon,
No. 17, was reduced to one officer and eight men, the centre
platoon, No. 16, to six men, and the left hand platoon, No.
18, to one officer and seven men.

Most of the casualties had been caused by the mines,
but the enemy had put up a stout resistance, and many of
them were found dead in their slit trenches. All three platoon
commanders had been wounded, and the platoons were almost
out of ammunition. However, it was not long before the
company carrier arrived with reserve ammunition, and soon
afterwards Major Hewitt was reinforced by two platoons
of " B " Company, and a platoon of machine-guns of the
Cheshire Regiment. Later in the day a platoon of the
Northamptonshire Regiment also arrived on the position.
Major Hewitt now proceeded to consolidate his positions,
and his command spent a comparatively quiet day until
it was counter-attacked in the evening.

Meanwhile Lt.-Col. Perreau had, at 6 a.m., given " C "
Company orders to take up the advance on L'Americano.
In spite of the preliminary artillery bombardment, " C "
Company, as soon as it started its long advance across the
scrub-covered sand towards L'Americano, encountered strong
opposition. Overcoming a series of enemy positions the
company reached and established itself on a ridge some
hundred and fifty yards short of L'Americano by about 7.30
a.m. No. 13 platoon, which had been advancing on the right
flank, had suffered particularly severely and was reduced to
twelve men, and the company had sustained some forty
casualties in all.

Capt. Roberts, at this stage, sent back a message to the
effect that he could assault L'Americano, but would not be
able to hold it with his present strength, even although the
troop of tanks was now coming up. There was no covered
approach to the houses, and the open ground, which the
company would have to cross, was covered by enemy machine-
guns from both flanks. A message was sent back to him that
No. 10 platoon of " B " Company was being sent up to reinforce his company.

Soon after 9 o'clock " C " Company launched an assault on L'Americano. Storming across the bullet swept ground, No. 14 platoon, with fixed bayonets, reached the foremost houses, killing seven Germans on the way. A section of No. 13 platoon, under Lt. Newton, followed them up, but this gallant officer and all his men were killed. The Commander of No. 14 platoon was wounded and the platoon was reduced to one Lance Corporal and six men, while all that was left of No. 13 platoon was one section.

Capt. Howell, who had been sent up to contact Capt. Roberts earlier in the morning, came back with one picture firmly imprinted on his mind. " I saw," he says, " in one place, five men of ' C ' Company, with an N.C.O. in the middle of his section, lying in perfect alignment on their faces, with their bayonets facing L'Americano—all dead."

Under these circumstances Capt. Roberts was forced to withdraw to his previous positions, to which he was ordered to hold on. At 11.30 Capt. Howell arrived with No. 10 platoon of " B " Company, consisting of fifteen men, and Capt. Roberts proceeded to consolidate as best he could. He was now holding a position approximately four hundred yards long, and some six hundred yards in front of " D " Company, and the enemy was putting down a heavy mortar and artillery bombardment. The tanks had arrived by this time, and proved to be invaluable in helping the Green Howards to cling on to their positions. Throughout the day a number of German counter-attacks were repulsed.

The Battalion was now in the unhappy position of having no reserve left, as " B " Company had been committed piece-meal to the battle as reinforcements for " C " and " D " Companies.

Line and wireless communication between Headquarters and the forward companies had broken down, and the situation as viewed from Battalion Headquarters was far from clear. Lt.-Col. Perreau had been instructed by the Brigade Commander not to leave his headquarters, and so he ordered Major Scrope to go forward and visit each company and platoon area, and to report the exact situation to him.

Major Scrope's own account of his mission gives a clear picture of the intensity of the fighting, which the leading companies had experienced. " I reached ' D ' Company," he states, " without incident, and found them well dug in with a good field of fire. Despite the casualties which the company had sustained, the men were in good heart and the position appeared to be securely held.

On going further forward I encountered a scene of

complete chaos. Dead and wounded British and German soldiers were lying all round, and there were a number of wounded men waiting to be evacuated. A 'brewed up' tank indicated our front line positions. 'C' Company had obviously had a very sticky time, and was now holding a very wide front with very few men. Capt. Roberts, who was killed a week later in the action near Ardea, told me that, with the invaluable assistance given by the remaining tanks, and by artillery support, he had already succeeded in repulsing several immediate counter-attacks of platoon or company strength. He was doubtful, however, of his ability to withstand a full scale deliberate attack." With no possibility of receiving further reinforcement, and with the tanks withdrawing at dusk to refuel and replenish their ammunition, Capt. Roberts' doubts were proved to be justified when the enemy launched a strong attack at about 9 'oclock that evening. Shouting and singing, the Germans advanced from the front and from both flanks, and, although "C" Company and No. 10 platoon of "B" Company took heavy toll of them, they were inevitably overrun.

The Germans completely surrounded No. 15 platoon on the right, and by sheer weight of numbers broke through Nos. 13 and 14 platoons in the centre.

In smoke, dust, and the failing light "C" Company Headquarters and a handful of survivors, about thirty in all, struggled back to "D" Company's positions.

Less than an hour later the enemy counter-attacked "D" Company's positions in what was estimated to be about battalion strength. No. 18 platoon on the left flank was overrun, and the remainder of the company, together with the remnants of "C" Company, were now strung out in a long line, with their backs to the river. At this juncture, in the opinion of Major Hewitt, the day was saved by the machine-guns of the Cheshire Regiment. Although one gun was knocked out early on, the other three fired their entire ammunition, and, in addition, eight thousand rounds borrowed from "C" Company. The 3-inch mortars, and guns of the supporting R.A. battery, fired until they were red hot, and the attack was finally beaten off, the enemy withdrawing leaving many dead on the field. During the night the Green Howards positions were subjected to shell fire from medium and heavy guns, but, owing to the good cover which they had dug, casualties were not heavy.

The situation, however, became serious again when it was discovered that the enemy was infiltrating through the gap between "D" Company and the sea, which had been made by the loss of No. 18 platoon. The Northamptonshire Regiment had been withdrawn from their original forward defence line, and there were no other troops between this gap, and " B " Echelon area and Anzio port.

Lt.-Col. Perreau, having no reserve, ordered Major Scrope to collect some men as best he could, and to move forward and close the gap. Major Scrope managed to raise a motley force of about twenty-five men, consisting of clerks, signallers, cooks, drivers and storemen, and set out towards the Moletta. The time was now about 1 a.m. on May 24, and, by the greatest 24 *May* 44 of luck, Major Scrope managed to get his party into the original forward defence lines a few minutes before the Germans arrived. A small arms duel ensued, but the gap was effectively blocked, and, with the exception of sending forward a patrol, the enemy made no serious attempt to cross the Moletta that night.

When daylight came on May 24 the situation was practically unaltered. Major Scrope's party was firmly established on the south bank of the Moletta, but being subjected to periodical shelling from light mortars, and to machine-gun fire from just across the river. " D " Company on the right was still north of the river, but uncomfortably placed with the enemy on three sides.

At 8 a.m. Lt.-Col. Perreau received orders to withdraw " D " Company, and at about 9 a.m., this tricky operation started. It entailed crossing the Moletta at a point which was covered by machine-gun fire from both flanks, and the enemy were by this time within grenade range, having crept up the ditches and behind bushes.

Major Hewitt sent his men off in batches with instructions to make a dash across the river. Unfortunately many of them were hit, and by the time the last man got across, there were more than a dozen men lying wounded in the shallow water. Stretcher bearers rushed forward, but they were in insufficient numbers, and so an officer called for volunteers, and, putting up the Geneva Cross, led them openly into the Moletta. This brave action was respected by the German machine-gunners, and they were able to go round to each wounded man, give him a shot of morphia, and get him away.

Major Hewitt was awarded the D.S.O. for his handling of " D " Company throughout this action. In the official words of his citation : " He showed outstanding leadership and resource, and it was due to his constant encouragement at times when the situation was gravest, that his very depleted force managed to drive off and hold its own against a very superior force of German Paratroopers."

Major Hewitt has asked that it should be recorded that, in his opinion as an officer of another regiment, the Green Howards were really terrific in this battle, and that he had never seen a company bayonet charge go in with such élan, as that carried out by the few survivors of his command.

Finally, an hour or so later, Major Scrope was relieved by a company of the Northamptonshire Regiment, and the Battalion found itself back where it had started from some thirty hours previously.

The Green Howards had suffered grievously, their casualties being one officer and twenty-six men killed, four officers and seventy-one men wounded, and one officer and fifty-two men missing. In the light of the intensity of the fighting it was considered that most of those reported missing had probably been killed.

Lt.-Col. Perreau, on the evening of the 23rd, received the following message from Brigadier Finlaison in his own handwriting : " I feel that your chaps did splendidly today, and regret very much your heavy casualties."

It is often unwise and unfair to criticise the higher command when things go wrong, as the critic seldom knows the whole story.

In the case of the Moletta battle, however, it appears that the Green Howards might have every justification in feeling bitterly the loss of the gallant lives which were sacrificed. They accomplished all that they were ordered to do but, owing to the losses sustained in securing their objectives, they could not possibly hold on to their gains. Moreover they suffered still further losses in extricating themselves from a position, in which they should never have been left unsupported. Had even one fresh company been at hand to consolidate the position in front of L'Americano, which " C " Company, reduced to one-third of its strength, was gallantly trying to hold, the result of the battle might have been very different.

Nevertheless, in this action, the 1st Battalion, Green Howards, added yet another chapter to the Regimental Record, and those who died, did not lay down their lives in vain. The spirit of those who fought at Alma was very much alive that day, and a tribute was paid by a tough German parachutist, who was captured, which may well make Yorkshiremen proud. " Your men," he said, " came in shouting and laughing to attack us. What can one do against men like these ? "

Doubtless many of the brave deeds performed in this battle were unseen, or else seen only by those who fell later

in the action and were unable to record them, but there
exist the records of those who were decorated for the part
which they played. Those men, whose stories we are about to
tell, would be the first to own that there were many others,
who fought as bravely, and who maintained the Green Howard
standard.

Mention has already been made of Lt. Newton and Cpl.
Arbuthnot, but at various times throughout the action Cpl.
A. G. Churms, Cpl. H. Dixon, Pte. C. Gill, L/Sgt. H. Woodall
and Pte. S. Shaw all performed deeds, which won for them the
Military Medal.

No mention has yet been made of the 3-inch Mortar
platoon, which, under the command of Lt. Whitehead,
rendered sterling service throughout the battle. The following
accounts of how L/Sgt. Woodall and Cpl. Churms gained their
Military Medals will serve to show the conditions under which
the Mortar platoon supported the forward Companies.

At about 10 a.m. on May 23 the enemy concentrated
heavy shell fire on to the area occupied by Battalion Headquarters, and the Mortar platoon. This resulted in communication between the Mortars and their observation post
being cut. L/Sgt. Woodall, realising that a critical situation
might result at a later stage, when it would be imperative to
maintain observed fire, immediately left the comparative
safety of his command post, and, under heavy shell fire, mended
four breaks in the cable. On his return journey he mended a
further break which had occurred since his journey up to the
observation post. When he arrived back at his post, he found
that the noise occasioned by enemy shell fire had increased
to such an extent as to render verbal communication between
the post and the mortars impossible. In order to ensure that
his section continued firing, L/Sgt. Woodall transmitted the
fire orders by running backwards and forwards despite the
heavy shell fire. L/Sgt. Woodall, by his complete disregard
of his own safety, set a magnificent example to his men, and
by his courage and ability to carry out the task allotted to him,
was largely responsible for the continuous support which
was given to the forward troops.

Cpl. Churms was in charge of a detached section of the
Mortar platoon when, during the night of May 23, enemy
shell fire was opened on to his position, in which a large
quantity of reserve ammunition had been stacked. One shell
landed so close that some of the secondary charges in the
bombs caught fire. The fire spread quickly to a large number
of the bombs, and soon over a ton of ammunition was in
danger of catching fire. Without a thought for his own safety,

T

Cpl. Churms ordered his crew to get out of the pit, and began personally to extinguish the burning bombs with sand. The heat generated, however, resulted in the explosion of one bomb, which wounded Cpl. Churms. In spite of his wound, he supervised the digging of a new position and continued to control the fire of his section under heavy shell fire throughout the action.

There is no doubt that the initiative and prompt action taken by Cpl. Churms prevented casualties amongst the remainder of his detachment, while his determination to carry on, although painfully wounded, when fire support was urgently needed, was typical of the courage and high sense of duty which had been characteristic of him throughout his active service.

Communications, of course, play a vital part in the success of any attack, and, with the very heavy fire which covered the battlefield, the work performed by the regimental signallers was arduous and dangerous. Cpl. H. Dixon, in particular, behaved with great valour, and was awarded the Military Medal. When, on the morning of May 24, the Commanding Officer wanted to recall " D " Company, it was found that wireless communication had been jammed, and the cable lines cut, Cpl. Dixon volunteered to attempt the repair of four hundred yards of cable, which crossed an area at that time under heavy artillery fire. Going out alone, he succeeded in reaching the bank of the Moletta having mended fifteen breaks in the line, but the line was still out of order. He therefore retraced his steps, and found a further four breaks, which had been made since his first journey. But the line was still out of order when he arrived back at Battalion Head-quarters, and it was therefore decided to establish an inter-mediate wireless station on the south bank of the Moletta. Cpl. Dixon at once volunteered to operate this, and succeeded, after repeated attempts, in establishing contact with " D " Company. It was largely due to his determination and perseverance that these vital orders were received in time by " D " Company. Not content with having accomplished this feat, while the company was making its way back across the river, and being hard pressed, Cpl. Dixon, while still operating his wireless set, undertook the loading of one of the 2-inch Mortars, the crew of which was short handed. Throughout the whole period he was under constant shell fire, and his courage and devotion to duty cannot be overestimated.

Finally the deeds of two of the regimental stretcher bearers must be recorded. Ptes. C. Gill and S. Shaw were attached to " D " Company in its initial assault, and, very soon after crossing the Moletta, the Company, as will be remembered, ran into an enemy minefield. Many of the wounded fell in the middle of the minefield, and Ptes. Gill and Shaw, without hesitation, walked into the minefield and succeeded in getting back several of the wounded to the Regimental Aid Post. Having completed this task, these two men collected other regimental stretcher bearers, who had only had a few days' training, and led them up into the forward lines. Here, in the face of heavy shelling, machine-gun fire, and close range fire from snipers, who were not respecting the Red Cross emblems, they continued, without rest throughout the thirty hours of the battle, to rescue the wounded and get them away, along tracks incompletely cleared of mines, to the Regimental Aid Post. The conduct of these two men was of the highest order, and had a tremendously encouraging effect upon the fighting troops. For their coolness and courage, Ptes. Gill and Shaw both received the Military Medal.

Other deeds worthy of mention are those of Lt. Ryrie, who, although wounded in the foot at the beginning of " C " Company's advance, continued to lead his platoon in the assault on L'Americano for the next four hours, and then asked for half an hour off to have his wound dressed, and of Sgt. W. E. Wickens who, when seven of his men were surrounded by ten Germans, seized a tommy-gun, and drove them off.

By May 25 the Battalion was back again in " B " Echelon 25/28 May 44 area for rest, re-equipment and reinforcement. During the short time it was there strenuous efforts were made to reweld the Battalion into an effective fighting unit. Large drafts of reinforcements arrived, and the companies were made up to strength in numbers, but the newcomers, who for the most part were anti-aircraft gunners, hastily converted into infantrymen, were, through no fault of their own, virtually untrained, and with no previous battle experience. The toll of experienced soldiers during the previous fighting had been very heavy, and a tremendous responsibility rested on the shoulders of those who were left, and who had to lead the new troops into action within a few days of their joining.

While the Green Howards were resting news came through that the main break-out from the beachhead by the Americans had been a great success, and that they had joined up with the advanced elements of the Army on their right, which had broken through at Cassino.

The 4th German Parachute Division at the seaward end of the line had, however, put up a very stubborn resistance, and, on May 29, the forward troops of the 5th Division were still a mile or so south-east of Ardea.

It was very important that this right German wing should be pushed back as quickly as possible, and there was little respite for the Green Howards. On May 28 they moved forward again, and on May 30 arrived close behind the 1st Battalion, K.O.Y.L.I., which, after stiff fighting, had established itself on some high ground along the line of the road leading from Ardea north-east to Campoleone.

The Germans had been displaying great skill in the art of withdrawal, and following them up was proving a difficult and dangerous task. Perhaps a company would advance several thousand yards against virtually no opposition, when, suddenly without warning, it would come under heavy machine-gun fire. Then a whole Battalion would possibly have to be deployed to overcome this resistance, and, shortly after the advance was resumed, the same thing would happen again. The Germans also showed great skill in the timing of their counter-attacks, which were frequently launched against an isolated company, before it could get up its supporting arms.

It was into this type of operation that the hastily reformed Green Howards battalion was flung on May 31.

Lt.-Col. Perreau was given orders on May 30 to take his Battalion forward through the 1st Battalion, K.O.Y.L.I., next day, and take up the advance. The ground held by this Battalion was covered with scrub and bushes, and overlooked a valley about half a mile in width, down the centre of which ran a mountain stream. Beyond the valley the ground rose steeply to Pt. 48. To the left of Pt. 48 was Pt. 51, whilst to the right of and slightly behind Pt. 48 was Pt. 55. All these features were steep, and covered with little or no scrub or any type of cover. Little was known of the enemy's dispositions on this front, in fact it was thought that he had withdrawn on the previous night.

At 9.30 a.m. on May 31 " B " Company (Major Scrope) moved forward towards Pt. 48. Major Scrope sent a fighting patrol of one platoon, under Lt. J. P. M. Horsburgh, forward on his left flank to report whether there were any enemy on Pt. 51. Unfortunately this patrol, owing to inexperience, kept to the low ground, and very soon came under heavy machine-gun fire. Practically the whole platoon was wiped out or taken prisoner, and only a few stragglers got back. Lt. Horsburgh was captured, but made his escape a week later and rejoined the battalion. It was now obvious that the opposition was far stronger than had been anticipated. After a short delay, in order to enable a fire plan to be laid on, " B " Company, less one platoon, assaulted and captured Pt. 48, but, owing

28/30 May 44

31 May 44

to almost complete lack of cover, found consolidation of the position extremely difficult. A number of casualties were caused by German machine-gun fire, and in the end, the Company was forced to occupy positions on the reverse slope of the hill, until it could dig itself in on the forward slopes under cover of darkness. Nevertheless " B " Company had done very well, and besides inflicting casualties on the enemy, had already sent back a number of prisoners which it had captured.

During this action Cpl. G. W. Gunn displayed initiative and gallantry of a very high order. He was the commander of one of the Sections of No. 10 platoon, " B " Company. After the capture of Pt. 48, the reorganisation of " B " Company on this feature proved very difficult. The enemy were on the next feature some four to five hundred yards away, well dug in and with good fields of fire. In order to be able to engage the enemy with fire, and to regain the initiative from him, it was necessary to try to establish positions on the forward slope. Pt. 48 was so bare, and lacked any form of cover such as scrub, that, the moment men tried to work forward over or round the crest, they came under heavy automatic fire. The result was that " B " Company dug in on the reverse slopes with very short fields of fire, and in positions from which it was unable to dominate the ground separating the enemy from its own positions, and from which it would have been very difficult to repel an enemy counter-attack.

Major Scrope, at this stage, visited No. 10 platoon and told Cpl. Gunn to move his Section some forty yards forward to a small patch of corn, which would afford a minimum of cover from view, and from which he would be able to engage the enemy with his Bren gun. Cpl. Gunn immediately worked forward with his Section and reached the patch of corn. Apparently the movement of the corn caused by the Section crawling through it was observed by the enemy, who opened fire and killed No. 1 on the Bren before he was able to get into a fire position. No. 2 took over and fired a few bursts, but shortly afterwards, he was wounded and had to be evacuated. Cpl. Gunn then took over the Bren himself, and from a fold in the ground engaged with fire enemy movement which he had seen. Another member of the Section scratched a bit of a hole in the ground for Cpl. Gunn which gave him a little better cover. He continued to engage the enemy intermittently for the next half-hour.

A little later the rapid fire of two enemy spandaus was heard and the slower " rat-tat " of Cpl. Gunn's Bren as he replied. A few moments later there was silence and Sgt. Parkin, the platoon commander, reported that Gunn had been shot through the head by one of the spandaus. Had Cpl. Gunn not been killed he would have certainly been recommended for a decoration.

Meanwhile " C " and " D " Companies had moved down into the valley, and soon after mid-day, " D " Company (Major Hewitt, D.S.O.) made a successful attack on Pt. 51. This company firmly established itself on Pt. 51, and remained there until withdrawn late in the evening of June 1. Later in the afternoon " C " Company (Capt. Roberts, M.C.) moved up into position immediately behind " B " Company on Pt. 48, preparatory to launching an attack on Pt. 55.

While Major Scrope and Capt. Roberts were discussing the line of the attack, and the best method by which " B " Company could support it, a very heavy concentration of enemy shell fire fell upon " C " Company. This caused a certain amount of disorganisation, and the attack was postponed for a short while. The men quickly recovered, however, and went gamely into the assault just before darkness began to fall.

The enemy on Pt. 55 fought stubbornly, and it was not until some fierce hand to hand fighting had taken place that the feature was eventually taken. However, taken it was, and " C " Company, having sent back a number of prisoners, firmly consolidated itself on the ground. In the course of the battle " C " Company had the misfortune to lose its commander, Capt. Roberts, M.C., who was killed instantaneously while leading his men with his customary courage and inspiration. Capt. O'Driscoll assumed command of the Company, and brought the remnants out of action the following day. After the Battalion had withdrawn " C " Company was taken over by Major J. S. Bade, who retained his command for the remainder of the war.

All three companies spent the night in strengthening their positions, and improving their dispositions. During the night the sounds of enemy armoured vehicles in considerable numbers could be heard in front of the Green Howard positions.

Urgent requests for anti-tank guns were sent back, but it was found impossible to get these across the steep banks of the intervening stream.

The forward companies, therefore, found themselves awaiting the dawn, with the unpleasant knowledge that an armoured attack was impending, and that the only defence they had were the P.I.A.T. guns, and some fire support from

British tanks in hull down positions some thousand yards in the rear.

As the first grey streaks of dawn appeared in the sky the enemy attacked with two troops of tanks, supported by infantry, which loomed up through the morning haze in front of Pts. 48 and 55. 1 *Jun* 44

The P.I.A.T. men of " C " Company on Pt. 55 fired as fast as they could, while the remainder opened up with their rifles and Bren guns, but not unnaturally this did not check the oncoming armour, and in a matter of minutes " C " Company was overrun. It was a nerve wracking experience even for seasoned troops, and " C " Company, composed as it was largely of untrained men, fought as best it could.

" B " Company on the hill behind did its best to support " C " Company with its fire, but a few minutes later No. 10, the forward platoon of this company, was also overrun. A P.I.A.T. man of " B " Company scored a direct hit on a German tank, but it still came on.

At this juncture, apart from Company Headquarters, No. 12 platoon of " B " Company, commanded by Lt. J. Storey, was the only sub-unit remaining on Pt. 48, and it was vital for it to hold on. Lt. Storey remained cool and imperturbable in the face of the oncoming enemy armour, and with the remnants of " C " Company, and No. 10 platoon of " B " Company, retiring in disorder in front of him. Regardless of his own safety, Lt. Storey moved about amongst his sections, and encouraged them by his example to stand firm, and continue to engage the enemy with their weapons. The best of troops might well have broken when faced with these conditions, and it was mainly due to the leadership of Lt. Storey and his example that they did not do so.

The position seemed to be desperate, but fortunately the light was now growing stronger, and the British tanks in support were able to see well enough to fire. They put down a barrage of fire on the enemy tanks and the latter withdrew.

In this action, and throughout the day, Major C. S. Scrope showed great qualities of leadership and courage for which he was awarded the Military Cross. When the enemy, having captured Pt. 55, were threatening the right flank of his company, Major Scrope went forward himself, and, collecting a handful of men, re-established this sector of his position. He then proceeded to collect some stragglers who had escaped from " C " Company's position, and led them on to his own positions. When his men saw their company commander walking coolly about under heavy machine-gun fire, and collecting reinforcements for them, they recovered their badly shaken morale and held gamely on to their positions.

Throughout the day Major Scrope moved from platoon to platoon under close machine-gun and mortar fire, encouraging his untrained men, who were experiencing their first action. By holding on to Pt. 48 all through the day of June 1, " B " Company undoubtedly saved " D " Company from being surrounded on Pt. 51.

In the words of Major Scrope's citation : " It was entirely due to this officer's exceptional leadership and fine example, at a time when there was a danger of inexperienced troops breaking up in the face of tanks, that the enemy counter-attacks failed to drive the remaining companies from their positions."

Throughout the remainder of June 1 the remnants of the Green Howards held on to their positions. They were subjected to heavy fire, but no further major attack was made.

" D " Company was firmly established on Pt. 51 and " B " Company, less two platoons, on Pt. 48, but Pt. 55 remained unoccupied, which made the positions of the remaining companies more uncomfortable.

At about 8 p.m. orders reached these two forward companies to withdraw some thousand yards back to the Ardea-Campoleone road. An hour later the 13th Brigade on the left withdrew, and, shortly afterwards, " D " Company abandoned Pt. 51. Finally the gallant " B " Company, which had proved itself the key to the defence, came back in the darkness at about 11 p.m. The Battalion then retired through the 1st Battalion, K.O.Y.L.I., who were still in their original positions on the ridge, and went into reserve.

2/19 Jun 44   After spending two or three days in great heat and discomfort in a wadi, news came that the Battalion was to go forward. The advance party moved up the disused railway line at the tail of the advancing army on June 4, and spent the night in some woods just north of Castel Porziano. Finding themselves very near the main road from Ostia to Rome the temptation proved too great, and on June 5 a jeep containing three Green Howard officers entered Rome with the American forces. And so, even if unofficially, the Green Howards were represented at the culmination of the long pilgrimage, which had started in the Western Desert of N. Africa in 1941.

So ended the fighting career of the 1st Battalion in Italy, since, soon after the fall of Rome on June 5, the 5th Division went back to Naples, and on June 20, sailed for the Middle East.

Since landing on the beaches of Sicily on July 10, 1943, the Green Howards had fought their way across that island, all the way from the toe of Italy to Lanciano on the east coast, across the Garigliano on the west coast, and finally crossed the Moletta River and pursued the enemy almost to the gates of Rome. It was the irony of fate that in their last four days fighting they should have suffered more casualties than in the whole of the previous eleven months, and that in these two actions they made no permanent forward progress. It was no fault of theirs that in the first case they were left unsupported, and in the second were faced with attacks from tough German paratroops, supported by armour, when at least half the Battalion consisted of gunners, untrained as infantrymen, who had only joined a few days before they went into action. Those men fought well, in fact they fought heroically, but the very greatest credit must be given to the old hands, the Green Howard officers, N.C.O.s and old soldiers, who led them and encouraged them. Even in that short time the regimental *esprit de corps* had done its work. Before leaving Italy, and while they were resting near Castel Porziano, and later near Pignataro, several organised parties were allowed to visit Rome, which had been their Mecca for so long.

On June 19 the Battalion embarked at Naples on the S.S. *Ascania*, and, sailing next day, arrived in the Grand Harbour of Valetta at Malta on June 22.

The following day it left for Alexandria, where it disembarked on June 25, and entrained next day for Cairo. There it was stationed in Mena Camp, and settled down to a period of rest and reorganisation.

The next few months were spent in training and carrying out security duties at various places in the Middle East, including Kafar Yona, Jebel Mazar, Ar Ramar, and Julis, until on February 24, 1945, the Battalion embarked at Haifa on H.M.T. *Highland Brigade*. *Jul 44/ Feb 45*

At the end of December, 1944, Lt.-Col. J. G. C. Waldron, O.B.E., The Gloucestershire Regiment, who had been second-in-command, took over the command of the Battalion from Lt.-Col. Perreau, with Major C. S. Scrope, M.C., as his second-in-command.

The story of how the 1st Battalion took part in the final stages of the war on the banks of the Elbe will be told in a later chapter.

CHAPTER TWELVE

"THE 6th AND 7th BATTALIONS"

"Training for 'D' Day"
"Landings in Normandy"
"La Rivière to Villers Bocage"

November 1943—*August* 1944

6 and 7 Bns
5 Nov 43

THE ships carrying the 6th and 7th Green Howards, with the remainder of the 50th Division, docked at Liverpool in the early hours of November 5, 1943. It was a dismal homecoming ; a wet and misty morning, a bomb-shattered city, and, since their arrival was covered by security regulations, there were no relations to meet them. But, although their return home was very different from that which they had so often pictured in the desert, the very austerity of the scene served to remind them that there was a job still to be done.

On November 8 they entrained and were taken to Riddlesworth Camp near Thetford in Norfolk. On arrival there, all ranks were immediately sent on two, three, or four weeks' leave according to the length of their service abroad, and it was not until the middle of December that the battalions were reassembled as complete units.

On leaving Sicily they had left behind all vehicles, stores, and weapons, other than personal arms, and so had to be completely re-equipped. The greater part of January 1944 was thus spent in re-equipping, and in individual training. On *1 Feb* 44 February 1 both battalions moved to billets in Southwold, where they were inspected by H.M. The King on February 23.

It was at about this time that Major F. H. Brunton, M.C. left the 6th Battalion to take up an instructional appointment. The 6th Green Howards, in their fighting career of the past three years, owed a great deal to Major Brunton. In the days when he was a Company Commander he led his company with such a cool and determined bearing that, on more than one occasion, it was singled out for special mention, while he himself received the Military Cross. Later on in the campaigns, on four separate occasions, he found himself commanding the Battalion at critical moments in battle, and never failed to display outstanding leadership. It is, however, as the vital link between the Battalion and the home town of Middlesbrough that we say farewell to Major Brunton in these pages.

282

There was scarcely a man, who joined the Battalion from Middlesbrough or the surrounding country, who was not known either directly or indirectly to Major Brunton. Commanding Officers came and went, and all will bear witness to the invaluable aid which he gave them as second-in-command, in helping to keep alive that very special *esprit-de-corps* of Middlesbrough and Cleveland, which was the hallmark of the 6th Battalion.

Training had now begun in earnest, but not under the best conditions. Certain factors concerned with training, and the supply of personnel, had so important an effect upon the operations in which these two battalions were due to take part, that it is worth while recording some of the comments made by their Commanding Officers concerning this period. It must be remembered that the battalions now consisted of a small proportion of war experienced, but in many cases " battle weary", troops, while the remainder were for the most part young recruits straight from Infantry Training Centres, or officers and men from disbanded anti-aircraft regiments. Few of the latter had taken part in more than platoon and company exercises, and none had had any battle experience.

It is not surprising, therefore, that Lt.-Col. Hastings gives it as his opinion that his battalion would have received greater benefit, if some of the time, which was expended on technical training for combined operations and large scale marshalling exercises, had been allotted to company, platoon and section training in the use of ground, and minor tactics. Lt.-Col. Richardson also makes this point, and states that the lack of this training definitely affected the fighting in the very close Normandy country, where good section and platoon leadership were essential.

Until February it had always been assumed that the 50th Division was to be one of the Divisions earmarked to land in Normandy on the third day of the invasion. Quite suddenly its role was changed into becoming the spearhead of the landings. This, as General Montgomery told them, was a great tribute to the fighting qualities of the Division, which had been proved on so many occasions in North Africa and Sicily.

This change entailed the complete re-equipping of the Division for the second time since its return to England, and the expenditure of a great deal of time on the specialised training for amphibious operations.

It was as long ago as 1940 that the Division had last had an opportunity of training in interior economy, drill, minor tactics and section leadership, since which time thousands of men had passed through its ranks.

In spite of the fact that the Division had spent many weeks in training for combined operations in Egypt, and had actually made landings from the sea on an occupied coast in Sicily in 1943, all the time between February and June 1944 was given over to this type of training.

From the point of view of training it appeared that the Division was being prepared solely for getting ashore, and tackling the immediate defences. When the day came, however, the 50th Division, not only carried the assault, but from June 6 to November 15 1944, fought its way through to Holland, and was only once, for about forty-eight hours, off the Order of Battle.

The Green Howards and their comrades in arms had to learn by bitter and expensive experience how to fight in close country ; but, as they had done before, they rose to the occasion, and proved themselves to be masters of the Germans, just as they had been in the wide open spaces of North Africa.

The next point made by both commanding officers was the question of personnel. Lt.-Col. Hastings remarks that it was very definitely a handicap from the point of view of team work and morale that reinforcements of officers and men came from any regiment except the Green Howards. Every infantry officer will agree with this statement, and, although it is recognised that towards the end of a long war the difficulties of replacing casualties from territorial sources increase, it does not seem that the wastage up to 1944 had been so severe, as to make it impossible to have supplied Green Howards, or at least Yorkshiremen, to the 6th and 7th Battalions.

One officer who played a large part in the training and supply of reinforcements, has given it as his opinion that the department of the War Office responsible for postings did not connect the name Green Howards with Yorkshire at all. This conjecture is more than possible, as the writer of this book was recently asked in all seriousness whether he was beginning it from the days of Robin Hood and his Merry Men !

Whatever the reason may have been, the Green Howards, although justly proud of those who fought so gallantly wearing their badge and upholding the honour of the Regiment, would have preferred it had the major part of the 6th and 7th Battalion consisted of officers and men who had passed through the Infantry Training Centre at Richmond, where they would have absorbed some of the Regimental traditions and *esprit de corps*.

At the outset the 6th Battalion was lucky in the fact that
all the Company Commanders and Company Sergeant
Majors were Yorkshiremen, but many key positions in the
Battalion were held by men from the Cameron Highlanders,
the remains of a draft of two hundred posted to the Battalion
after Dunkirk. Those of the Camerons who remained, having
fought with the Battalion so long, and so gallantly, had the
interests of the Green Howards at heart. Nevertheless, their
original allegiance was to their own regiment, and it is hard
to understand why it should have been necessary to post Highlanders to a Yorkshire Regiment at a time when the Infantry
Training Centre at Richmond contained hundreds of men who
came from the North Riding.

Lt.-Col. Richardson, commanding the 7th Battalion, was
faced with the problem of what to do with a certain number of
officers and other ranks who had fought valiantly in the past,
but who were obviously " battle weary ", and might crack
up at a vital moment. He decided to leave them behind, and
they were posted to battle schools and training centres,
where their experience was invaluable. He was then, however,
left with only two company commanders with considerable
experience in battle, one with slight experience, and two,
although regular officers, with no battle experience, and new
to the battalion. He also lost his adjutant and best fighting
patrol commander, while, on the very day of the invasion,
his second-in-command and one of the experienced company
commanders went down with malaria.

Incidentally, malaria played havoc during the period in
March, when the Battalion was training in combined operations at Inverary. In North Africa, and in Sicily, malaria
had been kept under control by the issue of one tablet of
mepacrine per day to each man. About a month after returning to England this issue was stopped, but the disease must
have been latent as, among the many who went down with it,
there were quite a number of men who had never had malaria
before. So many key men in the 50th Division developed
malaria that the issue of mepacrine was reintroduced before
" D " Day'

In the face of all these difficulties the Battalions continued *Feb/Jun* 44
to prepare themselves for the great day. On February 28, 1944,
they went to Inverary for training in combined operations,
returning on March 13 to Boscombe, where they were accommodated in billets. On April 6 they moved to Bushfield Camp
near Winchester, where they remained until May 16, when
they went to Romsey. From Romsey they moved to
Southampton under sealed orders, and embarked on their
landing ships on June 1.

Before beginning to relate the experiences of the Green Howard Battalions, which stormed the beaches of Normandy on June 6, 1944, we must endeavour to give the reader some idea of the whole vast operation called " Overlord ", in order that the movements of these two units can be followed as part of a much larger plan. There is no need in this story, which is primarily that of one Regiment, to go into details of the extensive planning and stupendous organisation which led to the success of this, the greatest combined operation in history. Many books exist, and doubtless many more will follow, in which the reader, if he wishes, can learn all about Mulberries, Gooseberries and Pluto, and can study the higher strategy of the campaign. For our purposes the tasks allotted to the 50th Division will suffice.

Early in 1944 Major-General S. G. Kirkman, O.B.E., M.C., who had commanded the Division since the closing stages of the North African campaign, left to command the 13th Corps, and was succeeded by Major-General D. A. H. Graham, C.B.E., D.S.O., M.C. At about the same time Brigadier E. C. Cooke-Collis, D.S.O., was transferred to command a brigade of the 49th Division. He was succeeded in command of the 69th Brigade by Brigadier F. Y. C. Knox, D.S.O.

When it was decided that the 50th would be one of the assault Divisions, it was greatly strengthened by the addition of a fourth infantry brigade, and also by other major units and formations. When it sailed from Southampton, on June 5, the strength of the Division was approximately 38,000 all told.

See MAP No. 16

With this force the first task of the 50th Division was to penetrate the beach defences between Le Hamel and La Rivière, and to secure a position inland stretching from Bayeux on the west to the neighbourhood of St. Leger, which lies on the Bayeux-Caen road, to the east.

The Divisional Commander allotted the Le Hamel sector to the 231st Brigade for assault, and the La Rivière sector to the 69th Brigade. After capturing the beaches and immediate hinterland, the assault brigades were to push on and enlarge the initial bridgeheads. The two reserve Brigades were to be prepared to land some two hours after the assault Brigades, on the orders of the Divisional Commander.

If the assault brigades were successful, the 56th Brigade was to follow up the 231st Brigade, and the 151st Brigade, the 69th. These two reserve Brigades were then, in conjunction with the 69th Brigade, to carry out the final stage of the assault, the capture of the Bayeux-St. Leger position.

The 69th Brigade, as will be seen when we come to the account of the 6th and 7th Green Howards, carried its first objectives, and, by the evening of June 6, was established in the neighbourhood of St. Gabriel, Brécy and Coulombs, having penetrated some seven miles inland, although it was still a mile or so short of the final planned objective. 6 *Jun* 44

The 231st Brigade met with very strong opposition, and it was not until 5 p.m. on June 6 that Le Hamel was finally cleared of the enemy by the 1st Battalion, Hampshire Regiment, which then proceeded on to Arromanches, which it captured by 6.30 p.m. At the end of the day, the 1st Battalion, Dorsetshire Regiment, was near Ryes, while the 2nd Battalion, Devonshire Regiment, had captured Ryes, and swung right towards Longues.

Meanwhile the two Reserve Brigades had landed at about 11 a.m., and the 56th Brigade, bypassing the 231st, which was fighting around Le Hamel and Ryes, had, by the evening of June 6, reached the outskirts of Bayeux. The 151st Brigade, following at first in the path of the 69th Brigade, on which it mopped up small detachments of the enemy which had been left behind by the assault troops, had reached the area of Esquay-sur-Seulles by 10 p.m., and there it dug in for the night.

By the morning of June 7 the Allied Armies were firmly established on French soil. On the right flank, the American forces, after meeting very strong opposition, had overcome it, and had started their advance across the Cotentin Peninsula. On the left, the Canadian forces and British 3rd Division had secured a firm footing, but had failed to reach Caen, their " D " Day objective. The 50th Division as we have seen, had reached Bayeux and was only a mile or so short of its final planned objective, the Bayeux-Caen highroad. 7 *Jun* 44

In the original planning of " Overlord " the early capture of Villers Bocage was considered to be of vital importance, and it had been hoped that this town would be captured shortly after " D " Day. Accordingly, the 50th Division had been ordered to have ready as soon as possible a strong force consisting of the 8th Armoured Brigade, the 1st Battalion, Dorsetshire Regiment (in vehicles), and supporting troops, to push ahead on this mission. This force, however, could not be assembled on " D " Day, as the component members were still fighting on some of the first objectives, and it was not until 11 p.m. on June 7 that orders were issued for this mobile column to assemble near Brécy by dawn on June 8.

In the meantime, on June 7, the remainder of the Division had advanced to, and in some cases across, their planned objective for June 6. For the next three days the remainder of the Division remained comparatively quietly in their positions, while the Mobile Column passed through them on the morning of June 8 on its way to capture Villers Bocage.

8 *Jun* 44   This mobile column ran into fairly strong opposition at the outset, and by the evening of June 8 was brought to a halt in the vicinity of Audrieu and Pt. 103. The 8th Battalion, Durham Light Infantry, added to the column during the day, had reached the outskirts of Tilly, but had been forced to withdraw by strong enemy pressure from the south and east. This pressure had been applied by the 130th Panzer Lehr and the 12th S.S. Hitler Jugend Divisions, and a counter-attack had been made with tanks and infantry.

Orders were then given for the Mobile Column to hold its ground, which proved no easy task in the face of a determined enemy, while the 7th Armoured Division made an attempt to reach Villers Bocage along roads further to the west. The 56th Brigade was taken from the 50th Division and lent to the 7th Armoured Division for this operation.

The 7th Armoured Division reached Villers Bocage on June 13, but arrived there almost simultaneously with the 2nd Panzer Division, which was on its way from east of the R. Seine to attack the Americans further west. A head-on collision between these two armoured forces ensued, with the result that the British forces had to withdraw from the town, and establish a defensive position on the high ground to the north west. Any immediate hopes of a sufficiently strong threat to the lines of communication of the enemy forces which faced the 50th Division to force their retreat were now gone, and the Division settled down to the task of containing as many of the enemy as possible, and harassing them by day and by night.

11/12 *Jun* 44   On June 11 Tilly was still being stubbornly held, and, on June 12, the 50th Division received orders to hold a line from Pt. 103 to La Belle Epine.

June 12, therefore, is a convenient date with which to mark the end of the first stage of the Normandy Campaign, and to which date we will now follow the fortunes of the two Green Howard Battalions from their initial embarkation on the landing ships at Southampton on June 1.

The assault of the 69th Brigade was to be led by the 6th Battalion Green Howards under Lt.-Col. Hastings, and by the 5th East Yorkshires. The 6th Green Howards were to land a quarter of a mile west of La Rivière, with the East Yorkshires on their left, and with the 7th Green Howards in reserve. Lt.-Col. Hastings had under his command for the

assault a squadron of the 4/7th Dragoon Guards with am-
phibious Sherman tanks, two teams of A.V.R.E. and Flail
Tanks, one platoon of Medium Machine Guns of the 2nd
Cheshire Regiment, and a detachment of Royal Engineers.
One battery of the Hertfordshire Yeomanry, self-propelled
25-pounders, was in support.

The enemy defences, as far as was known, consisted of a
strong point of about six pill-boxes manned with machine-guns,
(one with a 105 mm. gun), on the right of the Battalion front,
and a coastal battery of four 150 mm. guns, with its own
local defences, on the left. Some six hundred yards inland, on
the Meauvaines ridge, there was a line of shelter and fire
trenches, from which machine-guns could fire. There was a
marsh behind the beach, in which the Germans had dug an
anti-tank ditch, and laid a considerable number of minefields.
Another coastal battery about a mile inland near Ver-sur-Mer
was to be taken by the 7th Green Howards, whose final
objective for the day was a wireless station on the Bayeux-Caen
road near St. Leger. There were also a number of beach
obstacles, including floating mines, and mines on stakes which
were to be dealt with by the Royal Navy. The front allotted
to the Battalion was nine hundred yards in length, and the
depth of initial penetration was to be rather under two thous-
and yards ; although arrangements had been made to attack
a suspected rocket site about a further thousand yards inland.

In the first phase of the assault " A " Company was
ordered to attack the strong point on the right, and " D "
Company the coastal battery. " B " Company was to clear
the machine-gun positions on the Meauvaines ridge, while
" C " Company was to make for Pt. 52 on the high ground to
the west of Ver-sur-Mer, supported by the 4/7th Dragoon
Guards Squadron, and the Cheshires' machine-guns.

In the second phase " C " Company was to capture the
rocket site, while the Battalion advanced to Villiers Le Sec,
with a flankguard of carriers to the west.

The third phase, if all went well, was an advance by the
69th Brigade to a position south of St. Leger, between the
main road and the railway line from Bayeux to Caen.

On June 1 the 6th Green Howards had gone on board   6 *Bn*
their L.S.I. (Landing Ship Infantry) the " Empire Lance ", an 1/3 *Jun* 44
American built vessel which was very comfortably fitted out.
Slung from her davits were two tiers of L.C.A.'s, (Landing
Craft Assault), fourteen in all.

The days of waiting were spent in eating, sleeping, physical
training, cleaning weapons and studying aerial photographs.
These latter came in every day up to the last minute, and
U

showed new constructions and modifications of existing defences as they were carried out by the Germans. Services were also held on deck by the Ship's padre and were well attended.

The great armada assembled in the Solent and off Spithead, expecting some attention from the enemy, but receiving none whatever—a great tribute to the R.A.F.

6 Bn
4 Jun 44
On Sunday, June 4, the operation was postponed for twenty-four hours, owing to heavy storms. This was a trying decision for all ranks, whose nerves had been keyed up to the highest pitch during the past three days.

6 Bn
5 Jun 44
However, at 5 p.m. on Monday June 5, the Senior Naval Transport Officer announced over the loud-speaker :— " At 17.45 hours this ship will weigh anchor and, in passage with the remainder of the armada, sail for the coast of France ". A great silence fell over the ship as all realised that at last the invasion was on, and that tomorrow would be " D " Day.

6 Bn
6 Jun 44
The next morning reveille was sounded at 3.15 a.m., but few had slept that night, and many were up on deck watching the flashes from the coast, where the bombers were engaging the enemy's coastal batteries. The morning was misty and dull, and features on shore could not be picked out with any distinction. As a result, the beach defences were not demolished or neutralised by the bombing to the extent that had been anticipated.

The " Empire Lance " reached her lowering position for the assault craft at about 5 a.m., being then approximately seven miles from the coast. The Companies then transhipped and, as there was a heavy swell running—the aftermath of the storm—they spent two very uncomfortable hours in their assault craft, getting wet and being sick.

Battalion Headquarters embarked in a L.C.M. (Landing Craft Mechanised), which was attached to a derrick by a large hook weighing about half a ton. When the craft hit the water, the motion was such that the crew were unable to throw off the hook, which for a considerable time bounced up and down on the top of the command carrier. As this vehicle contained at one end a box of grenades, there were many sighs of relief when the hook was eventually released without damage. When the beach was reached, the door of the ramp would not open, and it seemed likely that Lt.-Col. Hastings and his tactical headquarters would have to sit on the beach being mortared, while his battalion fought the battle without him. However, the ramp yielded eventually to military and unprofessional pressure.

The experiences of Major C. M. Hull, M.C., who was second in command of the Battalion, were interesting. He, with two signallers and a runner, was aboard the main signal ship. This was a small craft carrying nothing but highly powered wireless sets. On this craft Major Hull was in direct communication with the higher military and naval commanders, both afloat and in England, with the Royal Air Force overhead, and with the Battalion on the assault beaches. The first task of the signal ship was to navigate the infantry assault craft to within six hundred yards of the shore, or, if visibility was bad, to lead them in until landmarks on the shore could be recognised.

It fell to Major Hull's lot to report that the 6th Battalion Green Howards had taken its first objective forty-eight minutes after landing, and this news was received in London a few minutes later. " I doubt ", says Major Hull, " whether the Green Howards have ever received such heartfelt congratulations from the Navy, as when this piece of news came through ".

Shortly after this a landing craft came up, as previously planned, and Major Hull and his small party joined the remainder of the Battalion on shore.

The naval bombardment was terrific. Salvos from H.M.S. *Warspite* sounded like express trains thundering overhead. Cruisers and destroyers joined in, and landing craft carrying 25 pounders fired unceasingly as they steamed ashore. In addition there were rocket ships, which came within a hundred yards of the shore, and each of which fired off four salvos a minute of ninety rockets each.

At 7.37 a.m. on June 6 1944 the leading companies of the Green Howards waded the last sixty yards on to the shore of France. Unfortunately several men of " A " Company were drowned before the shore was reached, including Sgt. Emmerson, an excellent N.C.O., whose death was a great loss to the Battalion. In the face of heavy mortar fire and machine-gun fire from the pill boxes Captain F. H. Honeyman led his company with great dash across the beaches, and, with the assistance of one tank of the 4/7th Dragoons, overcame this resistance.

The forward sections of the Company were then held up when they reached the sea wall, from behind which the enemy was lobbing grenades. Captain Honeyman, although he had been hit in the arm and leg by splinters, rushed forward, and by his personal courage and initiative, restored the impetus of the attack. In this daring action he was ably assisted by L/Sgt. H. Prenty and L/Cpl. A. Joyce, who leapt over the wall, and charged the enemy, firing sten guns and throwing grenades, until the latter were all dead or had surrendered.

The brilliant success of this Company's attack cleared the beach of small arms fire. These three brave men were all fated to be killed five days later in the action near Oristot, but all received posthumous awards for their gallantry. Captain Honeyman was awarded the Military Cross, and L/Sgt. Prenty and L/Cpl. Joyce the Military Medal. In addition to these three men, Lieuts. R. V. Mather, E. J. Hudson and L. A. Grosvenor, particularly distinguished themselves by their courage and leadership in this action.

" D " Company, commanded by Major R. Lofthouse, ran into deep water, mines, and heavy mortar fire as it landed, and suffered many casualties, including such good N.C.O.'s as Sgts. J. J. Hill, H. N. Scott, A. W. Lawson and W. Woolston.

Despite this unlucky start, Major Lofthouse collected the remainder of his Company, and personally led them across the protecting minefield into the enemy's positions. So swift had been his progress, the enemy troops defending the battery were taken by surprise, and were either killed or taken prisoner.

Major Lofthouse immediately exploited his success on the right flank, and had soon established his company in a position from which it was able to dominate the front of the whole battalion. The determination, initiative, and personal courage of Major Lofthouse enabled a track exit from the beach to be opened at an early stage in the proceedings, and had a direct bearing on the operation as a whole. Major Lofthouse was awarded the Military Cross.

It was during this assault, and for continuous bravery throughout the day, that C.S.M. S. E. Hollis was awarded the Victoria Cross. The official citation accompanying his award reads :—

" In Normandy, on June 6th, 1944, during the assualt on the beaches and the Mont Fleury battery, C.S.M. Hollis's Company Commander noticed that two of the pill-boxes had been by-passed, and went with C.S.M. Hollis to see that they were clear. When they were twenty yards from the pill-box a machine-gun opened fire from the slit, and C.S.M. Hollis instantly rushed straight at the pill-box, recharged his magazine, threw a grenade in through the door, and fired his Sten gun into it, killing two Germans and making the remainder prisoner. He then cleared several Germans from a neighbouring trench. By his action he undoubtedly saved his Company from being fired on heavily from the rear, and enabled them to open the main beach exit.

Later the same day, in the village of Crepon, the Company encountered a field gun and crew, armed with spandaus, at a hundred yards range. C.S.M. Hollis was put in command of a party to cover an attack on the gun, but the movement was held up. Seeing this, C.S.M. Hollis pushed right forward to engage the gun with a P.I.A.T. from a house at fifty yards range. He was observed by a sniper who fired and grazed his right cheek, and at the same moment the gun swung round and fired at point blank range into the house. To avoid the falling masonry C.S.M. Hollis moved his party to an alternative position. Two of the enemy gun crew had by this time been killed, and the gun was destroyed shortly afterwards. He later found that two of his men had stayed behind in the house, and immediately volunteered to get them out. In full view of the enemy, who were continually firing at him, he went forward alone using a Bren gun to distract their attention from the other men. Under cover of his diversion, the two men were able to get back.

Wherever fighting was heaviest C.S.M. Hollis appeared, and in the course of a magnificent day's work he displayed the utmost gallantry, and on two separate occasions his courage and intiative prevented the enemy from holding up the advance at critical stages. It was largely through his heroism and resource that the Company's objectives were gained and casualties were not heavier, and by his own bravery he saved the lives of many of his men ".

In addition to Major Lofthouse and C.S.M. Hollis, Lieuts. R. L. Fitzwilliam, L. Loxley and J. A. Kirkpatrick led their platoons with great gallantry, and contributed largely to " D " Company's success.

" B " Company, following behind the assault companies, rapidly secured its objective, clearing a quarry occupied by the enemy on the way and taking some prisoners.

" C " Company, led by Capt. J. C. Linn, waded ashore thirteen minutes behind the leading companies. By this time the enemy had recovered from his initial surprise and was plastering the high water mark with all the weapons at his disposal. Halfway up the beach Capt. Linn was wounded in the leg, but continued to direct operations from a sitting position until he was hit again and killed. This very gallant and popular company commander was a great loss to the Battalion. Several first class N.C.O.'s, including Sgts. W. Burns and A. Thompson, were also lost at this early stage in the proceedings.

The company was led on to its objective by the second in command, Capt. R. C. Chambers, despite the fact that he had been hit on the back of the head, and was bleeding profusely. When it reached the cover of the dunes at the top of the beach, it was temporarily immune from fire. On taking stock, it was found that the Company had sustained fairly heavy casualties, one platoon having already lost twelve men out of its original thirty-three.

During the half hour on the beaches, when the Company was under heavy mortar fire, Pte. T. Addis, a stretcher bearer, carried out his duties of rendering first aid, with complete disregard for his personal safety, and with unselfish devotion to his comrades. He was awarded the Military Medal.

" C " Company then proceeded to advance through " D " Company, which was firmly established on the site of the coastal battery, which it had captured. The next two objectives, well inland, were the 88 mm. gun position, and the unspecified rocket projector hidden in a wood.

When the Green Howards arrived at the gun position, they found that the crew had made good use of the gun's mobility, and had not waited for the arrival of the British troops. Accordingly " C " Company pushed straight on to the rocket projector site. This was in a wood, easy to recognise as there was a long tunnel running away from the wood to a nearby road. The Green Howards approached to within forty yards of the edge of the wood before the enemy opened fire. Capt. J. B. E. Franklyn then crawled over the back of an unoccupied firing position in the tunnel, and threw in a hand grenade. There was no movement after the explosion and the tunnel was found to be empty.

Meanwhile the 4/7th Dragoon Guards arrived with their tanks, and poured a heavy fire into the wood. One lucky shot set off an ammunition dump in the middle of the wood, and for a while it was better to watch from a distance. When the ammunition dump began to quieten down, Capt. Franklyn and Lt. G. A. Kenny led their men forward into the wood. On getting inside they found a maze of underground tunnels and strongrooms, into which they lobbed a few grenades. This was enough for the enemy, and forty sorry looking Germans, including a Lt.-Col, gave themselves up. " C " Company left behind at least a dozen enemy dead and twice that number wounded, its only casualty being one man wounded. It then proceeded on towards Crepon, and joined up with the rest of the Battalion.

The first objectives had now all been taken, but not without losses. In addition to those already mentioned, the Battalion suffered a severe blow when Major R. J. L. Jackson, one of the mainstays of the Battalion, was severely wounded as he stepped off his landing craft as Unit Landing Officer.

By mid-day the Battalion was pushing on fast towards Crepon with some of the 7th Green Howards in front. Little resistance had been anticipated inland of the coastal defences, but at Crepon the Green Howards had their first experience of really determined resistance in close country. Acting on instructions that any resistance encountered was to be bypassed, unless absolutely unavoidable, the Battalion ignored some snipers and a 75 mm. gun in the outskirts of Crepon, and pushed on towards Villiers Le Sec.

A further misfortune befell them in Crepon, when Capt. D. Jones, commanding the carriers, was killed by a shell, when passing through the village.

Soon after three o'clock in the afternoon the Green Howards arrived on the northern outskirts of Villers Le Sec. The 5th East Yorkshires were engaged in heavy fighting in the village, and Lt.-Col. Hastings sent " B " Company in to attack on the right side of the village and " D " Company on the left. This move caused the enemy to withdraw, but not before " D " Company had come under heavy mortar fire, and sustained some casualties, including Lieuts. Fitzwilliam and Kirkpatrick.

The Battalion then moved on towards St. Gabriel. Reports were received of considerable movement of enemy armoured forces moving west from Caen, and, at about 6 p.m., enemy tanks were reported to have reached Brécy. St. Gabriel was being heavily shelled by the enemy, and at 7.30 p.m. the Battalion was ordered to halt its advance towards this village. Later, at about 9 p.m., the Battalion moved to a position to the west and slightly south of St. Gabriel, where it passed a quiet night.

Although it was still some two miles short of its original planned objective for June 6, in view of the fact that the weather had prevented the maximum results from the naval and aerial bombardment, the Battalion could be considered to have been lucky to have landed, and moved five miles inland, with as few as eighty to ninety casualties. Even in this short time, however, the Green Howards had had experience of the chief problems of war in the bocage, namely the sniper and the mortar, both of which were provided with innumerable hiding places, and concealed lines of retreat. There were two kinds of sniper, the professional who hid well, shot well, and would not surrender, and the soldier who had been bypassed, and was prepared to show some resistance before surrendering to strong forces. The chief ambition of the latter was to pick off a sitting General passing by in his jeep, or even, as Major Hull feelingly says, a second in command passing to and fro between the beachhead and the Battalion inland. Fortunately, such shooting was inaccurate on the whole.

The day had been one of many heroic deeds, and it was also the first day on which the 6th Battalion had seen its commanding officer in action. No one who was there will forget the inspiring example set by Lt.-Col. Hastings, and it is true to say that from that moment the Green Howards would have followed him anywhere.

6 *Bn*   Early on the morning of June 7 the Battalion moved **7/11 *Jun* 44** forward again, and by 10 a.m. had passed through Rucqueville and was heading for Duoy Ste Marguerite. Shortly after crossing the main Bayeux-Caen road, the leading companies were held up by heavy mortar fire, and considerable sniping activity. At about mid-day the Brigadier came up and ordered the Battalion to withdraw to new positions about a thousand yards north of Duoy Ste Marguerite, and to conform with the rest of the Brigade.

The Battalion remained in this position until June 11, during which time patrols were sent out in various directions in search of information, including one led by Lieut. Mather, of " D " Company, which produced good results. On June 8 a joint post was established with the 8th Battalion Durham Light Infantry, of the 151st Brigade, at a bridge over the R. Seules near Conde-sur-Seules. This post was strongly attacked by the enemy, but they were driven off, one of the mortar crews having the satisfaction of scoring a direct hit on a German carrier. Unfortunately, Lieut. B. Hammer, who had only rejoined the Battalion a few hours before, was wounded, and Cpl. J. J. Jackson of " D " Company was killed by a sniper.

7 *Bn*   Leaving the 6th Battalion in these positions, we will **1/5 *Jun* 44** return to the beaches and bring the story of the 7th Battalion up to date. This Battalion, commanded by Lt.-Col. P. H. Richardson, D.S.O., O.B.E., went aboard its landing ships on June 1. Battalion Headquarters and " C " Company, Capt. D. H. Warrener, were on H.M.T. " *Empire Lance* ", " D " Company, Major S. M. Boyle on H.M.T. " *Rapier* ", " A " Company, Major A. D. Spark on H.M.T. " *Mace* ", and " B " Company, Major R. H. E. Hudson, on H.M.T. " *Halberd* ". Except for the Commanding Officer's carrier, the vehicles of the battalion were loaded separately on L.C.T.'s. Major H. E. Bowley was acting as 2nd i/c of the Battalion, as Major H. R. D. Oldman, M.C., did not embark on " D " Day.

Sailing with the remainder of the fleet on the evening of June 5, the companies of the battalion began getting into

their assault craft at 4.20 a.m. on June 6, and, by 5.30 a.m.,
all the latter had left the landing ships, and were on their way
towards the shore.

As they joined the hordes of other landing craft they could see the leading troops already on the beaches, and the under-water obstacles protruding from the sea. Lt.-Col. Richardson found it difficult to pick out which craft, amidst this mass, contained his own companies, and found that some of the landmarks on which he had been relying had been demolished by the bombardment. When the craft carrying his leading companies were in the middle of the water obstacles, Lt.-Col. Richardson suddenly realised that they were too far to the west. It was then too late to alter course, and the Battalion eventually landed, about four hundred yards to the right of its planned beach position, at about 8.15 a.m.

There was, not unnaturally, considerable confusion on the beaches at this moment, only forty-five minutes after the leading troops had landed ; tanks, S.P. guns, A.V.R.E.'s, carriers, and jeeps all seemed to be congregated on the narrow strip of muddy sand between the water's edge and the enemy's minefield. The beaches were being mortared at intervals, and some of the vehicles were on fire. Stretcher bearers were carrying the wounded down to the returning craft.

Leaving this unhealthy spot as rapidly as possible, the Battalion walked along the edge of the water to its own beach, and, in spite of clouds of smoke which billowed down over the shore from the burning dry grass, found the road leading inland towards Ver-sur-Mer, and set off along it. There were a few casualties at this stage, including Sgt. J. Ferguson of " B " Company.

The leading companies were soon in Ver-sur-Mer. They found that the coastal battery there had already been knocked out, and all that " C " Company had to do was to round up some fifty prisoners. The Battalion then pushed on to Crepon, supported by some of the 4/7 Dragoon Guards, and the 68th Field Battery, R.A. By this time, five carriers, the mortar platoon, and six anti-tank guns, had joined the Battalion.

" D " Company, became involved in clearing the enemy out of Crepon, so the remainder of the Battalion continued the advance towards Creuilly without them.

It was at Crepon that Pte. J. T. Thompson, a young soldier aged nineteen years, in his first action, displayed such courage and resource that he won the Military Medal. The section to which he belonged, working in close country, had to cross a gap, which was covered by enemy fire, and by a sniper up a tree. Pte. Thompson shot the sniper, and then, seizing a Bren gun, he rushed through the gap, firing on the enemy, and enabled his section to get through.

The capture of the bridge over the R. Seules at Creuilly was of vital importance, lying as it did on the main axis of the advance to the south. A mobile column was therefore formed under the command of Major H. E. Bowly, consisting of " B " Company, a squadron of tanks and a section of carriers. This column advanced as far as the cross roads north of Creuilly, where it had the satisfaction of knocking out a German staff car, and killing the officer inside it. The column then halted until the remainder of the Battalion, less " D " Company, came up.

Lt.-Col. Richardson then ordered the column to turn west and proceed along the road towards Villiers-Le-Sec, and to reconnoitre likely places for fording the river, in case the bridge at Creuilly was found to be blown up. At the same time he ordered " C " Company, under Capt. Warrener, to go forward and capture the bridge. " C " Company reached the bridge having encountered no opposition, and, having made sure that the bridge was not mined, and that there was no enemy in the village, information to this effect was wirelessed back to Lt.-Col. Richardson. The latter then recalled the mobile column, which joined up with " C " Company in Creuilly.

" C " Company had, in the meantime, made contact to the east with the Winnipeg Rifles of the 3rd Canadian Division.

As soon as the whole Battalion, less " D " Company, had arrived, the advance was continued towards Fresnay Le Crotteur, with " C " Company in the van. " D " Company, having finished its task in Crepon, was advancing along the road to St. Gabriel. On approaching Fresnay le Crotteur the supporting squadron of tanks of the 4/7 Dragoon Guards ran into some strong enemy opposition, and four of the tanks were hit. This opposition was, however, driven back, and the Battalion continued its advance towards Coulombs.

Shortly after this an unfortunate incident occurred, " C " Company, which was leading the Battalion, supported by the tanks, had just driven the enemy off a ridge when, without any warning, a salvo of naval gunfire landed right amongst them. Withdrawing slightly, they also received the next salvo, which landed short. No one knew who had asked for the fire, or how to stop it, since the bombardment officer, who had accompanied the Battalion in the early stages, had left. Fortunately, after three salvos, the gunfire stopped as suddenly as it had begun, but not before " C " Company had sustained several casualties. In all probability, the fire had been called for by an air-spotter who, not realising that British troops had advanced so far, mistook them for the enemy.

After a short period of re-organisation, the Battalion continued to advance towards Coulombs, with " C " Company still leading. The village was reported clear, and the advance guard pushed on towards the final objective, the wireless station. This was housed in a farm a few hundred yards west of the Coulombs-Loucelles road. The buildings had been strongly fortified and surrounded by a minefield. They stood on an open plateau with no covered line of approach. As dusk was approaching the leading troops came up against the minefield, and were fired on from the station itself.

By this time the 7th Battalion was some way ahead of the remainder of the Brigade, and orders were received to withdraw for the night to a position just north of Coulombs. " D " Company rejoined at 1 a.m. on June 7.

Early that morning Lt.-Col. Richardson made his plans for attacking the wireless station. Although the country surrounding the position was very open, there was a valley to the west which offered some initial cover for an advance. Accordingly " A " Company, with " B " Company in support, was ordered to move up this valley, with the object of cutting off the enemy's retreat, and giving supporting fire to the assaulting company, " C " Company. The assault was supported by artillery, mortars, medium machine-guns, and a squadron of tanks of the 4/7 Dragoon Guards. The task of the Infantry was not easy, as there was no natural cover, and pioneers with the leading troops had to make a lane through the minefield in broad daylight, under a very inadequate smoke-screen.

The attack was launched at 5.30 a.m., and was entirely successful. One section of " C " Company reached the entrance to the station on the east side, but was driven off for the moment. The remainder of the Company, however, supported by the tanks firing solid shot, and by machine-guns, quickly stormed the eastern entrance, while almost simultaneously " A " Company broke in through the defences on the west. Between fifty and sixty prisoners were captured, while the Battalion losses consisted of one officer, Lieut. J. D. Wilson, and six other ranks.

Sgt. W. Potterton, of " A " Company, throughout the action, displayed great courage and leadership, and was awarded the Military Medal. When his platoon was forming up for the assault it came under heavy mortar and spandau fire. Sgt. Potterton, standing upright with complete disregard

7 Bn
7 Jun 44

for his own safety, moved from section to section of his platoon, and eventually got them all into positions from which they could start the assault. Soon afterwards his platoon was held up by a minefield and by machine-gun fire. Sgt. Potterton immediately led the first section through the minefield, and, although three men of this section were blown up, he returned through the minefield and led forward his other section. He thus enabled the assaulting parties to reform, and contributed to the successful capture of the position.

Pte. S. Baldwin went forward, with another stretcher bearer, to give aid to some wounded men who were lying within twenty yards of an enemy machine-gun post. Whilst he was doing this the machine-gun crew surrendered, but at the same moment, another machine-gun opened fire at friend and foe alike from forty yards range. Pte Baldwin's companion was killed, but he carried on with his first aid work, and his courage proved a grand inspiration to all who saw him. He was awarded the Military Medal.

It was found that the station had been converted into a fortress, with concrete positions, and communication trenches. Barrack room huts were located in the rear. Much valuable wireless equipment, with stores and supplies, fell into the hands of the Green Howards. Later on in the day a German Staff car was knocked out at the cross roads a few hundred yards ahead, and a long range " Movie " Camera, complete with accessories was taken intact.

By noon the Battalion was consolidated in positions astride the cross roads, and facing south east. " D " Company was a short way across the main Bayeux-Caen road, with " B " Company in support near the wireless station. " A " Company was on the left, with a platoon forward towards Ste Croix Grand Tonne, with " C " Company in support.

During the afternoon a joint post was established with Canadian forces in a wood about half a mile north of Bronay. This post was commanded by Capt. D. J. Riches, and consisted of one platoon of " C " Company, one Anti-Tank gun, and one section of carriers, with one infantry platoon, two sections of carriers, and two Anti-Tank guns from the Winnipeg Rifles. Contact was also established with the 6th Green Howards on the right.

7 *Bn*
8/11 *Jun* 44

During June 8 the Canadians made an attack against the enemy holding the railway embankment near Bronay, but were driven back.

On June 9 a platoon from " B " Company, and one from " D " Company, established themselves on the railway embankment just north of Audrieu. The enemy were seen moving about in the woods near Audrieu, and an occasional sniper shot at these platoons. During the night of June 9/10, patrols went out to search the village of Ste Croix Grand Tonnerre, and to maintain contact with the joint post north of Bronay.

On the 10th a carrier patrol, and twelve men from " A " Company, went forward to Audrieu to deal with a party of enemy reported by civilians to be in the village. They returned without seeing any enemy but, on going out again the same night, they ran into heavy machine-gun fire, and were forced to withdraw.

At 1 a.m. on June 11 a report came in from the Canadians that enemy gliders had landed just south of the railway line at Bronay. A reconnaissance patrol went out, but found no trace of gliders or of parachute troops.

Leaving the 7th Battalion in these positions, we must take up the story of the 50th Division once more, and narrate the events which led to the 6th and 7th Green Howards resuming the offensive during the afternoon of June 11.

The 50th Division was now entering the real " bocage " country, so named from the French word for copse. It is an ancient land in which granite rock predominates. The houses and farms are built of granite, and each one is a ready-made fortress. During the centuries, in which the peasants of Normandy have developed every available yard of land for cultivation, they have taken the out-cropping granite blocks from the fields, and built them into the fences. The undergrowth has grown up through the rocks so that every hedge is also a naturally fortified obstacle. The fields are on the whole small, and there are many woods and orchards. In June the latter were in full foliage and gave wonderful cover to the defenders. In many of the fields standing crops obscured the field of fire, and the country was most unsuitable for tanks, since many of the banks, sunken roads and farm tracks, proved to be tank obstacles. The tanks had to be used singly to support platoons from one hedgerow to the next, but it proved extremely difficult to maintain contact. The infantry were liable to go to ground in the standing crops when fired upon, and so be lost to view of the tanks, and, owing to banks and sunken roads, the tanks could seldom follow the advance of the infantry. It was essentially a country for platoon and company battles, and good section leading was vital. Under such conditions the lack of such training in England made itself felt, and the well concealed German snipers took a steady toll of platoon and section leaders, who were difficult to replace.

In the face of these natural obstacles, and of a determined enemy who made the very best use of them, the Division spent the next few days endeavouring to enlarge its bridgehead before the enemy's reinforcements arrived in strength. Progress was, however, very slow, and the process of feeling their way forward, and probing for gaps in the enemy's defences, proved most exhausting to the leading troops, and especially to the platoon commanders.

It will be remembered that the 50th Division's mobile column consisting of the 8th Armoured Brigade, 1st Battalion, Dorsetshire Regiment, and 8th Battalion D.L.I., had been driven back from Tilly on June 9, and forced to take up a defensive position in the neighbourhood of Pt. 103.

6 Bn
11 Jun 44 At 8 a.m. on Sunday, June 11, Lt.-Col. Hastings was sent for by the Brigade Commander to accompany him to the headquarters of the 8th Armoured Brigade. The 69th Brigade had received orders to cross the main Bayeux-Caen railway line, and to secure the left flank of the Armoured Brigade, linking up with Canadian forces who were in Putot en Besin. Armoured patrols had already pushed forward towards Oristot, through a country which was exceptionally thick with high hedges on stone banks, deep ditches, belts of trees, and standing corn. They had met with a considerable amount of small arms fire, and the enemy appeared to be in strength, with some armoured forces at Fontenoy Le Pesnel.

The 6th Green Howards were ordered to advance, and occupy a position in the Oristot area. Support for the attack was to be given by the tanks of the 4/7 Dragoon Guards, guns of the Essex Yeomanry and 90th Field Regiment, R.A., while the machine-guns of " B " Company, 2nd Battalion, Cheshire Regiment, were available, if they could be used in this close country.

Lt.-Col. R. G. G. Byron of the Dragoon Guards, who had been out on reconnaissance earlier in the day towards Oristot, was most helpful on his return, but was naturally unable to give sufficient information as to the enemy's dispositions to make it possible to work out a complete artillery support programme.

After a hurried reconnaissance and conference in country where one could barely see a field ahead, Lt.-Col. Hastings made his plan of attack. This was to advance on a two company front, with one squadron of tanks supporting the leading companies. One squadron of tanks was to move with the reserve companies, while the remaining squadron was to be ready to escort the support weapons of the Battalion up to the objective, when it had been secured. The guns were to fire on any known target, and one hedge ahead of the advance. A line through the farm at Les Hauts Vents was chosen as the Battalion axis of advance.

The Battalion moved off through Duoy Ste Marguerite at 2.30 p.m., and by 4 p.m. had passed through Audrieu. By 6 p.m. it had come to grips with the Germans, who, waiting until the tanks had passed, opened up a withering fire on "B" Company, which was on the right. This company sustained fairly heavy casualties, but, largely owing to the efforts of Major J. M. Young, the Company Commander, who walked about the fields in full view of the enemy with a total disregard for his own safety, it pushed on until Major Young was wounded, his second in command, Capt. R. C. Mitchell, killed, and several N.C.O.'s became casualties.

Major Young was awarded the Military Cross for his leadership, determination and great personal courage.

In this action Lieut. P. C. Bawcombe, whose name readers will remember in connection with his gallant conduct as a Sergeant at the battles of Mareth and Akarit, and who was now attached to his old battalion, having received a commission in the East Yorkshire Regiment, so distinguished himself as to be awarded the Military Cross. In the words of the citation which accompanied the award :—" Lieut. Bawcombe was commanding the right forward platoon of "B" Company, when it was fired on by several spandaus from a hedge at short range. Although the left hand platoon was pinned down, Lieut. Bawcombe handled his men so ably that he advanced three hundred yards, and captured the immediate objective with only three casualties. When he heard that his Company Commander and the second in command had become casualties, he immediately took command of the company, and by his leadership and example rallied the other two platoons, who were temporarily disorganised, and led them forward to join up with "A" Company ".

Pte. J. M. Henson, a Bren gunner of "B" Company, set a great example to his comrades during this attack, and was awarded the Military Medal. Although wounded in the face, he continued to rush forward against an enemy spandau post, firing his gun from the hip, until the post was knocked out.

Pte. J. Leary, a company runner, although hit in the leg, continued to deliver his messages. Later, when Major Young was wounded, when up with the forward platoon, Pte. Leary went to him across fire swept ground, brought him back to cover, dressed his wounds, and then delivered his orders for continuing the attack. Later he tried to rejoin his platoon for the final assault, but was only just able to walk, and was ordered back to the Regimental Aid Post by an officer. For this remarkable tenacity and devotion to duty, Pte. Leary received the Military Medal.

" C " Company on the left was also pinned down by extremely heavy spandau fire from the orchards around Oristot. The Company Commander, Capt. Chambers, C.S.M. T. Ferguson, and Lieut. K. B. I. Rynning (a Norwegian Officer) were killed, and Lieut. Kenny was wounded. The Company was trapped in the middle of a cornfield, and, in addition to the heavy cross fire from the orchards on the left, and from a group of farm buildings about two hundred yards in front, snipers in the trees surrounding the cornfield were taking a heavy toll. The latter were almost impossible to locate, as they wore mottled green blouses and used smokeless ammunition.

Lt.-Col. Hastings now appeared on the scene, and ordered " A " Company to attack round the right flank of " B " Company, and to endeavour to outflank the group of farm buildings in front.

In the meantime, when he heard that Capt. Chambers had been killed, Capt. Franklyn, the second in command of " C " Company, went forward to restore the position. In his own words : " I found the fighting very confused, with Bren guns and spandaus firing in every direction, and, since the Company Commander and C.S.M. had both been killed, the Platoons had lost cohesion and were fighting individual battles. Fortunately, at about this time, " A " Company's attack came in and cleared the area of the farm buildings ".

Largely owing to the leadership of Major Honeyman, " A " Company got to within one field of its objective, when the supporting tanks came under heavy fire, and the squadron leader lost his tank. Two soldiers of " A " Company, Ptes. G. Backhouse and A. E. V. Clarke, were awarded the Military Medal for their great courage and determination during this attack.

" A " and " B " Companies then joined up, and " D " Company, having forced its way up through Les Hauts Vents, where it took about thirty prisoners, also joined up with " A " Company.

These moves helped " C " Company to advance a little further, and it reorganised near the farm buildings. Lieut. Rynning's platoon was left with only a L/Cpl. in charge. It had fought magnificently, although at a high price, and there were many German dead lying in their positions where this platoon had made its charge. A party of some twenty prisoners was rounded up and sent to the rear. They were all tough and arrogant looking young Nazis.

Lt.-Col. Hastings had now got his battalion together again, although losses had been heavy, and he had sent for the support weapons to come up. Information came in, however, at this juncture, to the effect that German tanks had broken through the 8th Armoured Brigade's positions on the Battalion's right flank, and had almost reached the line of the Battalion's axis of advance. In these circumstances Lt.-Col. Hastings exercised the discretion given to him by the Brigade Commander, and ordered a withdrawal. He sent Major Hull back to reconnoitre a position, in consultation with the Brigade Commander and the Officer Commanding the 5th East Yorkshires.

Soon after " A " Company had linked up with the rest of the Battalion, Major Honeyman told the commanding officer that C.S.M. G. Calvert, with a party of men, was pinned down in front, and asked permission to go forward to extricate them. He was ordered to do so, but not to get himself into trouble. With his usual gallant bearing Major Honeyman went forward and was shot through the head. Thus the Battalion lost a great company commander, whose record in command of " A " Company for more than one troubled year was tremendous. He had led his men in the landing with complete confidence and remarkable success, and his loss was deeply felt by the whole Battalion.

C.S.M. Calvert, meanwhile, had organised a support group of three Bren guns, and set about the task of extricating the platoon, which was cut off, and which was being subjected to heavy spandau fire. Only when two of the Bren gunners had been wounded, and the third gun had run out of ammunition did C.S.M. Calvert move back to " A " Company's position, carrying a wounded man himself and bringing up the rear of the party. His courage, leadership and example inspired all about him during three hours of desperate fighting, and he was awarded the Distinguished Conduct Medal.

The Battalion withdrew in good order, getting most of its wounded away riding on the tanks, but having to leave about eight of the more seriously wounded in enemy hands. At about 11 p.m. it dug in on the position which had been reconnoitred by Major Hull, between Audrieu and Pt. 103.

There was a high proportion of officers and N.C.O.'s amongst the two hundred to two hundred and fifty casualties which the Battalion suffered in this action. These included Major Honeyman, Capts. Chambers and Mitchell, Lieuts. Mather and Rynning killed, Major Young and others wounded. C.S.M. Ferguson of " C " Company was killed the day after he had been promoted, and Sgt. Dawson, M.M., who had

v

insisted on coming with the Battalion although he had lost the sight of one eye, also lost his life. Among other N.C.O.'s whom the Battalion lost that day were Sgt. Collins, D.C.M., Sgt. Walpole, Sgt. Prenty, M.M., Cpl. J. Alexander, and L/Cpl. Joyce, M.M.

6 *Bn*   Early the following morning, June 12, the Battalion
12/15 *Jun* 44 withdrew again, and dug in on a position north of the railway line south-west of Loucelles. At 11 a.m. Lt.-Col. Hastings issued the following message to be read to all ranks of the Battalion : " I want it to be clearly understood that I, who was there and saw it, have nothing but admiration for the way in which the Battalion fought yesterday afternoon. The withdrawal took place entirely on my order, it was carried out perfectly, and was rendered necessary because of the threat of enemy tanks to our line of communications. The men of the Battalion deserve more credit for their performance yesterday than for many other battles, for which we will—and have—received more credit ".

The remainder of June 12 was spent in improving the new positions, and in patrolling. Snipers were again very active. On the 13th many minor engagements took place along the whole of the Battalion's front, as the enemy were continually trying to infiltrate across the railway in small parties. In the evening the Battalion was relieved by a Hallamshire Battalion of the 49th Division. This relief was much disturbed by sniping and spandau fire, and the last company to leave had to crawl out ; but by 8.30 p.m. all companies were clear, and on their way to a rest area near Conde sur Seulles.

They arrived there at about 9.30 p.m. and bivouacked in the orchards adjoining the Manoir de Ghène, in which Battalion Headquarters was established. Here they spent the next thirty-six hours, and, in spite of being surrounded by medium and heavy artillery, managed to secure two good nights' sleep.

On the 14th some reinforcements arrived, including two Canadian officers. The other ranks came from all sorts of regiments, and included a large proportion of ration clerks, officers' mess waiters, and quartermaster's storemen from battalions in England, and who had never seen active service.

During the day the Battalion received a visit from Brigadier E. C. Cooke-Collis, D.S.O., who had commanded both the 6th Green Howards and the 69th Brigade in North Africa and Sicily, and was now commanding a Brigade of the 49th Division. He was given a great welcome by many of his old friends.

The 7th Battalion had also arrived in this rest area at about 10 p.m. on June 13, and we must now bring its story up to date.

On June 11 this Battalion was established in positions between St. Leger and Ste Croix Grand Tonne, with outposts as far forward as the main railway line, and the joint post established with the Canadians, under the command of Capt. D. J. Riches, still in the wood just north of Bronay. At 10 a.m. orders were received to advance towards Oristot, and at 2.30 p.m. the Battalion crossed the starting line on the main Bayeux-Caen road. The leading companies, " B " and " D ", were ordered to secure the south side of the railway embankment to the west of Bronay, while " A " and " C " Companies were to attack the village of Bronay itself. 7 *Bn* 11 *Jun* 44

" B " Company ran into very heavy machine-gun fire when on the line of the railway, and was pinned down. After making two attempts to advance further, and being forced back, this Company was eventually withdrawn at about 10.30 p.m. It had done a certain amount of execution to the enemy, one platoon claiming to have killed between twenty and thirty Germans, and had itself sustained about ten casualties. Lieut. G. Wilmot was wounded in the eye, Pte. M. W. Caris was badly wounded, and Lieut. P. H. O. Ruddock made two gallant, but unsuccessful, attempts to bring him in. " D " Company was also held on the embankment and eventually withdrawn.

" A " Company advanced through Capt. Riches' joint post, which was then disbanded, the Canadians returning to their own lines. Lt.-Col. Richardson accompanied " A " Company up to the high ground to the north-east of Bronay, and established mortar and artillery observation posts in order to enable fire to be brought on to the village. When the leading platoon had reached the outskirts of Bronay, the whole party came under heavy machine-gun fire from close range, and it was only after a smoke screen had been put down that they were able to extricate themselves.

Eventually, at about midnight, the whole Battalion withdrew to a position just north of the wood in which Capt. Riches' joint post had been located.

During this action, Pte. G. Goddard, a young soldier under nineteen years of age, who had only joined the Battalion a few days before it sailed for Normandy, performed an act of gallantry which won him a Military Medal. Pte. Goddard, who was a member of one of the leading sections, suddenly found that he and his comrades were ambushed. He immediately engaged the enemy with his rifle and then, with great daring and initiative, he seized the section's Bren gun and rushed at the enemy firing at point blank range. He killed fifteen Germans, and enabled some of his comrades, who were wounded, to be rescued. He himself was twice wounded by grenades, and, in the end, had to be carried away to safety.

7 *Bn* After this unsuccessful attack the Battalion spent June 12
12/15 *Jun* 44 and 13 in its new positions, taking aggressive action against the enemy but making no further progress. One patrol sent out at mid-day on June 13 ran into considerable opposition. Lieut. Fredriksen (a Norwegian officer attached to the Green Howards) was wounded, and only six of the twelve men who went out returned. On June 12 Major Oldman arrived, and took over the duties of 2nd i/c of the Battalion, while Major Bowley reassumed command of " C " Company.

At 3 p.m. on the 13th the Battalion began to hand over the position to a battalion of the K.O.Y.L.I. of the 49th Division. This relief was completed by 5.30 p.m., when the Battalion marched off to the rest area near Conde sur Seulles, where it arrived at 10 p.m. Here it remained resting, re-organising, and generally cleaning up until June 15.

Leaving the Green Howards enjoying a short but well-earned rest at Conde sur Seules, we must now make a brief survey of the general situation, and of the future movements of the 50th Division, up to August 4 when it eventually entered Villers Bocage.

On June 14 the 49th Division having taken over the left hand sector of the 50th Division's front from the 69th Brigade, the latter Division was free to concentrate its attention on an area embracing La Belle Epine—Longraye—Hottot—Tilly, in which it was destined to fight until July 19. Here it was faced by very tough opposition from the 130th Panzer Lehr Division, and many bitter engagements took place during the next month before the 50th Division finally secured Hottot and the enemy withdrew. All this time the Division, although primarily providing a firm base for the 30th Corps, was harassing the enemy and slowly making ground.

The first attack was made on June 14 by the 151st and 231st Brigades. The 151st Brigade, after a day of fierce attack and counter-attack, stabilised its positions by nightfall just west of Lingevres and Verrieres. The 231st Brigade, after equally heavy fighting, had forced its way through La Belle Epine, and joined up with the 151st Brigade near Lingevres.

On June 15 the 69th Brigade began to move up from Conde-sur-Seulles, and bivouacked that night in the neigh-bourhood of Bernieres Bocage. On the next day, it passed behind the 151st Brigade to the neighbourhood of Les Orailles, and on June 17 launched an attack from the north and east against Longraye, and the Lingevres—Longraye road. This led to a heavy counter-attack by the enemy, and the Brigade was thrown back on the defensive in this area until June 27, when it attacked again in the neighbourhood of La Taille.

Meanwhile, Tilly, on the Division's left flank, had been captured by troops of the 56th Brigade, while the 231st Brigade, having secured a foothold in Hottot, had been forced back, and established itself just north of the village.

On July 8 the 56th Brigade launched another attack towards Hottot, and made some ground. On July 11 the 50th Division made its final attack in this area, when the 231st Brigade advanced once more on the village of Hottot. After a day of very bitter fighting, the Brigade failed to secure its objective, and was brought to a halt just north of the village.

Big events, however, were now about to take place elsewhere, and, on the night of July 18/19, the enemy withdrew from the front of the 50th Division.

On July 18 the 8th Armoured Corps made a grand scale attack south-eastwards towards Caen, and on the 25th the American 1st Army broke through the German lines at the southern end of the Cherbourg Peninsula, and, swinging east through Le Mans and then north towards Argentan, began to form the southern half of the vast pincers, which eventually destroyed the greater part of the German armour in the " Falaise Pocket ". The British Second Army then advanced, on July 30, southwards towards the general line of Vire— Conde sur Noireau—Falaise to form the northern half of the pincers. The part played by the 50th Division in this operation consisted firstly in the capture of Villers Bocage, and secondly in the advance to Conde sur Noireau.

On August 2 the 69th Brigade captured a strong position to the north-east of Amaye-sur-Seules, and then Tracy Bocage.

Villers Bocage fell to the 50th Division on August 4, nearly two months later than had been hopefully anticipated.

We must now take the reader back to June 15 and narrate the deeds of the Green Howards in the actions fought by the 69th Brigade, which have been briefly described.

The 6th Battalion left Conde-sur-Seules early in the afternoon of June 15, and, after passing through the shattered village of Jerusalem, bivouacked for the night in the forward outskirts of Folliot. At 6.30 next morning it moved off through Bernières Bocage and La Senaudière, and by noon had occupied positions near Les Orailles.

6 Bn
15/17 *Jun* 44

The next morning, after being relieved by the 5th East Yorkshires, the Battalion moved across to a wooded area between La Belle Epine and Lingrèvres, and, soon after mid-day, started to advance in a southerly direction on both sides of the Lingèvres—Longraye road, with the cross-roads at La Taille as its objective. Supported by a squadron of tanks, the Battalion probed its way forward through very close country. The leading companies were continuously under mortar, spandau, or machine-gun fire. The leading platoon of " A " Company was ambushed, and two of the supporting tanks were put out of action. In this short advance, Major J. S. MacLaren, who had taken command of " A " Company the previous day, was wounded. The advance was completely held up by 4 p.m. in the vicinity of Pt. 113, a little more than a mile short of the crossroads at La Taille.

6 *Bn*
17/27 *Jun* 44   From June 17 until the 27th the position of the Battalion remained more or less unchanged. During this period, two further attempts were made to capture La Taille, and, although, in the first of these on June 19, the leading platoons of both " B " and " D " Companies got to within a few hundred yards of the crossroads, they came under very heavy fire, and were forced to withdraw.

These advances had been made with fighting patrols, generally one platoon strong, well out in front. Tanks were found to be useless except to meet enemy counter-attacks, and the enemy presented no suitable targets for artillery fire. It was warfare in which the sniper dominated the position, and the attacking infantry could only attempt to infiltrate up the hedgerows, avoiding any small areas of open ground where possible.

By nightfall on the 19th the companies were back in their positions, and proceeded to consolidate them. Here they remained being spasmodically shelled and mortared for the next seven days. Patrols went out at intervals towards Longraye and killed a few Germans, but it was obvious that a further advance was impossible unless the enemy withdrew or a full-scale attack with an artillery barrage was staged.

The short nights of this period, and the constant drain of casualties, caused a heavy strain on both officers and men, and they were very tired. Lieuts. P. C. Bawcombe, M.C. and A. Grosvenor did particularly good work in leading patrols under the most difficult and trying conditions. Capt. C. G. Rowlandson was killed by a sniper at this time, and the casualties continued to mount up. Reinforcements arrived who varied in quality, but were never Green Howards.

Nobody who was with the Battalion at that time will forget the great understanding and assistance given by the Padre, the Rev. T. H. Lovegrove, and by the doctor, Capt. J. M. Jones, and many a wounded man would like to acknowledge the debt which they owe to these two officers.

Another contributor to the excellent morale, which held the Battalion together during those trying days, was R.S.M. Dixon who, while temporarily resting with " B " Echelon transport, astonished the French peasants, and alien quartermasters, by carrying out at regular hours a daily programme of drill and physical training.

On June 27 the Battalion was ordered to make yet another attack on La Taille, this time under cover of a heavy artillery barrage and machine-gun concentration. _{6 Bn}

6 Bn
27 Jun 44

Early that morning a fighting patrol was sent out under Lt. A. Grosvenor with orders to shoot up any enemy who might be in two houses just north-west of La Taille. The patrol found the houses unoccupied, but, on a further reconnaissance, Lt. Grosvenor ran into some enemy at a cross roads near La Taille. On engaging them he soon discovered that their strength was approximately one platoon with four light machine-guns, and so, holding his ground, he sent back for the remainder of his platoon. When it arrived he placed his Bren guns in a position from which they could give covering fire, and then led two sections in an attack on the enemy's left flank. This was highly successful, and nine Germans were killed, and four captured. The enemy then counter-attacked, supported by mortars, and additional machine-guns. Lt. Grosvenor held on to his position, inflicting more casualties on the enemy, until it became untenable. He then made an organised withdrawal with his platoon to another position some two hundred yards to the rear, and engaged the enemy again. Eventually he arrived back in his Company's lines, having sustained only three casualties.

The captured Germans, and Lt. Grosvenor, gave information which proved invaluable in planning the attack, which took place later in the day. Lt. Grosvenor was awarded the Military Cross for his courage and leadership.

Cpl. B. Taylor, a section commander in the same patrol, won the Military Medal for his bravery and enterprise during this action. When his section was temporarily separated from the remainder of the patrol, he commanded it with great skill, and, at one moment, he tackled a German machine-gun post singlehanded with a Bren gun, knocking it out, killing the gunner, and capturing three of the crew.

At 5 p.m. the Battalion crossed the starting line. The known enemy opposition consisted of a Battalion of the 902nd P. G. Regiment of the 130th Panzer Lehr Division, who had one company in Longraye, one in La Taille, and one in a wood near the Chateau De Cordillion.

The Battalion attacked with " C " Company, Major D. A. Norton, leading on the right, followed by " A " Company, Capt. A. T. Semple. " D " Company, Capt. R. S. Baldon, led on the left flank, followed by " B " Company, Major F. Greensill.

" C " Company was soon held up by heavy fire from a group of houses. A squadron of Northamptonshire Yeomanry was sent to outflank this opposition, but, in the meantime, " C " Company had bypassed the houses on the left, and proceeded on towards its objective. At about 6 p.m., touch with " C " Company was temporarily lost.

Meanwhile, soon after the start, Capt. Baldon became a casualty, and, owing to a wireless breakdown and the closeness of the terrain, the second-in-command was delayed in taking over " D " Company, with the result that it lost the barrage.

At 5.30 the barrage was lifted, and Lt.-Col. Hastings moved across from " A " Company, on the right, to " B " Company.

The supporting tanks were unable to give much assistance, but " A " Company carried out a successful attack, all the more creditable as it was unsupported, against another group of houses. This attack resulted in contact being regained with " C " Company, and the general situation was cleared up.

Lt.-Col. Hastings now ordered " B " and " D " Companies to press on to their objectives, but shortly afterwards, at about 7 p.m., he and his signaller were wounded.

Major Lofthouse then took over command of the Battalion, and received orders from the Brigade Commander that, as it was getting late, he should consider taking up positions for the night, and not get any further involved with the enemy.

By this time all the companies were in trouble. " C " Company was asking for help against machine-guns and tanks in La Taille, and " D " Company was also asking for support against heavy machine-gun fire. " A " Company was held up by mines on the track ahead of it.

Major Lofthouse thereupon decided to consolidate on the positions which the Battalion had gained. The support weapons were ordered up, and soon after 10 p.m. the Battalion settled down for the night.

During this action the Battalion sustained thirty-two casualties and took twenty prisoners, but, although the

attack had been successful in so far as it was now finally
extablished within a few hundred yards of La Taille, it had
not been accomplished without the Battalion sustaining a
serious blow in the loss of its Commanding Officer, Lt.-Col.
Hastings, who was wounded in the thigh. Throughout the
past three weeks Lt.-Col. Hastings had been a great source of
inspiration to his men, and, when occasion demanded it, was
to be seen in the forefront of the battle. For his leadership
and gallantry he was awarded the Distinguished Service Order.

Before taking farewell of Lt.-Col. Hastings in these pages,
a few observations which he made on his return to England are
worthy of record. His first remarks throw a light on the type
of enemy against whom the Green Howards had fought with
such skill and daring in this very difficult country, and he then
goes on to pay a tribute to his men, which, coming from one
who was not himself a Green Howard, is all the more valuable.

Referring to the enemy he says : " The Germans met
during the last fortnight had been quite different from those
of the Coastal Divisions. They came mainly from the 12th
S.S. Hitler Jugend and the 130th Panzer Lehr Divisions, and
were, on the whole, young men who had been brought up as
Nazis, and were prepared to die rather than surrender. These
were the determined fighters who, aided by bad weather and
remarkably close country, helped the German Higher
Command once again out of a difficult situation, which was
largely of their own making. Whatever mistakes were made by
German Generals, the individual German behind a hedge
with a spandau was a difficult man to dislodge ".

Of his own battalion he says : " Our casualties for three
weeks were about twenty-six officers and three hundred men.
There was a high proportion of sergeants and corporals
amongst those killed. Of the total number of casualties very
few were missing, and the numbers of prisoners of war from
the Battalion must have been small—an indication of how well
the men of the battalion fought. Replacements of these
casualties were mainly from other divisions and regiments.
It was rare for a Yorkshireman to join the battalion. While
it was obviously impossible to arrange for Green Howard
reinforcements all the time, those responsible either forgot, or
never knew, how great is the importance to morale of the
territorial connection and regimental spirit. Men are not
numbers of nameless bodies concealed in large files, but
individuals who work much better with people from their
own county. It was not altogether a coincidence that C.S.M.
Hollis, who won the Victoria Cross, came from Middlesbrough,
the home of the 6th Battalion ".

Major Lofthouse was superseded in command of the Battalion at 6.30 next morning by Lt.-Col. Webster of the Essex Regiment. The latter officer's tenure of command was not, however, of long duration, since, at 2 o'clock on the same afternoon, the command passed to Lt.-Col. R. K. Exham, M.C., the Duke of Wellington's Regiment.

From June 28 to July 19, when the enemy withdrew and the Battalion moved forward, there is little of importance to relate about the 6th Battalion. It will be remembered that during this period two attacks were made on Hottot by the 56th and 231st Brigades, but the 69th Brigade remained comparatively static, patrolling and harassing the enemy around Longraye and La Taille. During this time the Battalion came in for a good deal of shelling and mortaring, and small groups of the enemy from time to time attempted to penetrate the forward company positions, but without success.

On July 3 the 6th Green Howards were relieved by the 7th Green Howards, and the former battalion went back to the Brigade Reserve area near La Gallette. Here it remained, sending patrols out daily towards Longraye, until, on July 10, it moved out to take over positions from the 2nd Essex Regt. about a mile south of Les Orailles, and a mile and a half south-west of Longraye. Here it remained, being intermittently shelled and mortared, until it moved forward in the early hours of July 19, the enemy having withdrawn during the previous night.

Before accompanying the 6th and 7th Battalions on the next stages of their advance to Villers Bocage, we must return to June 15, and give an account of the fighting by the 7th Battalion in the Longraye area.

At 2.30 p.m. on June 15 the 7th Battalion marched off from the rest area near Conde-sur-Seulles, in front of the 6th Battalion, and bivouacked for the night near Bernières Bocage. By 8 a.m. on the 16th the Battalion had reached Les Orailles, and at 9 a.m. began to advance along the road leading south-eastwards from that village.

Almost immediately it encountered strong opposition. After a mortar barrage had been put down, the Battalion moved forward with " D " Company on the left side of the road, followed by " B " Company, and with " C " Company on the right, followed by " A " Company. The flanks of the Battalion were protected by patrols of carriers and an armoured squadron.

Progress was slow, and an enemy 88 mm. gun firing directly down the road prevented any movement of vehicles along it. The leading companies soon came under heavy machine-gun and mortar fire, and their commanders, Major H. E. Bowly and Major S. M. Boyle were both killed, while Lt. G. O. Pearce was wounded. Capt. D. H. Warrener took over command of " C " Company, and Major Gullet that of " D " Company. Three enemy tanks were reported near the crossroads about a mile ahead, and by 4 p.m. the advance was completely halted, when the Battalion consolidated its positions, having gained only about half a mile of ground.

The Green Howards were on the forward side of a gentle slope, with the enemy on the forward slope of the next hill, and both sides had their outposts in the valley between. On the left of the road, the country was very close and wooded, and on the right, although it was a little more open, standing crops tended to obscure the view.

On the 17th the Battalion moved slightly to the north-east and took over from the 5th East Yorkshires, and during the afternoon " A " and " B " Companies managed to push forward to within a few hundred yards of the Longraye-Granville road. They were then held up by machine-gun fire, and consolidated their positions for the night. During this advance Lt. C. W. Keslick was wounded, and Capt. D. J. Riches took over the duties of Intelligence Officer.

7 Bn
17 Jun 44

On June 18 the Battalion received orders to make an attack, supported by one battery of the 90th Field Regiment R.A., and a troop of anti-tank guns. Its objective was the top of the ridge some six hundred yards in front, which the enemy was holding, and which lay across the line of advance.

7 Bn
18 Jun 44

The plan of attack was for " B " and " D " Companies to pass through " A " and " C " Companies, and to advance on the left and right hand sides of the road respectively. This road was still under direct enemy gun fire, and, as there was no lateral road, a bull-dozer was brought up to follow behind " D " Company and make a track for the anti-tank guns. The latter were to support " D " Company and protect the Battalion's right flank.

Both officers and men were very tired by this time and suffering from lack of sleep. The Battalion had lost, since landing, fifteen officers and over two hundred men. Two Company Commanders had been killed, and a third Company Commander, who had been left behind with malaria just before " D " Day, had not yet rejoined. Amongst the officers there were one Australian, two Canadians, and two Norwegians, but the two latter, both of them excellent platoon commanders, had been wounded. Frankly, the Commanding Officer, Lt.-Col. Richardson, felt that he had under him a somewhat heterogeneous body of men who were nearly exhausted, and

that it would require a very great effort on the part of the
officers and N.C.O.'s, both to reach the objective, and to
hold it if successful.

As it turned out, the objectives were taken with surprisingly
little opposition, the enemy having withdrawn into the thick
country behind them immediately the artillery and mortars
had opened fire. " A " Company moved up and took La
Vardière Farm, which " B " Company had bypassed, and
" C " Company came up to the Longraye-Granville road
behind " D " Company.

In the advance of " A " Company on La Vardière Farm,
Lt. F. F. Lawson displayed great skill, courage, and leadership
for which he was awarded the Military Cross. When the
Company was within two hundred yards of the farm, it
came under very heavy machine-gun and mortar fire. Major A.
D. Spark, the Company Commander, with about twenty men,
was pinned down in an isolated position and unable to control
the battle. Lt. Lawson then rose supremely to the occasion.
Gathering together the remnants of the Company, and his
own platoon, he attacked the enemy's position. He showed
inspiring leadership, controlling small engagements here and
there, and making his presence felt everywhere. He personally
killed a number of the enemy, and the remainder surrendered
after fierce fighting. Lt. Lawson then rallied his men, carried
out a most efficient reorganisation, and took up a position
beyond the farm.

Lt.-Col. Richardson, fearing a trap, and expecting a
counter-attack, went round urging the companies to consolidate their positions. Before this could be done, however,
the Germans counter-attacked heavily with infantry and
tanks. " B " Company bore the brunt of this attack and was
eventually cut off, and the wounded and few survivors were
taken prisoner. It so happened that Lt.-Col. Richardson
together with his Intelligence Officer, Capt. Riches, and the
Brigade Intelligence Officer, Lt. Warner, were visiting " B "
Company at the moment when the full force of the enemy's
attack struck them. Capt. Riches was killed outright, and
Lt.-Col. Richardson and Lt. Warner were both wounded and
taken prisoner.

Lt.-Col. Richardson managed to escape two months
later, and on his return to England wrote the following
account of this action. " Everything went surprisingly well,
chiefly due to the leadership of Major R. H. E. Hudson,
commanding " B " Company, and of Major Gullet commanding " D " Company. At the outset I went forward with

" B " Company, and, when it was well under way, I went across to " D " Company, and then to " C " Company, which was commanded by Capt. Warrener. After the attack had proved successful, I showed Warrener and Gullet the positions which I wanted their platoons to take up, and then went over to see Hudson, before going on to Major Spark, who was in command of " A " Company. I found that Hudson's forward men were in the bed of a very muddy stream with a hill in front of them—a very bad position. I was just giving orders for them to advance another hundred and fifty yards, and to secure some high ground, when a German tank from behind a hedge opened fire on us at point blank range. Capt. Riches was killed outright, Major Hudson was badly wounded, Lt. Warner wounded in both arms, and I myself was wounded in three places. Several men were also knocked out. I got them down into a ditch with Lt. Worley's platoon, where we were worried by another tank close on our right flank.

I gave Lt. Worley orders what to do, and then tried to crawl back to " B " Company's Headquarters in order to use their wireless set, as my own was out of action. On my way back I saw Sgt. Wilkinson and his platoon, who were in poor positions and about to be attacked by tanks and infantry. I gave him orders and then managed to get back to " B " Company's Headquarters, which were in charge of C.S.M. C. R. S. Bacon, but only to find that their wireless set was also out of action.

It was at just about this moment, in the failing light, that we found that the German infantry, all armed with automatics, had got round behind us, while their tanks were engaging us in front and on our flanks. I was with C.S.M. Bacon when I was caught. We were surrounded in a ditch, being shot at by some automatics and a tank at about thirty yards range. Before giving in, I think I got the Commander of one tank with a Bren gun. It was a most disheartening end to a successful advance ".

Throughout the day's fighting Lt. J. A. Clark behaved with the utmost coolness and gallantry. When his company was held up in front of a gap in a high wall, with a Tiger tank firing at close range from a flank, the men were temporarily disorganised, and inclined to waver. Lt. Clark, with great calmness, lit a cigarette, and walked slowly up to the gap in front of the whole company. His courageous example pulled the company together, and the leading troops followed him immediately.

The next stage of the advance was through a series of houses, farms, and thick trees. Once again Lt. Clark led his men through and around these obstacles in the face of heavy fire, and it was largely owing to his fearless enterprise that the company advanced as far as it did. For his leadership and personal courage Lt. Clark was awarded the Military Cross.*

The success of " D " Company's attack on the right flank was largely due to the bravery and dash of Pte. J. F. Crosson, a Bren gunner in one of the leading sections. When the company was nearing its objective, it came under heavy machine-gun fire, which caused confusion, and some hesitation. On his own initiative, Pte. Crosson rushed forward across the last two hundred yards, firing his Bren gun from the hip. By the accuracy of his fire, and his personal example, he turned what might have been an awkward situation into a most successful attack. Later, when the company's objective had been taken, the leading sections were threatened by an enemy gun on the flank. Pte. Crosson again went forward alone until he was able to find a position from which to engage this machine-gun. He silenced the machine-gun with well directed fire, killing two and wounding one of the crew, and the company's position was secured. Pte. Crosson was awarded the Military Medal.

Soon after Lt.-Col. Richardson had left " C " Company to go forward to " B " Company, Capt. Warrener went forward to visit his platoons, which were situated on each side of the road. He spotted a German tank, accompanied by an infantry section, approaching slowly down the road from the east. Hurrying back to his company headquarters, where there was a mobile anti-tank gun, which was sited to fire on the cross roads, he told the crew of the approaching target, which they had not seen. As the tank came onto the cross-roads, they put three or four rounds into it, and knocked it out. A section of No. 14 platoon of " C " Company, commanded by Sgt. W. H. Bell, M.M., then proceeded to wipe out completely the accompanying infantry section.

Eventually, under cover of darkness, the whole battalion withdrew, and took up positions in an area about a mile back, which was held by the 5th East Yorkshires.

Major H. R. D. Oldman, M.C., took over command of the Battalion. Casualties had been heavy and included Lt.-Col. Richardson, Major Hudson, Sgt. B. Horsfall wounded and prisoners of war, Capt. Riches killed, Lts. J. C. S. Worley, P. H. O. Ruddock, D. C. McConachie, C.S.M. Bacon and Sgts. Yarrow, D.C.M. and R. Wilkinson prisoners of war, and approximately a hundred and twenty others killed, wounded or captured.

*See reference in Appendix 2 page 391.

On the next day, June 19, the personnel who had been left out of battle rejoined the Battalion, and a draft of four officers and a hundred and fifty other rank reinforcements arrived at " B " Echelon. On June 22 Lt.-Col. W. R. Cox assumed command of the Battalion, and a new " B " Company was formed under the command of Capt. J. Hunter. At about this time Major Spark left the Battalion on transfer to the 59th Division, with which he was subsequently wounded in action, and Capt. F. W. M. Underhay took over command of " A " Company, with the rank of Major. Capt. A. W. Gray succeeded Major Underhay as Adjutant.

The Battalion had by this time moved to the neighbourhood of La Butte, where it remained under intermittent shell fire, and sending out patrols daily, until June 28.

The Battalion on that day moved over to new positions which it took over from the South Wales Borderers on the La Belle Epine-Lingèvres road, about a mile to the west of the latter village. Patrolling and harassing the enemy was again the order of the day, and useful work was done by Lts. W. Runer, F. V. Hall, Steinhoff and J. Pickford.

On July 3 the Battalion moved to relieve the 6th Green Howards north of La Taille. The story of the next fortnight is mainly one of shells dropping in the Battalion area, sometimes to the tune of two hundred and fifty a day, and of constant patrolling.

It is clearly impossible to describe all the countless patrols which went out by day and by night, often obtaining valuable information, and inflicting or receiving the odd casualty. The leader and members of every patrol are fully conscious of the importance of their task. The risks which they run as they probe into the enemy's country, peering through hedges, round buildings or out of ditches must not be underrated. It must be remembered, however, that in most cases a patrol works unseen by those who keep the records. Unless, therefore, his patrol has produced some particularly valuable information, or has become embroiled in a considerable engagement with the enemy, the patrol leader's report will not be of comparatively sufficient importance to be given in the Battalion diary. The many readers of this book who went out on patrol, and whose actions are not recorded, may console themselves in the knowledge that their deeds were just as important, and contributed as much to the success and honour of their Battalion, as those which can be related in this story.

One patrol, which went out to deal with the enemy near La Taille on July 5, is particularly interesting because so

much is left unsaid. Lt. J. R. Louis and twenty-five men left
the front lines of the Battalion at 9.30 p.m. and advanced
some distance. The entry in the War Diary then goes on:—
" The enemy immediately countered by mortar and artillery
fire on the forward positions. Spandaus fired continually at
the forward troops. Enemy machine-gun teams crept forward
to within grenade range of " D " Company, who replied
with small arms fire and grenades. It was estimated that two
hundred and fifty shells fell in the Battalion area, and the
Battalion had five men wounded ". And then we find the
laconic entry that Lt. Louis and his party returned complete
at 1.30 a.m. on July 6. The Battalion certainly had an unpleasant four hours, but one wonders what sort of experiences
Lt. Louis and his twenty-five men had, prowling about in
the darkness, away out in front amidst an enemy very much
on the alert. Patrolling might well be termed the " silent
service " of the Army.

When the enemy attacked " D " Company on this
occasion, L/Sgt. W. Hubble was commanding a forward
section of the left forward platoon. A spandau team crept up a
hedge, and opened fire at point blank range. L/Sgt. Hubble
went out alone and attacked it with grenades, and silenced it.
Although he was wounded in the leg, and suffering considerable
pain, he continued to direct his section, and refused medical
attention until the attack had been driven off. He was awarded
the Military Medal.

On July 7 Lt. Pickford took out a fighting patrol on a
similar mission. After proceeding some way, Lt. Pickford,
his platoon sergeant, and one or two men were all wounded
by machine-gun fire at close range, and the remainder of the
patrol returned. Immediately an N.C.O. and three men,
including two stretcher bearers, went out to bring in the
wounded. This party got pinned down and the N.C.O. was
wounded. The artillery then took a hand and fired smoke
shells to assist the men in their withdrawal, but without
success. Ten minutes later, mortars and artillery fired high
explosive and smoke shells in an endeavour to distract the
enemy's attention. In the end, all attempts had to be given up,
and only two men got back many hours later, and
independently.

On July 16 Lt. Louis took a fighting patrol further afield to
La Poterie, and had a brush with the enemy. After a short
duel with Brens versus spandaus, the patrol managed to put
two P.I.A.T. bombs through the roof of an occupied building,
and then returned to our lines without casualties.

The consistent courage, initiative, and determination
shown on so many occasions by Lt. Louis when serving with

the 7th Green Howards received the recognition which they
deserved after he had left the Battalion. When the 50th
Division returned to England in December 1944, Lt. Louis
was transferred to the 8th Battalion, Royal Scots Fusiliers and
was awarded the Military Cross for superb leadership and
great gallantry in an attack made by that battalion near Goch
in February 1945.

On the 18th Sgt. J. Midgely took out a platoon down the
Longraye-Granville road. They met no opposition, but
captured three Germans, and recovered the body of Capt.
Riches, who, it will be remembered, had been killed on June 18.

During the night of July 18/19 the enemy withdrew and
on the 19th, the Battalion resumed its advance.

Taking up the story of the 6th Battalion, during the night   6 *Bn*
of July 18/19 " B " Company was sent forward from its   19 *Jul* 44
position south of Les Orailles to occupy positions on the
road running south-west from Le Lion Vert to La Croix des
Landes, at a point about halfway between these two places.
This move was accomplished without incident. No enemy was
seen, but numerous booby traps and mines were encountered.

At 6.30 a.m. on July 19 " D " Company moved forward
and occupied positions in front of the Bois de St. Germain
to cover the right flank of the Battalion's advance. This
move was completed by 8 a.m., at which hour the remainder of
the Battalion started forward. By noon they had reached
the Le Lion Vert-La Croix des Landes road, and were soon
making good progress towards the woods just east of Les
Landes. At 1 p.m. news was received that the 56th Brigade,
which was advancing on the right of the 69th Brigade, was
encountering stiff opposition north-west of St. Germain
d'Ectot, and orders were received for the Battalion to consolidate its positions north of Les Landes. " A " Company
had encountered strong enemy resistance in some orchards
on the outskirts of Les Landes, but had, with the assistance
of a troop of tanks, cleared the place of the spandaus which
had held up its advance.

For the next seven days the Battalion remained in these   6 *Bn*
positions, subjected to considerable mortar and shell fire 20/27 *Jul* 44
which caused some casualties. Many patrols and reconnaissance parties went out to Les Landes and the adjacent
woods, and gradually a clear picture was built up of the
enemy's outpost line and forward defences.

At 10 p.m. on July 25 an air burst barrage was put down
over the enemy's forward positions. In the ensuing silence a
propaganda broadcast was sent out, in which the enemy were
informed of their awkward position, and promised honourable
w

treatment as prisoners of war if they surrendered. The sole result of this effort appears to have been a concentration of enemy shell fire an hour later resulting in further casualties to our own troops.

At 9 p.m. on July 27 the 1st Battalion, Devonshire Regiment, arrived to take over from the 6th Green Howards. The relief was completed by 11.30 p.m., and the Battalion marched off to a rest area at La Fiettées, about four miles south of Bayeux.

7 Bn
19 Jul 44 On July 19 the 7th Battalion also moved forward, on the left of the 6th Battalion. A mobile column consisting of " B " Company, the carrier platoon, and a troop of tanks and anti-tank guns, all under the command of Major H. R. D. Oldman, M.C., moved off first down the road leading south-east from Les Orailles. " A " Company, meanwhile, advanced across country to Le Lion Vert. Neither party met with any opposition, and, when Major Oldman's column reached Le Lion Vert, it proceeded to advance down the road leading to Orbois. Slight opposition was encountered from the Chateau du Bus, but this was brushed aside, and the column went on towards Orbois. By 6.30 p.m. Battalion Headquarters and the remaining companies had come up, and the Battalion began to organise a defensive position to conform with the 6th Battalion on its right.

" B " Company was now meeting opposition from the enemy, and was eventually withdrawn through " C " and " D " Companies, which had established themselves across the main road just in front of the wood which lies between the Chateau du Bus and Les Landes. The whole Battalion area was being shelled at intervals, and the crossroads at Le Lion Vert came in for particular attention. The Battalion now proceeded to strengthen its positions, and to probe the enemy's outposts.

7 Bn
21/27 Jul 44 On July 21 Sgt. Potterton, M.M., took out a patrol as far as the Orbois Chateau, and, by drawing the enemy's fire, enabled their positions to be located.

On the 25th Lt. G. Sherratt took out a fighting patrol towards a cottage in front of the left flank of the position. After going a little way they were spotted by the enemy, who opened fire. Making a detour, they crept round the next hedge to the east, where they saw a German officer and N.C.O. on the other side of the hedge. They killed them both with sten gun fire. Two spandau teams in the same field were fired on with Bren and Sten guns at very close range, and all were killed or severely wounded. After this excellent piece of work, the patrol returned, having suffered no casualties.

Throughout this period, the Battalion suffered casualties daily from mortar and shell fire. Late on the night of July 27 it was relieved by the 1st Battalion, Dorsetshire Regiment, and marched off to La Fiettées.

For the next four days both Battalions of the Green *6 and 7 Bns* Howards remained at La Fiettées. They were able to have *28/31 Jul 44* hot baths and overhaul their clothes and equipment. Recreation was provided in the form of films and E.N.S.A. entertainments.

On August 1 they were on the move again. The 69th *6 and 7 Bns* Brigade was ordered to take over from the 130th Brigade of *1 Aug 44* the 43rd Division in the neighbourhood of Caumont. The 6th and 7th Green Howards travelled in motor transport, and by 11 p.m. had completed their relief of the 5th and 4th Battalions of the Dorsetshire Regiment respectively. Their journey had been slow, as the 7th Armoured Division was using the same road, but going in the opposite direction.

On the next morning, August 2, the 7th Battalion moved *7 Bn* off at noon to attack the high ground to the east of Amaye *2 Aug 44* Sur Seulles. " D " Company led the way as advance guard as far as the starting line, and then the Battalion went into the attack with " D " Company on the left of the Brequessard-Amaye road, and " B " Company on the right, advancing across country parallel to the road. " A " and " C " Companies followed up on the left and right respectively, while Tactical Headquarters followed " D " Company along the road.

The forward companies advanced with tank support, meeting no opposition until they approached the high ground at about 5 p.m. They were then pinned down by spandau fire, and the support companies came up. For some little time the enemy put up a fight, but soon after 8 p.m. all companies had reached their objectives. Prisoners of war began to come in, all from the 751st Grenadier Regiment, and they admitted that they had been frightened by the tanks. Altogether a hundred and fifteen prisoners were taken by the Battalion, who found that the position had obviously been strongly held at the beginning of the attack. A number of spandau and other automatic weapons, as well as four heavy mortars, were taken intact. The Battalion's casualties during the day were five killed and twenty-five wounded.

During this action Lt. G. Sherratt commanded the platoon of " D " Company which led the attack. When it arrived within about seventy yards of the enemy positions, it was pinned down at the edge of an orchard by the fire of what subsequently proved to have been eight spandaus and four mortars. Beyond the orchard the ground was completely bare of cover, and so Lt. Sherratt called on the tanks for support. In full view of the enemy, and under heavy fire at close range, he went from one tank to another indicating targets. In the final phases of the attack Lt. Sherratt's bearing was an inspiration to all who saw him, and contributed in no small measure to the final capture of the objective by the Battalion. He was awarded the Military Cross.

Sgt. D. E. Gray, who was in command of the leading section of the carrier platoon, whose task was to cover the deployment of one of the assaulting companies, was awarded the Military Medal for the manner in which he commanded his section throughout the action. Taking up his position within a hundred and fifty yards of the enemy, under intense fire, he kept up a covering fire which materially assisted the attack. He himself operated a 2 in. mortar, until all the ammunition was expended.

Pte. F. Hudson, a company runner, was also awarded the Military Medal for conspicuous devotion to duty during this action.

7 Bn
3/8 Aug 44 During the next day the Battalion reorganised, and discovered a quantity of ammunition, documents and maps in a house which had clearly been a German Headquarters.

On August 4 the Battalion moved forward again and occupied Pt. 174, north of Tracy Bocage, without meeting any opposition. Late in the evening a patrol was sent forward into Villers Bocage, but found the town already occupied by British troops. In the town itself and in the area to the west, the enemy had not buried either his own or the British casualties resulting from the great armoured clash on June 13, and the country-side presented a terrible scene. He had also neglected, or been unable, to salvage the tanks which the 7th Armoured Division had left behind, and some of these were found to be in a condition to make salvage and repair possible.

The Battalion was now out of contact with the enemy, and remained resting near Tracy Bocage until August 8.

6 Bn
2/8 Aug 44 The 6th Green Howards, as reserve Battalion to the 69th Brigade, had followed up as far as Mesnil on August 2, and on the 4th it occupied the position on the high ground near Amaye, which had been taken by the 7th Green Howards on the 3rd. Here it remained until August 8.

And so, practically two months from the day on which they landed on the beaches, the Green Howards completed the first stage of the long journey, which was to take them on across France and Belgium into Holland. They had been two months of hard and bitter fighting in most difficult country. The front line Infantry soldier had had to endure for most of this time constant shelling and mortaring in country where the enemy was seldom visible. When he moved at all, either on patrol or often within his own lines, death from the concealed sniper was always round the corner. It is no wonder that those who survived this period were tired and feeling the strain. On the occasions when they really got to grips with the enemy, the Green Howards had acquitted themselves like heroes, and proved their superiority as man to man.

In this period, when, by virtue of their position in the larger field of operations, other units were taking part in more spectacular moves which filled the headlines, the 50th Division was doggedly holding on to, and harassing a portion of the German Army which, had it been available elsewhere, would have made the spectacular victories which were to follow very much more difficult, if not impossible.

The Green Howards had suffered severely. Both commanding officers had been wounded, most of the company commanders and senior N.C.O.'s had been killed or wounded, and of the original personnel who had made the landing, scarcely a half were left. They had been replaced by officers and men from a varied collection of regiments and even countries, but the Regimental spirit remained unquenched, and those who were now wearing the Green Howard badge carried it untarnished—indeed they added lustre to it—throughout the final stages of the campaign.

CHAPTER THIRTEEN

" THE 6th AND 7th BATTALIONS IN FRANCE, BELGIUM AND HOLLAND

" The Crossing of the Albert Canal "

August—December 1944

See MAP No. 18

6 *Aug* 44

AFTER a few days' rest—the first during which the Division had been relieved of front line responsibility since " D " Day—the 50th Division once again found itself in the forefront of the battle. On August 6 the 43rd Division captured the enemy's strongly fortified positions on Mt. Pincon, about eight miles south of Villers Bocage, thus opening up the way for an advance to Conde sur Noireau, a vital bottleneck on the German line of escape from the west to the Falaise Pocket, around which the pincers were rapidly closing.

Accordingly the 7th Armoured Division was ordered to move forward at once, followed by the 50th Division to mop up behind them. The armoured force, however, found it impossible to make sufficiently rapid progress in this enclosed country, and, on August 9, the 50th Division took over the lead. When the Division approached the village of St. Pierre la Vieille, some four miles south of Mt. Pincon, it ran into stubborn resistance.

9 *Aug* 44

At mid-day on August 9 the 151st Brigade attacked the enemy positions, but was pinned down, and at 2 p.m. the 69th Brigade passed through and took up the attack. The 6th and 7th Green Howards, the leading troops of the 69th Brigade, managed to advance another mile in the face of stiffening opposition, but by 8 p.m. the advance came to a halt, and positions were stabilised for the night.

10 *Aug* 44

Early the next morning, August 10, the 5th East Yorkshires took up the attack in a dense fog. They made some progress at first, but eventually the whole of the 69th Brigade was held short of St. Pierre la Vieille.

11/16 *Aug* 44

On August 11 the 231st Brigade was brought up, and launched an attack with a view to pushing on to the town of Conde sur Noireau. After a day of fierce fighting, this Brigade

326

drove the enemy back, and by 10 a.m. on August 12 was well south of St. Pierre la Vieille.

While this action was going on the 151st Brigade had been attacking the high ground to the south-east of St. Pierre, and succeeded in dislodging the enemy. During the next night, August 12/13, the 7th Green Howards finally threw the Germans out of St. Pierre la Vieille, and the way to Conde sur Noireau was open. The latter vital town was entered by British Armour on August 16.

By August 19 the pincers had closed, and there ensued *19 Aug 44* days of terrible slaughter when the trapped German armies were subjected day and night to a continuous hail of bombs, shells, and rockets from the air, and from massed artillery on the ground. Gradually the pocket shrank in size, a holocaust of men, animals, and vehicles, while the few Germans who escaped fled across the Seine, the Somme, and the Scarpe, back to the Low Countries and to the Fatherland itself. The 50th Division during those days pushed forward slowly with little opposition through Argentan and Laigle, until, in the last days of August, it had reached a line between Rugles and Conches.

Between August 25 and 28 the 43rd Division forced its *25/29 Aug 44* way across the R. Seine at Vernon, and, on the 28th, a general advance to Amiens was ordered by the 30th Corps. The Guards Armoured Division was to lead on the right, and the 11th Armoured Division on the left. The 50th Division was to follow the Armour on the right, and, at dawn on August 29, it set forth on the long chase which was to take it across France and Belgium into Holland.

On August 8 the 69th Brigade moved forward to an *69 Bde* assembly area near Ondefontaine, some six miles south of *8 Aug 44* Villers Bocage, where it spent the night. Early next morning it moved on to Posty, which lies under the northern slopes of Mt. Pincon, which, it will be remembered, had been taken by the 43rd Division on August 6.

The 151st Brigade, which was leading the 50th Division in its advance on Conde sur Noireau, had come up against the enemy positions in front of St. Pierre La Vieille, and been unable to make further progress. The 69th Brigade was ordered accordingly to pass through and take up the attack.

The 6th Battalion Green Howards moved forward to *6 Bn* battle from Posty soon after mid-day, with " A " and " B " *9 Aug 44* Companies riding on tanks. At 2.30 p.m. they got off the *See MAP* tanks about a mile south-west of Le Plessis Grimoult, and at *No. 17*

3.45 crossed their starting line a short way ahead. By 5 p.m. " A " and " B " Companies were fighting in and around Crapouville, and by 6 p.m. had overcome this resistance, and were proceeding to the higher ground across the river.

The attack by the 7th Green Howards on their left had not, however, gone so well, and the leading companies of the 6th Battalion were withdrawn to conform with the general line. The 6th Battalion then took up positions covering, and just in front of, Crapouville.

Throughout the afternoon and evening magnificent work was carried out by Pte. H. G. Birch, a stretcher bearer attached to " B " Company. Towards the end of the Company's advance beyond Crapouville, three casualties had to be left on the forward slope of the hillside in view of the enemy, who were little more than two hundred yards away. In the face of their fire, Pte. Birch visited each man in turn, dressed his wounds, and afterwards assisted in carrying them back to the Company lines.

Shortly after this he went out to an enemy machine-gun post, which had been overrun, and attended three badly wounded Germans. When the leading platoon was ordered to withdraw later in the evening, Pte. Birch went out a third time to rescue the wounded. On this occasion, the enemy respected his great bravery and forbore to fire.

Finally, when accompanying some of the wounded back to the Regimental Aid Post in a carrier, along a road which at that time was being accurately shelled, he met an N.C.O. who was seriously wounded. Stopping the carrier, Pte. Birch, despite shell fire, attended to his wounds, and took him with the other casualties back to the Regimental Aid Post.

His great personal bravery, and devotion to duty, was a source of inspiration to his comrades, and he was awarded the Military Medal.

6 *Bn*   At 1 a.m. on August 10 a patrol from " D " Company 10 *Aug* 44 went forward to the bridges on the left front, where the Le Plessis Grimoult—St. Pierre road crosses a stream, and, finding it intact and unoccupied, remained there until relieved by a platoon of the 5th East Yorkshires at 4.30 a.m. During the day enemy machine-guns opened fire at various points along the Battalion front. At 10.30 p.m. " A " and " D " Companies moved forward across the river, and established themselves just north-west of Rousseville. Later a fighting patrol of " A " Company went further forward, and confirmed that the enemy were still holding St. Pierre.

At 11 a.m. next morning, August 11, a heavy concentration   6 *Bn*
of artillery and mortar fire was brought to bear on " A " and   11 *Aug* 44
" D " Companies, who suffered casualties also from a tank,
and from machine-guns firing from their left flank. At midnight on August 11/12 the whole Battalion moved forward to
an area across the road south-east of Rousseville, sustaining
some casualties from heavy mortar fire as it emerged from the
village.

At 8.15 a.m. on August 12 it advanced further to Les   6 *Bn*
Forges, where it established a firm base to support an attack   12/13 *Aug* 44
which was being made by the 151st Brigade on the eastern
flank. From 9 o'clock onwards, until late in the afternoon, the
enemy put down a series of concentrations of mortar and
artillery fire on the Battalion area. At 5 p.m. orders were
received to move back and picquet the road north of Les
Forges. The whole of this stretch of road was under frequent
shell fire, and there were a good many casualties. Major D. A.
Norton, commanding " C " Company, and three of his men,
were wounded by snipers during this move. Throughout the
day the Regimental Aid Post did particularly good work in
dealing with the stream of casualties which came down the
road from the Battalion itself, the 9th Battalion, Durham Light
Infantry, and from other units.

On August 14 the Battalion was withdrawn to a rest area   6 *Bn*
about a mile south-west of Posty, where it remained until   14/18 *Aug* 44
the 18th.

The 7th Green Howards left Posty at about 2 p.m. on   7 *Bn*
August 9, and advanced to their starting line, which was   9 *Aug* 44
about a mile north of Rousseville, and north-west of Pt. 266,
which was their objective. Supported by a squadron of the
4/7th Dragoon Guards, and a machine-gun platoon of the
Cheshire Regiment, the leading companies crossed the
starting line at about 3.45 p.m. " B " Company led the
attack on the right, followed by " C " Company, while
" A " Company advanced on the left, followed by " D "
Company.

" B " and " C " Companies made good progress, and
" C " Company obtained a footing on its objective. " B "
Company was unlucky to lose its Company Commander,
Major N. Kirkman, who was wounded in this advance. Both
" A " and " B " Companies suffered a considerable number
of casualties.

Pt. 266 was at the top of quite a steep hill, with a stream
and deep ditch running round its northern side, and there were
numerous orchards on the lower slopes which gave excellent

cover to the enemy. The supporting tanks were held up by the stream and ditch and could not manoeuvre against the Tiger tanks, of which the Germans had quite a number hidden in the orchards. Three British tanks were knocked out in quick succession on a track, which they could not leave owing to a deep ditch on either side.

By 8 p.m. it had become obvious that the Battalion could not take its objectives that night, and so " C " Company was withdrawn to the north-west side of the valley to conform. " A " and " B " Companies were so depleted in strength by this time that they were combined to defend a one company position. " A " Company had also lost its Company Commander, Major Underhay, who was wounded by a shell, which killed Capt. F. V. Hall.

7 Bn
10 Aug 44
7 Bn
11/13 Aug 44
Early on August 10 " C " Company again moved forward to its previous position, and, during the afternoon, " A " and " D " Companies took possession of Pt. 266, which the enemy had abandoned during the night as the result of pressure elsewhere. All through the day, and for the next three days, the Battalion came under more or less continuous mortar and artillery fire.

7 Bn
4/18 Aug 44
On the evening of the 12th Capt. Sherratt, M.C. took forward a patrol into St. Pierre La Vieille, and reported that the village had been evacuated by the enemy. Accordingly, soon after midnight, the whole Battalion advanced to St. Pierre in a dense fog and intense darkness. When daylight came the village was found to be littered with German dead, and those left alive gave themselves up without a struggle. On August 14, the Battalion withdrew to the rest area near Posty.

This action, in which all the brigades of the 50th Division took part, opened up the road to the vital town of Conde sur Noireau, which was entered by British armour on August 16. The following message, which the Divisional Commander received from Lt.-Gen. B. G. Horrocks, commanding the 30th Corps, shows how important the success of the operations from August 9 to 13 had been in the general scheme of things, and the two Green Howard Battalions fully deserved their share of this praise.

" I would like all ranks of the 50th Division to realise how much their efforts of the last few days have contributed to the general plan for the encirclement and destruction of the German Army. The road Vire-Conde and to the east has been one of the main German supply routes, and recently the enemy has done his best to use it for the withdrawal of the large forces west of our present area. It was vital that this escape route should be closed, and the task was given initially to the 50th Division.

During the past week the Division has been fighting its way down towards Conde sur Noireau from Mt. Pincon. Although the country was well suited for defence, and although the enemy was fighting stubbornly, all the attacks launched by the 50th Division have been successful, and many prisoners have been taken. Owing to the scarcity of roads deployment was difficult, yet the Division never faltered, and we can now say that the escape route through Conde is closed to the Germans.

I cannot give you higher praise than by saying that the most experienced battle-fighting Division in the British Army has once more lived up to its reputation. Well done, 50 Div ! "

After four days of rest and reorganisation near Posty, the 69th Brigade moved forward again on August 18. The hunt was now up, and by August 28 was in full cry. The shattered remnants of the German forces were trickling back to the R. Seine, the bridges across which river were being systematically demolished by the British and American Air Forces. *See* **MAP No. 18**

The 50th Division did not meet any organised resistance again until September 8, when it fought its way across the Albert Canal near Gheel. During this period of three weeks, it advanced approximately five hundred miles, the pace gradually increasing as the British and American armies were able to spread out across northern France.

It is difficult to give a day to day account of the Green Howard Battalions throughout those hectic days. Those who took part in them will have mixed memories of relief at getting out of the bocage country, with its perpetual menace from snipers, mortars and ambushes, and of the tumultuous welcome which they received along the way from liberated French and Belgian citizens. They will remember too the torrential thunderstorms at the end of August, and their sense of frustration when, particularly in the earlier stages of their advance, their road was blocked by other British or American forces crossing their path.

In order to give the reader an idea of the atmosphere in which the troops moved forward, some of the incidents which befell the battalions on their long march will be narrated, but they will not necessarily be in chronological order. In the first place, however, a rough timetable will serve to show the route followed by the Green Howards, and the gathering tempo of the chase.

Date	Approx. Positions	Approx. Miles
Aug. 18	Posty-Athis	20
Aug. 19	Athis-La Carneille	4
Aug. 20	La Carneille-Vaux le Bardoult ..	15
Aug. 21	Vaux le Bardoult	
Aug. 22	Vaux le Bardoult-Laigle	40
Aug. 23	Laigle-Ambenay	10
Aug. 24	Ambenay	
Aug. 25	Ambenay	
Aug. 26	Ambenay-Pacy	45
Aug. 27	Pacy	
Aug. 28	Pacy	
Aug. 29	Pacy	
Aug. 30	Pacy-Beaugrenier	
Aug. 31	Beaugrenier-Villotran	80
Sept. 1	Villotran-Villers Bretonneux	
Sept. 2	Villers Bretonneux-Warlus	38
Sept. 3	Warlus-Arras	8
Sept. 4	Arras-Tournai (7th Battalion).. ..	50
	Arras-Alost (6th Battalion)	90
Sept. 5	Tournai (7th)-Alost (6th)	
Sept. 6	Tournai (7th)-Alost (6th)	
Sept. 7	Alost-Zammel (6th Battalion) ..	50
	Tournai-Zammel (7th Battalion) ..	90

In the first few days the Green Howards, although not in the van, were very close on the heels of the retreating Germans, as the following entry in the diary of the 6th Battalion for August 21 shows. " The Battalion arrived at Vaux le Bardoult after a most unpleasant journey in torrential rain, along a narrow lane on which a continuous stream of traffic was moving in the opposite direction. Progress was very slow. Our new area was littered with many hundreds of dead horses shot by the retreating Germans. There were also many German dead. We spent the rest of the day in this most unpleasant place."

Another example of the difficulties of progress and of discomfort is given in the following quotation a few days later. " Arriving just short of Conches at mid-day, we were dismayed to find the Americans moving four divisions from north to south across our route. We therefore " harboured " in the woods until such time as the road would be clear. This, as it turned out, entailed remaining in the woods all night.

During the night a most violent thunderstorm came upon us, and two men sleeping under a tree were struck by lightning."

On August 23 the 6th Green Howards took up the duties of advance guard to the 69th Brigade, and as such were the leading troops to enter the town of Rugles, amid tremendous enthusiasm. " The inhabitants brought out wine and spirits, besides showering us with bouquets and ribbons. The crowd, who were all dressed in uniform, or lacking that, in their best clothes, impeded our progress to some extent." *6 Bn 23 Aug 44*

Several Russian " volunteers " were captured during this period, including three very sheepish looking Mongolians, a somewhat surprising find in the middle of Normandy.

After crossing the R. Seine at Vernon soon after midnight on August 29/30, in artificial moonlight created by batteries of searchlights, the 6th Green Howards continued to lead the Brigade as far as Beaugrenier, where they halted for the night. *6 Bn 29/30 Aug 44*

While in this village, acting on reports from civilians, the Second in Command and the Intelligence Officer visited Nucourt, where there was said to be a depot for assembling and storing flying bombs. The village was deserted, but on the site were large tunnels with railway lines entering them. Overhead protection consisted of reinforced concrete up to twelve feet thick. No actual missiles were seen, but the civilians said that the bombs, when assembled, were launched from L'Isle Adam near Pontoise. It must not be forgotten that as rocket site after rocket site was overrun in this swift advance, the stream of " doodle-bugs " which for months had been doing great damage in London, its suburbs, and the home counties, dwindled with equal rapidity. The army in its triumphant progress must have been greatly cheered to feel that it was removing a great menace from the people at home.

On September 1 the 7th Green Howards took up the duties of advance guard to the 69th Brigade, and, passing through Beauvais, Boves and Villers Bretonneux, arrived at Morlancourt at about 2.30 p.m. Here they were informed by the local members of the " Maquis " that there was a strong enemy force in Albert. At 8 p.m. the Battalion deployed, and advanced towards Albert with " D " Company as advance guard, and the carrier platoon moving on the high ground to the east of the town *7 Bn 1/2 Sep 44*

On arrival near Becourt the Carrier Platoon commander, Capt. W. Murray, divided his command, and placed two sections on the Albert-Peronne road, and the other two on the Albert-Becourt track, accompanying the latter himself.

Soon after 10 p.m. loud explosions were heard in Albert, and an hour later enemy transport was heard approaching

Becourt along the track. The lorries were led by an armoured car, and a small scout car, and these were allowed to pass. They were closely followed by a tank and a half-track armoured vehicle. The two sections of carriers now opened fire ; the tank stopped and returned the fire, while the armoured vehicle advanced to within ten yards of the Green Howard party, who threw grenades at it, forcing it to withdraw. Before it had gone very far, however, Cpl. F. Senior scored a direct hit with a P.I.A.T. bomb, and the vehicle got out of control, and exploded. One Green Howard carrier had been set on fire by the German tank.

The two sections of carriers now withdrew to a position flanking the track, and spent some happy hours enfilading passing enemy columns with Bren gun fire. Much execution was done as the Germans were travelling, in many cases, astride the vehicles.

Later on Capt. Murray, with Sgt. D. E. Gray, Cpl. Senior and L/Cpl. A. Dow, went forward down the track. Here they met a German patrol of seven men at point blank range, and drove them back into a wood, which was then bombarded with mortar and P.I.A.T. bombs. On reconnoitring the wood next morning they found between thirty and forty vehicles packed head to tail, and all burnt out, while there were many signs of a panicky retreat.

In these operations the Platoon lost one Sergeant and one private killed, and one Sergeant missing.

The other two sections under Sgt. Rawson, when it was realised that their road was not being used, came across to assist the other half of the platoon. On approaching the wood they were heavily fired on, and, when making a detour, ran into a German armoured vehicle. A German Officer and private approached them on foot, and they wounded the former and killed the latter. Sgt. Rawson picked up the officer, took him back to Battalion Headquarters, and then rejoined the Platoon.

During the whole of these operations, which lasted for more than four hours, Capt. Murray displayed great powers of leadership and a very high standard of personal gallantry. He was a great inspiration to his men, who, during the night, inflicted many casualties on the enemy, and much destruction to his vehicles. The enemy were undoubtedly in considerable strength and in possession of a number of heavy weapons.

For his courage and leadership Capt. Murray was awarded the Military Cross.

" C " and " D " Companies, meanwhile, picquetted the roads leading south and east from Albert without seeing any enemy, while " A " and " B " Companies remained in reserve near Morlancourt. At 6 a.m., next morning, the Battalion " liberated " Albert. There was no opposition, and in the words of the war diary, they had " quite a celebration."

The 6th Battalion also arrived near Villers Brettoneux on the afternoon of September 1, and, having established " B " Company to hold the bridge over the R. Somme at Corbie, and " C " Company on a similar duty at Deaours, settled in for the night.   *6 Bn 1 Sep 44*

A considerable number of prisoners of war was handed over to the Battalions by the " Maquis ", and these were conducted back to the prisoners of war cage at Amiens.

On September 2 both Battalions moved forward in the afternoon to the neighbourhood of Arras, where many signs of the 1914-1918 war, and of the May, 1940, campaign were to be seen. They remained there during September 3, and then made a big stride forward on the 4th, the 6th Battalion going right through to Alost, about ninety miles, and the 7th to Tournai, about fifty miles.   *6 and 7 Bns 2/4 Sep 44*

When the 6th Battalion left Tournai, it was well ahead of troops on either flank, although the 11th Armoured Division was in front of them near Antwerp. " Once again madly enthusiastic crowds showered the troops with embraces, flowers, food and drink. The crowd in Alost made movement difficult, as they swarmed round every vehicle, and every soldier ".

The 6th Battalion remained in Alost until the afternoon of September 7, when it was rushed forward to make the crossing of the Albert Canal. Travelling through Malines and Westerloo it arrived at Zammel, its assembly area, at about 3 p.m.   *6 Bn 7 Sep 44*

Meanwhile, the 7th Battalion had remained in Tournai, where it took over from the 119th Regiment, United States Army. Here it stayed until September 7, its main role being to prevent Germans from escaping across the R. Escault. During this period it collected upwards of a thousand prisoners from the local " Maquis ", and on September 4 welcomed three Polish officers, who had been dropped by parachute for secret service work some two months previously.   *7 Bn 4/7 Sep 44*

In the afternoon of September 7 the Battalion was relieved in Tournai and proceeded to join up with the 6th Green Howards. Arriving at Zammel at about 10 p.m., it found the latter battalion close to the southern bank of the Albert Canal, making its final preparations for the crossing.

Shortly after leaving Alost on September 7 Lt.-Col. Exham, commanding the 6th Green Howards, was ordered to   *6 Bn 7 Sep 44*

See MAP
No. 19 move ahead and report to the Brigade Commander, who gave
him the following information and instructions. " It is
essential that two routes shall be opened without delay across
the Albert Canal. On the right of the 50th Division, the Guards
Armoured Division has secured a crossing, but the 11th
Armoured Division on the left has encountered stiff resistance
near Antwerp, and has failed to get across. The 50th Division
has therefore been ordered to make a bridgehead south-west
of Gheel. The operation is of the utmost importance, and
speed is vital."

The 69th Brigade was to make the assault, and the Brigade
Commander informed Lt.-Col. Exham that the task would
be carried out by the 6th Battalion Green Howards, followed
by the 7th Battalion. The situation was so urgent that orders
were given originally for the assault to take place before
midnight, but eventually it was launched at 1.30 a.m. on
September 8.

The first task given to Lt.-Col. Exham was to find out if
any of the bridges eastward from the main Gheel road bridge,
which was known to have been blown up, were still standing.
If they were, they were to be seized at once. If no bridges were
standing, the reconnaissance parties were to seize any civilian
boats they could find. The actual crossing place would depend
on the result of these reconnaissances, but, wherever it might
be, the ultimate bridgehead would have to cover the main Gheel
road, which was vital to future movements.

Having received his orders, Lt.-Col. Exham proceeded to
Zammel, at which place the Battalion arrived at approximately
3 p.m. As a result of a quick reconnaissance which he had
already made, Lt.-Col. Exham knew that the main bridge (A)
had been blown up, and had been told by the inhabitants that
the enemy were dug in on the far bank. As far as was known
there were no enemy troops on the near side at this point.

As soon as the Battalion arrived the Commanding
Officer immediately put into operation the following plan,
for obtaining information about the other six bridges (B-G).
Two groups, consisting of " A " and " B " Companies,
respectively, were sent forward to reconnoitre the canal
bank.   Each group was given a section of carriers,
a section of mortars, a detachment of engineers, and
an artillery observation officer, and allotted a section of the
canal approximately one mile in length. " A " Company
group was made responsible for " B " bridge, and " B "
Company group for " C " and " D " bridges. Each group
was given instructions that if any bridge was found to be still
intact, it was to cross, and secure an immediate bridgehead.

Should it be found that all the bridges were destroyed, a search was to be made for civilian boats, and, if possible, a landing was to be made on the far bank.

At the same time the Carrier platoon, less two sections, was sent off to reconnoitre the most distant bridges (E, F and G).

At about 4.30 p.m. the Brigade Commander arrived, and said that, if the Battalion found it impossible to secure a crossing during the late afternoon, then a night crossing would have to be carried out. He again stressed the fact that the opening of a second crossing over the canal was vital to subsequent operations.

As time was getting short, and he did not expect to get reports from all his reconnaissance parties before 6.30 p.m., Lt.-Col. Exham decided to go forward himself, and see where a night crossing could best be made if it became necessary. Taking his Intelligence Officer, and the officers commanding " C " and " D " Companies with him, he moved to a house (marked " H " on Map No. 19), from the roof of which he was able to get a good view of the canal. The canal at this point was about thirty yards wide, with a high and very steep bank on the near side. After discussion with the occupants of the house, it was concluded that it would be possible to carry assault boats down the bank. While this reconnaissance was being carried out, two parties of the enemy were seen on the far side, and extreme caution had to be exercised.

Leaving his two company commanders to make more detailed investigations, Lt.-Col. Exham then returned to his Headquarters, where he learned that reports had now come in from " A " Company group, and from the Carrier platoon. These reports showed that bridges " B ", " E ", " F " and " G " had all been blown up, and in each case the reconnaissance parties had come under fire from the far bank.

A despatch rider then arrived with a report that " B " Company group was actively engaged near bridge " D ".

Lt.-Col. Exham, failing to get in touch by wireless, decided to go and see for himself what was happening. He arrived at " B " Company's Headquarters. just north of Leissel at about 7 p.m. and found that both bridges, " C " and " D ", were destroyed. " B " Company, on approaching, had come under accurate mortar and spandau fire, and had sustained a number of casualties. The fire was being returned by our own mortars, and fighting patrols were just moving out to gain more information about the bridge approaches.

The Commanding Officer, before returning to his Headquarters, warned the officer commanding " B " Company

x

that a crossing might have to be made that night in the Gheel bridge area, and that he must be ready to move across at short notice.

It was quite dark when Lt.-Col. Exham arrived back at Headquarters, where he found the Brigade Commander. On hearing that all the bridges were destroyed, the latter confirmed his order for a night crossing, repeating his instructions that the bridgehead must include the village of Het Punt on the Gheel road, which, if held, would cover subsequent bridging operations. Lt.-Col. Exham gave out his orders at 9 p.m., and at the same time recalled " B " Company from Leissel.

The crossing places, of which there were two, lay about half way between bridges " B " and " C ", and had been reconnoitred by the officers commanding " C " and " D " Companies. These companies were therefore ordered to make the assault, covered, if necessary, by fire from " A " Company. One Mark II Assault boat and three reconnaissance boats were allotted to each of the leading companies. A provisional order of crossing for the remainder of the Battalion was laid down, but this was subject to alteration. A beachmaster was appointed for each crossing place, Capt. G. L. Carmichael carrying out this duty on the left where " D " Company crossed, and Capt. D. A. Spence on the right where " C " Company was in the van. Company objectives north-west of the village of Het Punt, were chosen, and compass bearings of the advance, subsequent to crossing, were given out. Finally, as it was not found possible to light or tape the route forward from the Assembly area, a control point was established on the main Zammel-Het Punt road, under the command of Major Hull, from which all units were directed to the off loading point on the western outskirts of Leissel, and thence to the canal bank.

Company Commanders then returned to their Companies, and at 10.30 p.m. met the Commanding Officer at the control point with their men.

6 Bn   At 1.30 on the morning of September 8 the 6th Green
8 Sep 44 Howards, the spearpoint of the 50th Division, began to cross the Albert Canal. The actual crossing was largely unopposed. No enemy were encountered on the far bank, and " C " and " D " Companies were safely across by about 2.30 a.m. Soon after this, however, spandaus opened up from both flanks, and lights were put up from the area of the neighbouring bridges. These did not, however, illuminate the actual crossing places, and only a few casualties were sustained.

Unfortunately touch by wireless with " C " and " D " Companies was lost almost at once, but from the noise of automatic fire, it was clear that the enemy was actively opposing the advance.

Battalion advanced headquarters reached Meulenberg at about 4 a.m., and soon afterwards reports were received that " D " Company had reached the main Gheel road, and was digging in, but that " C " Company was held up a short way in front of Meulenberg.

By 8 a.m. the whole Battalion was north of the canal, and making slow progress in the face of very determined opposition. " A " Company had by this time been ordered to move round the flank of " C " Company, and had managed to secure a footing amongst the houses of Het Punt.

Soon after daylight appeared Lt.-Col. Exham was wounded when carrying out a reconnaissance in an attempt to get news of the forward companies. Major Hull was called up from the control point behind the canal, and assumed command of the Battalion under very difficult conditions. There was no contact whatever at this juncture with either " A " or " D " Company, and it was some time since any report had been received from them.

Firing could be heard from the direction of the main Gheel road, and Major Hull set out with a small reconnaissance party in an attempt to gain contact with them. This party, however, had not gone very far before it ran into heavy machine-gun fire, which appeared to come from an enemy position between Battalion Headquarters in Meulenberg, and the estimated positions of " A " and " D " Companies, and was forced to withdraw.

Early in the afternoon " C " Company, 7th Green Howards, who had by this time arrived in the area, together with the Carrier Platoon, and elements of the 6th Battalion, delivered an attack on the village of Het Punt. The enemy responded to this threat by launching a counter-attack in considerable strength from a north-westerly direction across the main Gheel road, and towards Meulenberg.

One platoon of " A " Company, 6th Green Howards, which, during the morning had fought its way across the main road, was overrun, and the commander of " A " Company ordered the remainder of his company to withdraw towards Meulenberg. At the same time the commander of " D " Company, realising the seriousness of the situation, also decided to withdraw. The withdrawal of these two companies was well carried out, but they both suffered heavy casualties.

As darkness fell the 6th Battalion was regrouping in new positions covering Meulenberg, but, during the night, orders were received to make a silent night advance in a north-easterly direction, leaving the 7th Green Howards in the Meulenberg positions.

6 *Bn*
9 *Sep* 44
The 6th Battalion reached its new positions by first light on September 9, and, except for occasional spandau and mortar fire, spent a comparatively quiet day. Unfortunately, Capt. T. G. Richards, who had done excellent work as Intelligence Officer, was wounded when out on reconnaissance. His place was taken by Capt. E. J. Hudson.

On the night of September 9 the 5th East Yorkshires who, as will be related, had arrived south of the canal during the day, were ordered to make an assault across the canal to the west of Het Punt.

The 6th Green Howards received orders to strike west from their new positions across the main Gheel road coincidentally with the East Yorkshires' assault. This advance met with success, and a considerable number of prisoners was taken from the enemy forces, which were trapped between the two Battalions. The East Yorkshires, as they entered Het Punt from the west, released a number of men of " A " Company, 6th Green Howards, who had been captured on September 8, and kept in the village. Although most of the prisoners captured by the 6th Battalion were Germans trying to escape from Het Punt, two enemy staff cars, hurtling down the road from Gheel just after dawn, ran straight into the hands of the leading Company. Such was the fighting spirit of the German troops, whom the Green Howards were facing at this time, that two of the occupants of one car, although they must have known that they were surrounded, opened fire and badly wounded two men of the Battalion.

6 *Bn*
10/12 *Sep* 44
At 8 a.m. on September 10 the 6th Battalion was relieved by the 7th Battalion, and moved back to Steelen on the right flank. There it took over reserve positions from the 8th Battalion Durham Light Infantry. During the afternoon, Lt.-Col. C. F. Hutchinson, D.S.O., East Yorkshire Regiment, arrived, and took over command of the Battalion.

For the next two days, September 11 and 12, the 6th Battalion was out of direct contact with the enemy, but came under heavy shelling from the German guns, which were supporting strong counter-attacks against the Durham Light Infantry, who, after penetrating as far as Gheel, were fighting fiercely near Doornbloom.

The Battalion sent out constant patrols to contact the Durhams, and to reconnoitre the Canal further to the east. On September 12 Lt. P. C. Bawcombe, M.C., with a party of twelve men, went out on a daylight offensive patrol to the east. After going about a mile they attacked a house occupied by the enemy, and captured two prisoners whom they brought back. These supplied valuable information, and gave an accurate description of the layout of the German positions.

Later in the evening the Battalion was relieved by the 7th Royal Scots Fusiliers, and, after recrossing the Canal by ferry, proceeded in motor transport to a rest area near Veerle.

The 7th Green Howards, having, on September 7, travelled   7 *Bn*
some ninety miles from Tournai, and arrived at 10 p.m. on 7/9 *Sep* 44
the south bank of the Canal, started to cross the canal to the east of the 6th Battalion at 4 a.m. on the 8th. With only two assault boats at their disposal, they completed their crossing without opposition by 9 a.m., and proceeded to advance towards Meulenberg.

Soon after reaching the far bank Capt. Dennison was wounded, and, at about 11 a.m., Lt.-Col. Cox, commanding the 7th Battalion, was given command of both Green Howard Battalions, these being, at this juncture, the only troops across the Canal.

Early in the afternoon " C " Company, supported by the Carrier Platoon, joined with the 6th Battalion in an attack on the village of Het Punt. This resulted, as we have seen, in a fierce counter-attack by the enemy, and " C " Company was forced to withdraw.

In this action, Major H. Pye was killed, Lts. B. C. France, P. H. R. Taylor and P. J. Langdon wounded, while six other ranks were killed and twenty wounded.

Meanwhile the 151st Brigade, in the face of most determined opposition, had forced a passage across the Canal further to the east, and were involved in bitter fighting in and around Doornbloom.

On September 9 the 5th East Yorkshires arrived ,and were concentrated just south of the Canal. Brigadier F. Y. C. Knox, D.S.O., commanding the 69th Brigade, ordered them to make an assault crossing that night, slightly to the west of Het Punt, where enemy resistance was still strong on the Green Howards left flank. Launching their attack at 9 p.m. they reached their objectives by 4 a.m. on September 10, and the whole of the 69th Brigade was now across the Canal in an established bridgehead.

Meanwhile the 7th Battalion, having taken the place   7 *Bn*
of the 6th Battalion in the original bridgehead, advanced 10/11 *Sep* 44
during the night of September 10/11 to link up with the Durham Light Infantry on its right, and to enlarge the bridgehead.

This advance was successfully accomplished by 3 a.m. on the 11th, and the Battalion was consolidated in positions in the neighbourhood of Poyel.

In this advance a fighting patrol was sent out in front, one section of which was commanded by L/Cpl. J. Wilks. While searching some buildings over a mile from the nearest British positions, small groups of the enemy were discovered in trenches, which lay between the section and its line of withdrawal. With great boldness L/Cpl. Wilks approached a trench occupied by two Germans, and, taking them by surprise, compelled them to surrender. He then forced them to crawl in front of him back to his section. Throughout this time he was under fire from other enemy trenches, and it was only through his fighting skill and determined courage that the prisoners were brought back alive. Valuable identifications and information about enemy dispositions were obtained from them. For this action L/Cpl. Wilks was awarded the Military Medal.

At about 9 a.m. a carrier patrol joined up with the Durham Light Infantry near Stokt. The enemy were now showing signs of an impending attack. Ground troops and tanks were seen assembling in front, and at about 11 a.m. one enemy tank, which approached too close to " B " and " D " Companies, was knocked out by a P.I.A.T. bomb. An artillery barrage was brought down and this attack was broken up, but not before a party of Germans, trying to infiltrate from the east, had been mopped up by " C " Company and the carrier platoon. Of this party, four were known to have been killed, while one officer and forty-two men were captured, five of the latter being wounded. During the day the Battalion lost 2/Lt. J. E. Scrutton, who was killed, and one other rank killed and nine wounded.

7 *Bn*
12 *Sep* 44

On September 12, in the afternoon, a very determined counter-attack was made against the Battalion, in which, at one moment, the enemy broke through the Green Howards front. Owing, however, to a gallant attack by the carrier platoon, under Capt. Murray, M.C., the situation was restored, and, when darkness fell, the Green Howards were left in full possession of the field, with the enemy fleeing in confusion towards the north.

After a period of heavy shelling during the early afternoon, it was about 4 p.m. when a report was received from " D " Company that German infantry, supported by four tanks firing all their guns, were advancing within five hundred yards of its position. These troops were also seen by " A " Company who engaged them, and one tank was at once knocked out.

The remaining tanks then halted, and proceeded to bombard " A " and " D " Company areas with high explosive shells. Under cover of this fire enemy infantry crept up the hedges and, breaking into " A " Company's position, engaged No. 9 Platoon with grenades, rifle and spandau fire at twenty-five yards range. This platoon was forced back for a distance of some two hundred yards, leaving No. 8 Platoon on its right in an isolated position. No. 8 Platoon, therefore, withdrew and linked up with " D " Company, leaving a gap in the Battalion's line.

Immediate orders were given to Capt. Murray to block this gap with the carrier platoon and to engage the enemy. Capt. Murray, with his carriers, attacked with such dash that the enemy were driven back in disorder, suffering severe casualties, and all the lost ground on this flank was recovered.

Later, owing to misplaced fire from our own tanks, the carrier platoon was forced to withdraw, but eventually " C " Company reoccupied the positions. " D " Company beat off fierce enemy attacks on its front for some three hours, and, in the end, had the satisfaction of seeing the enemy extricate themselves with difficulty and flying in confusion.

This was an action fought with skill and determination by the 7th Green Howards, in which severe casualties were inflicted upon the enemy, and which put an end to any hopes he might have had of regaining the Canal crossings near Het Punt.

In the course of this action L/Sgt. E. F. A. Upperton and Pte. J. A. Reddington particularly distinguished themselves, and gained the Military Medal. L/Sgt. Upperton was the Platoon Sergeant of " D " Company's left forward platoon, which soon came under heavy fire from the advancing tanks. Some buildings immediately behind the platoon's position were set on fire, and one of them collapsed on to one of the section posts. The platoon was ordered to withdraw to an alternative position on the left flank. L/Sgt. Upperton at this point seized a P.I.A.T., and went forward alone under heavy fire in an endeavour to knock out the nearest tank. He failed, however, to get within range, and was ordered back by the platoon commander. When he saw that one wounded man had been left in the original position, L/Sgt. Upperton again went out alone and brought him in. The action continued for nearly four hours at very close quarters, and throughout this period, L/Sgt. Upperton continued to move about, directing fire and bringing up ammunition without any regard for his personal safety. L/Sgt. Upperton displayed leadership and personal bravery of a very high order, and he proved an inspiration to his men, who were at times in a very tight corner. He undoubtedly played a big part in helping to beat off a very determined counter-attack.

Pte. Reddington was in charge of the P.I.A.T. of the right hand forward platoon, and, as he fired it at an approaching tank, the first bomb exploded as it left the P.I.A.T., wounding him in the face and shoulder. Pte. Reddington then seized a rifle, and continued to fire it at the enemy. His platoon commander ordered him to go back to the Regimental Aid Post, but he asked permission to stay, and this was granted as he did not appear to be badly wounded. For the next four hours Pte. Reddington continued to do great execution with his rifle, but, when the attack was eventually beaten off, he was found to be in great pain, and, when he reached the Regimental Aid Post, he was found to be seriously wounded. Pte Reddington's determination to see the operation through with his comrades set an example which proved a great inspiration to them in future actions.

The Battalion's casualties consisted of Capt. R. E. Ellison and Lt. B. Wroe killed, four other ranks killed, twelve wounded and one missing.

Late in the evening the Battalion was relieved by the 9th Cameronians, and was taken back in transport to the rest area near Veerle.

The troops opposed to the 69th and 151st Brigades during these actions consisted at the onset of men from German Air Force regiments, and, in the latter stages, from the 2nd Parachute Division, which was brought up from Germany in a desperate effort to restore the situation. These were all tough troops, and, aided by tanks, they fought every inch of the ground with great determination and courage. They suffered very severe casualties—in some cases units virtually ceased to exist—and, on September 13, they voluntarily withdrew across the Escaut Canal.

By that time both the 69th and 151st Brigades had been withdrawn into reserve south of the Canal, after being relieved by the 15th (Scottish) Division, but not before they had once again inflicted a severe defeat on crack German troops.

6 *Bn* Both Green Howard Battalions went back to Veerle on 13/17 *Sep* 44 the 12th, and the next day the 6th Battalion moved to a defen-*See* MAP sive position near Mulzenheide, south of Beeringen, relieving No. 18 the 2nd Battalion, Devonshire Regiment, 231st Brigade. Here it remained for four days under comparatively peaceful conditions. Trips were made into Brussels, bathing parties were arranged, and most of the Battalion visited the concert party given by E.N.S.A. in Beeringen.

The 7th Battalion moved from Veerle to Pael on September 13 and to Oostram on the 15th. Here its task was to protect the left flank of the Beeringen bridgehead, but during the next three days it managed to find time for an intensive football season. At Rugger it was beaten by the 5th East Yorkshires by 9 points to 8, but overwhelmed the 6th Green Howards by 45 points to 6. A battalion soccer team, and one from " B " Company, played against two local Belgian teams, and in both matches Belgium proved victorious. 7 *Bn* 13/17 *Sep* 44

On September 18 both battalions moved forward some fifteen miles, and relieved the 151st Brigade in the bridgehead area just south of the Canal de Jonction. Here they were subjected to their first direct air attack since landing in France. Single aircraft flew over and dropped a quantity of Anti-Personnel bombs, but the only casualty in the two battalions was one German prisoner, who was wounded when with " B " Echelon of the 7th Battalion. 6 *and* 7 *Bns* 18 *Sep* 44

Before accompanying the 69th Brigade on its next step forward, a brief survey of the general situation is called for, in order that the reader may understand the importance of the part played by the Green Howard Battalions in the ensuing operations.

The Supreme Allied Command was now of the opinion that the German forces in the West had suffered so severely, that there was a very good chance of the next allied attack being sufficiently decisive to finish off the war. It was anticipated that the German Commander-in-Chief in the West might expect, at the most, twelve Divisions as reinforcements in the next two months, and the time was obviously ripe for daring. The operation known to those who took part in it as " Market Garden ", and which culminated in the grim battle of Arnhem, was therefore laid on.

" Market Garden " was planned to split Holland in two, and to cut off all the German forces in the western half from any chance of retreat to the Fatherland. The land troops were to make a rapid thrust northwards to the Zuyder-Zee, while, to help their advance, the largest airborne landing ever attempted was to be made in front of them.

Across the line of advance lay three main water obstacles, the Rivers Maas, Waal, and Neder Rijn. Two American airborne divisions, and the 1st British Airborne Division were to be used. The 101st American Division was to seize canal and river crossings around Eindhoven and Veghel, the 82nd American Division to capture the bridges over the Maas at Grave, and over the Waal at Nijmegen, while to the 1st British Airborne Division was given the task of securing the bridge across the Neder Rijn at Arnhem, the deepest penetration.

The 30th Corps was to form the spearhead of the land attack, with the 8th and 12th Corps protecting its flanks. The 30th Corps was to operate on a one-divisional front, and to advance with all speed to Nunspeet, on the shores of the Zuyder-Zee, by way of Arnhem. The Guards Armoured Division was to lead the Corps, followed by the 43rd Division, with the 50th Division in reserve.

It is a matter of history that this operation was not successful in accomplishing its objects to the full, but, nevertheless, in the bitter fighting which it produced, the enemy suffered so severely that his powers of resistance were further weakened. This was another of the glorious failures, of which there are so many in British Military History, and in which the spirit of the British soldier is seen at its best. The men who dropped from the skies at Arnhem and their comrades on the ground below, who fought their way grimly forward from Nijmegen, and then held on against desperate counter-attacks, wrote yet another chapter in military history which will never be forgotten.

At 3.30 a.m. on September 17 the great airborne armada was seen in the sky above the bridgehead position on the Escaut Canal, held at that time by the 151st and 231st Brigades of the 50th Division.

An hour later the Guards Armoured Division began to move forward, and the advance into Holland had begun. It was not long before stiff opposition was encountered, and the 231st Brigade had to be brought up to clear some woods just short of the frontier. By mid-day on September 18 the Guards had passed through Eindhoven, and on the 19th reached Nijmegen. There they found both the rail and road bridges still held by the enemy, who were strongly entrenched in concrete emplacements. The American airborne troops, who had met with great success at Zon, Veghel and Grave, had found the opposition at Nijmegen too strong. With the help of the Guards Division, however, they captured both bridges on September 20, after having spent three days of intensive fighting on their own.

The time-table was now sadly behind-hand, and the gallant British airborne troops at Arnhem, still some ten miles ahead, were tenaciously hanging on to their bridgehead against ferocious counter-attacks. Every effort was being made to come to their rescue, and to secure this last most important river crossing on the line of the 30th Corps advance.

69 *Bde*
21/23 *Sep* 44
On September 21 the 69th Brigade was ordered to push forward to Nijmegen with all speed, cross the R. Waal, and advance on Arnhem. For this purpose it was put under command of the Guards Division.

The road from Eindhoven to Nijmegen was choked with traffic, and the Brigade did not get away until 10 p.m. on the 21st. Early the next morning the Germans launched an attack with tanks and infantry designed to cut the main line of advance of the 30th Corps, and prevent the relief of the British force at Arnhem. This attack met with initial success, the enemy establishing himself across the main road near Uden, some eight miles south of Grave. This move resulted in the 69th Brigade being cut in two, with the 5th East Yorkshires to the north of the German troops, and the 6th and 7th Green Howards still to the south.

The British troops, and the American forces who were holding the crossings near St. Oedenrode, now got together, and, when, on September 23, the enemy attempted to strengthen their hold on the road by attacking Veghel, the combined American and British troops drove them back with heavy losses. As a result of this action the road was temporarily reopened, and the 69th Brigade, united once more, got through to Nijmegen, arriving there at about 8 a.m. on September 24. *69 Bde* *24 Sep 44*

It was now seven days since the airborne landings had been made, and the situation of the survivors of the 1st British Airborne Division was desperate. During the night of September 25/26 they were withdrawn from Arnhem. The next step forward from Nijmegen to Arnhem, and across the Neder Rijn, had therefore to be made by the troops on the ground. Accordingly the 69th Brigade attacked the village of *69 Bde* Bemmel north of Nijmegen on September 25, and on the *25/26 Sep 44* 26th a further attack was made towards Baal.

The position now, however, was drastically changed. Cheered by their success at Arnhem, the German troops, who had been carrying out a stiff resistance north of Nijmegen, now became aggressive and, reinforced by tanks and infantry released from Arnhem, they prepared to deliver a counter- *69 Bde* attack. This attack was launched on September 30 by a force *30 Sep/* estimated at an infantry division, and approximately seventy *2 Oct 44* tanks. The 69th Brigade, and in particular the 7th Green Howards, bore the brunt of this attack, and, for eighteen hours on October 1. they doggedly held on to their positions against fierce attacks from a numerically superior foe. On October 2 the 69th Brigade was relieved by the 151st Brigade, and withdrew to billets in Nijmegen.

We must now return to September 21 and follow the 6th *6 and 7 Bns* and 7th Green Howards in their advance into Holland, and *21/23 Sep 44* across the R. Waal at Nijmegen. September 19 and 20 passed quietly for the Green Howards, and it was not until 10 p.m. on the 21st that they eventually moved forward, and, making slow progress, passed through the first Dutch town of Valkens-waard soon after 8 a.m. on the 22nd. At noon they reached Eindhoven. Here they received an overwhelming welcome. Many souvenirs were given and received, and copies of a Dutch " underground " newspaper were handed out to all and sundry by some attractive girls.

When the Green Howards reached a point about a mile short of Oedenrode at about 5 p.m., they were halted and ordered to take up a defensive position. At this time, it will be remembered, the road ahead was cut by the enemy between Veghel and Uden, and the Brigadier and Battalion commanders were north of the enemy, the former having summoned bat-talion commanders to the head of the Brigade Column earlier in the day. The Battalions were temporarily put under command of the 231st Brigade, and, during the evening, Major-General Graham, commanding the 50th Division, paid them a visit and told them to remain where they were.

See MAP
No. 20
At 4 p.m. on the 23rd, the Commanding Officers arrived back, and, the road being now open again, the battalions resumed their advance at 3 a.m. on September 24. After passing through Veghel, Uden and Grave without incident, they arrived in Nijmegen at 8 a.m. The 6th Battalion estab-lished itself in a Convent School, which had recently been occupied by German troops. The 7th Battalion was ordered to guard the southern approaches to the road and railway bridges. Two platoons of " C " Company and the anti-tank platoon, less two guns, had been commandeered near Veghel by an American General to help repel a counter-attack by the enemy. They rejoined later in the day, having successfully accomplished their task.

6 *Bn*
24/25 *Sep* 44
At 2.30 p.m. the 6th Green Howards moved forward across the R. Waal, and took up positions near Ressen. At the same time the 7th Battalion moved forward to Merm. On arrival at Ressen patrols were sent out by the 6th Battalion but no contact was made with the enemy. After a quiet night enemy mortars began shelling the Battalion's positions, and Lt. H. W. Rushmere and three men of " C " Company were wounded. Throughout the 25th and the night of the 25/26th considerable patrolling took place but nothing was reported.

6 *Bn*
26 *Sep* 44
At about noon on September 26 the 7th Green Howards and 5th East Yorkshires launched an attack on Heuval. The role allotted to the 6th Battalion was to advance towards Baal on the right flank. The 6th Battalion moved forward at about 3 p.m. with " A " Company on the right and " B " Company on the left ; " C " and " D " Companies were in reserve. Soon after Battalion Headquarters started to move

a direct hit from a shell killed Capt. K. S. Dimmer, the Intelligence Officer, and Capt. A. T. Semple, commanding "A" Company, and wounded the Commanding Officer's signaller and driver. The shelling in this area was particularly heavy, and Battalion Headquarters withdrew slightly to the south of Ressen. Capt. Franklyn took over command of "A" Company.

At about 5 p.m. the advance was resumed, and by 7 p.m. "B" Company reported that its objective had been captured, while "A" Company reported that it was only two hundred yards short of its objective. These two companies were now within a quarter of a mile of Baal, "A" Company to the south-west and "B" Company to the north-west of the village. During the night "A" and "B" Companies linked up and consolidated their positions.

At 6 a.m. on September 27 the commanding officer, Lt.-Col. C. F. Hutchinson, called a conference and planned the next advance. "D" Company (Major F. Greensill) was ordered to pass through "B" Company, and renew the attack on Baal in conjunction with "A" Company. Artillery support was provided, and the Cheshire Machine guns were to fire a diversionary concentration to the south-east of Baal. The enemy had now brought up some tanks, and was covering the roads with 88 mm. and anti-tank guns. At 8 a.m. "D" Company reported that it was held up some thousand yards north of Baal. *6 Bn 27 Sep 44*

Although "A" Company had made a little progress, it was still short of the village. At 10 a.m. the news came back that two German tanks were firing on "A" Company from Baal, and that Capt. Franklyn had been killed. This was an irreparable loss to the Green Howards. Capt. Franklyn, whose father and grandfather had devoted their lives to the Regiment, and each of whom in turn had been honoured by being appointed Colonel of the Regiment, had now at the early age of twenty-one made the supreme sacrifice, and the line of succession, which it was his ambition to sustain, was broken.

"D" Company, which by 9 a.m. had advanced to within a few hundred yards of "A" Company, was ordered to press on to the assistance of "A" Company, but failed to make any further progress, and by 3 p.m. had been forced back towards Heuval. On September 28 "D" Company was placed under command of the 7th Green Howards. Meanwhile the position of "A" Company was becoming more and more precarious. Enemy tanks from Baal were firing on it, and the enemy infantry were attacking it from the north-east and the south-west. Major J. E. D. Maxwell was killed and Lt. R. F. Peters missing during the morning's fighting.

At noon " C " Company was given orders to advance with its right flank on the road running from Bemmel to Baal, and to occupy a position from which it could support " A " Company. " C " Company was given one troop of tanks to support this advance, but the Company Commander was told not to commit himself to full scale battle without reference to the Commanding Officer. " B " Company was given orders at the same time to work round the northern flank of Baal. Neither of these companies made a great deal of progress, and by the end of the day all companies had withdrawn slightly from the most forward points of their advance.

September 27 had been a day of strenuous fighting for the Green Howards. It will be remembered that the enemy were being strongly reinforced at this time, and, in all probability, the projected advance through and beyond Baal was a hopeless task from the outset. Nevertheless, they had made some progress, and, when counter-attacked, had held grimly on to the ground which they had gained.

6 Bn
28 Sep 44
It was not until 3.30 a.m. on September 28 that rations could be brought up to the exhausted troops. The day turned out to be very wet, but fortunately enemy activity died down, except for considerable artillery fire directed on the roads. At 9 p.m. the Battalion was withdrawn, with the exception of " D " Company, still with the 7th Green Howards, and moved back to Ressen as Brigade Reserve.

7 Bn
24/25 Sep 44
The 7th Battalion on its move forward to Merm during the afternoon of September 24 encountered slight opposition, and one man was killed and one wounded. During the night of the 24/25th patrols were sent out, which made contact with the 6th Green Howards on the right, and with troops on the left. On the night of the 25/26th patrols again went out as far as Aam, and the railway bridge north of Merm, but did not meet any enemy.

7 Bn
26 Sep 44
At noon on September 26 the Battalion began to advance towards Heuval, with " A " and " D ", Major K. A. Nash, Companies leading, followed by " B ", Major J. Hunter, and " C ", Capt. G. Sherratt, M.C., Companies respectively. The leading companies soon ran into opposition, and it was not until tanks were brought up in support at about 4.30 p.m. that they were able to penetrate into Heuval. The actual entry into the village was made by " B " Company, which moved round the flank of " A " Company. As it grew dark, " C " and " D " Companies moved forward in front of the village, and occupied positions in some orchards about a quarter of a mile to the north-west. During the night a patrol gained contact with the Welsh Guards on the left flank.

Casualties during the day consisted of two killed, two wounded and one missing, and the wounded included the Commanding Officer, Lt.-Col. Cox, and Major N. S. Atley. The command of the Battalion was taken by Major M. F. P. Lloyd.

Throughout September 27 and 28 the Battalion came under spasmodic shell and mortar fire, and engaged enemy snipers and spandau teams. Both " C " and " D " Companies sent forward patrols to the Canal de Ligne, but found the enemy in occupation of the south bank, and were forced to withdraw. At 8 p.m. on the 28th the line was shortened by the withdrawal of " C " and " D " Companies to positions in the forward outskirts of Heuval, and " D " Company, 6th Green Howards, who were in line on the right flank, came under command. 7 *Bn* 27/28 *Sep* 44

During these operations Pte. S. J. Riddle behaved with great gallantry, for which he was awarded the Military Medal. When his section was fired upon by a machine-gun at thirty yards range, and three of his comrades were lost, Pte. Riddle seized a bren gun, jumped out of a ditch, and, kneeling in the open, fired at the machine-gun post, killing two Germans. By that time he was being fired upon by several other Germans in a neighbouring farm but, springing to his feet, he dashed forward, firing from the hip. Shouting encouragement to the remainder of his section, he led them forward, and captured the position.

On September 29 the Battalion was shelled and mortared at intervals throughout the day, and the Germans could be seen moving quite openly on the banks of the canal about a quarter of a mile in front. All through the night of September 29/30, the rumble of tanks behind the canal could be heard, and the conclusion was drawn—quite correctly—that a large convoy of tanks and M.T. was moving down from Rykerswoerd. 7 *Bn* 29/30 *Sep* 44

At 5 a.m. on October 1, tanks were heard approaching from the north-west and at 5.30 a.m. the full fury of the German counter-attack struck the Battalion. Preceded by a heavy artillery and mortar barrage, groups of riflemen and spandau teams loomed up through the early morning mist, and were soon within fifty yards of the forward companies. These were later followed by tanks, twelve of which attacked on the front of " B " and " C " Companies. Two of these were knocked out but the remainder succeeded in forcing their way between these two companies. " C " Company was forced to give ground, thereby exposing " A " Company, which was left in an isolated position. This was the situation at 7 a.m., and from that hour until they were relieved by the 5th East Yorkshires at 11 p.m. that night, the Green Howards fought company by company, 7 *Bn* 1 *Oct* 44 and section by section, against continuous pressure from the enemy on all sides.

There can be no doubt that the main focus of this attack, for which the Germans had collected the equivalent of an infantry division and seventy tanks, was directed against the sector of the front held by the 7th Green Howards and the Irish Guards. The German Air Force had, on September 29, succeeded in seriously damaging both the rail and road bridges across the R. Waal at Nijmegen, and if the enemy had succeeded in breaking through the British front at that crucial point, it would probably have led to the destruction of all the British forces north of the river.

By the time that the Green Howards were relieved the counter-attack had definitely failed, and, as they moved back into Nijmegen next day, physically exhausted and licking their wounds, they must have been proud of the epic defence which they had put up during eighteen hours of ground fighting and artillery bombardment.

Many gallant deeds were performed that day. Pte. J. H. Adams, who had only been in action for three days previous to this battle, fought with the most outstanding bravery. In the initial attack two platoons on his company's flank were overrun, and the enemy infantry penetrated to within sixty yards of the positions of the platoon to which Pte. Adams belonged. After a brief interval two Panther tanks came forward to lead on the infantry, who had been stopped by rifle fire. Pte. Adams, taking the platoon P.I.A.T., crawled along a ditch, and coolly fired at them. This caused the leading tank to run into a ditch, from which position its crew kept up a heavy fire, as did the second tank in support. With a complete contempt for danger, Pte. Adams moved round the crippled tank, and hit it three times more. The crew got out, and abandoned their tank. The second tank then came up firing its gun and machine guns, but Pte. Adams fired his P.I.A.T. again, and secured a hit. This second tank quickly halted, then turned, and rapidly made off. For this magnificent single combat between Pte. Adams and two tanks, in which the latter were completely routed, he was awarded the Distinguished Conduct Medal.

C.S.M. P. Murphy was Company Sergeant-Major of " C " Company, which was the right forward company, with an exposed right flank. The company had one platoon forming a standing patrol at the end of an orchard some two hundred yards away from the main position. This platoon was heavily engaged at the outset of the counter-attack, and soon its ammunition began to run low. C.S.M. Murphy with great

Mopping up near Tracey Bocage.

A patrol being briefed near Taungup.

coolness and bravery, crossed the open and bullet-swept ground, carrying ammunition to this platoon. Later, enemy infantry, supported by two tanks, penetrated to within seventy yards of Company Headquarters. Nearby there was an anti-tank gun, the crew of which had become casualties. C.S.M. Murphy ran across the open to the gun, loaded it with the last round left, fired and hit the nearest tank, which caught fire. He had no sooner left the gun than it was hit by another tank and blown to pieces. Throughout the whole eighteen hours of this engagement C.S.M. Murphy moved about his company area with a complete disregard for danger, and proved a great source of inspiration to his men. He was awarded the Military Medal.

The following is an account of the day's fighting as seen by Major J. Hunter, commanding " B " Company, which, as one of the forward companies of the Battalion, bore the brunt of the battle.

" At about 10 p.m. on September 30 great enemy tank and transport movement was heard north of the canal. I went down to the standing patrol in the orchard north of our positions, and crept forward to " D " Company's old positions, but could see nothing, and the movement sounded to be well over the other side of the canal. Soon after midnight I had a report from the standing patrol that all was clear. This report was repeated again at 4 a.m. At 5 a.m., on receipt of a telephone message from Battalion Headquarters, I ordered the company to stand to. Only a few minutes previously to this Cpl. A. J. Williamson and three men of No. 11 platoon had gone off to relieve the standing patrol. This relief was completed, but no trace was ever found of Cpl. Williamson and his party, who must have been overrun by the enemy in their first onslaught.

At 5.15 a.m. the enemy attacked. It was a dark misty morning, and everything favoured the attackers. Groups of spandau teams and riflemen appeared through the mist about fifty yards in front of the company's forward positions. Our bren guns opened up and must have caused heavy casualties on the enemy, but they still came on in small parties.

At about 5.30 Capt. Thorne, R.A., from the Guards Armoured Division, appeared in his tank, on his way to his Observation Post. As he could not get up to his usual post in front of my left-hand platoon, I asked him if he would give us assistance with his tank. He immediately agreed, and, drawing his tank up on the road level with Company Head-quarters, began sweeping the orchard in front and the open ground on the left with his light automatics, at the same time
Y

bringing down heavy artillery fire on the orchard. By this time the enemy had infiltrated through a section of the right forward platoon (No. 10), killing the commander, Cpl. J. Dykes, and wounding Cpl. J. Brett.

C.S.M. D. Patterson, who acted with the greatest courage throughout the day, organised the defence of Company Headquarters, which were situated in a burnt out farmhouse in the village of Heuval. Ably assisted by Pte. F. Prior, he accounted for three of the enemy, who were about to rush the position.

By 6.45 a.m. the infantry attack had been halted, but I received a message from Battalion Headquarters to the effect that ' D ' Company had seen tanks moving up on our position through the orchards. I immediately called for an artillery barrage to be put down on the front of the orchard. About five minutes later the first enemy tank, a Tiger, appeared from the orchard. By this time all our positions were under heavy artillery and mortar fire. The first tank was closely followed by three others, and two self-propelled guns, which drew up in front of the orchard, and began to fire on the farm area.

Throughout the morning small parties of enemy infantry were seen on the open ground to our left, creeping down the ditches towards ' D ' Company. Whenever possible, I called down artillery and mortar fire on to them, and this accurate fire must have caused them some casualties. At about 10.30 the tanks started moving forward, and one Tiger came across the open field by Heuval Farm, where it got to within seventy yards of No. 11 platoon.

Pte. Edemenson, after firing about five P.I.A.T. bombs, brought it to a halt. One German got out, and waving his hand, shouted in broken English, ' You win this time ', and ran off as hard as he could. Another German got out and started firing from the turret, but he was soon accounted for. This seemed to deter the other tanks, and for the rest of the day they remained static in their positions, until about 6 p.m., when they started to pull out. Before leaving they attempted to salvage two tanks which had been knocked out, but I called for an artillery concentration, and simultaneously two Typhoons swooped down over the orchard. We took cover in our cellar while this was going on, and when we looked out later, we saw a large cloud of black smoke and a sheet of flame rising from the middle of the orchard. Another tank struck a mine on the road and heeled over.

At about 6.30 the artillery put down a magnificent barrage across our front and all round us, which must have caused heavy enemy casualties. From this time on, until we were ordered to withdraw at 10 p.m., things were comparatively quiet. Before leaving we counted twelve enemy dead within a radius of a hundred yards from Company Headquarters. Thus ended a most awful day, but the enemy had not broken through."

On October 2 both Green Howard Battalions moved back 6 *and* 7 *Bns* into billets in Nijmegen to rest and reorganise, their positions 2 *Oct* 44 having been taken over by the 151st and 231st Brigades.

The next two months were spent by the 50th Division in static warfare in the tract of country lying between the Rivers Neder Rijn and Waal, which became known as " The Island ". This was an area of low-lying country, with numerous orchards, and criss-crossed with dykes, roughly bisected by the Nijmegen-Arnhem road.

The allied troops and the German forces faced each other on a line which ran from Halderen on the northern bank of the R. Waal about three miles north-east of Nijmegen, through Bemmel to Elst. From Elst, the line ran due north along the railway as far as the bridge at Arnhem and then turned west along the southern bank of the R. Neder Rijn. The enemy positions north of the Neder Rijn were on an escarpment, which dominated the allied positions on the flat and open country of " The Island ". Consequently all major movements, such as the bringing up of supplies or reinforcements, had to be made by night. During this period, however, the enemy was singularly inactive, and confined his activities in the main to occasional shelling and mortaring. Beyond this there was little action except for patrolling, and a running competition between snipers on both sides.

The Green Howards, until they were withdrawn to Belgium on November 28, spent three periods in this line ; one in the northern sector near Driel, one near Elst, and made their final contact with the enemy in the Bemmel sector, which was considered to be the " hottest " spot on " The Island ", since our own and the enemy's positions were at really close quarters.

In between these bouts of duty the Battalions rested either in an area behind Elst, or in Nijmegen itself. The time was spent in training and recreation. Hot baths were available, and many football matches were played. Mobile cinemas and concert parties gave entertainment to the troops. On November 9 the 6th Battalion gave a dance in Nijmegen which was attended by the Brigade Commander and other distinguished guests. In the words of the War Diary : " There was good civilian support, which made the evening most enjoyable."

6 *and* 7 *Bns*
8/17 *Oct* 44

On October 8 the 6th Battalion moved forward from Nijmegen, and took over from the 1st Battalion, 502nd Regt. of the 101st American Airborne Division, in a sector of the line near Driel. The 7th Battalion, now commanded by Lt.-Col. D. R. Wilson, the Lincolnshire Regiment, who had succeeded Lt.-Col. W. R. Cox, promoted to command the 131st Brigade on October 5, was on the left of the 6th Battalion.

They remained in these positions until October 17, subjected to intermittent shelling and mortar fire from the enemy on the high ground across the river. No movement was possible by day, and the only people who were active during the daylight hours were snipers. The Battalion sniper sections had been reconstituted, and scarcely a day passed without their having added another German to the bag. Cpl. J. S. Latchford and Pte. M. Turner of the 6th Battalion received special congratulations from the Brigade Commander on the success of their sniping activities. At night, patrols went out to secure prisoners for identification purposes, and to harass the enemy in his forward positions.

On October 17 the Green Howards were relieved, the 6th Battalion going back to Nijmegen, and the 7th to a rest area near Elst.

6 *and* 7 *Bns*
22 *Oct*/
7 *Nov* 44

From October 22 to November 7 both Battalions were in the line again to the south and south-east of Elst. The only incident of note which occurred during this tour of duty, beyond the routine of patrolling, sniping, and enduring shell fire, took place on October 27.

7 *Bn*
27 *Oct* 44

The 7th Battalion was at that time occupying a position astride the unfinished Autobahn from Arnhem to Nijmegen. Across this road was a concrete bridge used by the enemy as an observation post. It was a strong position, mined and wired, surrounded by three hundred yards of flat open country. Repeated attempts had been made by various other battalions to destroy this point, but without success.

The 7th Battalion made an attempt to capture this bridge. One platoon succeeded in reaching the bridge, but its commander was captured, and the platoon sergeant was killed. The remainder of the platoon, being unable to get through the defensive wire, were subjected to severe and accurate shooting at point blank range and forced to withdraw. Capt. Rabbidge, commanding the Company, organised an immediate secondary attack under his own command, in order, if possible, to re-capture the missing officer and sergeant. The light had, however, by this time, become too strong, and the attack failed. Capt. Rabbidge and his two stretcher-bearers were both captured, but the German Officer in command of the post, with a courtesy seldom encountered, sent back the stretcher-bearers, with the body of the sergeant, to the Green Howard lines.

From November 7 to the 10th both Battalions were in Nijmegen resting and refitting for their next—and final—encounter with the enemy.

At 3 p.m. on November 10 the 6th Battalion, with the exception of " D " Company, which remained in Nijmegen for training, moved out across the road bridge towards Bemmel. The bridge and surrounding area was being heavily shelled. By 10.30 p.m. the Battalion had completed taking over from the 2nd Battalion, 508th Parachute Regiment, 101st American Airborne Division, in their positions about midway between Bemmel and Baal. Standing patrols were established in front of all company localities. Throughout the next day the enemy shelled and mortared the Battalion area, paying particular attention to the village of Bemmel and its church. On the 14th, " D " Company rejoined and relieved " A " Company. *6 Bn 10/27 Nov 44*

For the next fortnight the usual routine of trench warfare continued. On two occasions alarm was raised by the water rising in the dykes, once as much as three feet in one hour, but this was eventually ascribed to heavy rain during the night. At intervals large flashes were seen in the east, followed by a " noise in the air ", but it was noticed that the noise ceased at a point about a mile in front of the forward companies. These came from the V2 rockets, which, owing to their great speed, were to arrive in England unheralded by any sound until they exploded. During the last night in the line, that of November 26/27, " enemy spandaus were active, but caused no casualties ". At 8 p.m. the 6th Battalion was relieved by the 1st Battalion, Hampshire Regiment, and withdrew to rest billets in Nijmegen.

In the afternoon of November 10 the 7th Battalion, less " C " Company, left in Nijmegen for training, took over positions to the right of the 6th Green Howards, and about midway between Bemmel and Halderen. On the 13th " C " Company rejoined and relieved " D " Company, the latter returning to Nijmegen. *7 Bn 10/27 Nov 44*

A few minor clashes occurred during the next fortnight between patrols and enemy forward posts, and the Battalion snipers continued to do good work, but the record is mainly of spasmodic shelling and mortaring. In daylight, on the afternoon of November 27, the Battalion was relieved by the 2nd Battalion, The Devonshire Regiment, and went into billets in Nijmegen.

6 *and* 7 *Bns*   At 8 p.m. on November 28 the Green Howards left
28 *Nov* 44 Nijmegen, and, travelling by way of Alost, arrived at Roulers
during the afternoon of the 29th.   Here they were billeted in
the houses of a very friendly population.

It was now generally known that this was the end of the
fighting career of the 50th Division.   It had been decided
that the 21st Army Group should be reduced by one Division,
and the choice fell on the 50th Division.   In a letter to the
Divisional Commander Field-Marshal Montgomery said
that it was unthinkable that a Division with such a fine record
should lose its identity, and, therefore, it would become for
the time being a training division stationed at home.

Before leaving Roulers the task of dividing up the Battalions
into various categories had to be completed. A certain number
of men were to be posted direct to other units, the specialists
were to be sent to Northern Ireland to be trained as riflemen,
some men were to be sent to units doing garrison duties in
Europe, while the remainder were to return to England as the
nucleus of training battalions.

It was a difficult and somewhat heart-breaking task for
commanding officers, adjutants and company commanders.
In spite of the fact that during the course of the campaign
many old stagers had fallen by the way, and that quite a
number of those who were to be scattered far and wide had
not been wearing the Green Howard badge for very long, a
sense of comradeship had been inspired amongst the water-
logged positions in " The Island ".   Crouching together under
shellfire, or stealthily creeping forward on patrol in the
darkness, these men had seen death, and endured discomfort,
in each other's company, and when one has done that with a
companion, one does not part lightly from him.

Discipline, however, and the sense of duty, which had
sustained them through many a perilous hour, helped them
through this period of disintegration, and by December 12
all those who were leaving had gone their various ways.

6 *and* 7 *Bns*   On December 3 the Battalions held their last church parade
3/12 *Dec* 44 in Notre Dame in Roulers. The Divisional Commander and
the Brigade Commander came to say good-bye to those who
were leaving.   General Horrocks, commanding the 30th
Corps, sent a special message of good wishes for the future
ending with the words, " The T.T. boys will be much missed
by everyone."

At a parade on December 8 medal ribbons were presented
to Capt. W. Murray, M.C., R.S.M. P. Murphy, M.M., and
Cpl. J. McArthur, M.M., of the 7th Battalion.

At 7 a.m. on December 13 the cadres of the Battalions **6 and 7 Bns** left Roulers by train for Ostend, where they arrived soon after **13 Dec 44** 11 a.m. and embarked on H.M.T. *Lady of Man*, a ship which already knew the Green Howards, as she had evacuated the 6th Battalion from Dunkirk in 1940, and brought the 9th Battalion back from Lerwick to Newcastle in November, 1941.

Lt.-Col. D. R. Wilson said good-bye to his Battalion on the 12th, when he went off to command a battalion of the South Wales Borderers. Major J. M. Clift took command. Lt.-Col. Wilson wrote some time later : " . . . the atmosphere was oppressive, and it was a bitter blow to those who had come all the way from Alamein with the Division. I left the 7th Green Howards the day before they embarked at Ostend, and I was sad to leave such a loyal and courageous body of men."

The end is soon told. On December 14 they sailed up **6 and 7 Bns** Southampton Water, and disembarked at the spot from which **14/15 Dec 44** the Battalions had set forth with the great Armada the previous June. At 8.50 a.m. on December 15 they detrained at Malton, and two members of the Green Howard family were back in Yorkshire again.

The 6th Battalion went to Pickering, and the 7th to Scampston, and, after a period of leave, started their work of training recruits. At the end of the month Lt.-Col. F. F. S. Barlow, D.S.O. arrived to take over command of the 7th Battalion.

The young recruits who came to these Battalions were lucky, for they received more than mere technical training. What tales they must have heard in the barrack rooms, and the canteens ! Stories of Dunkirk, of Africa, Cyprus, Palestine, and Persia ; of the great days of the desert campaigns, when the men of Yorkshire and Durham stood up against Rommel ; of the epic battles of Mareth and Akarit, and Lt.-Col. Seagrim's Victoria Cross ; descriptions of the vineyards and olive groves of Sicily, of Mount Etna, and the voyage home by Malta, Algiers and Gibraltar : then of the landings on the beaches of Normandy, C.S.M. Hollis' Victoria Cross, the hidden dangers of the Bocage, and the victorious chase across France, Belgium and Holland—all these from the mouths of those who had been there, and who were proud to have enjoyed these experiences, endured the discomforts, and braved the dangers wearing the Green Howard Badge. Middlesbrough and Cleveland, Bridlington and Hull had good cause to be proud of their sons.

CHAPTER FOURTEEN

"THE 1st BATTALION FROM PALESTINE TO THE RIVER ELBE"

February—May 1945

1 Bn
26 Feb 45WHEN the 1st Battalion, Green Howards, sailed from Haifa on board H.M.T. *Highland Brigade* on February 26, 1945, the destination was Italy once more. The 5th Division had originally been ear-marked to return to the Italian theatre of war in December, 1944, and advance parties had been sent off during that month. The 1st Division, however, which had been ordered to relieve the 5th Division in its security role, had been diverted to Greece, and it was not until February, 1945, that the 5th Division could be relieved.

The 1st Battalion was now commanded by Lt.-Col. J. G. C. Waldron, O.B.E. (The Gloucestershire Regiment), with Major C. S. Scrope, M.C., as his second-in-command. The adjutant was Capt. J. B. Scott and the Quartermaster, Lt. E. D. Sleight. The Company Commanders were : " A " Company, Major P. J. Howell ; " B " Company, Major A. C. Blakley ; " C " Company, Major J. S. Bade, and " D " Company, Major A. T. Parkinson.

When the *Highland Brigade* arrived at Naples, much to the surprise of the Green Howards, they were informed that plans had been changed, and that the 5th Division was to join the British Liberation Army under General Eisenhower.
5 Mar/
16 April 45They remained on board the troopship accordingly, and sailed the next morning for Marseilles. There they disembarked, and, after spending two nights in a transit camp, entrained on March 5, and spent the next three days crossing France and Belgium, travelling by way of Lyons, Dijon, Chalons and Laon. On March 8 they detrained at Weteren, and went into billets at Schellebelle, and in neighbouring villages. There they spent the next few weeks, until April 16, in reorganisation and training, the main theme of the latter being the practice of " river crossing ".

Early in April all officers of the 5th Division were addressed by Field-Marshal Montgomery in Ghent. He informed them that he did not expect the war to end for a couple of months or so, and that the Division would shortly be moving up to the front to take part in the final operations.

On April 16 the Battalion moved off and, travelling partly 16/21 *Apr* 45 by road and partly by rail, through Brussels, Venlo, Geldern, Xanten, Borken and Osnabruck, arrived at a concentration area near Rabden. On the 20th it advanced again through Celle to Borne, where it arrived at 12.30 on the 21st. At 5 p.m. the same evening it moved again into forward positions in the vicinity of Grosse Thorndorf, a few miles south of the R. Elbe.

By this time the main German positions were on the north bank of the Elbe, but there were still a few isolated posts holding out on the south bank.

During the night of April 21/22 a German patrol attempted to enter Kettlestorf, which was held by " B " Company. The patrol was repulsed, and a corporal who had been wounded, was captured, together with fifteen other ranks.

On April 22 " C " Company made a raid on the village 22/28 *Apr* 45 of Ahndorf, with the object of " capturing " some German officers, who were suspected of being in hiding there. No officers were found, but three German W.A.A.F.s were " detained ". The precise distinction between " capturing " and " detaining " is interesting, and must be, presumably, attributed to the innate chivalry of the keeper of the War Diary towards the opposite sex.

Later in the day the Battalion marched to the area around Mucklingen, Headquarters, " B ", " C ", and the support companies taking up positions in Mucklingen itself, with " A " and " D " Companies in Suschendorf. The next few days were spent in patrolling and searching the surrounding villages and woods, in the course of which several more prisoners were taken, including two anti-aircraft officers of the Luftwaffe.

On April 27 it was found necessary, in order to maintain three rifle companies at the minimum fighting strength of five officers and a hundred and three other ranks, to cut down one Company. " A " Company was chosen for this purpose, and was reduced to two platoons.

On April 29 the Battalion moved to Hittenbergen, just 29/30 *Apr* 45 south of the Elbe. In the early hours of the 30th an assault was made across the Elbe, in front of the Green Howards, by the Commandos, the 15th (Scottish) Division, and the 6th (Airborne) Division. This attack was highly successful, and by 11 a.m. a bridgehead on the north bank of the river, some two thousand yards in depth, had been formed.

At this hour, 11 a.m., the 5th Division started forward to cross the river to enlarge the bridgehead.

The Green Howards crossed on a hastily constructed floating bridge at Lauenberg, and by one o'clock were concentrated behind troops of the 15th (Scottish) Division near Basedow, about a thousand yards north of the Elbe. Orders were then received for the Battalion to advance through the forward troops, and to capture two woods, some eight hundred yards in front, prior to an advance on Dahldorf.

Whilst Lt.-Col. Waldron was preparing his orders for the attack, Major Scrope led all the company commanders up to a forward observation post, and showed them their company objectives. This party was seen by the Germans and heavily shelled, but, fortunately, no casualties resulted.

The Commanding Officer then gave out his orders. The Battalion was to form up in Basedow, and the start line was to be a hedgerow immediately north of the village. The leading companies were " C " Company on the right and " B " Company on the left, with " A " and " D " Companies in reserve. The attack was to be supported by artillery and mortar fire, with machine-guns covering the south-east flank.

Whilst moving up to Basedow village the Battalion was shelled, and Major P. J. Howell (" A " Company) was seriously wounded.

The attack was launched at 6.30 p.m., and by 8 p.m. both the woods were in the hands of " B " and " C " Companies. Fairly strong opposition had been encountered and thirty-four prisoners were taken.

During this action L/Cpl. L. Miller of " C " Company led his section with great gallantry against a machine-gun post, which was dug in behind a mound in a hedgerow. Three of his men were killed, and two wounded, leaving L/Cpl. Miller alone, still about fifty yards short of the post. Single-handed, and firing his sten gun, he silenced the post, killing three Germans, whilst two more were taken prisoner. For his inspiring courage L/Cpl. Miller was awarded the Military Medal.

The Battalion then reorganised, and prepared to make a night attack on Dahldorf.

1 *May* 45   " D " Company led the attack, and, by 2.30 a.m. on May 1, had captured a wood, which lay on the line of approach. " B " and " C " Companies then passed through, and by 4 a.m. had captured Dahldorf against relatively slight opposition. Forty prisoners were taken in the village. Soon after daylight, the 1st Battalions of the K.O.Y.L.I. and the York and Lancaster Regiment, took up the advance, and, at 11 o'clock, the Green Howards moved forward to the village of Witzeeze, where it was accommodated in billets. It seemed improbable

that the Battalion would be required again that day, and so the men settled down to get some sleep after their activities of the previous night.

However, all had not gone too well in front, and at 5 p.m., Lt.-Col. Waldron was sent for to proceed to Brigade Headquarters. There he was informed that the 1st Battalion, K.O.Y.L.I., having successfully captured Poltau, was finding it impossible to advance further towards the important road, rail, and canal junction at Buchen. The Divisional Commander, Major-General R. A. Hull, had told the Brigadier that it was most important that Buchen should be captured before dark, as, until it was cleared, the advance of the remainder of the Division would be held up.

It later transpired that Buchen was being held by about two hundred German S.S. troops, who had orders, and were prepared, to fight to the last round and the last man. They had no artillery support, but possessed, in addition to their automatic weapons, several heavy mortars.

Lt.-Col Waldron received orders to make an immediate attack, to be launched at 8.45 p.m. There was no time for reconnaissance, but for this, the last attack of the war on this sector of the front, a terrific concentration of support fire was available. In addition to the fire of mortars and machine-guns, the enemy position in Buchen was subjected to the concentrated shelling of the 5th Divisional artillery, medium artillery from positions south of the Elbe, the artillery of the 6th (Airborne) Division on the right, and a squadron of tanks.

It is little wonder that the Green Howards, when they finally entered Buchen, found the majority of the survivors cowering in the cellars.

The Battalion plan of attack was for " D " Company on the right, and " B " Company on the left to assault and capture the town. " C " Company was then to pass through, and secure the far side of the railway yards.

The light was just beginning to fail when the leading companies crossed the start line. They soon encountered a river, which was deeper than had been anticipated, but the attack went according to plan, except that the wireless sets were put out of action by water in the crossing, and all communication had to be carried out by runner. By 9 p.m. all companies had captured their objectives, and about eighty prisoners had been taken.

" B " Company on the left suffered most casualties in this action, including the commander, Major Blakely, who was killed, and Capt. D. W. Gillespie, the 2nd I./C., and Lt. R. M. Briggs, who were wounded. As a result of these casualties C.S.M. C. Peacock was left in charge of the Company, before the objectives were actually taken. He first of all personally led the right hand forward platoon on to the objective, and then went back to Company Headquarters where the wounded officers were lying. He arranged for their evacuation, carrying one of them himself on his back to a position of safety. Throughout all this time snipers and well concealed machine-guns were bringing accurate fire to bear on all gaps between the buildings. The successful establishment of " B " Company was vital to the effective deployment of " C " Company. By his quick appreciation of the situation, his immediate assumption of control, and his personal initiative and courage, C.S.M. Peacock was largely instrumental in ensuring the success of the whole Battalion.

C.S.M. Peacock was awarded the Distinguished Conduct Medal, a fitting climax, on the last day of fighting, to a distinguished career with the 1st Battalion, during which he had won the Military Medal in Palestine (just before this story opens), the Norwegian Military Cross in the Battalion's first engagement at Otta in 1940, and had been mentioned in despatches.

The quick success of " D " Company in gaining its objective was largely due to the forceful and aggressive leadership of Major Parkinson, who was awarded the Military Cross. Major Parkinson had commanded a company in all the battles fought by the 1st Battalion, since it landed in Italy. He had always shown great bravery and devotion to duty, and his award was certainly well deserved.

" C " Company, in securing the objectives on the far side of the railway yards, also met with strong resistance, in the course of overcoming which, Pte. C. H. Loughren distinguished himself and won the Military Medal. When the Company was moving over an exposed piece of ground, it was held up by intense machine-gun fire from a house. Without hesitation, Pte. Loughren ran forward with his P.I.A.T., through close range fire, and, completely destroyed the post with one well aimed shot, killing the entire garrison.

The capture of Buchen virtually saw the end of the campaign, as the German Divisions on this sector of the front capitulated a day or so later. The Battalion then entered on a period of carrying out the various duties of an internal security roll, which included tackling the refugee problem, rounding up prisoners, and controlling canal and river crossings.

8 *May* 45   On May 8, at 3.30 p.m., the 5th Division held a ceremonial parade in Lubeck, at which the Union Jack was hoisted by the Divisional Commander, Major-General R. A. Hull. The

Green Howards were represented at this function by a party of fifty men, commanded by Major J. S. Bade, with Capt. J. B. Scott, Lt. G. H. Whittaker and C.S.M. C. Peacock, D.C.M., M.M.

And so ended another campaign of the 1st Battalion, The Green Howards, which had lasted for more than five and a half years. Although chance had not decreed that it should take part in the spectacular campaign in North Africa, or in the epic landings and battles of Normandy, the Battalion had added further laurels to the Regimental record in Norway, Sicily, Italy and finally in Germany itself.

CHAPTER FIFTEEN

" THE 2nd BATTALION IN INDIA AND BURMA "

1939—1945

THE story of the 2nd Battalion, Green Howards, during the war years can be divided conveniently into three parts. Firstly the period from September, 1939, to October, 1942, during which the Battalion remained on a peace footing, and was mainly employed in dealing with intermittent riots in India. Secondly the period from October, 1942, to December, 1943, which was spent at Razmak on the North-West Frontier, and thirdly, from September, 1944, when it left India to go to Arakan, where it took part in the coastal operations which led to the recapture of Rangoon in May, 1945, and whence it returned to India in July, 1945.

The intermediate months of 1944 were spent by the Battalion in Peshawar, and in May of that year, it moved to Ranchi, at which place, and later at Lohardaga, it underwent a course of training in jungle warfare, and made preparations for taking the field in Burma.

Sep 39/
Oct 42 Of the first period there is little to be written. In 1942, in particular, the riots were especially bad, and the Battalion played an active part in suppressing them, frequently having to open fire on the rioters.

The Battalion was at this time commanded by Lt.-Col. A. W. Hawkins, with Major J. S. G. Branscombe as his second in command, Capt. W. O. Walton as Adjutant, and Capt. (Q.M.) W. J. Lipscombe as Quartermaster.

During these years, and indeed up to the end of 1943, the Battalion was called upon to provide a very large number of officers, N.C.O.s and trained soldiers for extra regimental employment in India and Burma, and for drafting to the United Kingdom to train the new armies. Practically every officer, who was with the Battalion in September, 1939, was sent away at one time or another, with the exception of the four officers mentioned above, who were not allowed to leave. Their places were largely taken by volunteer and somewhat untrained men from the United Kingdom, who, when the time came, displayed the individual gallantry which was to be expected of them, and great powers of endurance under the trying conditions of jungle warfare. Continual change in command posts is, however, not good for morale, and, in addition, the Battalion was never, from the early days, up to full strength. In fact, when the Green Howards landed on Ramree Island, in January, 1945, the Battalion was less than five hundred strong, as compared with another British battalion, also in the landing, which mustered over one thousand men. These facts should be borne in mind when reading the account which follows of the actions of the 2nd Battalion.

At the end of October, 1942, the Battalion moved at *Oct* 42 seventy-two hours' notice from Jubblepore to Razmak, where it relieved the 2nd Battalion, King's Own Scottish Borderers. It was still on a peace scale. No mechanical transport was taken, and the Battalion reverted to the use of mule transport. The Green Howards had been rushed up into Wazirstan since they were the only British battalion in India at that time with recent experience of frontier warfare, having completed a successful tour of duty there in 1938. Except, however, for Lt.-Col. Hawkins, Capt. A. M. Jordan, Lt. J. F. Atkinson, and a few N.C.O.s, none of the battalion, as it was constituted by this time, had had any training whatever in mountain warfare. The remainder, however, soon learned and proved most efficient.

The force based on Razmak consisted of the 2nd Green Howards, a Gurkha Battalion, four Indian Battalions, and supporting arms. Its duties consisted of manning the frontier post, of supplying piquets on certain days on the hills covering a sector of the Bannu-Razmak road, and of forming columns, which went out from time to time into tribal territory, generally for a period of about ten days.

At this time Capt. A. W. Stansfeld was performing the duties of Adjutant, and the companies were commanded by Capts. Jordan, M. W. T. Roberts, Trinder, and N. Swan, the latter having his company, " D " Company, on detachment at Nagpur. The regimental sergeant-major was R.S.M. C. Scott. In December Capt. A. D. Mathewson took over " C " Company from Capt. Trinder.

Apart from a certain amount of sniping from the tribesmen into the camp, and when the troops were out on picquet duties, little of importance occurred during the first half of 1943. In May, Lt.-Col. Hawkins left the Battalion on appointment as G.S.O.1 at Simla, and Lt.-Col. W. O. Walton arrived to take over command.

The only actions of note, which occurred before the Battalion left the frontier for Peshawar on December 20, took place on June 6 and 7, when Capt. D. C. Siddall and twelve 6/7 *Jun* 43 men had a sharp encounter with a party of tribesmen near

Dosali, in which they inflicted casualties on the enemy without loss to themselves, and for which they received the congratulations of the Army Commander ; and a brief clash in

23 *Jun* 43 the hills on July 23, in which L/Cpl. G. Jackson was killed, and L/Cpl. C. V. Linney and Pte. F. Pattison won the Military Medal for rescuing wounded under fire.

20 *Dec* 43/
17 *Sep* 44 On December 20 the Battalion was relieved, and went to Peshawar, where it remained until moving to Ranchi in May, 1944. In July, 1944, it moved again to Lohardaga.

See MAP
No. 21 Although in this story we are only concerned with that period of the Burma campaign between September, 1944, and July, 1945, during which the Green Howards fought in Arakan, it is necessary to give a very brief account of the events which led up to the situation as they found it when they entered Burma. The Japanese first invaded Burma on January 10, 1942, and, by the end of May, 1942, had driven forward practically to the frontiers of Bengal, Assam and China. They then proceeded to consolidate their positions, and generally build up a firm base from which to launch an invasion of India. The allied armies, meanwhile, concentrated on securing their frontiers, and on making preparations for the ultimate recapture of Burma. Broadly speaking, the allied armies were on the defensive from the middle of 1942 until December, 1944, with the exception of Brigadier Wingate's long range penetration troops, who, supplied and reinforced by air, kept the offensive going, deep in the jungle of North Burma, within and behind the enemy's lines; and General Stilwell's northern army, which began to move forward from Ledo at the end of 1943.

In March, 1944, the Japanese struck in the central sector across the R. Chindwin, and began their " march on Delhi ". Advancing with great speed, they forced the allied troops on this sector back across the frontier, and, by April, had cut off the two main bases of Imphal and Kohima. For some time the situation was extremely perilous, but, reinforced and supplied by air, the defenders held on, and eventually struck back. Kohima was relieved in May, and, after further months of hard fighting, the enemy was finally cleared out of Manipur, and, by December, was in retreat.

Meanwhile, in the north, General Stilwell had started, towards the end of 1943, on his tremendous task of building a road from Ledo towards Myitkyina, and fighting his way forward at the same time. In March, 1944, a force of Brigadier Wingate's " Chindits ", consisting of 10,000 men and 1,000 pack animals, was flown over the mountains by night, and set down far behind the enemy lines across the Mandalay-Myitkyina railway line to the south-east of Myitkyina. Acting in co-operation, these forces recaptured Myitkyina on August 3, 1944. In the Arakan district, the 14th Indian Division counter-attacked in the autumn of 1942, but, in May, 1943, the 26th Indian Division, which had just relieved the 14th Indian Division, withdrew to positions in the area of Bawli Bazaar and Goppe Bazaar, and consolidated defence positions there.

It was to this area that the Green Howards moved when *17 Sep* 44 they left Lohardaga on September 17, 1944, as part of the 4th Indian Brigade, of the 26th Indian Division, the latter being commanded by Major-General C. E. N. Lomax, C.B.E., D.S.O., M.C. The Battalion, commanded by Lt.-Col. W. O. Walton, with Major C. E. B. Acland as second in command, arrived at Bawli Bazaar on September 23, and, during the *23/30 Sep* 44 night of September 29/30, moved up to Goppe Bazaar, taking over a sector of the perimeter defences, with " D " Company on detachment at Kyaundaung Bazaar. Intensive patrolling was the order of the day, and, on the night of October 5, *5/6 Oct* 44 three patrols went out, commanded respectively by Lts. W. C. Downie, K. C. McCarthy, and L. Ward. The latter was accompanied by a Canadian officer, Lt. Trites, who had joined the Battalion on October 1. Early on the morning of October 6 a wireless message was received from Lt. McCarthy to the effect that a large force of Japanese had passed him going in the direction of Goppe. At about 8 a.m. the Japanese, estimated to be about five hundred strong, advanced against Goppe in close formations, supported by mortar fire and grenades. The Green Howard mortar platoon, under Capt. N. Botham, broke the back of the attack and, although fighting continued all the morning, the enemy was completely routed, and suffered severe casualties from Bren gun and rifle fire.

The Battalion suffered some casualties, including Lt.-Col. Walton, who was slightly wounded but not evacuated, and Lt. W. M. H. Green, whose leg was shattered.

The trench, in which Lt. Green lay wounded, was in an exposed position, and under enemy fire. Sgt. T. E. Storey, who was in charge of the stretcher bearers, went forward without hesitation across the bullet swept ground, dressed Lt. Green's wounds, and carried him back to safety. For this action, and for continuous devotion to duty in bringing in wounded men from outside the perimeter, Sgt. Storey was awarded the Military Medal.

While this action was in progress the three fighting patrols *7/8 Oct* 44 were still out in the jungle. Lt. Downie made his way through to join " D " Company at Kyaungdaung, while Lt. McCarthy brought his patrol safely back to Goppe on October 7.

z

Lt. Ward's patrol, however, was not so lucky, and fell into an ambush as it was returning to the Battalion lines. Lt. Ward, Sgt. Turner and two other members of the patrol were killed, while Lt. Trites was seriously wounded. The latter officer, assisted by Pte. Chamberlain, found cover very close to the enemy, and, after lying up for two days, came in safely on October 8.

It was discovered later that, in this action, four Japanese companies had made the attack on Goppe, and that at least two hundred of them had been killed.

3 *Nov* 44/
16 *Jan* 45

For the remainder of the month the Green Howards kept up their patrolling activities, until, on November 3, they were relieved and withdrew to Colaba, the Divisional rest area. At the beginning of December they moved to Nidania, where they remained until January 16, 1945, when they left for Chittagong to embark for operations on Ramree Island.

During this period Lt. E. Hudson took over the duties of Adjutant, and Major K. Y. Hewitson took over " B " Company from Major H. J. Clifford. R.S.M. Jessamine also left the Battalion at about this time on repatriation, and was succeeded by R.S.M. Ashmore.

On January 12, 1945, Major Acland left the Battalion on promotion and, on the 15th, Major G. Herbert joined as second in command.

While at Colaba, and later at Nidania, the Green Howards underwent intensive training in combined operations.

Early in December, 1944, the allied armies took up the offensive on all fronts. In the north American and Chinese forces, and the British 36th Division, advanced on Katha and Lashio, and so towards Mandalay from the north-east. In the centre the 4th and 33rd Corps crossed the R. Chindwin, and, fighting their way across the central plains of Burma, recaptured Mandalay on March 20, 1945. In Arakan the 15th Corps launched its attack on December 10, 1944, towards Akyab. This attack was designed to secure the airfields in Arakan, which the enemy had been using to threaten Calcutta, and the possession of which would enable the allied air forces to bomb Rangoon, and the Japanese lines of communications from Mandalay back into Siam and Malaya. It was also essential to secure Arakan as a supply base for the 4th and 33rd Corps in their advance from Mandalay on Rangoon.

While the remainder of the 15th Corps, which had secured Akyab on January 3, 1945, was still fighting its way down the coastal strip towards An and Ru-ywa, an assault landing from the sea was made on Ramree Island by the 26th Indian Division on January 21.

The Green Howards embarked on the S.S. *Nevassa* at 16/31 *Jan* 45 Chittagong on January 16, and, sailing with the invasion fleet, arrived off Kyaukpyu in the early hours of January 21. Under the powerful support of the battleship *Queen Elizabeth*, four cruisers, four destroyers, four sloops, and a cloud of Thunderbolts, Hurricanes, Hurribombers, Liberators, Mitchells, Lightnings and Seasprites, the 71st Indian Brigade landed at about 9.30 a.m. There was practically no opposition, and the second wave of the assault, the 4th Indian Brigade, began to land at about 4 o'clock in the afternoon. The Green Howards, on landing, pushed on through Kyaukpyu, and took up positions south of the town. On the 24th they marched to Minbyin, where they took up perimeter defences, and sent out patrols.

The Battalion was now spread out over a very wide front, with companies acting independently, searching for individuals, or small parties of the disintegrated Japanese garrison of the island. The majority of these, however, had tried to escape to the mainland, and those of their boats, which were not sunk by the Navy or by aircraft, drifted into the swamps, where their occupants, without food or water, met a terrible death from scorpions and crocodiles, drowning, hunger or thirst.

On February 1 the Green Howards moved forward a 1/14 *Feb* 45 further ten miles to the neighbourhood of Sane, and later to Kondwbe.

On February 14 Tactical Headquarters, with " C " and 14/26 *Feb* 45 " D " Companies, made an unopposed landing on the Kalabon peninsula on the mainland, some six miles across the water.

On the night of February 26/27 the Green Howards were 26 *Feb*/ relieved by the 1st Battalion, Lincolnshire Regiment, and 12 *Mar* 45 moved back to Gonchwein at the northern end of Ramree Island.

On March 12 the Battalion embarked once more at 12 *Mar* 45 Kyaukpyu for the mainland, with the objective of continuing the advance southwards through Taungup, which had become the main Japanese base in Arakan. At dawn on March 13 the Green Howards transferred to assault craft, and, proceeding up the Kaleindaung River, entered the Ma-i Chaung. The chaungs of Burma are tidal waterways running circuitous courses for miles inland between mango swamps, and, in defence, were a sniper's paradise.

This voyage of the Green Howards was a hair-raising experience as there was very little information regarding the enemy's dispositions, and it had been learned from the inhabitants that the Japanese had two or three 75 mm. guns covering the chaung, and they expected to be ambushed at any moment. All went well, however, and, at about 9.30 a.m., the Battalion made an unopposed landing on the north bank at Pyin-Wan, and, pushing through the village, took up 12/25 *Mar* 45 pre-arranged positions inland covering the beachhead. For the next twelve days the Battalion remained in this vicinity as lines of communication troops, while other units took up the southward drive, but, on March 25, the Green Howards began to move, being now on the south side of Ma I Chaung.

1 *Apr* 45 Pushing south along the Taungup road they met little opposition until, on April 1, they reached a position some four miles north of Taungup, where a patrol of " B " Company, on coming into the open, was met by machine-gun fire. " B " Company took up positions astride the road for the night, and the next morning " C " Company, supported by tanks and machine-guns, made an assault on the enemy position, but was repulsed by heavy fire from strong positions on the 2/4 *Apr* 45 hill. The following morning " D " Company, Major D. C. Siddall, reinforced " C " Company in a further attack, and the enemy was driven back. In this fierce encounter Lt. T. Evans, Cpl. Church, and several men were killed, while amongst those who were wounded or died of wounds was Cpl. Lacey.

Major Siddall, during the ascent of the hill to the enemy's positions, fell and broke his shoulder, and Capt. J. R. Allen took over command of " D " Company.

With " A " and " B " Companies in the lead, the Battalion then pushed on to within two miles of Taungup. A patrol under Lt. A. H. M. Scott had a successful skirmish with the enemy, in which six Japanese were killed, and Lt. Scott was slightly wounded.

The Battalion now dug itself in, as there was considerable shelling activity.

5 *Apr* 45 On April 5 the enemy launched a counter-attack which, in its initial phases, overran a platoon of " D " Company. The battle went on all night, and " D " Company, very ably commanded by Capt. Allen, held on until its ammunition was 6/16 *Apr* 45 exhausted, and it was forced to withdraw at dawn on April 6. Later the same morning, however, with support from tanks, " D " Company counter-attacked, and regained its positions. Lt. F. Parrott was killed, while gallantly leading this counter-attack, and the company also lost six other ranks killed, and seven wounded.

For the next few days the companies held on to their

positions under intermittent shell fire. On April 8 Capt. N. Botham received shrapnel wounds from which he died five days later.

On April 17 the Battalion moved to Kyetkaing, and came under command of the 82nd West African Division. *17/27 Apr 45*

On April 28 the Battalion moved south through Taungup, and began patrolling along the road to Prome. Small enemy parties were seen, and a certain amount of shelling experienced, but no casualties were sustained by the Green Howards. The enemy had, in fact, by this time, ceased to put up any organised resistance, and, on May 2, troops of the 33rd Corps, moving down from Meiktila, entered Prome. *28/30 Apl 45*

On May 1 Lt.-Col. Walton left the Battalion for another appointment, and was succeeded in command by Lt.-Col. G. Philpots Green, of the York and Lancaster Regiment. *1 May 45*

On May 4 the Green Howards turned towards the sea once more, and marched to Sandoway, arriving there on May 10. Here they remained until June 27, when they left for Ramree Island, disembarking at Kyaukpyu on June 28. *4 May/ 28 Jun 45*

On July 12 they embarked once more on the S.S. *Nevassa* and sailed to Madras. On July 27 they arrived at Meerut, where, on August 16, they celebrated V.J. Day. *12/27 Jul 45*

Owing to the fact that they only arrived in Burma for the tail end of the campaign, the 2nd Battalion did not have an opportunity of taking part in any major action. In addition to Sgt. Storey, who received the Military Medal, Major K. Y. Hewitson and Sgt. Casey were mentioned in despatches.

Several officers and men, however, who were originally in the 2nd Battalion, Green Howards, and who left to fight with other units in the earlier stages of the Burma campaign, gained distinction in battle, including Lt. W. B. Weston, who won the Victoria Cross. Their actions do not come within the scope of this story, but their names will be found on the Roll of Honour.

The dangers and discomforts of war, however, are not all attributable to the enemy, and, in fairness to those Green Howards who spent months in the malaria ridden swamps of Arakan, it must be recorded that the conditions under which they lived, and fought, were appalling. The weather, just before the breaking of the Monsoon, was terribly hot, and the water problem was acute. The chaungs amongst which they spent much of their time, were tidal, and the only source of " fresh " water was a dirty brackish liquid obtained from holes dug in the lowest lying areas. They had to wash, shave, and wash out socks in rather less than half a mess tin of water. Thousands of salt tablets were consumed as an antidote to heat exhaustion, while mepacrine tablets, as an anti-malarial precaution, were administered personally to every man by an officer.

When it is remembered that the Battalion was never at more than half strength, and that, in addition to the climatic conditions under which they lived, the Green Howards were fighting a ruthless, savage and uncivilised enemy in country extremely favourable to ambushes and sniping activities the Regiment should be proud of the manner in which *esprit de corps* and discipline were maintained throughout the campaign.

CHAPTER SIXTEEN

THE REGIMENTAL DEPOT

THE story of the Green Howards during the war years cannot be complete without reference to the Depot at Richmond. This story opened at Richmond and it is fitting that it should close there.

It was at The Barracks, the Green Howards' Depot, that officers and men received their first training for war, learnt discipline, and the history and traditions of their Regiment, and became imbued with the *esprit de corps*, which was to stand them in such good stead when they took their places in the fighting battalions.

The Green Howards first came to Richmond in 1873, when the Barracks were being built on the top of Richmond Hill, more familiarly known as " the bank ". From then onwards Richmond has been the home of the Regiment in every sense of the word.

To Richmond and these Barracks, so steeped in Regimental pride and interest, men have come from every part of the North Riding and from the boundaries beyond, from the dales and the wolds, from the towns, the boroughs and the villages. There can scarcely be a single community which has not produced either a son, brother or husband to serve in its County Regiment.

Indeed the Regiment is a large county family, supported in no uncertain way with an intense interest and pride by the whole North Riding, an interest which has found expression in many deeds of generosity and friendliness.

At the Depot one is made very aware of the strong bonds of affection between County and Regiment, which, combined with the setting, atmosphere, and visible signs of past glory and tradition, produce a spirit of comradeship strong enough to endure and triumph over discomfort or disaster.

Richmond is also the true spiritual home of the Regiment. Therein lies the lovely old twelfth century Parish Church of St. Mary's, standing in a commanding position on the hillside overlooking the Swale, and containing the Green Howards Memorial Chapel. It is in this Church that so many Green Howards have prayed and dedicated themselves before going out to battle.

County interest has been expressed by the granting to the Regiment of the Freedom of the Boroughs of Middlesbrough,

Bridlington, Beverley and Scarborough, which confers the ancient right to march through the streets with colours flying, bands playing and bayonets fixed. The illuminated addresses marking these occasions are a source of pride, and are to be found in the Officers Mess at the Depot.

It is a matter of historical interest, however, that the Regiment does not officially enjoy the Freedom of the Borough of Richmond, although this honour and distinction was conferred upon their Colonel-in-Chief, Haakon VII, King of Norway, in January, 1945. The reason for this apparent omission is that, when the matter was being considered in Council by Richmond Borough, it was decided that : " there was no purport in conferring upon its Regiment a privilege which it had freely enjoyed for more than seventy years ".

The Depot also houses the Regimental Museum which, with all its relics, souvenirs and trophies of past campaigns, and sentimental treasures beyond all price, is a source of interest and inspiration to soldiers both young and old.

Such, in brief, is the background of the Regimental Depot.

When war broke out in September, 1939, it was carrying out its normal function of training volunteer regular recruits and militiamen for the 1st and 2nd Battalions, under the command of Major A. E. I. Belcher, M.C., but on mobilisation he handed over to Lt.-Col. B. V. Ramsden, a retired officer, who remained in command until July, 1944, when he was succeeded by Lt.-Col. C. E. Brockhurst, M.C. In June, 1945, the latter officer handed over to Lt.-Col. C. W. D. Chads.

When Lt.-Col. Ramsden arrived the Depot was furnished to accommodate 350 all ranks, and he was informed that he would shortly be receiving up to 2,000 men, with an unpredictable proportion of officers, N.C.O.s and men of all ages. At the same time the title of the Depot was changed to The Infantry Training Centre, The Green Howards, the I.T.C. as it was generally known, although some still clung to the good old word Depot.

During 1939 No. 40 Company, North Riding A.T.S., reported for duty as clerks, storewomen, waitresses and cooks, to form part of the permanent staff. In those days woman soldiers were something new at the Depot, an innovation breaking with the long traditions of the past, which was at first looked upon somewhat askance. However, they soon made their presence felt, taking over their many tasks with great efficiency, thereby releasing men for fighting, and they soon became a very welcome part of the Depot life, voluntarily adopting the pride, *esprit de corps* and badge of the Regiment as their own personal concern.

Beyond the duty of receiving and training recruits, and of providing N.C.O.s, there were no definite instructions at that time, and the I.T.C. Commander was left a fairly free hand to do what he thought best. Later a spate of official guidance corrected, or otherwise, this state of affairs.

One of the major problems at the time was that of accommodation. It was not until 1942 that a satellite camp was thrown up at Gallowgate, the most exposed site possible in the neighbourhood. The words " thrown up " are used with intention, as it has never been a camp of particularly happy memories for the occupants, especially in winter.

To deal with the surge of recalled reservists and new recruits it was necessary to resort to billeting, for which purpose Richmond was not very well provided with buildings of a suitable size. Many men will no doubt have grim memories of Castle dungeons, barns, lofts, wynds, and the old mill along the Reeth road during that bitter winter of 1939-40 ; although others perhaps may have happier memories of Aske, Brough Hall and Oglethorpe House, the last of which later became a second Officers' Mess.

The I.T.C. was very lucky in one way. It was in a peaceful situation far from any industrial centre. The sights and sounds of war seldom penetrated to Richmond, and this may have been a determining factor in its survival at a time when the I.T.C.s of many other regiments were disbanded. Such a fate befell the East Yorkshire Regiment I.T.C. at Beverley, which, after a heavy air raid in 1941, was amalgamated with the Green Howards at Richmond. The Green Howards I.T.C. was designated No. 5 I.T.C., and from that time on served both Regiments.

Richmond had better facilities than most training centres, with plenty of open country and an eight target rifle range at Aislabeck, which, although ricochets sped over the Marske road, was an invaluable adjunct, and deemed safe enough for war time needs.

No. 5 I.T.C. was organised into sufficient recruit companies to meet the requirements of both Regiments, and the training period varied between twelve and sixteen weeks, before the recruits were drafted to Battalions, or, later on, to certain holding units.

Originally each Regiment provided the staff for its own recruit companies, but later on the staffs were amicably and efficiently mixed.

The normal fortnightly intake and output of recruits was about 270 for each Regiment. For a Regiment with five battalions in the field this number seemed strangely inadequate even in 1939, but, when the real fighting began in 1940, it was even more so. At this time recruits were actually despatched to battalions of their own regiment, in striking contrast to later procedure.

Quite early on the Stables of Aske Hall, the home of the Lord Lieutenant of the North Riding—Lord Zetland—were taken over, and converted into a company detachment for the training of specialists. The I.T.C. also set up its own Cookery School there, with S/Sgt. Hurley and Sgt. Dunkley as instructors, with the object of replacing casualties amongst Battalion cooks at the time of Dunkirk. This later developed into an Emergency Cookery Training Centre, where large numbers of cooks of both sexes were trained. Much of the work of conversion into suitable premises was undertaken by the I.T.C. Pioneers, under Major T. K. Bower—an invaluable body of men composed of masons, bricklayers, carpenters, plumbers and painters, which took everything in its stride.

Under the expansion scheme on mobilisation battalions were supposed to send some of their best Warrant Officers and N.C.O.s to the Depot, to assist the I.T.C. in training recruits. This procedure placed an unenviable onus on Commanding Officers, whose primary interest was the efficiency of their own units. In order to avoid the necessity of fighting battalions being stripped of their best N.C.O.s, No. 5 I.T.C. started a succession of N.C.O. Training Cadres, which produced many men, who were to distinguish themselves later on. Many young officers and N.C.O.s owe a great debt of gratitude to R.S.M. A. Richardson, who was primarily responsible for teaching them their duties and inspiring them with discipline. His outstanding leadership was infectious, and, although the lessons were learnt in a hard practical school, they proved lasting and invaluable in many theatres of war.

During 1942 and 1943 the total strength of the I.T.C. at times exceeded 3,000, excluding training companies of the A.T.S. which began to arrive at the Depot in 1942.

These A.T.S. companies took possession of the Howard and Hulse Blocks, ousting the soldiers to Gallowgate Camp, but thereby ensuring certain modern equipment in the barrack blocks not normally found in soldiers quarters. They remained for about a year, when, on reorganisation of the A.T.S., they disappeared to their own Training Depots, leaving behind the female members of the permanent staff, who remained until demobilisation.

In the summer of 1942 there was an alteration of Army organisation, when the General Service Scheme came into operation. Under this scheme all recruits were put through a Primary Training period of six weeks, during which they underwent basic training in drill, weapons, field craft and discipline, regardless of the arm of the service for which they were destined. They were also subjected to " personnel selection " by a specially trained team of the " Personnel Selection Staff ", in order to ascertain for what type of work each recruit was best fitted, so that he could be posted to the arm of the Service most suitable to his natural bent.

The I.T.C. now took on the additional duties of a Primary Training Centre, with a fortnightly intake of three hundred general service recruits.

With the exception of those who had enlisted voluntarily prior to being called up, or who had strong family or territorial claims for a certain regiment or branch of the Service, the recruits had little say in the matter, and at the end of six weeks were despatched to the Corps Training Centres of their future units for the next stage of training.

Once a fortnight the Green Howards and the East Yorkshires received about thirty men each from the Primary Training Companies, and these, after being given their regimental badges, were posted to Infantry Training Companies for a further ten weeks training. After this period they were normally drafted to Home Service Battalions of their own Regiment for final polish. In the case of the Green Howards the 11th Battalion carried out this function.

In 1943, however, this excellent system was changed for one less satisfactory. Army Group Pools were formed whereby there was no guarantee that the recruit, who left Richmond proudly wearing the Green Howard badge and full of his own Regimental pride, would ever join a Green Howard battalion. This system was very unpopular and often meant that a man had to serve and fight as a stranger among strangers.

Some of these men died, some were wounded, while others gained distinction in battle, but, although they were still Green Howards at heart, it has been impossible to tell their stories in this book, so widely scattered were they throughout the many regiments of the British Army.

Whatever was to be the destiny of the men who passed through their hands, however, the permanent staff of the Depot went on year after year with unflagging energy, welcoming, training, and supervising the welfare of those under their temporary charge. Many officers, N.C.O.s and old soldiers, who were not considered fit for the fighting line, spent those years repeating over and over again to each fresh batch of recruits the primary lessons of military citizenship, and, above all, imbuing them with the traditions of the Green Howards.

To each new squad, platoon or company, they managed to impart the same enthusiasm as they had given at the beginning. It was no easy task to maintain interest for so long in what must have become a monotonous form of life, far away from the limelight and excitement of war, and the Regiment owes these men a great debt of gratitude.

They are entitled to a share of the reflected glory from the deeds chronicled in these pages. It is obviously impossible to mention all their names, but, in addition to those of the Commanding Officer and the Regimental Sergeant Major, already referred to, no story of the Depot at Richmond could be complete without paying a tribute to Major H. W. Ibbetson.

Throughout the pages of this book the use of nicknames, with very rare exceptions, has been purposely avoided, but a further exception must be made in the case of Major Ibbetson, so affectionately known as " Musso " by thousands of Green Howards. Throughout the war years " Musso " looked after the comfort and well being of all those who passed through Richmond Barracks or Gallowgate Camp, a task which covered a multitude of functions too numerous to be listed here. His personal interest in each individual, in their families, and in any subject affecting the well being of the regiment are well known. It is probable that there is no one alive today who knows so many Green Howards personally, or so much about the Regiment. He is, happily, still carrying on what he has made his life's work, and now helps to administer, under the Regimental Council, the Green Howards Association and the Benevolent Fund. The latter Fund grew out of the Regimental Comforts Fund, later including the Prisoners of War Fund, which was started by Mrs. Belcher at the beginning of the war. With the able assistance of Sgt. Woodall, later a Councillor of Richmond, the fund prospered exceedingly. In the summer of 1944 its administration was taken over by Capt. H. E. Thornton, M.C., another prominent citizen of Richmond, and at one time the monthly subscriptions amounted to nearly £800. Members of the Green Howards Battalions of the Home Guard were very generous donors to the Fund, and were actually responsible for raising more than £20,000. With so much money available the Depot was a byword in prison camps everywhere, and considered second only to the British Red Cross.

The number of clothing parcels despatched to Prisoners of War was, 7,395 ; Cigarettes ordered for Prisoners of War, 3,887,710 ; Tobacco ordered for Prisoners of War, 3,779 lb. ; Wool knitted by voluntary workers exceeded, 1¼ tons. The Value of Stores purchased (1942-1945) was, £20,096 11s. 4d.

A great debt of gratitude is due to the small band of tireless workers for their wonderful efforts. In the end the handsome sum of more than £17,000 was subsequently transferred to the Regimental Benevolent Fund.

In addition to the training of recruits, the I.T.C. had many other duties to perform, including the provision of guards for the satellite aerodromes, which were being opened up alongside the Great North Road, and of mobile columns to take their place in local defence schemes. The garrison at Catterick Camp also called frequently on the I.T.C. for troops to take part in training exercises, and the role of the Green Howards ranged from the perimeter defence of Richmond to counter-attacking trained parachutists, who were alleged to have captured neighbouring aerodromes. There were also various A.R.P. schemes for Richmond, in which the I.T.C. played its part.

The training of the Home Guard Battalions, of which there were thirteen, became another partial responsibility of the I.T.C., and involved considerable activity in the evenings, and at weekends particularly so far as adjacent battalions were concerned. In addition, various courses were continually in operation. This imposed a considerable strain on the I.T.C. instructors, but the time spent with the Home Guard was never grudged, in fact it was generally well enjoyed in the company of men so eager to learn and to become proficient in their particular role. The spirit of the Regiment was absorbed with splendid enthusiasm, and the Home Guard became an integral part of the Regiment, and such help as was forthcoming from the I.T.C. was amply reciprocated by the magnificent generosity of all units to the Prisoners of War Fund, which was saved thereby from any financial embarrassment that might have arisen in those critical days in 1942. At the end of the War all units of the North Riding of Yorkshire Home Guard joined together in making a presentation to the Officers' Mess of an antique writing desk, and of a silver rose-bowl to the Sergeants' Mess.

Amidst all these activities engendered by War the Depot never forgot its responsibilities for keeping up, as far as possible, the amenities of peace time. The Green Howards Gazette was published throughout the war, and, owing to the ever-changing and varied population of the Depot, there was an unusual amount of talent available, and the paper probably saw its best days during the war years.

The playing fields were kept up and enlarged, and, subject to the increased hours of work, games and sports were enjoyed with the same keenness as in peace time.

Throughout the war years the shooting and fishing along the Skeeby valley were a great solace to many officers and men. Barely fifteen minutes' walk from the barracks, it was possible to snatch an hour's sport there at any time, and to get away from the atmosphere of war and all its preparations.

Another very important function carried out by the I.T.C. was the reincarnation of the skeleton band of the 1st Battalion, which had been left behind at the Depot when the Battalion went overseas in 1939. Early in 1940 Bandmaster R. Lester began collecting recruit and reservist musicians, and by the end of the war the Band was well up to pre-war standards, and was rewarded by a tour of Germany after the cessation of hostilities.

The band of the East Yorkshires paid periodical visits to Richmond, and the spectacle of the combined bands marching through the town to the Parish Church on Sundays, and beating Retreat together, was one which the townspeople will not easily forget.

Between 1939 and 1945 the Depot received numerous distinguished visitors, the chief of whom were their Majesties the King and Queen, who honoured the Regiment with a visit in August, 1940. After inspecting the troops and the barracks, their Majesties took tea in the Officers' Mess. The two dining room chairs, which they used, have now been suitably inscribed, and form a unique memento of their visit.

Next in order of importance was the visit paid by H.M. King Haakon of Norway, Colonel-in-Chief of the Regiment. He came up to Richmond in August, 1943, and displayed an interest in every phase of regimental life which greatly impressed all who came in contact with him. When he left he presented the Officers' Mess with a magnificent silver bowl. On a later visit in January, 1945, King Haakon was presented with the Freedom of Richmond.

As Commandant of the A.T.S. the Princess Royal paid more than one visit to the I.T.C. from her neighbouring home at Harewood.

The Memorial to those of the Regiment who gave their lives during the years of battle, which have been related in these chapters, is concentrated in the Regimental Memorial Chapel in the Parish Church of St. Mary's at Richmond.

The Chapel itself is a fine example of beautiful simplicity, and is situated to the South of the Chancel. The restoration of the Chapel formed part of the Regiment's Memorial for the 1914/1918 War, and involved excavating to a depth of three and a half feet to reach the original floor level, and uncover the thirteenth century Sedilia, Piscina and Aumbry.

The new floor, steps and screen are all in Yorkshire stone with the altar in Hopton Wood stone. To the north side of the altar a shrine let in to the wall contains the Roll of Honour Book of the 1914/1918 War. Along the whole length of the north wall there is a panelled screen dedicated " In Memory of Queen Alexandra, Colonel-in-Chief of the Regiment 1914-1925 ", with, emblazoned in the centre, Her Majesty's Coat of Arms. Across the entrance on the west side is a carved screen in English oak in memory of a former Rector, and acting Chaplain to the Regiment, Canon Neville Egerton Leigh.

In the angle of the walls above the Altar are the oldest of the colours carried by the Regiment—the Crimea colours carried by the 1st Battalion at the battle of the Alma (where the bearer of the Regimental Colour, Ensign Stockwell, was killed), and at the battle of Inkerman. This was the last occasion when Colours were carried in battle by the 19th Foot.

On either side, on the north and south walls, hang the old Colours of the Regiment since the Crimea War.

Beautiful as the Chapel was, it was incomplete, especially above the altar. The Memorial to this War has been devoted to adding to the Chapel. Over the altar has been added a carved oak reredos of somewhat unusual design, to fit the large shallow space available. The theme of the design was conceived by the then Depot Commander, Lt.-Col. C. W. D. Chads, and drawn by his Adjutant, Capt. J. B. Oldfield. The figures were sketched from life, all being Green Howards. It purports to depict a group of soldiers moving across the panorama of any battlefield and engaged upon their lawful occasions ; a very normal group which might be met anywhere during the war, but without depicting the horrors of war. The centre and focus of the scene is the figure of Christ on the Cross—a silent reminder that only in the light of His Supreme Sacrifice can our lesser sacrifices be of any avail.

The work has been exquisitely carved in English oak, in three-quarter relief, by Robert Thompson of Kilburn, who also made the screen and Chapel chairs.

In addition, another shrine has been added on the other side of the Altar to hold the new Roll of Honour and Book of Remembrance for those who gave their lives in this War. The stone panelling of the north wall has also been reproduced on the south wall, and the Battle Honours carved in gold in the panels of the Queen Alexandra Memorial. All that now remains to be done is to add the Battle Honours of this War, when decided, to the panels of the south wall.

The Reredos, the Shrine, the Roll of Honour and Book of Remembrance, and the stone screen were Dedicated by His Grace the Lord Archbishop of York at a most impressive Service on Sunday, September 19, 1948. The Roll of Honour and Book of Remembrance was received by the Rector, The Rev. Stuart MacPherson, from the Colonel of the Regiment, General Sir Harold Franklyn, K.C.B., D.S.O., M.C.

Since then, on every Sunday, before beginning the morning Service, a special prayer for the Regiment is said on the Chapel steps, and one page of one of the Books of the Roll of Honour is turned.

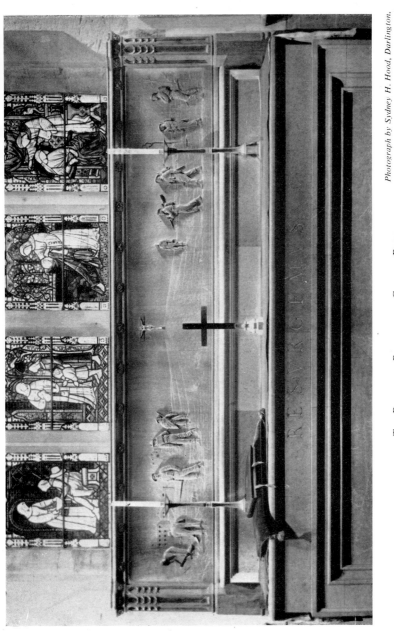

The REREDOS—REGIMENTAL CHAPEL, RICHMOND.

Photograph by Sydney H. Hood, Darlington.

Face page 384

APPENDIX 1

CITATION OF V.C's

No. 4390973 W.O. Class II (Company Sergeant Major)
STANLEY ELTON HOLLIS

In Normandy on 6th June, 1944, during the assault on the
beaches and the Mont Fleury battery, C.S.M. Hollis's Company
Commander noticed that two of the pill-boxes had been by-passed
and went with C.S.M. Hollis to see that they were clear. When they
were 20 yards from the pill-box, a machine-gun opened fire from the
slit and C.S.M. Hollis instantly rushed straight at the pill-box,
recharged his magazine, threw a grenade in through the door and
fired his Sten gun into it killing two Germans and making the
remainder prisoner. He then cleared several Germans from a
neighbouring trench. By his action he undoubtedly saved his
Company from being fired on heavily from the rear and enabled
them to open the main beach exit.

Later the same day in the village of Crepon the Company
encountered a field gun and crew armed with Spandaus at 100 yards
range. C.S.M. Hollis was put in command of a party to cover an
attack on the gun but the movement was held up. Seeing this,
C.S.M. Hollis pushed right forward to engage the gun with a
P.I.A.T. from a house at 50 yards range. He was observed by a
sniper who fired and grazed his right cheek and at the same moment
the gun swung round and fired at point blank range into the house.
To avoid the falling masonry C.S.M. Hollis moved his party to an
alternative position. Two of the enemy gun crew had by this time
been killed and the gun was destroyed shortly afterwards. He later
found that two of his men had stayed behind in the house and
immediately volunteered to get them out. In full view of the enemy
who were continually firing at him he went forward alone using a
Bren gun to distract their attention from the other men. Under
cover of his diversion, the two men were able to get back.

Wherever fighting was heaviest C.S.M. Hollis appeared and in the course of a magnificent day's work he displayed the utmost gallantry and on two separate occasions his courage and initiative prevented the enemy from holding up the advance at critical stages.

It was largely through his heroism and resource that the Company's objectives were gained and casualties were not heavier and by his own bravery he saved the lives of many of his men.

Major (Temp. Lieutenant Colonel) DEREK ANTHONY SEAGRIM
(26914)

On the night of the 20/21st March, 1943, the task of a battalion of The Green Howards was to attack and capture an important feature on the left flank of the main attack on the Mareth Line. The defence of this feature was very strong and it was protected by an anti-tank ditch twelve feet wide and eight feet deep with minefields on both sides. It formed a new part of the main defences of the Mareth Line and the successful capture of this feature was vital to the success of the main attack.

From the time the attack was launched the battalion was subjected to the most intense fire from artillery, machine-guns and mortars and it appeared more than probable that the battalion would be held up entailing failure of the main attack.

Realising the seriousness of the situation, Lieutenant Colonel Seagrim placed himself at the head of his battalion which was at the time suffering heavy casualties and led it through the hail of fire. He personally helped the team which was placing the scaling ladder over the anti-tank ditch and was himself the first to cross it. He led the assault firing his pistol, throwing grenades, and personally assaulting two machine-gun posts which were holding up the advance of one of his companies. It is estimated that in this phase he killed or captured twenty Germans. This display of leadership and personal courage led directly to the capture of the objective. When dawn broke the battalion was firmly established on the position which was of obvious importance to the enemy, who immediately made every effort to regain it. Every post was mortared and machine-gunned unmercifully and movement became practically impossible, but Lieutenant Colonel Seagrim was quite undeterred. He moved from post to post organising and directing the fire until the attackers were wiped out to a man.

By his valour, disregard for personal safety and outstanding example, he so inspired his men that the battalion successfully took and held its objective thereby allowing the attack to proceed. Lieutenant Colonel Seagrim subsequently died of wounds received in action.

Lieutenant WILLIAM BASIL WESTON
(311376)

In Burma on 3rd March, 1945, during the battalion's attack on the town of Meiktila, this officer was commanding a platoon. The task of his Company was to clear through the town from the North to the waters edge in the South, a distance of about 1600 yards of which the last 800 yards was not only very strongly held but was a labyrinth of minor roads and well constructed buildings. The Company was working with tanks and Lieutenant Weston's platoon was one of the two platoons leading the attack. The clearing of the final 800 yards was commenced at 1330 hours and was to be completed by dusk. Practically every man in Lieutenant Weston's platoon was seeing active service for the first time and under the most difficult conditions.

From the start, Lieutenant Weston realised that only by the highest personal example on his part could he hope to carry out his task within the time given.

As the advance continued the already determined opposition increased until in the final stages it reached a stage when it can only be described as fanatical. Fire from guns and light automatics was heavy from well bunkered positions and concrete emplacements. Each bunker position had to be dealt with separately and super-imposed on the enemy's fire from the front was accurate sniping from well selected positions on the flanks. The fighting throughout the day was at very close quarters and at times was hand to hand.

With magnificent bravery Lieutenant Weston inspired the men of his platoon to superb achievements. Without thought of his personal safety, he personally led his men into position after position exterminating the enemy whenever found. Throughout, the leadership was superb, encouraging his platoon to the same fanatical zeal as that shown by the enemy. His bravery, his coolness under fire and enthusiasm inspired his platoon. There was no hesitation on his part and no matter how heavy or sustained the enemy's fire, he boldly and resolutely led his men on from bunker position to bunker position. It was at 1700 hours, within sight of the water's edge which marked the completion of the patoon's task that he was held up by a very strong bunker position. Lieutenant Weston, appreciating the limited time now at his disposal and the necessity of clearing the area before nightfall, quickly directed the fire of the tanks with him on to the position. He then led a party with bayonets and grenades to eliminate the enemy within the bunker. As on many occasions before, he was the first into the bunker. At the entrance to the bunker he was shot at by the enemy inside and fell forward wounded. As he lay on the ground and still fired by the undaunted courage that he had shown throughout the day, he withdrew the pin from a grenade in his hand and by doing so killed himself and most of the enemy in the bunker. It is possible that he could have attempted to reach safety but to do so would have endangered the lives of his men who were following him into the bunker and throughout the final $3\frac{1}{2}$ hours of battle, Lieutenant Weston set an example which seldom can have been equalled. His bravery and inspiring leadership was beyond question. At no time during the day did he relax and inspired by the deeds of valour which he continually performed, he personally led on his men as an irresistible force. The final supreme self-sacrifice of this gallant young officer within sight of victory was typical of the courage and bravery so magnificently displayed and sustained throughout the day's operation.

APPENDIX 2

Roll of Valour

NOTICE

This Roll consists purely of British gallantry awards, and makes no mention of those British Orders of Chivalry and decorations which are not bestowed specifically for gallantry in the Field. No foreign awards, for valour or otherwise have been included.

No effort has been spared to make it as accurate and complete a list as possible. Errors and omissions may have occurred, however, and for any such the compiler apologises. The Officer Commanding The Regimental Depot would be glad to receive amendments and additions to this list.

The citations for the decorations mentioned in this Roll may be seen in " The Green Howards Book of Valour " which is deposited in the Regimental Museum at Richmond.

The Victoria Cross

4390973	C.S.M. HOLLIS, S. E.	6th Bn	6 Jun 44	MONT FLEURY, France
Lt.-Col.	D. A. SEAGRIM	7th Bn	20/21 Mar 43	MARETH, Tunisia
Lt.	W. B. WESTON	1st Bn West Yorkshire Regt.	3 Mar 45	MEIKTILA, Burma

Bar to The Distinguished Service Order

Brig.	E. C. COOKE-COLLIS, D.S.O.	HQ 69th Inf Bde.	16-21 Mar 43	MARETH, Tunisia
Lt.-Col.	M. R. STEEL, D.S.O., M.C.	6th Bn	23 May 40	GRAVELINES, France

The Distinguished Service Order

Lt.-Col.	P. G. BULFIN	1st Bn	19/20 Jan 44	MINTURNO and TRIMONSUOLI, Italy
Capt.	A. BURNS	1st Bn Duke of Wellingtons Regt.	9 Oct 44	MONTE CECE, Italy
Lt.-Col.	W. E. BUSH, M.C.	5th Bn	May 40	ARRAS, France
Lt.-Col.	E. C. COOKE-COLLIS	{ 6th Bn / HQ 69th Inf Bde	27-29 Mar 42 / 26-28 Jun 42	KNIGHTSBRIDGE, Lybia / MATRUH, Egypt
Major	J. W. DUNNILL	2nd Bn London Irish Rifles	23 Apr 43	HEIDOUS, Tunisia
Lt.-Col.	A. F. P. EVANS	2nd Bn Royal Fusiliers	13 May 44	CASSINO, Italy
Major	P. H. D. FOX	5th Bn	30 May 42	UALEB, Lybia
Lt.-Col.	D. S. GORDON	1/7th Bn Queen's Royal Regt.	7 May 43	TUNIS, Tunisia
Lt.-Col.	M. L. P. JACKSON	8th Bn Durham Light Infantry	14 Jun 42	GAZALA, Lybia
Lt.-Col.	C. N. LITTLEBOY, M.C., T.D.	4th Bn	20-23 May 40	ATHIES, France
Lt.-Col.	F. E. A. MACDONNELL	7th Bn	28/29 Jun 42	MATRUH, Egypt

Rank	Name	Unit	Date	Location
Major	D'A J. D. MANDER	Escaped Prisoner of War	Dec 43-Jun 44	ROME, Italy
Colonel	R. G. PARKER	12th (Yorkshire) Bn Parachute Regt.	12/13 Jun 44	BREVILLE, France
Lt.-Col.	A. E. ROBINSON	1st Bn	27-29 Apr 40	OTTA, Norway
Lt.-Col.	A. L. SHAW	1st Bn	12 Jul-6 Aug 43	SICILY
Lt.-Col.	T. W. G. STANSFELD	5th Bn East Yorkshire Regt.	28 Jun 42	MATRUH, Egypt
Capt.	P. B. WATSON	4th Bn	27 May 42	TRIGH CAPUZZO, Lybia

Bar to The Military Cross

Rank	Name	Unit	Date	Location
Major	C. M. HULL, M.C.	6th Bn	6 Apr 43	WADI AKARIT, Tunisia

The Military Cross

Rank	Name	Unit	Date	Location
Lt.	L. ATKINSON	2nd Bn Nigeria Regt., R.W.A.F.F.	21 Dec 44	DODAN, Burma
Lt.	T. S. ATKINSON	1st Bn Devonshire Regt.	11 Apr 44	TENGNOUPAL, Burma
Lt.	R. BELL	1st Bn	19/20 Jul 43	CATANIA PLAIN, Sicily
2/Lt.	J. R. BOOTH	4th Bn	28/29 May 40	YPRES, Belgium
Major	J. W. BOTTELL	1st Bn	28 Jan 44	MOUNT TURLITO, Italy
Lt.	J. E. BRABBS	1st Bn King's Own Royal Regt.	11 Dec 44	PIDEURA, Italy
Lt.	P. E. BRAY	5th Bn	1 Jun 42	UALEB, Lybia
Major	F. H. BRUNTON	6th Bn	27-29 May 42 / 21 Jul 42	GAZALA, Lybia and MATRUH, Egypt / TAQA PLATEAU, Egypt
2/Lt.	P. CARR	6th Bn	24 May 40	GRAVELINES, France
Lt.	J. A. CLARK*	2nd Bn Royal Warwickshire Regt.	18 Jul 44	LE QUAI, France

*Since the text was printed, it has been discovered that Lt. J. A. Clark earned his decoration while fighting with the Royal Warwickshire Regiment in the same vicinity, but at a later date.

Rank	Name	Unit	Date	Place
Lt.	R. N. Cockburn	6th Bn	16/17 Mar 43	Mareth, Tunisia
Capt.	P. H. D. Dessain	1st Bn	26 Apr 40	Kvam, Norway
Lt.	A. N. Drake	11th Bn King's African Rifles	{ 16 Nov 44 / 18/19 Nov 44	Sage, Burma / Indainngyi, Burma
Capt.	W. G. Dumville	5th Bn	28/29 May 40	Ypres, Belgium
2/Lt.	V. Evans	7th Bn	15 Jun 42	M'rassus, Lybia
4380801	R.S.M. Exall, J.	4th Bn	28-29 May 42	Trigh Capuzzo, Lybia
Major	L. A. Fitzroy-Smith	6th Bn Parachute Regt.	25 Oct 44	Khalkis, Greece
Capt.	K. H. Forster	Escaped Prisoner of War	Sep 43-Nov 43	Prescina, Italy
Capt.	A. Graham	Iraq Levies	22 May 41	Fallujah, Iraq
Lt.	L. A. Grosvenor	6th Bn	27 Jun 44	La Taille, France
Capt.	I. T. R. Hay	7th Bn	6 Apr 43	Wadi Akarit, Tunisia
Lt.	R. Henderson	1st Bn West Yorkshire Regt.	9 Mar 44- 11 May 44	Seksih-Potsangban, Burma
Lt.	W. T. Holdsworth	8th Bn Manchester Regt.	18 Aug 44	San Sepolcro, Italy
Major	F. H. Honeyman	6th Bn	6 Jun 44	La Rivière, France
2/Lt.	J. L. Hughes	6th Bn	24 May 40	Gravelines, France
Capt.	C. M. Hull	6th Bn	27 Jun 42	Matruh, Egypt
2/Lt.	E. L. Kirby	4th Bn	21 May 40	Athies, France
Capt.	F. F. Lawson	7th Bn	16-18 Jun 44	La Vardiere, France
Major	R. Lofthouse	6th Bn	6 Jun 44	Mont Fleury, France
Lt.	G. R. Louis	8th Bn Royal Scots Fusiliers	23 Feb 45	Goch, Germany
Major	J. B. Mansell	7th Bn	{ 16-21 Mar 43 / 6 Apr 43	Mareth, Tunisia / Wadi Akarit, Tunisia
Capt.	P. S. Marsden	1st Bn Highland Light Infantry	22 Oct 44	Helzenhoek
Capt.	W. Murray	7th Bn	1 Sep 44	Albert, France
Lt.	G. W. Nosotti	7th Bn	20/21 May 43	Mareth, Tunisia

Rank	Name	Unit	Date	Location
Major	A. T. PARKINSON	1st Bn	1 May 45	BUCHEN, Germany
Major	G. S. POWELL	12th (Yorkshire) Bn Parachute Regt.	Sep 44	ARNHEM, The Netherlands
Major	C. R. PULLINGER	6th Bn	25/26 Oct 42	MUNASSIB DEPRESSION, Egypt
Capt.	A. J. C. REEVES	2nd Bn The King's Regt.	11/12 May 44 / 23 Jul 44	River GARI, Italy / MELETO, Italy
Lt.	G. V. RICHLEY	7th Bn	20/21 Mar 43	MARETH, Tunisia
Major	G. RITCHIE	12th (Yorkshire) Bn Parachute Regt.	24 Mar 45- 3 Apr 45	DZ East of River RHINE— OSNABRUCK, Germany
Capt.	E. S. ROBERTS	1st Bn	19 Jan 44	MINTURNO, Italy
Major	C. S. SCROPE	1st Bn	31 May-1 June 44	ARDEA, Italy
Lt.	G. SHERRATT	7th Bn	2 Aug 44	AMAYE SUR SEULLES, France
Lt.	C. G. SMITH	7th Bn	14 Jul 43	MOUNT. PANCALI, Sicily
Major	A. R. M. TANNER	1st Bn	20 Jan 44	TRIMONSUOLI, Italy
Major	R. H. TURTON, M.P.	HQ 50th Div.	27/28 May 42	GAZALA—TOBRUK, Lybia
Capt.	G. H. WALKER	6th Bn	25/26 Oct 42	MUNASSIB Depression, Egypt
Capt.	W. WARRENER	GHQ 8th Army	7 Nov 42	MATRUH, Egypt
Capt.	H. D. WHITEHEAD	5th Bn	24 May 40	GAVRELLE
Lt.	G. D. WING	7th Bn	20/21 Mar 43	MARETH, Tunisia
Major	G. M. YOUNG	6th Bn	11 Jun 44	ORISTOT, France

The Distinguished Conduct Medal

Number	Rank	Name	Unit	Date	Location
14716652	Pte.	ADAMS, J. H.	7th Bn	1 Oct 44	HEUVAL, The Netherlands
12925024	Cpl.	ARBUTHNOT, E.	1st Bn	23 May 44	MOLETTA River, Italy
4393111	Pte.	ARMSTRONG, J.	6th Bn	25/26 Oct 42	MUNASSIB Depression, Egypt
4388271	P.S.M.	ASKEW, W. H. B.	1st Bn	28 Apr 40	OTTA, Norway
4387223	Sgt.	BLACKHAM, L.	6th Bn	16/17 Mar 43	MARETH, Tunisia
4389328	C.S.M.	CALVERT, G. E.	6th Bn	11 Jun 44	ORISTOT, France
4390829	L/Sgt.	CASS, R.	5th Bn	29 May-1 Jun 42	UALEB, Lybia
4393999	L/Sgt.	COLLINS, N.	6th Bn	16/17 Mar 43	MARETH, Tunisia
4389360	Sgt.	HUGGINS, A., M.M.	6th Bn	25/26 Oct 42	MUNASSIB Depression, Egypt

4380815	LENG, J.	Sgt.	5th Bn	17 May-2 Jun 42	UALEB, Lybia
3757247	MACDONALD, J.	C.S.M.	9th Bn	29 Jul 40-27 Sep 40	DOVER, England
4340914	McLOUGHLIN, M.	C.S.M.	7th Bn	20 Mar 43	MARETH, Tunisia
2653740	PEACOCK, C., M.M.	C.S.M.	1st Bn	1 May 45	BUCHEN, Germany
4386986	ROBINSON, H.	L/Sgt.	1st Bn	7/8 Feb 44	MINTURNO, Italy
4388769	WALLER, J.	Pte.	Escaped Prisoner of War	Sep 40-Feb 41	KONITZ, Poland—OSTROU, Russia
4386530	YARROW, J.	L/Sgt.	7th Bn	20/21 Mar 43	MARETH, Tunisia

Bar to The Military Medal

| 4392429 | CRADDOCK, C., M.M. | Sgt. | 7th Bn | 6 Apr 43 | WADI AKARIT, Tunisia |
| 4386724 | ROCHE, F. M., M.M. | Sgt. | 1st Bn | 22 Jan 44 | MINTURNO, Italy |

The Military Medal

5260175	ADDIS, T.	Pte.	7th Bn	6 Jun 44	LA RIVIÈRE, France
4394374	ALEXANDER, W. J.	L/Cpl.	4th Bn	23 May 40	ATHIES, France
14508415	ARCHER, H. C.	L/Cpl.	1st Bn	22 Jan 44	MINTURNO, Italy
4394761	BACKHOUSE, G.	Pte.	6th Bn	11 Jun 44	ORISTOT, France
14655373	BALDWIN, S.	Pte.	7th Bn	7 Jun 44	ST. LEGER, France
4392097	BELL, W. H.	Cpl.	7th Bn	16/17 Mar 43	MARETH, Tunisia
5889820	BIRCH, H. G.	Pte.	6th Bn	9 Aug 44	ST. PIERRE, France
4749380	BLACKMORE, H. J.	Sgt.	7th Bn	16/17 Mar 43	MARETH, Tunisia
6895188	BURDETT, W.	Sgt.	5th Bn	27 May-1 Jun 42	UALEB, Lybia
4385854	BUTLER, B.	Sgt.	10th Bn Lancashire Fusiliers	13-15 Mar 43	HTIZWE, Burma
4392868	CHURMS, A. G.	Cpl.	1st Bn	23 May 44	ANZIO Bridgehead, Italy
4393117	CLARKE, A. E. V.	Pte.	6th Bn	11 Jun 44	ORISTOT, France
4393108	CLAYTON, J.	Sgt.	6th Bn	16/17 Mar 43	MARETH, Tunisia
4394496	COOPER, R.	Cpl.	7th Bn	16/17 Mar 43	MARETH, Tunisia
4392429	CRADDOCK, C.	Sgt.	7th Bn	16/17 Mar 43	MARETH, Tunisia
4386294	CROSSON, J. F.	Pte.	7th Bn	18 Jun 44	Near LA VARDIERE, France

4391008	Pte.	DALE, A. N.	7th Bn	15 Aug 43	FORGO DE AGRO, Sicily
4392704	Sgt.	DAWSON, W.	6th Bn	19/20 Jul 43	PRIMOSOLE Bridgehead, Sicily
4749516	L/Cpl.	DIXON, A.	7th Bn	20/21 Mar 43	MARETH, Tunisia
4387748	Cpl.	DIXON, H.	1st Bn	23 May 44	MOLETTA River, Italy
4264080	Sgt.	DOCHERTY, A. E.	6th Bn	22 Jul 42	TAQA Plateau, Egypt
4753817	Pte.	FOREMAN, D. J.	7th Bn	5 Jun 42	SIDRA, Lybia
5830049	Pte.	FULCHER, A. L.	4th Bn	28 May 40	YPRES, Belgium
4345586	L/Cpl.	GIBSON, S.	1st Bn	28/29 Mar 44	ANZIO Bridgehead, Italy
4395171	Pte.	GILBERT, E.	1st Bn	22 Jan 44	MINTURNO, Italy
14598284	Pte.	GILL, C.	1st Bn	23 May 44	MOLETTA River, Italy.
14660505	Sgt.	GODDARD, G.	7th Bn	11/12 Jun 44	BRONAY, France
4391159	Sgt.	GRAY, D. E.	7th Bn	2 Aug 44	AMAYE SUR SEULLES, France
4393879	Pte.	HARE, C.	6th Bn	16/17 Mar 43	MARETH, Tunisia
5953857	Pte.	HARPER, H.	6th Bn	6 Apr 43	WADI AKARIT, Tunisia
4396546	L/Cpl.	HEATLEY, H.	6th Bn	6 Aug 43	SAN GIOVANNI, Sicily
4999507	Pte.	HENSON, J. M.	6th Bn	11 Jun 44	ORISTOT, France
4388054	L/Cpl.	HILL, A.	1st Bn	30 Dec 43	ARIELE, Italy
4391447	L/Cpl.	HOLTBY, R.	Escaped Prisoner of War	9 Sep 43- 23 May 44	FARA NEL SABINA—SAN SILVANO, Italy
5054699	L/Sgt.	HOOD, E. A.	7th Bn	18 Jul 43	PRIMOSOLE Bridgehead, Sicily
5107145	L/Sgt.	HUBBLE, W.	7th Bn	5/6 Jul 44	LA TAILLE, France
14426301	Pte.	HUDSON, F.	7th Bn	2 Aug 44	AMAYE SUR SEULLES, France
4389360	Sgt.	HUGGINS, A.	6th Bn	29 Jun 42	MATRUH—ALAMEIN, Egypt
4389962	Sgt.	JACKSON, R. M.	Escaped Prisoner of War	27 Feb 43- 31 Mar 44	OZZANO—SANTA CATERINA, Italy
5435034	L/Cpl.	JOYCE, A.	6th Bn	6 Jun 44	LA RIVIERE, France
4387153	Pte.	LAIDLER, R.	6th Bn	24 May 40	GRAVELINES, France
4384537	Sgt.	LAMBERT, W. C.	1st Bn	13/14 Oct 43	MORRONE, Italy
4389924	Pte.	LAWSON, J. W. A.	4th Bn The Buffs	14 Nov 43	LEROS, Dodecanese
14335289	Pte.	LEARY, J.	6th Bn	11 Jun 44	ORISTOT, France
5947239	L/Cpl.	LINNEY, C. V.	2nd Bn	23 Jul 43	RAZMAK, Waziristan
4390070	Pte.	LOUGHREN, C. H.	1st Bn	1 May 45	BUCHEN, Germany

2934936	Pte.	MACKINNON, C.	6th Bn	25/26 Oct 42	MUNASSIB Depression, Egypt
4386933	L/Sgt.	MADDOX, J. R.	1st Bn	19 Jan 44	MINTURNO, Italy
4392001	Pte.	McCURRY, J.	7th Bn	20 Jul 43	PRIMOSOLE Bridgehead, Sicily
4393217	L/Cpl.	MILLAR, L.	1st Bn	30 Apr 45	PENKBERG WOOD, Germany
4390614	L/Sgt.	MUIR, J. A.	7th Bn	20-23 Mar 43	MARETH, Tunisia
7047537	Cpl.	MURPHY, J.	1st Bn	22 Jan 44	MINTURNO, Italy
7014424	C.S.M.	MURPHY, P.	7th Bn	1 Oct 44	HEUVAL, The Netherlands
4389350	Pte.	NEEDHAM, J. R.	5th Bn	31 May 40	HOUTHEN, Belgium
14660562	Pte.	OLDHAM, V.	1st Bn	23-26 Apr 44	ANZIO Bridgehead, Italy
4387081	C/Sgt.	OLIVER, J. G.	6th Bn	14 & 28 Jun 42	GAZALA, Lybia–MATRUH, Egypt
4391249	Cpl.	O'ROURKE, J.	7th Bn	6 Apr 43	WADI AKARIT, Tunisia
4391132	Pte.	OWEN, T. B.	5th Bn	24 May 40	GAVRELLE, France
4391884	L/Sgt.	PARKIN, J. W.	1st Bn	6 Sep 43	CERIMODO, Italy
4393153	Pte.	PATTERSON, T. G.	7th Bn	16/17 Mar 43	MARETH, Tunisia
4387960	Pte.	PATTISON, F.	2nd Bn	23 Jul 43	RAZMAK, Waziristan
4390667	L/Sgt.	PEACOCK, J. W.	4th Bn	23 May-2 Jun 40	ATHIES–DUNKIRK, France
4390075	Cpl.	PEARS, T.	1st Bn	18/19 Oct 43	LUCITO, Italy
4387058	Cpl.	PEEL, R.	1st Bn	22 Jan 44	MINTURNO, Italy
4393084	L/Sgt.	PLUCK, W. L.	6th Bn	27 Jun 42	MATRUH, Egypt
4751978	Sgt.	POTTERTON, W.	7th Bn	7 Jun 44	ST. LÉGER, France
2934980	L/Sgt.	PRENTY, H.	6th Bn	6 Jun 44	LA RIVIÈRE, France
4397603	Pte.	RALPH, R. T.	7th Bn	5 Jun 42	SIDRA, Lybia
14427480	Pte.	REDDINGTON, J. A.	7th Bn	12 Sep 44	ALBERT Canal, Belgium
5388512	Pte.	RIDDLE, F. J.	7th Bn	29 Sep 44	HEUVAL, The Netherlands
4386724	Sgt.	ROCHE, F. M.	1st Bn	28 Apr 40	OTTA, Norway
4391158	Sgt.	RODGERS, J. R.	6th Bn	25/26 Oct 42	MUNASSIB Depression, Egypt
4389287	Pte.	SCUFFHAM, J. A.	4th Bn	21-24 May 40	ATHIES, France
534780	Pte.	SHAW, S.	1st Bn	23 May 44	ANZIO Bridgehead, Italy
4384274	Sgt.	SISSONS, H.	1st Bn	22 Jan 44	MINTURNO, Italy
3658454	Pte.	SMITH, J.	Escaped Prisoner of War	12 Sep 43	SULMONA,—AQUILA,—TERNI, Italy
2935111	Sgt.	SMITH, L.	6th Bn	16-17 Mar 43	MARETH, Tunisia

4397133	L/Cpl.	Smith, R. W.	6th Bn	6 Apr 43	Wadi Akarit, Tunisia
4397612	Pte.	Snowdon, L.	6th Bn	20 Jul 43	Primosole Bridgehead, Sicily
4386304	Sgt.	Storey, T. E.	2nd Bn	6 Oct 44	Goppe, Burma
4914549	Cpl.	Taylor, B.	6th Bn	27 Jun 44	La Taille, France
4394951	Cpl.	Tierney, J.	1st Bn	27 Apr 44	Anzio Bridgehead, Italy
14428214	Pte.	Thompson, J. T.	6th Bn	6 Jun 44	Crepon, France
6100031	L/Sgt.	Upperton, E. F. A.	7th Bn	12 Sep 44	Albert Canal, Belgium
4391050	Sgt.	Usher, G. F.	7th Bn	15 Jun 42	M'Rassus, Lybia
4389371	L/Cpl.	Vickers, F. W.	6th Bn	16-17 Mar 43	Mareth, Tunisia
4386033	Pte.	Walker, A.	5th Bn	27 May 40	Vyfeg, Belgium
1465457	L/Cpl.	Wilks, J.	7th Bn	11 Sep 44	Albert Canal, Belgium
5260354	L/Cpl.	Winterbottom, A.	6th Bn	6 Apr 43	Wadi Akarit, Tunisia
4388644	L/Sgt.	Woodall, H.	1st Bn	23 May 44	Anzio Bridgehead, Italy

INDEX

PART 1. GREEN HOWARD BATTALIONS

1st Battalion

	Date	Year	Pages
On Mobilisation	3 Sep	1939	3
Sails for France	5 Oct	1939	6
Returns to England	17 Apr	1940	7
Sails for Norway	24 Apr	1940	7/9
Arrives at Dombaas	26 Apr	1940	11
" B " Company at Kvam and Sjoia	26/28 Apr	1940	11/15
In action at Otta	28/29 Apr	1940	15/21
Withdraws to Aandalsnes	30 Apr/2 Mar	1940	21/23
Sails for England	2 May	1940	23
Service at Home	Jun 1940/Mar	1942	58, 59
Sails for India—Service in India and Persia	Mar 1942/Mar	1943	59, 60
Arrives at Kabrit	16 Mar	1943	199
Training at Kabrit, Damascus, and El Shatt	Mar/Jul	1943	199/202
Sails for Sicily	5 Jul	1943	202
Lands in Sicily	10/11 Jul	1943	203/205
Advances to Floridia	11 Jul	1943	205
Advances to R. Gornalunga	12/19 Jul	1943	206/208
Attacks north of R. Simeto	19/20 Jul	1943	222, 223
In positions on R. Simeto, and in Reserve	20 Jul/3 Aug	1943	223
Advances to, and captures, Motta	3/4 Aug	1943	223, 224
Advances to, and captures, Belpasso	5/10 Aug	1943	225, 226
Advances to R. Nigro	10/12 Aug	1943	226
Resting and reorganising at Paterno	16/31 Aug	1943	226
Crosses to Italian mainland	3 Sep	1943	239
Advances to Picerno	3/23 Sep	1943	239/242
Resting and training at Picerno	24 Sep/8 Oct	1943	242
Moves across to R. Biferno	8/12 Oct	1943	242, 243
In action on R. Biferno	12/31 Oct	1943	243/246
Moves forward to Rionero	31 Oct/11 Nov	1943	246
In positions at Rionero	11/25 Nov	1943	246, 247
At Castelpetroso, Capracotta, and Castiglione	25 Nov/19 Dec	1943	247, 248
Moves across to Lanciano	19 Dec	1943	248
In positions in front of Lanciano	21 Dec 1943/ 3 Jan	1944	248/250
Moves across to R. Garigliano	6 Jan	1944	250
Training behind R. Garigliano	9/18 Jan	1944	250
Attacks at Minturno	19 Jan	1944	250, 251
Attacks at Trimonsuoli	20/24 Jan	1944	251/255
In reserve, and in positions near Minturno	24 Jan/10 Feb	1944	255
In reserve, and in positions near Trimonsuoli	10 Feb/3 Mar	1944	256
Sails for Anzio	5 Mar	1944	257
In positions at " The Fortress "	6/15 Mar	1944	258, 259
In positions at Lorenzo	23 Mar/15 Apr	1944	259/261
In positions at " The Fortress "	20/28 Apr	1944	261/264
In positions at " The Fortress "	6/15 May	1944	264, 265
Attacks across R. Moletta	22/24 May	1944	266/275

2B

1st Battalion—*contd.*

	Date	Year	Pages
Reorganising at " B " Echelon	25/28 May	1944	275
Attacks near Ardea	31 May/1 Jun	1944	276/280
Sails for Egypt	20 Jun	1944	281
Reorganising and on duties in the Middle East	Jun 1944/Feb	1945	281
Sails from Haifa	26 Feb	1945	360
Arrives at Marseilles	3 Mar	1945	360
Arrives at Schellbelle—at Schellbelle	8 Mar/16 Apr	1945	360
Moves to Grosse Thorndorf	16/21 Apr	1945	361
Raid on Ahndorf	22 Apr	1945	361
Moves to Mucklingen and Hittenbergen	22/29 Apr	1945	361
Crosses R. Elbe	30 Apr	1945	361
Advances from Basedow	30 Apr	1945	362
Attacks at Dahldorf	1 May	1945	362
Attacks at Buchen	1/2 May	1945	363, 364
Ceremonial parade at Lubeck	8 May	1945	364, 365

2nd Battalion

	Date	Year	Pages
In India	Sep 39/Oct 42		366, 367
Moves to Razmak	Oct	1942	367
In action at Dosali	6/7 Jun	1943	367, 378
Moves to Peshawar	20 Dec	1943	368
Moves to Ranchi	May	1944	368
Moves to Lohardaga	Jul	1944	368
Moves to Bawli Bazaar	17/23 Sep	1944	369
Moves to Goppe Bazaar	29/30 Sep	1944	369
In action at Goppe Bazaar	5 Oct/3 Nov	1944	369, 370
Moves to Colaba	3/4 Nov	1944	370
At Colaba and Nidania	4 Nov 1944/ 16 Jan	1945	370
Moves to Chittagong	16 Jan	1945	370
Sails from Chittagong	16 Jan	1945	371
Lands on Ramree Island	21 Jan	1945	371
On Ramree Island	21 Jan/14 Feb	1945	371
Lands at Kalabon	14 Feb	1945	371
Moves to Gonchwein	26/27 Feb	1945	371
Sails from Kyaukpyu	12 Mar	1945	371
Lands at Pyin Wan	13 Mar	1945	372
Advances towards Taungup	25 Mar	1945	372
In action on Taungup road	1/17 Apr	1945	372, 373
Moves to Kyetkaing	17 Apr	1945	373
Advances towards Prome	28 Apr/3 May	1945	373
Moves to Sandoway	4/10 May	1945	373
At Sandoway	10 May/27 Jun	1945	373
Sails for Kyaukpyu	27 Jun	1945	373
Sails for Madras	2 Jul	1945	373
Arrives at Meerut	27 Jul	1945	373

4th Battalion

5th Battalion

5th Battalion—*contd.*

	Date	Year	Pages
In action on Bergues-Furnes Canal	30/31 May	1940	54, 55
Withdraws to Bray Dunes	31 May	1940	55
Embarkation at Dunkirk	1/3 Jun.	1940	56, 57
Service at Home	Jun. 1940/Apr	1941	60, 61
Sails for Middle East	25 Apr	1941	68
Arrives at Port Tewfik	Jun	1941	69
At El Daba	3 Jul/15 Aug	1941	69
Sails for Cyprus	15 Aug	1941	70
Service in Cyprus	15 Aug/6 Nov	1941	70, 71
Sails for Palestine—at Mount Carmel	7/29 Nov	1941	71
Moves to Amiriya	29 Nov	1941	72
At Sidi Haneish and Bir Thalata	3 Dec. 1941/		
	25 Jan	1942	72/75
Crosses the Libyan Frontier	27 Jan	1942	75
At Garat el Auda	29 Jan./2 Feb	1942	75/77
At Bir Hacheim	3/17 Feb	1942	78
At Bir el Naghia	17 Feb/20 Apr	1942	79, 80, 81, 82
Moves to Got el Ualeb	20 Apr	1942	82
At Got el Ualeb	26/27 May	1942	90
At Got el Ualeb	27/28 May	1942	92, 93, 94, 96
At Got el Ualeb	29/30 May	1942	98, 99, 100, 101
At Got el Ualeb	31 May	1942	101, 102
At Got el Ualeb—the final battle	1 Jun	1942	104, 105
The Cadre	Jun/Nov	1942	107, 108

6th Battalion

	Date	Year	Pages
On Mobilisation	Sep	1939	3, 4
Sails for France	24 Apr	1940	39
Moves to Canal du Nord—at Saude-mont	16/19 May	1940	39/41
In action on R. Scarpe	19/21 May	1940	41, 42
Withdraws to Gondecourt	22 May	1940	42
Withdraws to Gravelines—in action at Gravelines	22/24 May	1940	42/45
In action in front of Dunkirk	25/29 May	1940	45/47
Embarkation at Dunkirk	30/31 May	1940	47, 48
Service at Home	Jun 1940/Jun	1941	60, 61
Sails for Middle East	3 Jun	1941	69
Arrives at Port Tewfik	21 Jul	1941	69
Sails for Cyprus	7 Aug	1941	70
Service in Cyprus	8 Aug/6 Nov	1941	70, 71
Sails for Palestine—at Acre	7/28 Nov	1941	71
Moves to Persia and Syria	28 Nov 1941/		
	12 Feb	1942	71, 72
Moves to Libya	12/22 Feb	1942	72

6th Battalion—*contd.*

	Date	Year	Pages
Arrives in Gazala Line	22 Feb	1942	83
Near Alem Hamza	Feb/May	1942	83, 84
In action with 50th Division Mobile Column	27/29 May	1942	91, 92, 94/96
Near Alem Hamza	30 May/14 Jun	1942	89, 90
Breaks out from Gazala Line	14/16 Jun	1942	119/121
At Bir Thalata	16/21 Jun	1942	121
Rearguard action from Buq Buq to Mersah Matruh	21/26 Jun	1942	121, 122
Attacks from Mersah Matruh	27/28 Jun	1942	122/125
Breaks out from Mersah Matruh	28/30 Jun	1942	125/128
At Mareopolis	2/12 Jul	1942	128
At Ruweisat	12/19 Jul	1942	134
Attacks at the Taqa Plateau	20/24 Jul	1942	137/140
Attacks at Alem Dakar	25/27 Jul	1942	140, 141
Behind the Alamein defences	28 Jul/13 Oct	1942	142/143
Moves up to the Alamein Line	13 Oct	1942	148
In positions in front of the Munassib Depression	13/25 Oct	1942	150,151
Attacks " The Moor "	25/26 Oct	1942	151/156
In positions at Munafid and Ruweisat	29 Oct/4 Nov	1942	156
Pursuit to Mersah Matruh-Siwa track	4/13 Nov	1942	156
Advances to Mareth, via El Adem and Benghazi	Dec 1942/Mar	1943	158, 159
Arrives in front of Mareth outposts	12 Mar	1943	164
Attacks the Mareth outposts	16/17 Mar	1943	165/174
Attacks on the Wadi Zigaou	22/23 Mar	1943	182/184
Enters Mareth	28 Mar	1943	185
Moves up to Oudref	3 Apr	1943	185
Attacks at Akarit	5/6 Apr	1943	191/196
Advances to Enfidaville	14/23 Apr	1943	197
Moves back to Egypt	25 Apr/6 May	1943	197
Reorganising and training in Egypt	May/Jul	1943	202
Sails for Sicily	5 Jul	1943	202
Lands in Sicily—advances to Floridia	10/12 Jul	1943	205, 206
Advances to, and attacks near, Mount Pancali	12/14 Jul	1943	209/211
In positions near Lentini	14/17 Jul	1943	215
Moves forward to Primosole Bridge	17 Jul	1943	215
Attacks in the Primosole Bridgehead	17/21 Jul	1943	219/221
In Reserve and in positions in the Primosole Bridgehead	21 Jul/4 Aug	1943	227, 228
Advances on Catania	4 Aug	1943	229
Advances towards Riposto	5/12 Aug	1943	229, 230
Advances to Capo d'Ali	13/17 Aug	1943	233, 234
Sails for England	17 Oct	1943	235
At home, training for " D " Day	5 Nov 1943/5 Jun	1944	282/285
Sails for Normandy	5 Jun	1944	290, 291
The landing and first day's fighting	6 Jun	1944	291/296
In positions near Duoy Ste. Marguerite	7/11 Jun	1944	296
Attacks at Oristot	11 Jun	1944	302/306
At Loucelles and Conde sur Seulles	12/15 Jun	1944	306

6th Battalion—*contd.*

7th Battalion

7th Battalion—*contd.*

7th Battalion—*contd.*

	Date	Year	Pages
Attacks at St. Pierre la Vieille	9/14 Aug	1944	329, 330
Advances to Morlancourt	18 Aug/1 Sep	1944	331/333
In action near Albert	1/2 Sep	1944	333/335
Advances to Tournai	2/7 Sep	1944	335
Advances to Zammel	7 Sep	1944	335
Attacks across the Albert Canal	8/12 Sep	1944	341/344
In reserve, and moving up to Canal de Jonction	12/21 Sep	1944	344/346
Moves up to Nijmegen	21/24 Sep	1944	347, 348
Crosses R. Waal	24 Sep	1944	350
Attacks at Heuval	26/30 Sep	1944	350, 351
German counter-attack at Heuval	1 Oct	1944	351/355
In positions on " The Island "	8 Oct/27 Nov	1944	355/357
Moves to Roulers—at Roulers	29 Nov/12 Dec	1944	358
Sails for England	13 Dec	1944	359
Arrives at Malton	15 Dec	1944	359

8th Battalion (13th and 30th)

	Date	Year	Pages
On Formation	Nov	1939	4
At Doncaster and Spalding	Jun 1940/Sep	1943	62
In North Africa and Italy	Sep 1943/	1945	62, 63

9th Battalion

	Date	Year	Pages
On Formation	Mar	1940	4
At Dover and Deal	Mar 1940/Mar	1941	63
In Shetland Islands and Northumberland	Mar/Dec	1941	63
Conversion to 108th Light Anti-Aircraft Regiment	31 Dec	1941	63

10th Battalion

	Date	Year	Pages
On Formation	Jun	1940	4
At Tidworth	Jun 1940/Feb	1941	63
In Kent	Feb 1941/Dec	1942	63
At Truro	Dec 1942/May	1943	63, 64
Conversion to Parachute Regiment	May	1943	64
Operations as Parachute Troops	May 1943/	1945	64

11th Battalion

	Date	Year	Pages
On Formation	Jul	1940	4
In Northumberland	Oct 1940/Nov	1941	64
In Lincolnshire	Nov 1941/	1945	64, 65

12th Battalion

	Date	Year	Pages
On Formation	Oct	1940	4
In Yorkshire	Oct 1940/Jul.	1942	65
Redesignated 161st Reconnaissance Regiment	Jul	1942	65
" Green Howard " Squadron in action	Jul 1944/	1945	65

The Regimental Depot

	Date	Year	Pages
		1939/	4, 375/
		1945	384

The Home Guard Battalions

	Date	Year	Pages
		1940/	65/67
		1945	Chapter 16

PART 2. OTHER UNITS

Armies	Pages
1st (French) Army	26
2nd Army	309
8th Army	84, 86, 109/111, 121, 126, 137, 144/146 158, 160, 161, 164, 196, 200, 236/238, 250
21st Army Group	358
1st U.S. Army	309
5th U.S. Army	236, 237, 238, 240, 250, 265

Corps and other formations	Pages
Afrika Corps	96, 158, 160, 186, 197
8th Armoured Corps	309
10th Armoured Corps	145, 147, 148
1st Corps	26
2nd Corps	25, 26
3rd Corps	60
4th Corps	370
5th Corps	61, 236/239, 242, 248
8th Corps	61, 346
10th Corps	111, 158, 188, 236
12th Corps	346
13th Corps	144/147, 158, 198, 200, 202, 221, 224, 236/238, 286
15th Corps	370
30th Corps	113, 145, 147, 158, 159, 186, 198, 205, 221, 223, 228, 232, 308, 327, 330, 346, 347, 358
33rd Corps	370, 373
G.H.Q. Reserve (France)	25, 26
G.H.Q. Reserve (Middle East)	72
Frankforce	29
Goldforce	77
Group Fischer	11
Group Pellenghar	15
Petreforce	34
Reesforce	107
Silverforce	77
Usherforce	44

Divisions	Pages
1st Airborne Division	345, 347
6th Airborne Division	250, 361, 363
82nd U.S. Airborne Division	345
101st U.S. Airborne Division	345, 356, 357
1st Armoured Division	86, 95
7th Armoured Division	86, 107, 135, 142, 143, 146, 147, 181, 184, 194, 288, 323, 324, 326
11th Armoured Division	327, 335, 336
9th Australian Division	113, 136
Ariete Division	95
Brescia Division	109, 148, 156, 157
Canadian Divisions	236, 237, 239, 241, 242, 248, 287, 298, 300/302, 307

411

PART 3. INDIVIDUAL NAMES

A

Acland, C. E. B., Major, 369, 370
Adams, J. H., Pte., 352
Addis, T., Pte., 294
Alexander, U., 2/Lt., 31, 49, 50
Alexander, W. J., L/Cpl., 34
Alexander, J., Cpl., 306
Allen, F. V., Capt., 54, 55
Allen, J. R., Capt., 372
Ambler, Lt., 244, 245
Anderson, D., Sir., Lt.-Gen., 60
Anderson, W., L/Cpl., 124, 138
Angel, R. C., Cpl., 18
Arbuthnot, E., Cpl., 267, 273
Archer, H. C., L/Cpl., 254
Armitage, E. R. P., Capt., 16, 18/21
Armstrong, J., Pte., 155
Arnott, A. I., Lt., 245
Ashmore, F., R.S.M., 370
Askew, W. H. B., P.S.M./C.S.M., 18
Atkinson, J. F., Lt., 367
Atley, N. S., Major, 351
Auchinleck, C. J., Sir, Gen., 70, 72, 111

B

Backhouse, G., Pte., 304
Bacon, C. R. S., C.S.M., 317, 318
Bade, J. S., Lt./Major, 12/14, 19, 242, 245, 278, 360, 365
Baldon, R. S., Capt., 312
Baldwin, S., Pte., 300
Barber, A. A., Capt., 52, 102
Barber, V. J., Lt.-Col., 4, 62
Barlow, F. F. S., Lt.-Col., 354
Barnes, J., L/Sgt., 17
Barnley, G. W., Lt.-Col., 67
Barwick, J., Pte., 180
Barwick, J. M., Capt., 199, 246
Bateman, G. M., Lt./Capt., 80, 93
Bawcombe, P. C., Sgt./Lt., 167, 183, 184, 192/194, 303, 310, 340
Bayerlein, Gen., 106
Belcher, A. E. I., Lt.-Col., 4, 63, 376
Belcher, Mrs., 380
Bell, R., Lt., 204, 222, 223
Bell, W. H., Cpl., 169, 318
Benson, Pte., 138
Berny, Lt., 255
Berney-Ficklin, H. P. M., Maj.-Gen., 59
Best, A. G., Capt., 107
Bevan, H. E., Cpl., 175, 180

Birch, H. G., Pte., 328
Black, A., Lt., 68
Blackham, L., Sgt., 171
Blackmore, H. J., Sgt., 169, 180
Blakely, A. C., Major, 360, 363
Blunt, N., Lt., 80/82
Booth, J. R., 2/Lt./Capt., 33, 48, 49, 82
Botham, N., Capt., 369, 373
Bower, T. K., Major, 378
Bowley, H. E., Major, 296, 298, 308, 315
Bown, E. L., Lt., 82
Boyle, S. M., Major, 296, 315
Bradford, E., L/Cpl., 189
Branscombe, J. S. G., Major, 366
Bray, P. E., Lt., 105
Breckon, F. E., Pte., 167, 168
Brennan, E., Pte., 189
Brett, J., Cpl., 354
Briggs, R. M., Lt., 363
Bright, H. N., Lt.-Col., 4, 65
Brockhurst, C. E., Lt.-Col., 376
Brown, W. N., Cpl., 18
Browning, C. G., Lt., 93
Brunton, F. H., Capt./Major, 91, 120, 123, 125, 126, 137, 139, 141, 142, 151, 157, 159, 164, 191, 210, 211, 220, 282, 283
Bucknall, F. N., Pte., 138
Bulfin, P. G. J. M. D., Capt./Lt.-Col., 6, 11/15, 19, 199, 208, 226, 239, 241, 249/251, 253, 256
Bull, C., L/Cpl., 193
Burdett, W., Sgt., 94
Burn, H. B., 2/Lt./Lt., 92, 120
Burns, W., Sgt., 293
Bush, W. E., Lt.-Col., 25, 28, 36, 37, 68, 80, 102
Byron, R. G. G., Lt.-Col., 302

C

Caden, H. T., Capt., 214
Calvert, A., C.S.M., 305
Capps, A. J., 2/Lt., 32
Caris, M. W., Pte., 307
Carmichael, G. L., Capt., 164, 338
Carr, P. J., 2/Lt./Capt., 44, 164
Carter, D., R.S.M., 191, 196
Carton, H., Sgt., 55
Carton de Wiart, A., Gen., 10
Carver, J. M., Cpl., 180
Casey, T., Sgt., 373
Cass, H., Lt., 129
Cass, R., L/Sgt., 100

PART 4. SELECTED PLACE NAMES